CREATING ENTREPRENEURS

Making Miracles Happen

CREATING ENTREPRENEURS

Making Miracles Happen

edited by

Fred Kiesner
Loyola Marymount University, USA

World Scientific

NEW JERSEY · LONDON · SINGAPORE · BEIJING · SHANGHAI · HONG KONG · TAIPEI · CHENNAI

Published by

World Scientific Publishing Co. Pte. Ltd.

5 Toh Tuck Link, Singapore 596224

USA office: 27 Warren Street, Suite 401-402, Hackensack, NJ 07601

UK office: 57 Shelton Street, Covent Garden, London WC2H 9HE

British Library Cataloguing-in-Publication Data
A catalogue record for this book is available from the British Library.

CREATING ENTREPRENEURS
Making Miracles Happen

ISBN-13 978-981-4261-11-1
ISBN-10 981-4261-11-4

Typeset by Stallion Press
Email: enquiries@stallionpress.com

Printed in Singapore by Mainland Press Pte Ltd

Life is all about family and friends!

This book is dedicated to:

My wife Elaine, who has truly been the wind beneath
my wings!

My daughter Andrea, and my grandson Stevie,
who are the reason for my life!

My old friend and mentor Howard Drollinger who enabled
me to become a good teacher by his support, encouragement,
kindness and example!

Ron Valenta, an outstanding student I had the pleasure to
teach some 30+ years ago, and a wonderful entrepreneur who
inspires me and motivates me to achieve much, much more.

And finally, to Fr. Ray Morman and Sgt. Schue, who both
died before I could tell them what an impact they had on
my life as a young man! Perhaps they are reading this
book now, from above!

Contents

Acknowledgements

This is the first (and last) book I have ever written! It has been a delightful experience for the most part, and I owe my supreme thanks to many in my life that have helped me with this project. I name only a few here, but my gratitude goes out to all!

To my sister, **Diane M. Hammill**, of Indiana, USA, the creative graphic artist behind the cover of this book, thanks for sharing the beauty of your work with your totally un-artistic brother!

Obviously I owe a great debt to the **many authors** of chapters in this book, from a half-dozen countries, for being willing to share the beauty of their thinking with the readers of this book. They have dedicated their lives to achievement and doing good things. Sharing their power with the reader is an act of good!

To **Raymond Kao**, an Educator of great intellect who got me involved in this project, I offer my deepest gratitude for believing in me! I might also say, you owe me for getting me involved in all this work!

To wonderful **Sandhya**, my editor at World Scientific Publishing! A lady who believed in me and had the utmost patience and kindness as severe health problems in my life caused delay after delay in finishing this book! She always gave positive support!

To the grand and exciting **Entrepreneurs** I have known in this world, my deepest appreciation for letting me hang with you! Oh what a beautiful and fulfilling life you have given me!

To **Austin Kurtz** and **Alicia Mikolaycik**, two wonderful former students who took the time to read this book and catch this old Professor's grammar, spelling, and typo errors!

Introduction

WARNING! DANGER ALERT! This book is about action, doing, and making things happen!

It is **not an academic treatise** for academics and ivory tower folks, full of textbook mumbo jumbo!

It is for those that want to **make things happen in their lives, and the lives of others, any place in this wonderful world of ours!**

The target audience is all who are included in Entrepreneurship education, coaching, mentoring and development.

It is also extremely useful for existing Entrepreneurs, and hopeful future Entrepreneurs, as it gives neat insights into what it takes to create, and be an Entrepreneur!

It is our fervent hope that you, the reader (a teacher, mentor, student, entrepreneur, or future entrepreneur) will be able to gain great insight into educational activities and entrepreneurial thinking that will help you to **translate the thoughts, experiences, ideas and "doable" action activities presented in this book to your everyday ACTIONS** in helping to prepare the future for entrepreneurial success!!!!!

Start with any chapter. It is designed to give you short, action oriented snippets of thoughts and ideas from some of the finest thinkers in the area of entrepreneurship in all shapes and forms in the world!!!!! All of these authors have extensive **streetwise experience** in entrepreneurship and developing entrepreneurs internationally.

If you added up all of the years these authors have cumulatively impacted the field of entrepreneurship, the total would be **hundreds and hundreds of years of real world, doing it, experience!!!!!**

What a **grand resource of talent** from a field of endeavor that has been formally acknowledged for perhaps only 35 years, and is still in its infancy!!

The editor of this book has participated in the field of entrepreneurship and entrepreneurship education for more than 40 years throughout the world! He has **watched entrepreneurship revolutionize and shape the world** in such diverse environments as the Soviet Union (now Russia), China, Singapore, Ireland, Eastern Europe, the Southern Hemisphere, and the USA!

Entrepreneurship is the future! It can truly solve the ills of the world, if we help to fulfill its full potential!!!!!

You will notice that there is a chapter of this book that deals with the Entrepreneurial miracle of Ireland! Why? Because **Ireland, the "Celtic Tiger", represents the realized potential of entrepreneurship!** This country went from a wonderful sleepy little rural economy with unemployment in the mid twenty percent range and severe under-employment, to a major player in the entrepreneurial world economy in just twenty years! The best and brightest young talent of the country was fleeing overseas to find their destiny, Ireland's population was declining several percentage points a year! Today Ireland is a mover and shaker in the technology game, and those who fled are returning home to help with the entrepreneurial and technological miracle that is happening there. As a Fulbright Scholar in Ireland in the "tough years" your editor has marveled at what key educators and leaders have been able to accomplish in this tiny country!

The lessons of Ireland's "Celtic Miracle" can teach us a great deal about how we can "Survive and Thrive" in today's dire, worldwide economic chaos.

Entrepreneurship and Entrepreneurs are the path out of the world's economic troubles and Chaos!

Ireland has proved that entrepreneurship can help any other country in the world to achieve the same miracle. It doesn't matter if it is the poorest country in Africa, a country trying to recover from a tragic civil war, or a country just trying to enter into the 21st century, or ALL of the countries in the world facing the deep world economic recession!

Ireland has clearly shown that developing the entrepreneurial spirit, and the entrepreneurs to carry it out, can, indeed, produce economic miracles in a very short time span.

You will also note there is a chapter on the subject of corporate entrepreneurship! You bet!!!!!! **Being entrepreneurial in the large corporate business sector is essential to the future of the economies of the world.** The leaders of the corporate world can no longer devote their time to protecting what they have! They must always be creating the future in an entrepreneurial way!

General Motors has certainly taught us that!

We can never allow the world to suffer through the excesses and stupidity of another General Motors!

Encouraging Entrepreneurship, and truly exciting **"Intrapreneurs" (Entrepreneurs within the larger corporation and business entity)**, in the larger firms of the world will play a major role in redeeming businesses of all sizes in the next few decades!

I am also very delighted to have a chapter on ethics and social responsibility in this book, and a chapter about Social Entrepreneurship! We proudly proclaim our mission in the Entrepreneurship Program at Loyola Marymount University as "teaching entrepreneurship with ethics and social responsibility!"

This must be an essential ingredient in entrepreneurship education or we will spoil the chance we have to make the world better.

Look at what many large corporate leaders, bankers and supposed Wall Street financial wizards have done to spoil the world! **Somehow they never learned about ethics and social responsibility, did they!**

We must now, more than ever, imbed ethics and social responsibility in all that we do.

Yes, I am an idealist and very proud of it!!!!!

If you are involved in developing Entrepreneurs, hopefully this book will provide the reader with the "warp" and "woof" with which to weave one's own entrepreneurial tapestry in the grand endeavor of guiding and developing the entrepreneurial leaders and winners and miracle makers of the future!!!!!

Of most importance, we hope that as you read between the lines, you truly learn that to be a really effective entrepreneurial educator and mentor, **you must be entrepreneurial yourself!**

You are setting the stage for greatness among those who learn from you and those you guide. You are whetting their appetite for what they can be and achieve! You must not only give them the knowledge and methodology of entrepreneurship, **you must also convey the passion, street smarts and fire in the belly it takes to create winning entrepreneurial success stories!**

We believe the authors in this book will help you give your "customers" just that!!!!!

If you are a fledgling Entrepreneur, Wow! You will find a myriad of key, exciting, doable and implementable action oriented ideas and methodologies that will help you to jump start your career as an Entrepreneur! **You can learn from some of the world's best entrepreneurial minds in this book!**

Finally, you will notice many, many, many "!!!!!!" exclamation points used in this book! Why? Because that is what entrepreneurship and entrepreneurship education are all about!!!!! You must be excited about it!!!!! **You must be passionate** as a standard bearer for developing tomorrow's entrepreneurs, including yourself, if you are a fledgling Entrepreneur!!!!!

Entrepreneurs are exciting and excited!!!!! To help them to fulfill their destiny, **you must be excited and exciting in all you do** with them!!!!!

Make it happen for those you teach, help and guide!

Help them to make their lives into exclamation!!!!!!!!!

I ask the reader to:

Read this book in Small Snippets! Never more than a chapter at a time!

Learn! There is so much in this book that will help you!

"Borrow" and make better anything you want from this book! That is what we want, for you to use what we have provided for you!

Adopt the ideas we have given you, as they fit your unique ambiance!

Adapt its content to your life, culture and situation! We have provided some wonderful, neat action oriented material in this book!

But of most importance, after reading this book, **go out and do something wonderful, fun, majestic, and powerful for yourself and your corner of the world!**

"A rock pile ceases to be a rock pile the moment a single man contemplates it, bearing with him the image of a cathedral."

Antoine de Saint-Exupery

Chapter One

Setting the Entrepreneurial Stage: This is the Age of the Entrepreneur!

We Are Living in "Wow!!!" Times

By Fred Kiesner

Fred Kiesner was an entrepreneur in the import/export business, ran a small country newspaper, and he had a fun business as a freelance writer and photographer! He began teaching courses in how to start your own business while an entrepreneur, in 1969. A heart attack in 1974 encouraged him to switch to a full-time career as an educator at Loyola Marymount University! He is still proud to be a full-time entrepreneurship professor, holder of the Conrad Hilton Chair of Entrepreneurship, and Director of the LMU Entrepreneurship program! The LMU Entrepreneurship Program that he heads

1

has been ranked in the Top Twenty Five Entrepreneurship Programs in the USA for over a decade, and for the past several years has been in the Top 10 rankings! He is so very pleased to have been able to witness — and play a small role in the growth of Entrepreneurship Education over the past 40 years!

INTRODUCTION

The purpose of this chapter is to get you, as an entrepreneur or a teacher of entrepreneurs, to think positively about the absolutely wonderful ambiance in which entrepreneurs are operating, **and how you, as a creator of entrepreneurs, must think!**

We are living in an age of exceptional opportunity for folks of all ages, sizes, shapes, heritage, and personal persuasions. **The game is wide open for anybody!!!!!!!!!!** There are so few limits to finding their way to exceptional success in life if they truly want it.

The key is, we are truly living in the **AGE OF THE ENTREPRENEUR!!!!!**

No, it is not because the economy is good or bad at the time you are reading this book (but in my opinion it does not matter if times are good or bad, opportunity is always knocking)!

Nope, it is not because there are plenty of jobs available (but even in times of high unemployment, the future looks absolutely wonderful, anyway from the entrepreneurial viewpoint)!

It doesn't matter how old you are. I have met young entrepreneurs who have sold their businesses for millions of dollars while they are still in high school, and for hundreds of millions of dollars just a few years out of school. And there are many wonderful entrepreneurs who are staying young by fulfilling their dreams by starting their businesses in their golden years, often finding the power they never knew they had within them for the first 60 or 70 years of their lives.

Color does not matter, poverty does not matter in the entrepreneurship game. Nobody can blame their failure to thrive in life on anything at all, **except their own failure to take control of their own life and destiny**, through entrepreneurship.

Education is not the key (though often it does help a lot) but learning and knowledge are critical ingredients.

It doesn't even matter if the world is at relative peace or at war!!!!!

Without question, more than at any other time in the history of mankind, everybody, anywhere in the world, has a wonderful chance to find their successful niche in the world through entrepreneurship.

It is an incredible time we live in, a time when even the poorest of the poor, in the most inaccessible most remote location in the world, can become successful by **finding a need, taking the first steps to starting their own business, and solving the problems around them.**

Entrepreneurship allows the willing, the eager, the excited, the passionate, the bright, the "believing" to find fulfillment through earning their living and impacting the world through their own **wits**, and through the wonderful powerful brains we each possess, if we stretch them.

Entrepreneurship provides the vehicle and process for mankind to fully utilize the power of our minds.

Cool, huh!?!?

Entrepreneurship is the potential mega change in the power structure of the world, truly! Anyone now can find success and have the power to make an impact on the world through entrepreneurship.

The key is, they **must take action, they must choose to take the first step and try their luck at Entrepreneurship!!!!!**

They may fail, but so what? Entrepreneurship tolerates failure, and entrepreneurs learn so very, very much from their failures.

It is the age of the quick, the young acting and thinking, the knowledgeable!

In the "good old days" of just a decade or two ago, young people world wide had to spend decades learning the ropes and trudging up the ladder before they got the power to control their own destiny, if they ever reached that position!!!!! Their future was in the hands of those above them. If they made a single mistake, or didn't play the game right, their future careers could be destroyed, period!

Today, as entrepreneurs, they create their own destiny!!!

They can't wait!!!

They don't have to wait!!!

We are clearly in the age of knowledge, information, and action. Things change incredibly fast now. Look at how fast the economies of the world tumbled — in just months! Those who know how to gain knowledge and information and **act upon it have no limits!!!**

If you come up with a new idea that solves a problem, fills a need, and has a niche that you can identify and target, you

may have a real shot at making it, regardless of whether the world's economy is flying high or crash landing.

The **winners** of the future are those who **create their own future!**

Those who just keep doing things "as we always did them" are the losers of the future.

Look at everything you interact with today and how fast it is changing. I can clearly attest to that, really. I used outhouses, inkwells and crank telephones when I was a kid.

It is estimated that **knowledge (what we know) doubles every two years**, and with technology changes, this will soon happen every six months (if it isn't true already). This should remove any wonderment you may have as to why the big old cumbersome companies of the past are decaying. Many are dead, they just haven't rolled over yet and collapsed. (Hello, GM, are you still awake?)

Don't fight it, enjoy it and join it! Join the Age of the Entrepreneur! Be entrepreneurial in all you do. You must ensure that you are the one in charge of causing some of the exciting changes of the future, not just a bystander wondering what happened!

THE KEY IS IN YOUR MIND AND HEART

There are several keys to making it in the future, wonderful world of Entrepreneurship.

1. **Stop worrying about bad times and troubles!** Don't read the fear mongering in the papers! **Disruption, change, churn, chaos are the breeding places of the future. That is where the action and opportunities are. Embrace chaotic change, it is the entrepreneur's friend.**

2. **Think like an entrepreneur 24 hours a day**, in all you do, in everything you are involved in! Look for an opportunity, a problem you can conquer, a path to something new in all you do, then act on it.

3. **Do not forget that even the biggest firms need entrepreneurial thinking to survive!** Save them by your entrepreneurial thinking (but be aware of the fact that many big firms fear entrepreneurial thinking and want protect their past glories, fearing change). You may get fired for being entrepreneurial, but then you will be free to chart your own course. Many grand entrepreneurial success stories have been created by folks who were fired from big firms for thinking entrepreneurially!

4. **Don't be negative!** The entrepreneurial mind is **always positive**. If you get fired, remember, that losing your job provides a grand incentive to take that first step on the business idea you have always had deep within you.

5. When you catch yourself saying "they ought to do something about this," remember, I have never met "they." You must be the "they," **be the entrepreneur who recognizes opportunity in problems!** So do something about it yourself.

6. Constantly thrive on and seek knowledge in life. It is the lifeblood of the successful entrepreneur. But then, it is critically important to act on it and figure out how to use it to fulfill a need or solve a problem.

7. **Keep thinking BIG, always!**

8. **Seek out challenge and risk!** But be sure it is a risk you can impact and mitigate by your ability, knowledge and leadership. Only a fool plays the lottery. The successful entrepreneur

only bets on a deal where they can impact the outcome by their action, wits, and knowledge!

9. **Action is the key ingredient for entrepreneurial success**. There are millions of timid souls out there who had great ideas, but never took the first step to pursue them and see if they really were good enough to be born.

10. **You must BELIEVE!** You must **BELIEVE in yourself!** So very many opportunities go unfulfilled because people hesitate and do not think they are "good enough" to do it. How can you possibly know that, if you don't try it? And, if it works, **WOW!, what a grand ride you will have.** If you don't believe, and don't at least take the first few steps, you are guaranteeing that you are not good enough to be an entrepreneur. **Don't fail by omission!** At least go down trying, and having fun, and learning. Then, if you do fail, start another business and succeed. Most billionaires I know have failed at least two or three times before winning. **Winning comes from growing! Failure is a part of the growth experience.** I teach failure. Don't be afraid of it, embrace it and learn from it. Certainly you are good enough to test the waters and find out if you are entrepreneurial, and if your idea flies. How can you doubt that?

11. **Stop making excuses!** "Just do it" is the old adage that has heavy truth to it. If nothing else, experiment with starting a business on the side. Don't invest the mortgage money, but pursue it with the play money you have that you would have blown anyway on toys and trinkets and Café-Latte-Frappe-Crape! If you make it, think of how many, much better, toys and trinkets you can buy, and you can own a coffee plantation of your own!

12. If you are a winner at entrepreneurship, you know inherently that **you just have to control your own destiny**, and

you act. Losers spend their lives making excuses and blaming others for what they didn't do! **<u>Which are you?</u>**

13. Finally, entrepreneurs, and winners, have **<u>fun</u>** in all they do. Find your passion in life that excites you, and be sure it is something you really enjoy doing!

Now, please say the following ten times, quietly, within your heart and soul, and do this every day until this medicine takes full effect on your heart, mind, and soul, and you win:

I am a winner! I can achieve whatever I want!!!!!

"Creativity requires the courage to let go of certainties."

Erich Fromm

Chapter Two

The Crazy Entrepreneurial Professor! Crazy Like a Fox!

By Fred Kiesner

Adapted from an article of the same title published in the International Journal of Entrepreneurship and Innovation, Volume 4, Number 1, 2003, pp. 77–79. Copyright © 2003 IP Publishing Ltd. Used by permission."

Why is this chapter right up front in this book? Because it is your editor's belief that the single most important ingredient for success in an entrepreneurship educator and developer of winners is the persona that they project to their "customers," the entrepreneurs, and future entrepreneurs!!!!! Hopefully this article will stimulate you to think about the image your customers have about you and your methods!

Start thinking heavily on this now, regardless of what is going on in the world economy and situation!

Have You Ever Met A Boooooooring Entrepreneur?

You can call them a lot of things, but "boring" and "uninteresting" are not adjectives that normally fit the entrepreneurial creators of the future in any way at all.

No way, no how!!!!!!

> **You can call them passionate, weirdoes, failures-made-good, successes made into failures, nuts, out of control, unorthodox, impatient, quirky, creative, innovative, action-oriented, unique, outlandish, rule breakers, troublemakers, irreverent, winners, oddballs, extroverts, eccentric, way-out, cool dudes, characters, controversial, non-conformist, etc., etc., etc.,. But absolutely, positively, never, never, never, ever call them boring!!!!!**

The above descriptors are all **terms that are regularly used to describe entrepreneurial types!** We could add many dozens more of exciting and passionate words to this list. Clearly the entrepreneur is not a "normal" person! If that is the case, then clearly they should not be treated as a normal person in the classroom!

They are special, and they need to be treated in a super special manner by academia, coaches, mentors, and those who guide them, or **we will lose them totally as our customers.**

Thus, if you accept the premise that entrepreneurs are different and unique, then frankly, if you are going to teach, consult with, train, develop, help, or build entrepreneurs, you must, simply, **gain their trust and interest!**

How do you do that?

Damned if I know, cuz it is different for every single person. Nobody can do exactly what I do, nor should they. And without doubt, I certainly can't copy and be like anyone else if I am to be truly entrepreneurial.

THE SECRET FORMULA (YOU BETCHA, SVEN)

What I can tell you is that one way of teaching that works well for me is to get into the entrepreneurs' minds by being like them, by being entrepreneurial in how I teach!

The following are **a few words that I have often heard used to describe me** and my teaching methodologies (hopefully sometimes in an affectionate manner) by students at my own university, and in schools throughout the world where I have taught. Here they are:

> **I am passionate, a weirdo, a failure-made-good, a success made into a failure, nuts, out of control, unorthodox, impatient, quirky, creative, innovative, action-oriented, unique, outlandish, rule breaker, troublemaker, irreverent, a winner, an oddball, an extrovert, eccentric, way-out, cool dude, a true character, controversial, non-conformist, etc. etc. etc. But absolutely, positively, never, never, never, ever call me boring!!!!!**

Does this sound familiar? If so, maybe you will get my point (hint, hint, look back above in this article to the fifth paragraph). **A teacher of entrepreneurship must be an entrepreneur!** Teachers of entrepreneurs must be "one of their own" if they are to have a tremendous impact on the future entrepreneurial leaders of the world.

You want to teach entrepreneurship? You had best totally infuse the entrepreneurial spirit into your class, your personality, your being, and your life!

Translated to street talk, this means you must **Keep Entrepreneurs Awake!** They have fast minds that wander quickly, and if you don't keep them riveted totally on you, as their teacher, and what you are trying to impart to them, you will rapidly lose them.

You must become totally entrepreneurial in everything you do! Again, please refer to the adjectives above for a refresher course in what that means.

In my view, you must become an entertainer, through and through!

This is obscene blasphemy to many academic teachers. How awful! Do you mean to say teachers should entertain their audience, especially if they are entrepreneurial characters?

You bet! No other way to do it.

We often hear how successful entrepreneurs dropped out of school, mostly because they had things to do and places to go, were misunderstood, under-served, and felt school was adding nothing to their preparation for their destiny. In short, they were **booooored** and didn't want to waste any more time **with boooooooring professors** and the often petrifying, booooooring academic book learning methodology.

BREEDING OR TRAINING

Are entrepreneurs born, or are they made? There "ain't" no answer to that one, and it doesn't matter anyway. I personally believe it is a little bit of both sides! Entrepreneurs seem to have some inborn genes that make them different, **and we can hone and develop their talents** to help them be better entrepreneurs, and better able to realize their potential.

> **A winner of an entrepreneur is like a fine racehorse, breeding certainly counts, but heart is the critical ingredient, and training and development is the difference between the winners and the also-rans!**

I believe with all my heart that we can train entrepreneurs and be of tremendous value to them. But to do it, we must get by their impatience, their quirks, and their "weirdiocity!"

We must get their attention. With a racehorse you can perhaps do that with the whip and a few sugar cubes. Nice idea, but all that does for entrepreneurs is create angry, fat people.

The best advice I can give you? **Don't fight 'em, join 'em!**

Yes, be entrepreneurs, be like they are, and entertain them. Don't whip them and beat them to death with the normal dull classroom methodology! Don't blunt their minds with sugar coated, mostly worthless recitations from dull, dim-witted textbooks.

Be an actor or actress (unleash your "hidden thespian,") and every now and then you can slip in some incredibly useful words of wisdom while entertaining them with good stuff. Actually, with a little practice, you can actually impart knowledge and useful information while being entertaining!

Now there is **a startling revelation and concept!!!!!!!!!!!!!!**

The True Word! A Partial, Incomplete, And Still Growing List of "How To's"

(Warranted to work for exactly 33 seconds for you. They work for me, they might work for you, try them.)

Now I am going to be like the accountants and give you a warning that what I am about to tell you might probably be wrong for some, that I can't guarantee it is correct, and that it will work for me, but might not for you. In short, here is a bit of a capsule look at what works for me, in teaching in the classroom, and in seminars and one on one consulting:

1. Turn them on! Get them excited!

2. Get them excited! Turn them on!

3. Refer to #1 and #2 regularly, and intermix and stir them constantly, adding new excitement daily, hourly, and by the minute!

Well, good folks, that is the formula that works for me.

You say you want more specifics? OK, here goes the good old college try!

- **Passion and excitement are the key words!** Sometimes I scream and yell at my students to make a point, not in anger, but rather in passion! I sometimes even swear and am a bit profane (as an old army sergeant and an Irishman, this comes naturally, but I never ever use the **real bad words**). I have even been known to tell a slightly off-color joke or two, but mostly my jokes are just plain fun and often so bad they are good! At other key moments I am soft and serious, and speak in a whisper (neat technique for gaining the attention of those whose minds wander). Move around the classroom a lot too, if your arthritis allows it!

- **Be totally, completely different from anything else they have ever seen or met!** Have the *"huevos rancheros"* (look it up in a Spanish dictionary, and then use your imagination). Every thing I do, every fiber of my body screams to be different! As an example, my personal email address is not my name, it is "himself@frazmtn.com" If you can't respect yourself enough to be different and a bit odd, and poke fun at yourself, how can you ask your students to respect you as somebody they can learn from?

Don't be part of the herd!

- **Have Fun!** Often I do crazy things in the classroom to make a point! My students never know what I will do next, and thus they never miss class and are always watchful of what is going on. In the process, they tune in, not out! I have a whole closet full of costumes, wigs, and silly things! One day I might wear my Willie Nelson wig (goes well with my beard, gray hair, and awful singing voice). Another time I might go in my head-to-toe yellow chicken costume with orange pantyhose. (I am famous on campus for wearing orange pantyhose. The costume was a gift of that entrepreneurial great Stew Leonard, who always knew how to get the attention and achieve the results he wanted.)

For evidence of my weirdiocity, take a look at the pictures included with my chapters in this book!

Students who come into my office are wowed by a weird assortment of strange pictures of me, for example, as Santa Claus sitting on the President's lap (the president of our university, a Jesuit priest, at that. I certainly would never sit on the lap of President Clinton, President Bush, or President Obama! I don't take this weird stuff that seriously)! There is the picture of me as a hippie, teaching in the sixties and seventies (my God, we wore awful clothes then), and the picture of their Prof. as an idiotic looking seventeen year old in the army, trying to look macho and heroic! I love the picture the students did of me, digitally transposing my head onto Arnold Schwarzenegger's body (close, but doesn't quite fit right). In short, show them that you can be fun as a Prof. and that it is OK to have fun in business and as an entrepreneur, so long as you also work like hell!

Early in my career I quickly learned that if you can't make fun of yourself, and make others happy, and not take life too seriously, then life just isn't worth living! Many Entrepreneurs entertain such revolutionary thinking!

- **Feed them a constantly changing mixture** of jokes and tiny bits of good and useful information in a constantly fast-moving, always exciting, always passionate series of one-act plays that illustrate your subject and the point you want to make. One might call my lectures and teaching disjointed, but I plan it that way. You can't teach and lecture from the book, with Entrepreneurs, therefore don't let your teaching methodology look like, or act like, you are regurgitating a book! Know your subject and material, and constantly repackage it for the entrepreneurial mind! I never use notes. At most I take one 3×5 card to the classroom that has a few key word prompts in case I forget a subject area I want to cover.

- **Get under their skins, get in their minds!** Make them think, test, and fail, not memorize and regurgitate! Let them know you are one of them, an oddball like they are! A good entrepreneur believes nobody else is anything like them, and they love being different. They also totally respect others who think and act in that manner! So, does this give you a clue as to what you must be?

- **Force them to discover themselves** and their strengths! The most important single assignment I give my students is a "self-assessment" assignment (presented in a later chapter). They must review their lives in the past, identify their experiences and failures, assess their present strengths, and then set their road-map for the future, setting a target of activities and actions they must take to make their life special and of great impact! It forces them to dream, and **DREAM BIG!!!!!**

I am convinced that at least 50% of the ingredients for success in the world of entrepreneurial endeavor are composed of a total and unflinching belief on the part of the entrepreneur that they are good, and that they have something to add to the world. Sadly we seldom "teach" this in school. Rather we often value conformity, being bean counters, and specializing in working in the shadows of others rather than creating a new shadow.

Entrepreneurs make themselves great! It doesn't happen by accident! They must find their path, we just try to give them a nudge or two!

In my self-assessment theory they must then embark on a serious and thoughtful discussion of who they are, and why they are here on this earth. Surely it can't be to just have fun and party!

Then they are encouraged to dream the dream and predict the future, telling themselves who they will be, and what they will achieve in life! I do this with little sections of the assignment such as forcing them to write their own obituary (dreaming of what will be said of them at the end of their fruitful career! Wow, does this get you thinking of where you have been and what the road ahead must be if you are to have real impact). And they must also write their own seven or eight word epitaph, what few words will be put on their tombstone that will sum up the essence and core of their life and their accomplishments!

- **Toss out the book!** When teaching entrepreneurs, the book, if you do use one, is only a reference source, the place you go to get a few ideas you can build upon, change, and improve. Yes, I have a book for my classes, two of them, in fact. One is a serious book that my students can refer to when they are stumped about how entrepreneurs might do something. The other is the Dr. Seuss book, *"Oh The Places You'll Go,"* a wonderful book children of all ages should read! It makes them think about who they are, and where they can go. Frankly, the Seuss book is much more useful in getting entrepreneurial students to understand what their role is in the world than any textbook.

- **Trashcan the tests and the traditional papers!** Every single thing I do in the class has practical use in getting my students to know themselves and their inner power! Reading classical textbooks and memorizing timeworn techniques is a waste of time for the Entrepreneur. What the textbooks have in them is just a basic summary of what has happened, and what worked yesterday. Use that as a reference mainly, and a basic foundation for building future success, and never make students memorize material for tests! What works changes much too fast! If it works today, it probably won't work tomorrow. What you must teach them is to think, experiment, try, fail, and try again! They are re-inventing themselves constantly, while inventing the future.

- **Yes, teach them to fail!** Failure is the life's blood of the entrepreneur! They grow from it, they learn from it, they succeed from it! I don't wish my students "good luck" at the end of the term! I wish them many, many failures, and one more success than their failures! Then they will be very big winners in life!!!!! Perfectionists and bean counters are the arch-enemy of the successful entrepreneur. Teach them to fail fast, fail often, and fail spectacularly. That is the fodder and manure from which magnificent successes are fertilized!

- **Be a storyteller, not a "lecturer"!** Those who dream of changing the world can get involved in stories, especially if they have a powerful point that they can visualize and use and apply right away!

Every single thing you do in your teaching and your classes must have value to the entrepreneur. Every story you tell must teach them something they can use and apply tomorrow, or even tonight. Storytelling is an immensely useful tool to impart knowledge. Tell them stories about the entrepreneurial winners and losers of the world. However, I seldom have guest speakers **in my classes!** I like to make the points of the stories quickly, and an entrepreneurial winner/speaker wants to take the whole period to convince the audience they are great. They are, but time waits for no man, and for my students, every minute is important.

I do bring living entrepreneurial winners to the campus for special monthly seminars and presentations which are open to the entire campus. This works!

I also demand that my students go out and find an entrepreneur in the field they are pursuing who is a big, big winner that has had an impact on changing the world, and their field. They must interview them, and then give the class a brief, two-page summary of what their minds are like (not a history lesson of what they did, rather, an in depth study of what makes them tick). Boy, does this work in teaching students how to make cold calls, how to get close to the very best, how to gain the attention of potential mentors, about rejection, and most of all, it teaches them that they are just as good as their interviewees and entrepreneurial role models. It is just that they are still in training, and a few years behind on the time line of their inevitable success!

If your students can **stand toe-to-toe, and eye-to-eye with great entrepreneurial winners,** you will marvel at how they leave the encounter with a much stronger belief in their own future and pride in what they are made of.

- **Exult and cheer** with your students at their victories! You must only allow them 24 hours to celebrate a great victory, then it is time for them to build the next victory upon this current victory. Too many people have early victories, think they are magnificent, do no more, and never achieve their true destiny!

- **Cry** with your students, and share their defeats! Be a shoulder for them to lean on, and a powerful role model for them to emulate! Be someone they can touch, hug, and learn from and with! But teach them to waste no more than 24 hours mourning a failure. Then they must move on to greater things!!!!!

- **Be truly an entrepreneur!** As a teacher of entrepreneurs, your product is the future success of your students! Build the best products you can!

I like to start off the first chat of a course or seminar by telling my students that I am still an entrepreneur, that I am still in the manufacturing business, **that I manufacture the future yuppies and winners of the world!**

Please note, I did say **chat** above. You must talk with your customers from the heart and soul, not as a lecturer! When they leave my classroom, I want them to think they have each just had a one on one chat with me, no matter how many people may have been in the class or seminar. You do this with total and complete eye contact, always working the room from side to side and front to back. Every now and then I focus on one student, get in their face (in a friendly manner), make a point, and move on!

- **Be you!** Don't be me. Don't be anybody else! Develop your own style. Test constantly what strengths and innovative ideas and methodologies you have in your guts, heart, and soul, and then try them out. **Don't be afraid of failing, yourself.** It only hurts for a little while, and wow, do you grow from it!

- **Remember that Entrepreneurship is universal!** In your teaching, counseling, mentoring, remember, Entrepreneurship fits in all fields and endeavors. The engineer or the piccolo player could be tomorrow's world class Entrepreneur! Teach and help them all!

Where To Now? Who Knows? Don't Ask Me, Ask Yourself!

Will this stuff work for you? Probably not, at least not in the exact form it does for me!

It has worked for me! I have had a wonderful, productive, and exciting life teaching entrepreneurs throughout the world. (Ireland, Singapore, China, Russia, France, Eastern Europe, etc.) I have taught at the biggest schools (UCLA and the Univeristy of Michigan) and at the small schools (LMU and junior colleges!) Oh! How I love to teach at the smaller schools. I have had wonderful victories and honors, and my products (students) are winners in life all over the world!

Most of all, I have had an incredible amount of fun hanging out with successful entrepreneurial types, and helping them to fulfill their destiny!

My fervent prayer is that what I (and other great minds) have written here will inspire you to experiment just a little bit with being entrepreneurial and absolutely exciting, creative, and stimulating in the classroom. Once again, let me repeat the formula or description of what you must be to be successful as an entrepreneurial educator:

> You must be passionate, a weirdo, a failure-made-good, a success made-into-a-failure, nuts, out of control, unorthodox, impatient, quirky, creative, innovative, action-oriented, unique, outlandish, a rule breaker, troublemaker, irreverent, a winner, an oddball, an extrovert, eccentric, way-out, cool dude, a true character, controversial, nonconformist, etc. etc. etc. But absolutely, positively, never, never, never, ever let yourself be called boring!!!!!

Be an Entrepreneurial Teacher!!!!!

You can be!

You must be!

Will you be?

Honestly check the answer here, please: ___ Yes! ___ No.

If you answered yes, send me an email with news about your successes and defeats, and give me a war story or two about your victories in creating tomorrow's entrepreneurial leaders and winners!

"It takes courage to grow up and turn out to be who you really are."

E. E. Cummings

Chapter Three

Creating The 21st Century Entrepreneurial Campus

By Donald F. Kuratko

Professor Kuratko is a prominent scholar and leader in Entrepreneurship Education in the US and internationally. He has authored 24 books, including several of the leading books in the field of entrepreneurship internationally. He has been honored by Entrepreneur Magazine as the #1 Entrepreneur Professor in America. He has published more than 180 articles on Entrepreneurship around the world. Dr. Kuratko is a consultant on Corporate Innovation to a number of major Fortune 100 corporations. He is the founder and Executive Director of the Global Consortium of Entrepreneurship Centers (GCEC), an organization of top university Entrepreneurship centers throughout the world. Under his leadership, the Indiana University Entrepreneurship Program has been ranked #1 for Graduate and Undergraduate

Entrepreneurship Programs (Public Institutions) by "U.S. News & World Report." In addition, Dr. Kuratko and his Entrepreneurship Programs have earned a myriad of honors and awards from academic, governmental, and journalist organizations throughout the world.

INTRODUCTION

Indiana University's Kelley School of Business has established a model program in cross-campus entrepreneurial development at Indiana University-Bloomington. The Johnson Center for Entrepreneurship & Innovation (JCEI) leadership team works to implement projects and initiatives to further the **development of entrepreneurial growth across the Bloomington campus.** The vision has been to create the "21st Century Entrepreneurial Campus" by establishing offices, programs, initiatives, and experiential entrepreneurship curriculum in the diverse schools across the campus.

Rather than take the "virtual" approach that many universities have taken, our approach is much more a "hands-on" material approach to establishing the entrepreneurial mindset throughout the campus. **The focus is on the IU School of Medicine, the IU College of Arts & Sciences, the IU School of Informatics, the IU Jacobs School of Music, The IU School of Law, the IU School of Journalism, and the IU School of Public & Environmental Affairs.** The impact for the students at Indiana University could be immense, and the economic benefit of this initiative will be harvested in the generations to come.

OVERVIEW

The Entrepreneurship Program at Indiana University was founded in 1989, although individual courses in entrepreneurship were introduced at Indiana University in 1959.

We have now developed one of the world's largest entrepreneurship faculties **with some of the world's most** recognized entrepreneurship thought leaders **from departments in Management, Finance, and Marketing in the Kelley School of Business, as well as the School of Public & Environmental Affairs.**

Indiana University offers one of the most comprehensive **entrepreneurship curriculums** and includes an undergraduate major in entrepreneurship, an MBA in Entrepreneurship, a PhD in Entrepreneurship, and an Entrepreneurship Academy for MBA students.

The Entrepreneurship program has **multiple offices** in the School of Business, the Medical School, the School of Law, and the College of Arts & Sciences, as well as affiliations with the Jacobs School of Music and the School of Informatics!

Our programs provide students with a wide range of classroom and experiential opportunities to discover and **develop the "entrepreneurial perspective"** throughout the entire campus. The Johnson **Center** for Entrepreneurship & Innovation is the **focal point** for all entrepreneurship activities.

MISSION AND FOCUS OF THE IU ENTREPRENEURSHIP PROGRAM

Primary Mission

The Entrepreneurship degree bridges the classroom theory and the real business world and emphasizes the **development of an "entrepreneurial perspective" in each and every student** by incorporating the fundamentals of business creation and innovation with the importance of **interacting and networking with the entrepreneurial community.**

Primary Audience

The Entrepreneurship Program is aimed primarily at full-time students enrolled in a comprehensive degree program on the campus. The research based PhD Program in Entrepreneurship contains cohorts totaling eight students carefully selected. Of the 400 MBA students admitted (first and second years) to the MBA program, more than 120 MBAs actively participate in the entrepreneurship program. There are 200 undergraduate majors/minors in entrepreneurship.

DEGREES IN ENTREPRENEURSHIP

PhD Program in Entrepreneurship

Launched in 2000, the PhD program in Entrepreneurship is one of only six such entrepreneurship programs in the country.

MBA Program in Entrepreneurship & Corporate Innovation

The MBA Entrepreneurship curriculum **focuses on new venture creation as well as innovative development inside existing corporations.** Students may major or minor in Entrepreneurship & Corporate Innovation, taking courses in entrepreneurship leadership and practice, corporate entrepreneurship, new venture strategy, new venture business planning, growth management, and strategic management of innovation and technology.

Bachelors Degree Program in Entrepreneurship & Corporate Innovation

This major involves the study of the special skills and knowledge needed by entrepreneurs and managers of **small to medium-sized firms.** In a **collaborative effort** with other schools on the IU campus, the Management & Entrepreneurship Department also offers an **Entrepreneurship minor** to non-business students.

By weaving entrepreneurial themes through core business courses, IU students can combine their areas of expertise with sound business principles.

SPECIAL AND UNIQUE PROGRAMS IN ENTREPRENEURSHIP

The Entrepreneurial Management Academy (EMA)

The Academy is a required **Experiential Component** of the MBA in Entrepreneurship. One thing that makes the Indiana University MBA experience unique is the **ability for students to customize their degree plan**. The "Academies" offer a unique feature where students focus on a particular industry and/or career option and experience intensive immersion into that particular area of interest.

The Academy offers exposure to the emerging life sciences, high-tech and fast growth companies, as well as venture capitalists, angel investors, and professionals involved in the entrepreneurial process. It is designed to help students develop the skills and contacts needed to pursue entrepreneurial leadership careers such as working in developing new businesses within large corporations, leading their own independent businesses, or starting-up or buying an existing business, and some students will seek senior management positions with small, growing ventures or corporate entrepreneurial positions in established corporations.

Other students may develop their interests in the emerging life sciences field. Finally, some students will pursue positions in private equity firms, venture capital firms, or consulting to the entrepreneurial community. The Academy is combined with the Entrepreneurship and Corporate Innovation major or minor so that classroom knowledge is then translated into practice.

EMA "Intensive Weeks"

Each "Academy" is assigned **four "Academy Intensive Weeks"** for the two-year, full-time MBA students. These weeks occur either before or between the seven-week course sessions in the MBA program. These four weeks are required and students earn **full course credit for each completed week.** The following sections briefly describe the general activities contained in each Intensive Week.

Academy Intensive Week #1

Introduction to the field, career guidance and career panels, professional assessment, typical issues facing the leaders of new ventures, and professional development activities. Guest speakers are utilized along with a field trip to Indianapolis where the MBAs interact with company CEOs in the Indiana University Emerging Technology Center (an incubator for high-tech and life science companies). The week also includes a "Bio-Tech Primer," conducted by two experts in the life sciences industry so the students gain a perspective on this emerging area of new venture development, and a due dilligence primer conducted by venture capitalists for students to understand the decision process in funding a view venture.

Academy Intensive Week #2

Intensive Immersion Experiences are conducted by the MBAs during the seven weeks leading up to this week. These unique seven-week project experiences provide MBA student teams an immediate immersion into the specific challenges facing emerging life science or high technology companies.

Acting as an **"Entrepreneurial Action Team,"** each challenge much be assessed, defined, and solved within the reduced time frame in order to provide real-time solutions to the fast moving company. Final presentations are made to the clients during intensive week #2.

Another important component of the second Academy Intensive Week is **The Velocity Conference.** This annual event, organized by the Kelley School of Business, is held every year in partnership with other universities for the purpose of "accelerating entrepreneurial careers." Students have the opportunity to meet CEOs from high-potential businesses, venture capitalists funding them, and other individuals instrumental in launching them. Past host schools have included Stanford University, the University of Texas-Austin, Rice University, Boston University, MIT, the University of California-Berkeley, Syracuse University, the University of Southern California, and Texas A&M University.

Academy Intensive Week #3

The Live Case Study **"Innovation Competition"** provides a chance for students to practice venture analysis, strategy development, and venture planning skills from an investor's viewpoint. MBA "Action Teams" must spend an intensive week reviewing and researching the commercial potential of applicants to the state of Indiana's $75 million 21st Century Research & Technology Fund. **"Kelley Action Teams" present their conclusions to a judging panel** comprised of members of the Indiana Economic Development Corporation.

Academy Intensive Week #4

Here the MBAs from all of the academies integrate back together for a **final school-wide case competition**. This is a comprehensive challenge case with the actual business entrepreneur/founder present to explain the challenges involved with the case and then witness the students' resulting work.

Other Activities During Intensive Weeks

The students interact here with successful entrepreneurs, corporate innovators, and venture capitalists through the Entrepreneur-in-Residence program, the Dye Speaker Series, the IU Angel Network, the Entrepreneurship Law Clinic, and the Indiana University Entrepreneur Day.

Some of the past speakers have included: Dr. Jack Gill, founding partner of Vanguard Ventures; Dr. Roger Newton, founder of Esperion Therapeutics; Todd Wagner, founder of Broadcast.com; Patricia Miller, founder of Vera Bradley; Herb Kelleher, founder of Southwest Airlines; and Irwin Jacobs, founder of Qualcomm; Jack Stack, CEO of SEC Holdings; and Michael Uslan, Producer of the Batman movies.

ADDITIONAL EXPERIENTIAL COMPONENTS

The Entrepreneurial Innovations Lab

It was established for the purpose of supporting the commercialization of life sciences and other high potential research technologies developed by Indiana University faculty. Students have the opportunity to bridge the gap between scientific research and business opportunities by conducting feasibility studies, extensive marketing and competitor analyses, and preparing in-depth business plans.

Intensive Immersion Experiences

These **unique seven-week project experiences** provide MBA student teams an immediate immersion into the specific challenges facing emerging life science or high technology companies. Acting as an **"Entrepreneurial Action Team,"** each challenge must be assessed, defined, and solved within the reduced time frame in order to provide **real-time solutions to the fast moving company.**

THE JOHNSON CENTER FOR ENTREPRENEURSHIP & INNOVATION (JCEI)

We believe this center is the premier entrepreneurship entity facilitating entrepreneurial knowledge creation through entrepreneurial research, teaching, and practice. **It is the hub of action for cross-campus entrepreneurial initiatives in the life sciences, biotechnology, informatics, law, music,** and other entrepreneurial departments that foster the development of aspects of entrepreneurial research or commercially viable enterprises. Its goal is to develop and support knowledge creation and transfer that will advance the fundamental understanding of entrepreneurship, thus increasing the potential for entrepreneurial growth and development.

OTHER UNIQUE ELEMENTS OF THE ENTREPRENEURSHIP PROGRAM

Entrepreneurship Law Clinic

Collaboration between the IU Law Maurev School and the Kelley School of Business that allows business and law students an opportunity to work together on **intellectual property protection issues** with emerging companies.

The Indiana Entrepreneurial Leadership Awards

An outreach program of the Johnson Center for Entrepreneurship & Innovation that **identifies and awards the finest entrepreneurial companies in the region.** This initiative allows students the opportunity to interact with leaders of these emerging companies, as well as develop potential consulting assignments to assist their firms.

The Chambers Internship Program

An **elite internship program** supported by the generosity of John Chambers, CEO of Cisco, designed for entrepreneurship students to immerse themselves into summer experiences with fast growth, high technology firms.

Regular Internship Program

The Johnson Center for Entrepreneurship and Innovation has been able to provide entrepreneurial internship experiences to students across campus during the last few years. MBA and MPA students from the Kelley School of Business and the School of Public & Environmental Affairs, along with undergraduates from the Kelley School of Business and School of Informatics, were able to work for various start-up companies and organizations across the state of Indiana, The Johnson Center for Entrepreneurship and Innovation (JCEI) will continue to secure additional funding resources in order to provide entrepreneurial internship opportunities to more students from across campus.

The Distinguished Entrepreneur-In-Residence Program

The Center for Entrepreneurship also brings guest speakers to campus as part of the Distinguished Entrepreneur-In-Residence program so students can learn from and network with successful entrepreneurs. Students from all across campus are invited to participate in this event to help them explore the various entrepreneurial career paths from which they may choose.

Campus-Wide Special Programs

The Entrepreneurship Program has created offices and affiliations across the Indiana University campus in order to immerse the entrepreneurial perspective throughout the schools and colleges.

JCEI has its home office in the Kelley School of Business and satellite offices with the School of Medicine, the School of Law, and the College of Arts & Sciences, as well as affiliations with the Jacobs School of Music, the School of Journalism, and the School of Informatics. Our programs aim to provide students with a wide range of classroom and experiential opportunities to discover and develop the **"entrepreneurial perspective" throughout the entire campus.** The Johnson Center for Entrepreneurship & Innovation is recognized as the focal point for entrepreneurial development of technologies and potential ventures within any discipline at Indiana University.

The Johnson Center for Entrepreneurship & Science Innovations

Located in the new Science Complex, this satellite office of the JCEI is dedicated to the emerging science projects emanating from the laboratories of Indiana University's top scientists. Through this collaboration, MBA students, in conjunction with science students, **embark on a research journey** into the investigation of the commercial potential of technologies developed in the laboratories.

The Johnson Center for Entrepreneurship & Medical Science Innovations

Located in the Emerging Technology Center (IUETC) in Indianapolis near the School of Medicine Complex, this satellite office of JCEI focuses on the medical life sciences developments being created by the physicians and researchers at the School of Medicine. It is the result of a partnership between the MBA in Entrepreneurship Program, the School of Medicine, and the Research & Technology Center.

In a departure from standard practice at business schools, teams of Kelley MBAs are not simply assigned to a company for the semester. Rather, they focus on individual strategic projects for companies and doctors. Through market research and discovery, MBA students, in conjunction with medical science experts, work together to establish the potential commercial viability of the newest medical technologies developed by the medical faculty.

These "intensive immersion experiences" have been developed so that the MBAs can step into projects on a shorter-term basis. MBA Action Teams are involved in researching the market potential for findings coming out the labs. They **look for potential patent conflicts and conduct other business analysis**, which doctors and companies often find time consuming. The students benefit from having an **array of shorter consulting projects**, giving them knowledge that enhances what they're learning in classes. They are exposed to the unique challenges facing life science start-ups and are exposed to emerging technologies and opportunities.

Life Sciences have become an integral part of the entrepreneurial efforts at Indiana University. There has been much excitement surrounding the collaboration between the Kelley School of Business's JCEI and the IU School of Medicine.

Biomedical Dinner Series

This program operates on a quarterly basis. This dinner series provides medical faculty researchers the chance to meet and learn about how to get their discoveries to market. The researchers have the opportunity to work with the Kelley School of Business MBA entrepreneurship students to put together business analyses. The Biomedical Dinner Series averages thirty medical school faculty focusing on topics such as SBIR and STTR grants and technology transfer policies. In addition, Dr. McDonald and Dr. Kuratko authored "Complete Business Planning Guide" and provided all participants with a copy to give them a feel for what is involved in marketing their research.

The Entrepreneurship Law Clinic

Located inside the JCEI office at the Kelley School of Business, this specialized clinic provides unique legal challenges for JD/MBAs, as well as JDs working alongside MBAs in relation to emerging venture initiatives in the Indiana University Emerging Technology Center and from laboratories across the campus.

The Entrepreneurship Law Clinic (ELC) is a joint program of the Maurev Law School and the Kelley School of Business. The purpose of ELC is to provide law and business students with a unique opportunity to **work on actual business formation, planning, and strategy issues in a multidisciplinary setting**. In terms of educational and clinical experience, the ELC is designed to

* expose students to the practical legal and business realities of start-up and early-stage businesses, and

* provide opportunities for active participation in the legal and business challenges facing such companies.

Students entering the ELC will be primarily fourth-year JD/MBA candidates. The Clinic will focus largely on legal tasks related to early-stage businesses, including

* obtaining permits and licenses

* researching and registering intellectual property rights

* negotiating contracts and leases

* advising on appropriate business form

* drafting necessary formation documents.

ELC students will also draw on the resources and expertise of the Kelley School of Business's Johnson Center for Entrepreneurship while participating in the evaluation, development, and financing of such companies.

These students have worked on projects for various Indiana companies such as Cook, Inc., a start-up company called BioConvergence, IU School of Medicine, and more. Projects have included patent mapping, researching logistical legal issues, business plan refinement, negotiation review, and development of employment policies for rapidly-growing companies, to name a few.

During this collaboration a major academic breakthrough was accomplished. A couple of the ELC students approached the ELC director about implementing a fast track, three year JD/MBA program to offer in addition to the traditional four year program. They put together a program specific to Indiana University and presented it to both the Maurev Law School and Kelley Business School faculty. The program was unanimously approved and has proven to be a successful marketing tool to encourage talented students from around the globe to come to Indiana University.

The Social Entrepreneurship Program

The **Graduate Program in Social Entrepreneurship** combines the top-ranked programs in nonprofit and public management of the School of Public and Environmental Affairs and in entrepreneurship of the Kelley School of Business. It also combines resources with the Center on Philanthropy at Indiana University. It is open to master's degree students on both the Bloomington and Indianapolis campuses to obtain a Certificate in Social Entrepreneurship.

The Social Entrepreneurship Program prepares students for innovatively approaching public needs by applying entrepreneurial practices to social purposes, through the for-profit, nonprofit, and governmental sectors. Students wishing to earn the certificate must take a course on the principles and practices of social entrepreneurship in addition to selected courses designed specifically for this field of study. The certificate includes an internship in the field of social enterprise.

Center for Entrepreneurship & Cultural Leadership

"The Center for Entrepreneurship & Cultural Leadership" is being developed as a collaboration between the Jacobs School of Music and the Johnson Center for Entrepreneurship & Innovation. This extracurricular program is enthusiastically supported by the IU Jacobs Music School. It offers students in the musical arts an opportunity to learn some of the business principles necessary to enhance their careers, as well as exploring entrepreneurial options that exist for their talents.

Informatics and Entrepreneurship Program

The Johnson Center has established a presence in the new incubator on the Bloomington Campus. Working with the IU School of Informatics, it will be the focus of the Johnson Center to provide MBA analysis to the emerging information technologies that stem from IU today.

Certificate in Entrepreneurship and Journalism

A "Certificate in Entrepreneurship & Journalism" is being considered for 2011. This concept has been discussed with and has the support of the School of Journalism. This program would offer students in journalism an opportunity to learn some of the business principles critical to their career field.

WORLD CLASS RANKINGS AND RECOGNITIONS

The Entrepreneurship Program at Indiana University has achieved dozens of the most notable national rankings and recognitions in recent years, demonstrating the thought leadership in entrepreneurship emanating from its faculty and programs.

WORLD CLASS FACULTY

The School of Business features one of the largest and most recognized entrepreneurship faculties in the world. It is ranked among the most prolific business schools for research productivity. Many of the faculty members are among the most recognized thought leaders in their respective areas of research. Fourteen faculty members are associated with the entrepreneurship program.

It is our goal to provide the students of Indiana University, from all colleges and schools, with the most comprehensive immersion program of Entrepreneurship Education in the world! We believe we are well on our way down that path.

"We are not what we know, but what we are willing to learn."

Mary Catherine Bateson

Chapter Four

Developing Effective Business Plans

By Charles W. Hofer

Dr. Charles Hofer is a specialist in New Enterprise Development and has taught at Northwestern, Stanford, Columbia, NYU, the University of Georgia, and Kennesaw State University, where he teaches now. He received a BS in Theoretical Physics (summa cum laude) from Lehigh University, an MS in Applied Mathematics from Harvard University, an MBA in Marketing (with distinction) from Harvard, and a DBA in Business Policy from the Harvard Business School. He has written a number of books, has made over one hundred major presentations, and has had many articles published in academic and trade publications in the field of Entrepreneurship. He has won dozens of awards and honors for his work, including: Fortune Small Business naming him

one of the top 18 professors in America, a Lifetime Achievement Award from the Academy of Management, The International Hall of Fame Entrepreneur's Award from the Inventors Club of America, he was the first recipient of the U.S. Association for Small Business & Entrepreneurship (USASBE) Educator of the Year Award, and he has received a Leavey Award for Excellence in Private Enterprise Education and the Cherry Award for Great Teachers — an award from Baylor University for English Speaking Faculty throughout the entire world. He is a past President of the USASBE organization. His business experience includes being Vice President of Marketing of the Power Ski Corp. and Executive Vice President of the Chicago Strategy Group. He is currently President of the Strategic Management Group, an Atlanta based consulting company specializing in strategy and entrepreneurship issues. Finally (though many of his major accomplishments are not mentioned here), and of most importance to the subject of this Chapter, Dr. Hofer's teams have been ranked as being the winningest teams among universities competing in Business Plan Competitions internationally, including two Grand Champion wins in the Moot Corp. International Business Plan Competition.

THE PURPOSE OF BUSINESS PLANS

The most important questions that MUST be answered when developing a Business Plan for a new venture is:

- What is its purpose?

- Why are you writing it?

There are two major reasons given for writing Business Plans,

1. To formalize your thinking about the business that you intend to start, and

2. To assist in raising money for the start (launch) of your venture.

It is critically important that you understand which is the primary *raison-d'être* of your plan <u>before</u> you begin to develop it.

Plans Developed to Formalize Your Thinking About Your Venture: If the primary purpose of your Plan is to help you formalize your thinking about your venture, you need to make sure that its **content is sufficiently detailed and complete to make sure that you and your startup team have not overlooked any critically important factors related to the launch of your business.** Organization, Style, and Grammar are not crucial, though.

Plans Developed to Raise Money: However, if your primary purpose is to raise money, then **organization, style, and grammar** become much more important. Not more important than content, but, to paraphrase Dr. Steven Nichols of the University of Texas, your **plan needs to be written so well that not only can everyone understand it, it needs to be written so well that no one can misunderstand it.** Among other things, this means that you should have a "trusted" friend or other non-expert read your plan to make sure that they "get" all that you are trying to say.

If your primary purpose is to use your plan to raise money, there are two important facts that you need to remember.

First, **nobody will give you money based on your plan**. All that your plan can do is to get you an interview. Put differently, the primary goal of your plan (from a financial perspective) **is to get you an interview with an investor who will then make the decision on whether or not to fund (in full or in part) your venture** based on:

1. your presentation,

2. your ability to answer questions about your venture,

3. the Due Diligence that they (or the consultants they hire) do on all aspects of your proposed venture.

Second, **the optimal format for your plan will depend on precisely who your proposed investors are**. For instance, if you expect to fund your business with loans, most bankers will not require or expect a "full" business plan. What they will want is an **Executive Summary, plus a set of fully developed financial projections for your venture**.

Why? Because they are making you a loan, not investing equity capital in your venture. So, they need to verify that your proposed venture has the capacity of paying back this loan with interest, and with very little risk of default. By contrast, most VCs will expect and/or require a full business plan at some point during the fund-raising process.

THE STYLE, ORGANIZATION, AND CONTENT OF EFFECTIVE BUSINESS PLANS

The Style, Organization, and Content of **all** effective business plans are determined, or at least influenced, by the "goal" of using the plan to assist in the fund raising process.

The Plan's Style

The three major "Stylistic" considerations of all plans are their:

- Basic Look and Feel,

- Use of Pictures and Colors,

- Professional **PIZZAZ**.

The Plan's Basic Look and Feel

In general, a business plan should convey a very positive impression to its readers (potential investors) that makes them want to ask the startup team in to make a presentation of their venture idea. This "requirement" translates into several very practical parameters regarding the overall "look and feel" of the Plan. These include:

1. Page Margins & Numbering,

2. Font Type and Size,

3. Length and Line Spacing,

4. Exhibits and Appendices,

5. Use of Index Tabs, Headings, and Sub-Headings,

6. Grammar, Spelling, and Numbers.

- **The Plan's Page Margins and Numbers.** In general, good plans should have a reasonable amount of white space, just as good ads do. I recommend one-inch margins all around. Less looks too crowded, and more does not use space (and paper) effectively. These are also the required Margins for almost all Moot Corp® Feeder Business Plan Competitions, with a few exceptions (Moot Corp is the grand daddy of all business plan competitions; it is international in scope, and only winners of other competitions are invited). In general, Covers and the Table of Contents are not numbered. I also recommend numbering the plan's Exhibits separately from its Text. Usually, I prefer to put the page numbers at the bottom of the page on the right. This allows one to insert the venture's "corporate slogan" in the Footer on the left side of the bottom of the page. One-inch margins also allow the insertion of the venture's "corporate logo" (if it has one) in the margin in the upper right part of the page.

- **The Plan's Font Type and Size.** In general, plans should not make readers use magnifying glasses to read them. Both Font Size and Font Type should be selected for ease of reading. For most plans, I recommend either 12-Point Times New Roman font, or the 11.5 or 12-Point Arial font. Almost all Moot Corp® Feeder Business Plan Competitions require 12-Point font. Times New Roman font has the two advantages that it gets more text into a given space than just about any other font and is also familiar to readers because it is used in newspapers and magazines, so it is what I usually recommend, even though I personally prefer the "look" of Arial.

- **The Plan's Length and Line Spacing.** In general, plans should be short. Remember that their principal purpose is to get one an interview with an investor. Also remember that investors want some confidence that the entrepreneur in whom they invest will use their money wisely in order to maximize the likelihood of successfully launching the venture. A 100-page plan bound in leather with gold embossed letters would say just the opposite. So keep it short. My preference is for single-spaced plans with double-spacing between paragraphs. The Total Length of such plans will vary depending on the complexity of the venture's products, markets, and technology. In general, though, such plans should have between 10 and 15 pages of text MAXIMUM. Sometimes I will also use 1.5 line spacing, and such plans should have, in general, 15 to 20 pages of text. Moot Corp® Feeder Business Plan Competitions require double-spacing, something which I personally believe to be a waste of paper. Their Maximum Length for the plan's text is 20 pages.

- **The Plan's Exhibits and Appendices.** Exhibits are Charts, Figures, Graphs, Pictures, Tables, etc. of one page (or less) that are part of the plan that are used to supplement and extend the Plan's Text. The two types of Exhibits found in almost all plans are:

1. pictures of the venture's products and,

2. the venture's pro-forma financial statements i.e., the plan's Net Income by year for five Years, Cash Flows by year for five Years, Balance Sheets by year for five Years, and Cash Flows by month until the venture becomes Cash Flow positive.

I prefer to number Exhibits separately from the Text, usually E-1 to E-n, where *n* is the last page number for the exhibits. I also prefer to put exhibits at the end of the plan's section in which they are referenced. Others prefer to put all exhibits at the end of the plan. In general, there should be fewer pages of exhibits than there are of text. Moot Corp® Feeder Business Plan Competitions limit the total length of the plan to 30 pages with a maximum of 20 pages of text. So, they implicitly provide 10 pages for Exhibits, although one could have more Exhibits if one's text is less than 20 pages.

Appendices, by contrast, should be bound separately. They are the various materials that one can assemble in the preparation of one's plan that an Investor might want to see during a verbal interview with the Entrepreneur. These include copies of the venture's:

1. Articles of Organization or Incorporation,

2. Business Licenses,

3. Patents and/or Patent applications,

4. Trademark and Copyright Filings,

5. Market and Competitive Information collected as part of the team's research,

6. Management and Advisor Resumes,

7. Rapid Growth and Worst Case Financial projections, etc.

- **The Plan's Use of Index Tabs, Headings, and Subheadings.** All investors differ from one another, yet each wants to read precisely that part of the plan in which they have the greatest interest. One of the best ways to achieve this is to use Index Tabs to separate plan sections in the "final" versions of your plan. I also generally recommend starting each new section of a plan at the top of a new page. This can extend the length of the overall plan by a page or two, but the investors and reviewers with whom I have spoken prefer it.

  Note: this can be difficult to do if one is trying to meet the page limits imposed by most business plan competitions.

  One of the best ways to assist the reader, though, is through the use of Headings and Subheadings throughout every macro-section of the plan. My general recommendation is to treat such Headings and Subheadings as "Newspaper Headlines" whose purpose is to "telegraph" the overall structure of your plan while moving your story forward. Note: all plans should have a story or theme, a topic that will be covered shortly. As a consequence, I usually recommend that all Section heading be put in **Bold Type**, Subsection Headings in ***Bold Italic Type***, and Sub-Subsection heading in *Underlined Italic Type*.

- **The Plan's Grammar, Spelling, and Numbers.** Generally, plans should be written in the active voice with simple, short, direct sentences. Earlier, I noted that investors want some confidence that the Entrepreneur in whom they invest will use their money wisely in order to maximize the likelihood of successfully launching the venture. This also means that they expect you, the prospective entrepreneur, to have done your homework in the preparation of your plan — in other words, that you have "invested" the same degree of care in the preparation of your plan that you would in the use of their money. This means that you **must** double (and triple) check your spelling. This is particularly true since computer "Spell Checks" do not catch all mistakes. (For instance, have you used the right "principle"/"principal"?) It also means that you need to double (and triple) check the numbers throughout your entire plan for consistency. Most plans go through multiple "drafts." It is quite easy to miss "correcting a number" in some part of the plan when you get new information, especially if several people are involved in the preparation of the plan. This is one reason that at least one member of the team should be assigned the responsibility of checking everything for accuracy before the plan is sent out to prospective investors, or even to a competition.

THE PLAN'S USE OF PICTURES AND COLOR

The old saw that **"a picture is worth a thousand words"** is absolutely true for business plans. However, given the fact that effective plans have very severe Length requirements, one MUST be very judicious in the choice of the pictures and "picture-like" materials such as Charts, Diagrams, Figures, Graphs, and Tables that should be included in the plan. I usually recommend the use of an eye-catching picture on the plan's front cover that is directly related to the plan's central focus. The front cover should also contain the venture's name, the name and address of the person who should be contacted regarding the plan, and, if it has them, the venture's "corporate slogan" and "corporate logo."

Small pictures (Charts, Diagrams, Figures, Graphs, and Tables) can be inserted in the body of the plan; larger ones should usually be put into Exhibits. All pictures (Charts, Diagrams, Figures, Graphs, and Tables) that are used should be self-explanatory. Each should also "make, explain, and/or confirm" some important point related to the venture's success directly and dramatically.

Color is also an important tool for increasing the overall impact of the plan. However, many **if** not most business men and women, including investors, will develop "negative" reactions to the excessive use of color. Also remember that most major companies have "corporate logos" that contain one, two, or at most three colors, and the same is true of the flags of most countries. So, while color is a useful tool, it must be used wisely, and its use should be directly related to an important aspect of the venture's identity and/or products. Finally, remember to "vet" any tentative color choices with the venture's potential target customers because some colors can create negative rather than positive impressions with their intended audience.

For example, early in my career I was involved in a campaign for the U.S. Congress. Since the candidate involved had a limited budget, a decision was made to choose campaign colors that would uniquely identify "our" candidate. This meant choosing colors that no one else had ever used in that Congressional district. The colors also had to be distinctive, noticeable at a distance, and produce a positive reaction with the voters. The most distinctive and noticeable color was the "lime greenish yellow" used on some fire trucks. Unfortunately, it created negative reactions with almost everyone we interviewed. So, the next most distinctive and noticeable color was the "bright neon orange" used on many Air Force vehicles. When we placed it on a deep auburn red background, it stood out at great distances, and yet also created a very positive image with most voters in this District. And no one else had ever used these colors in this district. Every billboard, bumper sticker, campaign letter, TV advertisement, etc, used these colors. In the opinion of everyone associated with the campaign, this simple color choice was worth tens, if not hundreds, of thousands of dollars in PR, and was one of the factors that led to the election of "our" candidate.

The Plan's Professional PIZZAZ

* Professional PIZZAZ refers to a number of small "touches," professionally done, that add to the plan's overall impact and credibility. They are the written equivalents of handing out "Sample Menus" and "Sample Dishes" during an investor presentation for a new restaurant. The insertion of the venture's "corporate slogan" in page footers and its "corporate logo" in the top right margins of pages is one example of such PIZZAZ. A few other such small touches are putting clear plastic covers on the front and back of the plan, spiral binding it, and using index tabs to separate the plan's various sections for ease of reference. Clearly, the possibilities are limited only by one's imagination and creativity. One must remember, though, that they are "extras" and do not compensate in any way for weaknesses in the plan's "fundamentals." The one "touch" that I try to include on most plans is "upgrades" on both the front and back covers. Far too many plans have plain black plastic or cardstock sheets as their back cover. For consistency, I recommend making the back cover out of the same color cardstock as the front cover, which allows one to use it to add to the plan.

* So, what should one add? I usually recommend a "List" of the Plan's Appendices on the "inside" of the back cover. As noted above, appendices should not be part of the plan because of length considerations. Listing them on the inside of the back cover lets the reader know that they do exist, and gives a rough idea of what they contain.

- My preferences for the outside of the back cover are either a
"Set of Customer Comments" on the venture's products gathered during market research or, if you can find one, a copy of
a cover from a well know magazine (e.g., Time, Newsweek,
Business Week, etc) that emphasizes the importance of the
problem that the proposed venture proposes to solve.

- The inside of the plan's front cover can be used in the same way.

The Plan's Organization

The five major Organization considerations of **all** plans are its:

1. Theme

2. Macro-Structure & Topical Sequencing

3. Completeness

4. Prioritization

5. Simplicity.

The first thing that needs to be said about a plan's Organization
is that it is simultaneously the most important and least important aspect of writing a plan. How can both of these statements
be true? Both can be true because of a fact that many individuals do not realize i.e., that the **"determinants of success" are
different from the "determinants of failure."** Many people
think that differences in performance are mostly due to differences in "how well" a particular thing is done. The reality is that
most differences in performance are due to differences in "what
is actually done," not in "how well" these things are done.

So, how does this reality apply to the organization of one's business plan? Quite simply, poor organization will destroy much

if not most of the value of the plan, so it is extremely important that a plan have a reasonably strong Organization. However, once a plan is well organized, additional efforts to further improve its organization will add little to its value. Once it is well organized, most future efforts should be focused on improvements in its content and style rather than on further improvements in its organization.

- **The Plan's Theme**. All effective plans should tell a story, and the ultimate conclusion of all such stories is that prospective investors in the venture will make money if they invest in your venture. There are myriad themes that can be used to organize the plan's Content. Four of the most effective themes are *Successful Business*, in which the focus is on the reasons why the proposed venture will be a "successful business;" *Venture Opportunity*, in which the focus is on the market opportunity that the proposed venture will address and solve; *Problem → Solution*, in which the focus is on the "fact" that the venture's products and/or services will "solve" some major problem facing its target customers; and *Outstanding Investment*, in which the focus is on the factors that make the proposed venture a truly outstanding investment opportunity. Exhibit 1 contains sample outlines of plans organized around:

  1. A Successful Business theme

  2. A Venture Opportunity theme

  3. A Problem → Solution theme

  4. An Outstanding Investment theme.

The challenge is to determine the Theme that best fits your specific venture. Very few ventures, for example, offer high enough returns to use the *Outstanding Investment* theme.

Exhibit 1

Sample Macro-Outlines of Three Possible Business Plan Themes

Successful Business Theme	T*	E†	Venture Opportunity Theme	T*	E†	Problem → Solution Theme	T*	E†
Executive Summary	2	0	Executive Summary	2	0	Executive Summary	2	0
Company Overview	1	0	Situation X: A NV Opportunity	2	2–3	The Problem: Size, Growth	1	2–3
Products and/or Services	2–3	2–3	Market & Industry	1–2	1–2	The Solution: Our Products	2–3	3–4
Market & Industry	2–3	2–3	Services and/or Products	2–3	2–3	Market & Industry	2–3	1–3
Sales & Marketing	1–2	2–3	Goals, Strategies & Plans	1	0	Company Overview	1	0
Operations	1	1	Operations & Outsourcing	2	2–3	Sales & Marketing	2–3	1–3
Product Development	1	1	Marketing & Sales	2	1	Operations	1	1
Management & Key Advisors	2	0	Management & Key Advisors	2	0	Management & Key Advisors	2	0
Financials	1–2	4–5	Financials & Investor Returns	1–2	4–5	Financials & Investor Returns	1–2	4–5
Key Risks & Contingencies	1	0	Key Risks & Contingencies	1	0	Key Risks & Contingencies	1	0
Future Growth	1	0	Future Growth	1	0	Future Growth	1	0
Total Pages	15–19	12–14	Total Pages	17–20	12–17	Total Pages	16–20	12–19

* T = Text Pages.

† E = # of Exhibit Pages.

In fact, in the 30+ years that I have helped individuals develop business plans, fewer than five have had sufficiently high returns to warrant the use of an *Outstanding Investment* theme.

The *Problem → Solution* theme is very compelling. Thus, three of the four student teams that I have had that finished First (2) or Second (2) at the Global Challenge of Moot Corp® or the Rice International Competition used a *Problem → Solution* theme. But the *Problem → Solution* theme can **not** be used effectively unless there is **truly some major "problem"** facing the venture's target customers that **must** be solved.

For instance, if you were to ask ten potential customers **"What are the most significant problems that you face today?"** the problem around which you "plan" to build your plan **must** be among the top 3 problems mentioned on each customers' list or you should **not** try to use *Problem → Solution* as the theme of your plan because it will lack credibility. Put differently, choosing the "wrong" theme for your plan could be one of the **biggest mistakes** that you'll ever make. **You do not choose a theme because it's powerful, you choose a theme because it fits your venture.**

- **The Plan's Macro-Structure and Topical Sequencing.** All effective business plans contain four sections:

  a. A one- to two-page **Executive Summary**, which briefly **summarizes the key points in the body of the plan**.

  b. **The Body of the Plan** will cover descriptions of the:

    1. venture's goals and objectives,

    2. startup and growth strategies,

    3. products and services,

4. sales and marketing strategies,

5. operational strategies,

6. over-perfect development plans,

7. management teams and key advisors,

8. financial strategies,

9. progress to date,

10. target markets and customers,

11. key competitors,

12. industry trends,

13. major suppliers.

The specific Sequencing of Topical Areas in the Body of the Plan will depend on several factors, including:

- the plan's theme,

- the specific markets that your venture is proposing to enter,

- your venture's Strengths and Weaknesses.

c. A one-page **Specification of the Key Risks** that the venture may face in Years 1–5 and the venture's **Contingency Plans for dealing with them**.

d. A one-page **Description of the venture's Future Growth and Development Plans** for Years 6–10.

The reason that plans need to be "logically" organized according to their theme is that this is the way that most potential investors are used to thinking. So, even though the entrepreneur may have developed the ideas that will make them wealthy in a way that most investors do not understand and cannot duplicate, the entrepreneur MUST, nonetheless, describe how they plan to capitalize on their creative insights "logically and sequentially" if they want to get funding — at least for their first venture. Once they have a track record of success, this record can be substituted for a more formal plan as they seek financial backing.

- **The Plan's Completeness.** Effective Plans should address all of the major issues and answer most, if not all, of the major questions that the potential investor will have about the proposed venture. These include:

1. How much money do you want?

2. When do you want it?

3. Will I get my money back?

4. How much will I make?

Note that almost all of the "investor questions" are usually answered in the Finance Section of the business plan. So, what is the rest of the plan for? The answer depends on who the potential investor is.

In those instances in which one is seeking loans to finance all or most of the venture's launch, about all that one needs is a one-page Executive Summary, a one-page Financial Summary, and a set of well thought out pro-forma financial statements. The rest of the plan is needed only to help guide your actions in the launch of your business.

Quite simply, the rest of the Plan exists to answer the questions "Will I get my money back?" and "How much will I make?" since for equity investors there are no "adequate" returns unless

a. the venture goes public or is sold to another company, which requires that,

b. the venture must not only generate sales and profits, but must grow into a reasonably large enterprise in a reasonably short period of time.

To provide compelling evidence that both conditions are not only possible, but highly likely, one must discuss the venture's Goals and Objectives, its Startup and Growth Strategies, Products and Services, Target Markets and Customers, Key Competitors and Industry Trends, Sales and Marketing Strategies, Operations Strategies and major Suppliers, Management Team and Key Advisors, Financial Strategies, and Progress to Date — which is to say that one must complete the rest of the venture's business plan.

- **The Plan's Prioritization.** Given the page limits that investors and business plan competitions impose on all plans, there is no way that any plan can cover all that one might want to know about any proposed new venture. Some might regard this as a problem. It is not. It is, in fact, a major positive for at least two very important reasons.

First, your ultimate objective is to start a business, NOT to write a plan. Far too many have forgotten Edison's observation that success is "1% inspiration and 99% perspiration." Thus, while a plan needs to be relatively complete, **you need to spend far more time making your business happen than writing about how great it will be.**

Second, this means that in the writing of your plan you will be able to show that you can differentiate between those things that are truly important and those that are of lesser importance, i.e., that you possess "good judgment" by including only what is needed.

There is, however, at least one exception to the general rule that a plan should include "all of the important information that's fit to print" relative to the proposed venture. This happens in situations where extremely complex explanations are needed to fully communicate the reasons for a particular conclusion. In such circumstances, one should **tell the conclusion, but refrain from trying to explain it** since it will be almost impossible to do within the space available.

- **The Plan's Simplicity.** Finally, it is important to realize that few investors will be as knowledgeable about your business as you are. Even more importantly, remember that **your job is to educate them about your business, not to "snow" them with your technical expertise**. In short, you need to KISS (Keep It Simple, Stupid) your plan to increase its readability. Use simple, direct "Peter Rabbit" language to describe all aspects of your venture. Never use a $10 word, when a five-cent word is available. **Your goal is not to write your plan so well that everyone can understand it, it is to write it so well that no one can misunderstand any aspect of it**. And that is very difficult to do.

The Plan's Content

The five major Content considerations of all plans are:

1. Accuracy,

2. Documentation,

3. The Use of Precise, Specific Information,

4. Internal Consistency,

5. Believability.

- **The Plan's Accuracy.** The **most important aspect of any plan is its Accuracy**, a fact that one of my MBA business plan teams found out the hard way about 10 years ago. This team had come up with a novel idea for addressing a very large "niche" market. Unfortunately, there was no way to patent any aspect of their product or business processes. It would be some time before the venture would be able to develop a well known brand name, and even this would do little since brand reputation was not a critical factor in the market involved.

So, the team decided to seek long-term (2- to 4-year) contracts with their major customers. Most of their potential customers had expressed a willingness to enter into such contracts. The team wanted to do more than just get an expression of interest, and encouraged their sales manager to try to sign at least one contract before the team went to its first competition, which is what he did. And he briefly communicated this fact to the person responsible for finalizing the team's plan.

But to get the contract, he had to agree to run the team's system side-by-side with the customer's existing system for a year, at which time the customer would either sign a multi-year contract or go back to their existing system. The person finalizing the plan did not include all of these details, however, saying simply that the team had secured its first multi-year contract.

From the time its plan was submitted through the date of the competition, the team spent most of its time polishing its verbal presentation, which it presented with great energy and confidence. At the conclusion of its presentation, the major venture capitalist on the panel asked the team if it wanted to add anything. The team responded "NO." At this point the VC said two things. First, because of the potential of the team's idea, he had done some "due diligence" on the plan and project. Among other things, he had called the first customer and found out that, while the team did have a contract, it was for only one year. He then said "I gave you an opportunity to 'correct' any errors that you may have made in your plan, but you did not do so, and what you did present was a 'lie' so why should I believe another word that you have said?" Needless to say, the team finished last in its bracket in that competition.

The difficulty of being accurate in "everything" that you say in your plan is one of the reasons that many individuals use "generalities" rather than "specifics" in much of their plans. Unfortunately, this is not a solution. Why not? Because almost all "professional" investors want you to communicate your knowledge of and capabilities relative to the industry that you are proposing to enter through the use of "detailed, specific information" about that industry in your plan and presentation.

- **The Plan's Documentation.** Since the key to writing effective plans is to tell compelling stories, one very important requirement is that **one should document all really important information in the plan through the use of extremely credible sources**. Thus, the statement that "<u>According to Business Week</u> (January xy, 200z), 'ABC is a $2 billion market growing at over 20% per year'" has far more credibility than the almost identical statement that "ABC is a $2 billion market growing at over 20% per year."

In short, all critical information in both the text of the plan and the plan's exhibits should contain credible references. Further, in the plan's text it is usually far more effective to incorporate a brief reference to the credible source in the text itself as was done above than to just insert footnotes throughout the plan. Do not misunderstand. Either footnotes or a Set of References with complete documentation of sources should be contained somewhere in the plan. As noted earlier, I sometimes like to place this Reference List on the inside of the plan's back cover along with the list of appendices.

A key point here is that it is the job of the plan's authors to make the sources of all references used in the plan absolutely clear. This is **not the responsibility of the plan's readers** (the prospective investors). Also, if this has not been done well, this fact is a perfectly reasonable basis for concluding that one does not want to invest in this business. Put differently, **prospective entrepreneurs must make it easy, not hard**, for potential investors to invest in their business.

Two further observations. First, the presence of a large number of references in a plan is also an indicator that these prospective Entrepreneurs have done their homework while preparing their plan. Second, you should **not include any references that you have not actually read**. This may sound crazy, but some people (including both students and entrepreneurs) have been known to try to "stuff" more than just ballot boxes. Thus, I once received a plan for a small import business similar to Pier One. In the competition section of this plan, the authors listed all of the "similar" products carried by other similar import businesses in the community involved including both Pier One and Kubota. Before I could give the authors an "F," it was necessary to visit the Kubota dealer to verify that he carried only backhoes, bulldozers, and other earthmoving equipment, not scented candles, silk flowers, and wicker baskets. Oooooops!

- **The Plan's Use of Specific, Precise Information.** As noted above, many individuals make a major mistake when they write business plans by using far too many "generalities" throughout their plan. What they have done is forgotten who their audience is, namely, professional investors. In general, these individuals are both well educated and have substantial business experience. They also know from experience that what works in one market may not work in another. Consequently, **they are looking for mastery of the "specific knowledge" associated with the market and industry** that the proposed venture will enter. Statements such as "This is a huge market that is growing rapidly" are absolute "turnoffs." Far better are statements like "This is a $200 million market that is growing at 18% annually." Such specifics are "music" to the professional investor's ears. However, it is far more difficult to make statements of the latter type, because to do so requires a very detailed knowledge of the markets and industries that one is proposing to enter. But this is what the preparation of an effective business plan is all about.

One starts with secondary research about the market, the industry, and the competitors currently in the industry. **In almost all instances, one will then need to gather primary research also**, through the use of interviews, focus groups, questionnaires, etc. This data then needs to be integrated into a simple, coherent picture of the specific opportunities facing the venture.

The specific process that one must go through to get such data will vary by market and industry. There are two approaches that I have found to be very useful in making developing of such market knowledge:

1. The first is to ask **"Who already knows this information?"**

2. As well as the natural follow-on question **"How do I get to talk with this person?"**

Quite often, this approach has led to one or more interviews with people who have the information needed to develop a great plan for the venture involved.

There is one very important caveat that needs to be followed when using this approach, though. It is to **do your homework before interviewing these key people**. If you have done you homework, you will be able to ask intelligent questions about the market, the industry, your potential competitors, etc., and in most cases this will get you the information that you need.

Of course, there are always some people who will not speak with you no matter what you do or how well you prepare. My experience, however, is that 90% or more of the people with whom you talk will help you if you have done your homework. Put differently and more directly, **it is your job to get the information, not theirs**, so you need to avoid wasting their time. This means that you must have done enough homework so that you can fully understand almost everything that they will tell you, and so that you can ask intelligent questions in those few instances when you do not.

If you have not done your homework, I have also found that most will not talk to you for long or provide you with all of the specifics that you need. Note: My doctoral dissertation data gathering was an example of this point. To get the data that I needed, I was going to have to interview "in depth" several of the senior executives of the General Electric Company. These were individuals who were making well over $500,000 per year in today's dollars, and whose value to GE was at least 25 times that. In short, their time was worth over $5,000 per hour to GE's shareholders. And I wanted at least ten hours of their time. I got it, but I had to do two things to get it.

First, I had to begin by interviewing their subordinates, starting at the bottom.

Second, and more importantly, I had to estimate how much time each and every interview that I did was going to take and then keep a log of how much time each interview actually took. Eventually, I got to the top of the pyramid, but not until well after I completed over 150 hours of interviews that had been budgeted to take almost 200 hours, i.e., I got to the top after I had proven that I had done my homework and was not going to waste anyone's time.

Another approach that I have found very useful is to build up one or more "detailed" models of the market(s) involved by using all of the data gathered from secondary sources, and then **filling in the gaps with a series of key assumptions** that are consistent with this secondary information. It is, in fact, amazing how accurate such models can be. I used this approach when writing a series of Harvard Business School cases on the farm equipment industry. Among other things, I used this approach to "guesstimate" the sales by product line by geographic area of the companies on which I was writing the cases.

All such cases required "in-person" CEO sign-off before they could be used. At the first company, the CEO asked me to tell him who had provided me with the information that I had included in the case because it was considered to be company confidential. When I explained that I had "guesstimated" these numbers, he initially did not believe me because almost all of my guesstimates were apparently within a few percent of the actual numbers. So, using one product, I showed him how I had done it. He asked one further question "Had I done the same thing on his competitors?" I said I had. The price of case approval was to explain to his VP of Strategic Planning how I had done it.

The important point here is that there is lots and lots of data out there. Your job is to gather it, analyze it, and then use it to generate insights on the industry that you are about to enter. It is not to do a few Google searches, and then conclude that you have gotten all of the information that's worth getting.

- **The Plan's Internal Consistency.** The need for internal consistency in all of the materials contained in your plan is both critically important and exceedingly difficult. There are numerous ways that internal inconsistencies can arise in a plan. The two most common are (1) inconsistencies among the various "external" data gathered for and used in the plan and (2) inconsistencies among various elements of the Plan's Business Model.

  Inconsistencies among the Plan's "External" Data. All plans use a variety of "external" data gathered from a variety of sources to "estimate" market and market segment size, market and market segment growth rates, competitive behaviors, etc. Unfortunately, these data and data sources are not necessarily consistent with one another. Documenting one's sources will alert readers (your prospective investors) to the efforts you have made to try to gather relevant and accurate data. But this not enough! If there are "major" inconsistencies among these data, potential investors will expect that you will have identified these inconsistencies and tried to resolve them in some reasonable way.

  Inconsistencies among Elements of the Plan's Business Model. All the figures that appear in a venture's financial statements are linked together by various aspects of its Business Model. However, these linkages are not always obvious to those who put together the venture's financial statements. Nonetheless, all such linkages must be checked to make sure that they are accurate.

For example, a venture that plans to sell its products through direct sales calls on its primary target customers might list its *Selling Expenses* as $200,000 based on its plan to use two sales persons who will each be paid $75,000, plus an estimated $25,000 each for travel and other associated sales expenses. Even if these salary and expense numbers are accurate for the industry involved, this does NOT mean that the venture's forecast for *Selling Expenses* is reasonable. Why? Because these estimates are also linked to the venture's *Revenue* forecasts. How? By the linkages contained in questions such as the following: How long does a "typical" sales call take? How much travel and preparation time must be spent for each call? Given these estimates, how many sales calls can each sales person make in a year? Also, how many calls are needed before a customer will say YES? And, what percentage of customers will actually say YES?

Taken together, these numbers determine the number of orders that each sales person can generate per year. Further, what is the typical order size? This gives the revenues that each sales person can generate each year. Multiplying this number by the number of sales persons (2) should equal the venture's *Revenue* forecast for the year. But frequently these numbers do NOT match, which means that the Venture has either overestimated its *Revenues*, underestimated its *Sales Costs*, or both.

There are similar linkages among most of the major *Cost* and *Revenue* categories in the venture's financial statements, and ALL of these linkages MUST be checked for accuracy. What many entrepreneurs do not realize is that most professional investors will know all of these numbers and linkages for the industries in which they invest. One of the key points here is that the use of "spreadsheet" programs will not necessarily save you. On dozens of occasions, **I have**

seen professional investors catch major "flaws" in a venture's numbers with "back-of-the-envelope" calculations that were far more accurate than the numbers that the plan's authors developed over weeks or months of developing "spreadsheet" forecasts.

- **The Plan's Believability.** There is one last check to do before completing your plan. It is to assess its "believability." As mentioned earlier, the primary purpose of your plan is to get you an in-person interview with your potential investor. That means that your plan must compellingly tell a powerful story. To be compelling, however, your plan must be believable to your potential investors. If you have done your homework carefully, you might think that you have done all that's needed. Usually, this is true, but not always.

The key point here is that businesses come in all shapes and sizes. So, what will work in one business will not always work in another. All sophisticated investors know this. But they do not always know their own limitations. Specifically, what they may not know is that the general investment guidelines that they have developed over a lifetime of experience may not apply to the specific industry in which you plan to launch your venture. Alternately, they may not recognize the changes that have taken place in an industry since their last experience with it.

Potential investors will not tell you of these potential limitations on their part, because they can't. It is your job as an Entrepreneur, not theirs as potential investors, to recognize when this may be the case, and to take the necessary steps to provide whatever additional information may be needed for them to assess your plan appropriately.

In the early 1990s, one of my student teams developed a plan for the launch of a truly innovative semi-recumbent bicycle that they helped design. Their plan was well organized, with carefully researched and documented content, and they had some exciting PIZZAZ in the form of three functioning prototypes and a lot of customer feedback about their designs. They also had over $25,000 in customer orders in today's dollars.

Yet they did not do as well as they had hoped. Why not? Because they did not realize that their judges and potential investors did not fully realize the changes that had taken place in the U.S. bicycle market since they had last purchased and ridden bicycles. The team planned to sell its innovative bike for about $1,200. What the judges did not fully understand — in part because the team never explicitly addressed the issue — was what a $1,200 bike was in the U.S. bicycle market in the early 1990s. The team understood that a $1,200 bike was, in car terms, a Buick or Chrysler. However, the judges thought that a $1,200 bike was a Rolls Royce or Ferrari, a step above even a Mercedes. Consequently, the judges' perceptions of the size of the market that this business was addressing was significantly different than the market size described by the team.

And why did this hurt so much? Because **Market Potential is the first criterion that most VCs use to separate the thousand of business plans that they receive every year into those that will go into the "circular file" and those that they will examine more carefully.** Put differently, VCs "fish" for whales, not for minnows, and most of those on the judging panel though that the team's $1,200 bike market was a minnow.

Most VCs "claim" that their "ultimate" criterion is the quality of the venture's Management Team. This may or may not be true. The semi-recumbent bike team never got to find out because they got cut earlier in the VC's screening process because they did not realize that the judges were "not buying" their arguments about the size of the U.S. market for their bike — mostly because the last time that the judges had bought or ridden a bike was 30+ years ago when almost all bikes had "fat wheels" and when one "stepped backward on the peddles" to put on the brakes.

SUMMARY AND CONCLUSIONS

The primary purpose of most business plans is to help you gain an audience with prospective investors for your venture. Therefore, you need to put careful thought into its development. First, you should choose a "theme" that fits your venture and lay out the rest of the plan's organization. Most of your attention needs to go into its content, since this is the most critical component of all plans. Then you "put the icing on the cake" by strengthening its style and adding a dash of PIZZAZ. And after it's all done, you ask a friend with absolutely no knowledge of your products or markets to read it and tell you what they think since this is the only way to get a quick check on the plan's overall effectiveness and believability. Then you figure out how to incorporate their observations to further improve your plan. **And, after doing this for four or five times, you may be ready for the big time.**

Does the amount of work needed scare you off????? Why? Remember often how BIG the reward down the road can be for excellent work put forth now!

NOTES & OBSERVATIONS

1. <u>The Macro-Structure of every Plan should be customized to the particular specifics of the venture's market and industry.</u>

First, Sections can be added or dropped depending on the nature of the business or the importance of the Topic. For instance, a Section on "Product Development" may be absolutely essential for a technology-based venture, but irrelevant for businesses like a restaurant. On the other hand, it is sometimes useful to add Sections in order to make important points. For example, for health care products it is frequently useful to add a Section on the "FDA Approval" process.

Second, one should "craft" the names of Section Titles by using "specifics" such as company or industry names. Thus, instead of "Situation X: A NV Opportunity" one would say "Tax Prep Outsourcing: A Venture Opportunity." Likewise, instead of "Market & Industry" one would say "The Tax Preparation Market & Industry." Even the choice and sequencing of words can communicate useful information. For B2B markets with a limited number of customers, the title "Sales & Marketing" indicates that direct selling is more important than advertising, while for B2C markets with large numbers of customers, the title "Marketing & Sales" implies that advertising and other forms of marketing take precedence over direct selling. Also, the word "Sales" could be dropped if there are no direct selling activities.

2. <u>The Macro-Structure of every Plan should be customized to the venture's specific strengths and weaknesses.</u>

Every successful venture has some Key Strengths. These should always be covered as early in the Plan as possible, even if this means changing the "normal" sequencing of Section Topics. For instance, for most ventures "Marketing & Sales" is more important than "Operations," so it is covered first. However, there are exceptions to almost every rule, and when they occur one must change the Macro-Structure of one's Plan accordingly.

3.   Did it "bother" you that the "sequencing of topics" covered in the body of the business plan listed on pages 15 & 16 was different from the sequencing contained in paragraph 2 on page 18? Or did you even notice that they were different'! People think ditlerently. Many, including most entrepreneurs, have a "flowing stream of consciousness" thought process. Most such individuals would not have noticed the differences or would not consider it a BIG DEAL if they did notice it. However, many others have a more "sequential, tightly logical" thought process. More of these individuals will have noticed the difference and some may even be "bothered" by it. Since many professional investors have the latter types of thought processes, you need to write your plan so that the macro-aspects of its organization and grammar do not "turn off" potential investors before they fully appreciate the "attractiveness" of your new business idea.

"I was always looking outside myself for strength and confidence, but it comes from within. It is there all the time."

Anna Freud

Chapter Five

Self-Assessment for the Entrepreneur!

Know Thyself First!

By Fred Kiesner

It is because I firmly believe that the number-one **key to success is understanding yourself and your own power, and having dreams that you can chase**, that I have had every single student I have ever taught do the following assignment. It is demanding, but if done well, and with passion and heart and soul, it will be of great value to the entrepreneur!

I present it here hoping it will help you understand yourself (try doing it, it really won't hurt), and help you and those you help develop inner strength, power, and understanding and guide you into the wonderful world of entrepreneurship.

This assignment contains some ideas and thoughts that were developed with the wonderful help and guidance of Don Kuratko, Entrepreneurship Educator *par excellence*!

THE ASSIGNMENT

This is a very tough assignment. Take it very seriously, and put a good deal of careful thought into it. Stretch your brain beyond your present thinking about yourself and your abilities and future. Think in terms of what you are really capable of if you get excited about it, and are willing to commit fully to it. Please read the assignment, and then provide what is required. There is no page limit, up or down, to this assignment. You are doing this assignment for yourself, and for me as a secondary target.

Despite the fact that we study things like the need for strategic and long-term planning in business, we seldom practice what we preach in the most important business of our lives — our careers. We tend to have vague, haphazard, generalized thoughts about what life will hold for us, but we don't take the time to sit down and think about what we are really all about, and what we **SHOULD** be doing in life. The career paths we set out upon are often determined by outside and relatively unimportant influences, such as our parents, what a friend is doing in life, what interviewer shows up on campus, or happens to like us and invites us to a second interview, or other such relatively unimportant details. In short, the most important single activity in our lives, our career, is often plotted and determined by totally unimportant factors and influences outside of ourselves. You must not allow that to happen. You, and you alone, must control your destiny!!!!!

This assignment can have serious impact on your life! Don't just do it as a required assignment for Kiesner's class, or for an "A". Do it for YOU, because it can start you thinking along the right track about your future. If you approach this assignment from that viewpoint, it will be fun, and even easy, for you will really get into it, and that will show. Be honest with yourself, and me! I am the only one who will read this report, and I will keep it totally private between us.

Please carefully follow the suggested format and schedule below:

Front Page

The first page of the paper you turn in will include only the following:

1. Name

2. Course number

3. Date submitted

Please **do not use covers**. Use normal writing methods, **including the use of headings and subheadings for each section**, proper English, grammar, spelling, and no typos. This is of great importance in everything you do. The work you submit is, **truly**, a portrait of you and your talents! Sloppy work gives a real message! Please try to follow the format I have provided in this assignment summary, wherever possible.

Double space your writing for this paper, please.

Please proofread your own work carefully before you turn it in. Stupid and careless spelling and type and grammar errors really detract from the quality of your brain and your thinking. Don't shoot yourself in the foot by making dumb mistakes of carelessness.

Briefly list your work experience from birth to the present. Provide the **earliest in outline form**, only discuss the most critically important learning experiences in any detail. What have you done that prepares you to be a winner in life, and have a successful career? Don't be modest, and don't you dare say you have no experience. You do, list it, and discuss briefly those entries that have real impact. These experiences could well include things like babysitting, lemonade stands, volunteer work at social entrepreneur establishments, etc.

A Sense of Self

To survive in the world, and achieve a major impact, we must have a strong "sense of self," a feeling and comfortable understanding of who we are, and what our power and talents are, realistically, that will propel us towards achievement and impact in the future. Who are you? What makes you unique, powerful, interesting, good, and capable of being a major leader of the wonderful future world? What are your core values. What makes you say to yourself, "gee, I am a neat person who **will** have an impact in the future, and **I am very proud of who I am!**"

The Future — Life Goals

Briefly discuss your goals in life with regard to your **career path**, in the following three categories. Be **specific**, not vague and generalized — I want you to seriously look at what makes you tick, what you **can** and **should** expect from life, and what you want to achieve from your efforts in this world. Please note this section applies particularly to your career goals and hoped-for achievements in society. Of much less importance, for the purposes of this paper, is how many children you have, what a wonderful spouse you marry, or other such details. Those items are nice and should be a real part of your future career, but please, for this paper, concentrate primarily on your career achievements, goals, and targets. The critical factor here, in this paper, is your career, your impact on the world, and where you will go.

Please do not waste my time and yours with other incidentals. Talk about the critical subject of this paper, the path you will take through life that will allow you to use your talents and direct and control your own life. I consider this section to be the major thrust of this paper. Other sections flow from it and support it. Please do not insult yourself, and me, by blowing the assignment off by saying, "duh, gee, I don't know where I am going, but I am sure something wonderful will happen." Think and write realistically about what you are going to **make happen in your life!**

Short-Term, the next five years

Intermediate-Term, the next twenty-five years

Long-Term, the next fifty to seventy years

Agonize over where you are going, and get a real fuzzy vision of YOU in the future! This is a key element of this paper, and it should be of critical importance for you. There is a big hint here! Don't try to slip through this section without doing some deep soul searching about who you are, what you are capable of, how you should start your path, and where your path might take you.

If I Could Dream

If you knew you could not fail, what would your dream job/ career/purpose/passion be in life? Disregard any potential barriers such as education, or anything else that might, in real life, prevent you from getting this job. You can assume you have the requirements for this job, and you can ignore all such mundane things as money. In short, assume nothing would stop you from getting this job, and nothing would hold you back from being successful at it. Please be serious here! No jokes. Also explain why this would be your dream job.

Successes

List and discuss your greatest accomplishments in life to date. **FIRST** tell about your single most important victory or achievement in life that you are the most proud of, in some detail. How has it impacted your thinking, what did you learn from it, and how will it help you achieve your future success? Then, in descending order, briefly discuss one or two other achievements you consider very important. Please think currently and in your recent history. **Do not** go back and tell me your greatest victory in life to date was when you won the spelling bee in third grade, or when you hit a double in little league play that won the game. We are talking here about your more recent successes and victories that will have true impact on your life, your dreams, and your achievements.

Think carefully about this, and I think you will surprise yourself with the quality and quantity of the successes you already have. Remember, you are the cream of the crop, or you wouldn't be here. That may sound a bit elitist, but you must remember and accept the fact that you are among the very best. You will, therefore, have accomplished a good deal! Tell me about it. Of more importance, recognize it in yourself. We often overlook or downplay our achievements because we were taught from childhood to be modest. Be modest, but also in your heart recognize and rejoice over your wonderful victories, and let them shape and impact your future!

Failures

Failure, in my estimation, is not a negative. It is merely a stepping-stone in life, and one of the most potent teaching tools there is, if used in a positive manner. Briefly (I repeat, briefly) list your greatest failures in life, and how they impacted what you have done in life since then (what lessons you learned, in other words). Again, list your **greatest single most wonderful**

and glorious failure first, the one magnificent failure that has had the most impact on your life. Again, stay in recent years. While it may have had an impact, I am not really looking for what you did in kindergarden here.

Don't be shy! This is between you and me, and I won't tell! Don't just look at the failure from a negative viewpoint, look at it from a positive attitude, and learn from it. Forget your ego here, be honest, let it out! Tell me about the most wonderful failures you have had, what you learned from them, and how they will impact what you **will and can** do in the future.

Why Are You Here?

Please give some very serious thinking and effort here as to why you are on this earth. I somehow don't think any of us could be so arrogant as to think that the sole purpose of our being is to have pleasure and enjoyment for ourselves, only. What do you feel your purpose in life is? What is the meaning of your being on this earth? I am not really looking for a religious treatise here, though that may be a powerful part of your thinking.

In short, from a **career** and **impact on the world** viewpoint, tell me **briefly** why you think you are here! We seldom give much thought to this, and yet it should be the real essence of our being. It must play a major role in where we are going, and the paths **we choose** to follow in life. Success is not an accident. Those who achieve true success and impact in life usually do so because they have a comprehension of who they are, where they are, and why they are here. They have a **vision** of themselves in the role they will play in the future, then they fulfill that vision. You must gain that clearly-defined sense of self! It is the critical factor that will determine if you fulfill your potential in life, and are a giver, rather than a taker in society. Give this some very serious and critical thought, please.

Now What on Earth Do I Do?

In a bit of a twist of the above thought stimulator, consider this situation. You are merrily going along through life. Life is good. **Ooooops!** The doctor just told you that **you have one year or less to live!** Now what would you do? What would become important to you? How would you conduct your last months? How would you change in the ways you think and operate? I don't mean to be maudlin and depressing. This is a serious question. I have faced this situation four times in my life (goes to show you doctors don't know what they are talking about sometimes), and it had a profound impact on me, how I think, and what is important to me. Think on how it would impact you, who you are, what you would do. Don't you dare tell me you would get stoned and go on a twelve-month binge until you died! You are better than that.

Who are Your Heroes?

As we begin setting our course for the future, and embarking on the initial path towards our goals, it is critically important that we have real and meaningful **HEROES** that give us inspiration and focus on what we want and can do in life. If you prefer, call them **ROLE MODELS**, who inspire us, motivate us, and guide us towards reaching our potential, capturing our power, and truly impacting the world we will operate within.

Briefly identify one or two genuine, certified, undeniable **HEROES** for you that make you sit up and say **WOW!!!!!** Please identify why they are your **HEROES**, and what impact they have had upon you in propelling you towards your wonderful future success! By the way, often our real heroes that have a true impact upon us are not celebrities or well-known people. Think about the person that has propelled you the most into molding and shaping yourself to be a person of real, positive impact in the future! It would be appreciated if you would talk about real people who are able to directly impact you. While Babe Ruth was a neat guy, I would appreciate your talking about someone that has had a solid and direct impact upon you. Also, don't tell me about some dumb rap crap rock band, or someone like that. I want to hear about the people who bring out the deep-seated power and strength you have within you to have a real and meaningful impact upon the world.

Yippee!!!!!

You Made It Big In Life !!!!!

Now what will your impact on the World be from a Social Responsibility Viewpoint?

Fantastic. You are now fabulously successful beyond your wildest dreams, from both a financial and personal happiness viewpoint. Being successful gives you **power! Isn't it wonderful?**

How will you use this power to truly help the world? What would you do to cause improvement and change in the world with the wealth and power you achieved? Many believe that when one gains tremendous personal success, they have an obligation to make life better for others.

In short, in my opinion, once you have made it over the tall and tough wall of life and have achieved personal success, I think you are **obligated to toss the rope back over the wall to help the next folks trying to win in life.**

What will be your pet **"social responsibility"** project and interest once you become a winner? I would hope it would be something slightly more substantial than writing an annual check for $100 to the United Way and putting $5 a week into the collection plate.

Briefly, but specifically, write about what your dream impact on the world would be. Make it real and realistic, not just some pipe dream from smoking too much of that funny (and really dumb) stuff!

Your Obituary

You are **one hundred twenty (120)** years old, and have just died. How sad. I want you to write your obituary as you realistically expect it might appear at age 120. Make it a narration of what you realistically might have accomplished in this wonderful life, and what you will be remembered for, if you follow the career path you are charting now. Be reasonable! Think in terms of what you really can, and probably will, accomplish in life if you put the proper effort and dedication into it! Namely, 110% effort.

Please **do not** include details about your wife or husband and kids, and stuff about how much people will miss you, or where the funeral service will be, or how you died, etc. We will assume you will all die while doing something thrilling and daring, like skydiving from a rocket ship over Mount Everest on a mile long bungee cord! This is not the key material I want here, so forget about including how you died. I want "future think" here on your effect on the world, and how the world will remember you. Put down a serious, **DETAILED** obit that well might appear in a newspaper many years from now after you have had your impact on the world.

Do include a specific narration about what you will have accomplished in life from a career viewpoint, and your impact on society. What influence will you have had on life, your career, and the world? Realistically assess your potential, the mark you can, truthfully, make on the world if you truly commit to it. This should summarize your dreams, the fuzzy view you have of yourself as a real leader in the world. Don't just put in blue sky BS.

Make it real! Make it be something that you can and should achieve, if you want it.

It is expected, obviously, that what you include here will have a **direct tie-in** with what you discussed in your goals section.

We seldom set long-term goals for ourselves. This exercise is designed to force you to think in terms of what life can hold for you, and what you can offer to life. Students and those in their early career years seldom give much thought to drawing up their **road map of life**, where they are going, and what their ultimate goals in life are. You tend to be thinking in the now, only about the tremendous demands and strains of being a student, or building your early career, and about whatever jobs you might have in the next few years. **Go beyond that in doing your obituary**. Draw your road map of life by using this obituary as the **summary** of what you expect to be known for at the end of your life. Describe the essence of your life as you think it really might unfold. Yes, it will be a fuzzy picture, especially in your later years, but **without a fuzzy picture of where we are going, and some focus on what we can be, we will be nothing** compared to what we could have been.

I would strongly urge you to **read an actual obituary** or two on some real winners in life who have had an impact! This will give you an idea of how a real, well done, detailed obit might read **for someone who has a big impact,** not just some "ordinary" person. **You can, should, and will be extraordinary!**

I should warn you, **most students just blow off this section on their obituary!** Why, I do not know. Don't let yourself fall prey to that problem and ruin the impact and value of the paper in the end. One might suspect that the last image or impression the reader gets of a paper has a fair amount of impact, thus make sure your obit is powerful, and I get a really strong feeling **you have your life's dream well in hand**. Think this section through carefully. **Have a powerful ending, not a wimpy collapse** because you are afraid to really dream of what you truly could be, and **will be**!

Your Epitaph

Now summarize the totality of what you expect your life to mean by providing me with a **very brief** one-line epitaph. Make it **four to eight words, or less, maximum**. Put down here what you would like carved on your tombstone. **Make it count**.

What are the few words future generations will have to note your having been in this world, and to remember and judge you by? This is a difficult part of this assignment, so put some serious thought into it. You want it to represent your life and say a lot about what you are, what you stood for, and what you achieved with your talents. It must summarize what you are (were) and what you achieved in life!

Please have this epitaph summarize your impact on the business world, your career, and society. Please don't waste these incredibly important **few** words on cutsie pie silly things that describe your partying ability, your drinking capacity, or your sexual prowess! This is a serious effort to summarize the core of your existence. These few words must have **substance**, and truly summarize what you were all about.

Make sure this epitaph is a **clear and concise summary of what you are and will be all about in life!**

Any Final Comments or Additions

This is an optional section. If you wish, add anything else you want that might be appropriate to this assignment. Was there anything that was missed that is important to you? Any other comments you might want to make?

The Key Word

Your final, final, **final** assignment — on a **last, single, empty piece of paper**, in fairly large bold print, put the **one, single word that would best describe you, and your power to have an impact on the world!** If you do more than one word, you will get no credit for this section. What single word sums up the absolute core of your existence, your power, your essence!

HAVE FUN EXPLORING YOU, AND CLARIFYING YOUR FUZZY VISION OF WHO YOU ARE, AND WHO YOU CAN BE!

Make this paper be a wonderful **painting or portrait** of where you have been, who you are, where you are going, who you will be, and the impact you will have on life. Will this effort be a masterpiece that shows the writer has a powerful comprehension of who they are and where **they will take life?** Or will it be a booooooooring, half-hearted attempt to barely fulfill an assignment for class and a grade? **This paper is for you! Make it count like nothing else you have ever done before!**

Don't run and hide from the issues raised in this assignment! Embrace them, think them through, and make this paper work for you as an instrument that helps you **take charge** of where you are going.

You own the quality of this effort! Will it be stunningly good, and an effort that will help you to achieve your future and your destiny? **Or will it be a weak, lily-livered, half-hearted effort** from a weak-kneed chicken who wants somebody else to control where they go in life, and is afraid to accept the fact that they must take the action needed to make sure they achieve their destiny and power? **The decision IS yours.**

There is no limit to the length of this assignment. Though I have flunked students who turned in five pages (if it takes me seven pages to tell you what I want, how can you do it in five pages?), and one who turned in nearly 300 pages of pure junk that was not his thinking, just chapters lifted from books.

Now make a copy of this paper and tuck it away in some place where you will find it every ten years or so in your life. When you find it, enjoy how you thought now, and then do a new self-assessment for the next ten years of your life.

"I have an irrepressible desire to live till I can be assured that the world is a little better for my having lived in it."

Abraham Lincoln

Chapter Six

Training Programs for Fledgling Entrepreneurs

By George Solomon

Dr. Solomon is currently Associate Professor of Management at The George Washington University School of Business and is the Director for the Center for Entrepreneurial Excellence (CFEE). Dr. Solomon is the Past President of the United States Association for Small Business and Entrepreneurship (USASBE) and the International Council for Small Business (ICSB). He also serves as the Senior Policy Advisor to the Associate Administrator for Business and Community Initiatives, US Small Business Administration (SBA). From 1976 until 2004, Dr. Solomon held various managerial positions at the SBA, including Director of the Office of Special Initiatives and Deputy Associate Administrator for Business Initiatives Education and Training.

Dr. Solomon has published and edited over 130 articles, books of readings, book chapters, reference materials, and proceedings articles in both the areas of Entrepreneurship /Small Business Management and Organizational Behavior & Dynamics. He is a colleague of the Creative Education Foundation, a fellow of the United States Association for Small Business and Entrepreneurship and the Small Business Institute Director's Association, and a Wilford White Fellow of the ICSB. He is one of only four individuals in the United States to be so honored by all three organizations. In 2008, the Acton Foundation honored him as one of 28 outstanding entrepreneurship educators. In 2009, the United States Association for Small Business and Entrepreneurship selected Dr. Solomon to received the Innovative Teaching Pedagogy Award for developing the small business multi-role playing pedagogy. He also was selected by the Freedom Foundation to receive the prestigious Leavey Award for excellnec in free enterprise education.

In 1984, he was one of five federal employees worldwide to receive the Arthur S. Flemming award for excellence in government management. In 1986 and 1993, he received the George Washington Freedom Medal in Economic Education from the Freedom Foundation. Dr. Solomon has been elected to Beta Gamma Sigma and Delta Mu Delta, National Business Honor Societies, and Omicron Delta Kappa, National Honor Leadership Society. He was awarded the Small Business Institute Director Association's Distinguished Service Award in 1988. In 1997, the United States Association for Small Business and Entrepreneurship selected Dr. Solomon as the "Entrepreneurial Educator of the Year" for Small Business and Entrepreneurship. In 1996, Dr. Solomon and two colleagues were awarded the Best Graduate Entrepreneurship Program in the United States from the United States Association for Small Business and Entrepreneurship.

Dr. Solomon received his Doctorate of Business Administration (DBA) from The George Washington University School of Government and Business Administration, 1982, with a major in Entrepreneurship/ Small Business Management and Organizational Behavior & Development. He was the first individual at that time to receive a doctorate in entrepreneurship/ small business management from a major accredited school of business. He received his: (MBA) from Suffolk University in 1972; (BBS) from Central Connecticut State University in 1971 and (AS) from Norwalk Community College in 1969.

Editor's Note: *If one were to try to determine who the founders were of our wonderful field of Entrepreneurship and Entrepreneurship Education, certainly George Solomon would be among the absolute **TOP FIVE!** For almost thirty-five years, he has been a major leader and innovator in the field. He is a coach, mentor, inspiration, and fabulous creator of the most incredible, exciting, and creative programs in entrepreneurship education. He showed us the way, he guided us, then cajoled us to do more, and he made sure what we did was really exciting. This one man has been a beacon and rallying point for Entrepreneurship Education in America and the world. He has created dozens of outstanding entrepreneurial development programs over the years. I have asked him to briefly outline several of them in this chapter. I think they will give you some food for thought on what you can develop for your program. The programs below were all developed by Dr. Solomon, while he was an official with the U.S. Small Business Administration, and while in the academic world.*

INTRODUCTION

For the last fifty years (1958–2008), educators, trainers, and public managers have reported that small business managers and entrepreneurs, both young and old, needed a smorgasbord of programs, outreach activities, and electronic delivery systems capable of meeting their diverse and constant need for relevant and practical information and knowledge. This chapter reports on a number of government and academic programs designed to assist entrepreneurs in recognizing opportunities and acting upon them.

The dilemma in the small business and entrepreneurship sectors has always been that, although **the demand for knowledge and information is high, focused training programs designed to meet the innovative and creative mindset of present and potential entrepreneurs have been lacking**. Thus, the challenge has been to design and offer programs both in the government and academic sectors that are **reality-based**, paying attention to both the uniqueness of small business ownership (income generation) and the innovation and creativity of the entrepreneur (wealth generation) in an **interactive learning environment**.

This chapter will first examine the government sector — with particular focus on programs developed by the US Small Business Administration (SBA), whose mission is to aid and assist America's small businesses. We will then consider programs developed in the academic sector, focusing on programs created at The George Washington University Center for Entrepreneurial Excellence (CFEE).

GOVERNMENT PROGRAMS

During the later part of the twentieth century (1980–2000), the US Small Business Administration (SBA) attempted, with limited resources, to develop comprehensive training outreach programs to supplement their existing efforts through three resource partners:

SCORE

The National SCORE Association (NSA), established in 1964, is a resource partner of the SBA dedicated to entrepreneur education and the formation, growth, and success of small businesses nationwide. There are more than 10,500 SCORE volunteers in 374 chapters operating in over 800 locations who assist nascent and early start-up small businesses with business counseling and training. SCORE also operates an active online counseling initiative.

Small Business Development Centers (SBDCs)

The Small Business Development Centers (SBDC), established in 1978, provide management assistance to current and growing small business owners. SBDCs, through their 76 lead centers and over 1,000 outreach locations, offer one-stop assistance to individuals and small businesses by providing a wide variety of information and guidance in central and easily accessible branch locations. The program is a cooperative effort of the private sector, the educational community, and federal, state, and local governments and is an integral component of Entrepreneurial Development's network of training and counseling services.

Small Business Institute (SBI)

The Small Business Institute (SBI), established in 1972 as a pilot program, began in large part as a cooperative venture, funded by the United States Small Business Administration (SBA) and approximately 20 universities. The program developed to include as many as 500 programs at colleges and universities in the 50 states and several U.S. territories. Through the Small Business Institute program, students participate in hands-on learning experience by conducting field case studies and providing consulting services to local small business owners. Teams of qualified senior-level and graduate students, under the expert faculty, provide consulting to small business owners and managers as part of their educational training.

The first such effort was the development of the annual Creativity, Innovation, and Entrepreneurship Conference (CIEC).

The Creativity Innovation, and Entrepreneurship Conference

As stated above, the annual Creativity, Innovation, and Entrepreneurship Conference (CIEC) was developed by the U.S. Small Business Administration (SBA) in 1983, with a partnership among academic and private sector sponsors and the Creative Education Foundation (CEF). The annual conferences, supported through private sector support, were attended by over 1,500 entrepreneurs, educators, government officials, and students over the ten year period (1983–1993). The purpose of the conferences was to support research, discussions, and presentations across the topics of creativity, innovation, and entrepreneurship.

During the ten years the conference existed, the veritable Who's Who of entrepreneurs who spoke and interacted with the audiences included:

- Stew Leonard, Founder and CEO of Stew Leonard's

- Wally "Famous" Amos, Founder of Famous Amos Cookies

- Fred DeLuca, Co-Founder and CEO of Subway Sandwich and Salad Co.

- Arthur Lipper, III, Chairman of British Far East Holdings

- Edward Lowe, CEO and Founder of Kitty Litter

- William C. W. Mow, Founder and CEO of Bugle Boy Clothing

- Neil Balter, Founder and CEO of California Closet Co.

- Max DePree, CEO of Herman Miller Company.

New approaches to train and educate entrepreneurs resulted from these conferences and discussions. The Journal of Creative Behavior launched an annual issue to further explore the issues talked about at the conferences.

Based on the CIEC conferences, the SBA developed a strategy of leveraging, using diverse community-based resources to expand the SBA's delivery capabilities and use the credibility and knowledge of these community-based organizations. This strategy lead to the creation of the Small Business National Training Network (SBNTN).

Small Business National Training Network (SBNTN)

The concept of the Small Business National Training Network (SBNTN) was proposed and developed by the SBA in the mid 1980s. The concept was modeled after the Small Business Institute (SBI) program developed and managed by the SBA working with four-year colleges and universities.

SBNTN was created and directed at two-year colleges to provide focus training to small businesses. The American Association of Community and Junior Colleges (AACJC) coordinated the activity for the SBA, with over 200 junior and community colleges enrolled in the network with the understanding that they would provide focused and directed training to current and potential small business entrepreneurs. The program was phased out in the late 1980s as priorities changed and funding from the U.S. Congress was no longer available to support the program.

At its zenith, the SBNTN provided training to over 100,000 individuals on a variety of topics. No direct funding was provided to the individual sites. The AACJC was provided funds to administer and coordinate the SBNTN with the SBA, and sites charged current market rates.

In 1993, the SBA revisited the concept of the Small Business National Training Network and awarded a grant to the Small Business National Advancement Center (SBANC) in Conway, Arkansas to coordinate the operational aspects of the SBNTN. In its reincarnation, the SBNTN was to provide initial seed money — $1,250 to about 100 two-year colleges. The colleges would use this seed money to offset the costs of developing and presenting five training programs. Each of the five programs required a minimum of twenty attendees.

- Steps to Starting a Small Business

- How to Finance Your Small Business

- The Ins and Outs of Government Contracting

- Developing a Sound Marketing Plan

- Steps to Improving Your Cash Flow.

The SBA was hoping to increase its overall training participation by 10,000 new attendees. In order to fulfill their obligations to the SBA and the SBANC, each school was required to develop the training, present the training, and evaluate the training. Evaluations conducted on this program and feedback from entrepreneurs attending the training showed that the program was ranked very favorably.

Even though this program was successful, it was discontinued due to a lack of funding support from the U.S. Congress. In 1988, the SBA focused its attention on the growing youth market and created YES — the Young Entrepreneurs Seminars.

Young Entrepreneurs Seminars (YES)

In 1988, the SBA launched the Young Entrepreneurs Seminars (YES) program — a nationwide series of workshops that were held simultaneously in 113 locations on October 22, 1988. This one-day event attracted almost 11,000 young people nationwide in the USA. They heard local business professionals present the "pros and cons" of owning a small business.

These seminars included lectures, workshops, and question-and-answer sessions covering topics such as getting started, developing a business plan, marketing, and franchising. Local young entrepreneurs discussed the rewards and difficulties of business ownership.

The purpose of YES was to:

- Provide a forum of motivation and counsel in which the SBA could deliver (en mass) an overview of its mission, programs, and objectives.

- Engage SBA's business development resource base, SCORE, SBDC, SBI, and community organizations, with the goal of increasing youth awareness of entrepreneurship.

- Develop linkages with national youth groups such as Distributive Education Clubs of America (DECA), Students in Free Enterprise (SIFE), Junior Achievement (JA), Future Business Leaders of America (FLBA), and Future Farmers of America (FFA).

- Introduce, educate, and demonstrate the process, issues, and factors to be considered by youth in developing and operating a small business.

Overall, the Young Entrepreneurs Seminars were extremely successful in their mission. Nearly 11,000 young people across the country set aside one Saturday and attended the program. To make it all come together, the Small Business Administration leveraged private-sector support from companies including A.L. Williams, Pacific Bell Directory, Bell Atlantic, Bell South, Southwestern Bell, and Southern New England Telephone. Funding for the production of the introductory film, student manuals, posters, and direct marketing brochures was provided by the private sector firms.

In 1992, the SBA again engaged in a national Young Entrepreneur Seminars (YES) program on a lesser scale. Although the overall results in terms of corporate sponsorship and attendance was less than that in 1988, the overall evaluation of participants was again very high. Unfortunately, the SBA discontinued this programmatic thrust due to a lack of internal support and Congressional funding.

In the early 1990s, the SBA turned its attention toward technology-enhanced resources given its diminished fiscal and human resources. In 1991, the SBA began to commit to establishing a technologically-based delivery system to better serve not only the current and prospective entrepreneurs, but also educators and students nationwide. The SBA's first foray into this direction was the creation of Business Information Centers (BICs).

Business Information Centers (BICs)

The SBA's Seattle district office began a pilot program in 1991 by offering a computerized Business Information Center (BIC) staffed by SCORE volunteers. It was an actual storefront location. The BIC provided databases, computerized business plans, and a reference library along with a limited bulletin board. The flexibility of meeting today's entrepreneurs' needs required a diversity of both community-based resources offering high-quality solutions and the latest technology and information sources.

Based on this pilot, the SBA realized the trend toward technology and information and decided to implement the BIC program nationwide. The SBA embarked on a new automation effort to provide small businesses with access to vital information using the latest personal computer and audio-visual technology.

They provided a full range of management and technical assistance, printed materials and access to databases and business software capable of providing financial and management information. By the end of 2001, the SBA had in operation 100 BICs throughout the United States and Puerto Rico.

By offering easy access to a large universe of data in print and electronic form, the Business Information Centers (BICs) assist the SBA's professional staff with updated tools necessary to better inform and educate present and potential entrepreneurs. It also provided an ongoing learning environment for the counselors and a non-threatening environment for small business owners.

The latter permits small business owners to become comfortable with using computers and computer technology in making both sound business decisions and market projections. BICs provide SBA's management counselors with the tools they need to better inform and educate small business clients. Among the features — products and services — and benefits a BIC offer are as follows:

- Reference Materials and Textbooks

- Online Information Exchange

- Computer Tutorials

- Video Tapes

- Start-up Guides

- Internet Access

- Computer Databases

- Periodicals and Brochures

- Applications Software

- Interactive Multimedia

- Internet Access

- Contact Information.

The Major Benefits of BICs

- Made small business information more accessible to the public

- Established a foundation for information networking among SBA resources and small businesses

- Created a focal point for private sector partnerships in SBA's mission to transfer management knowledge to entrepreneurs

- Provided a full range of management and technical assistance, printed materials, and access to databases and business computer software needed for financial and managerial decision-making

- Offered easy access to large universes of databases, which assist SBA's business counselors to better inform and educate present and potential small business entrepreneurs.

Although these special initiatives were highly successful, no overall strategy was identified and implemented. More importantly,

senior SBA officials and the U.S. Congress were never sufficiently influenced to support the continuance of these efforts.

ACADEMIA

In the early 1990s, the Center for Family Enterprise (CFE) submitted a grant proposal to the Coleman Foundation to develop a
web-based knowledge portal dedicated to providing an online
entrepreneurship education curriculum to high school students
involved in the national Distributive Education Clubs of
America (DECA) high school program. CFE proposed to create
and launch a twelve-module online curriculum in entrepreneurship for over 3,000 high school teachers and 150,000 high school
students.

The George Washington University (GWU) DECA Project

The main objective of the GW-DECA (Distributive Education
Clubs of America) project was to disseminate information on
Entrepreneurship Education to DECA participants. DECA is a
national association of marketing education students. It provides teachers and members with educational and leadership
development activities to merge with the education classroom
instructional program.

DECA chapters attracted students across the United States who
were interested in preparing for entrepreneurial, marketing, or
management careers. The George Washington University, in
partnership with The Coleman Foundation, developed a knowledge portal as a resource area for teachers in assisting in the
entrepreneurial education of DECA student members. The
twelve-module, four-tiered training covered the following areas
as displayed in Table 1.

The curriculum was pilot tested at a series of regional and
national DECA Conferences over a three-year period from

Table 1   George Washington University DECA.org Curriculum.

1: Fantasy to Reality	1 Who and What Are Entrepreneurs? 2 Is Your Idea Really a Business? 3 Tapping Your Entrepreneurship Creativity
2: Getting Started	1 Know Your Market 2 Writing a Winning Feasibility Plan 3 Using the Internet to Launch Your Business Venture
3: Nuts and Bolts	1 Elements of a Successful Business Plan 2 Sources of Funding 3 Financial Issues for Your Entrepreneurial Venture
4: Let's Roll	1 Building Your Entrepreneurial Team 2 Effective Marketing Strategies for a Successful Entrepreneurial Venture 3 Using the Internet to Grow Your Venture

1997–2000. Based on the feedback, the web site was launched in early 2000. Modifications to the topics covered and the support materials enhanced the usefulness and relevancy for both students and teachers.

Based on this successful partnership, DECA approached The Center for Entrepreneurial Excellence (CFEE) in 2003 to launch a project targeted at their college-age members enrolled in Delta Epsilon Chi. CFEE had evolved from the Centre for Family Enterprise founded in 1988 at GWU.

The Entrepreneurship Challenge

In September 2003, Dr. Edward Davis, Executive Director of Distributive Education Clubs of America (DECA), met with the directors of CFEE to discuss how to build upon the successful GWUDECA.org web site project. Due to the successful collaboration between DECA and CFEE, Dr. Davis was looking for a program, activity, and/or event targeted to the college division of DECA — Delta Epsilon Chi. The intent was that the program,

activity, and/or event would stimulate interest in entrepreneurship, free enterprise, and small business among the over 2,300
high school students attending Delta Epsilon Chi's
International Career Development Conference annually.

Based on conversations, CFEE developed "The Entrepreneurship
Challenge." The purpose of the challenge was to educate and
inform students and their collegiate advisors about basic principles underlying the concepts and theories of entrepreneurship
and small business management education. Modeled after the
concept of the "elevator pitch," students would be exposed to a
select number of informative sessions delivered by educators
and entrepreneurs over two days. An outline of the program is
displayed in Table 2 below.

Table 2   Entrepreneurial Challenge Program.

* Opening Session: "The Entrepreneurial Spirit"
* Presented by an Entrepreneur
* Introduction of the Entrepreneurship Challenge and a Discussion on
  Environmental Scanning   ﾠ᠂
* Know Your Market
* Pricing and Promotional Strategies
* Entrepreneurial Financing
* Franchising Opportunities
* During and after the information session, time is allocated to allow stu-
  dents, working individually or in teams, to formulate their game plan
  and develop their pitch. Teams and individuals would be assigned tables
  where as many as twenty judges — SCORE volunteers, local business
  leaders, educators and entrepreneurs — would judge each presentation
  based on the following eight criteria:

  1. Purpose/mission statement   20 points
  2. Description of business concept   15 points
  3. Concept was innovative   10 points
  4. Concept was creative   10 points
  5. Concept was doable   10 points
  6. Concept was well-presented   15 points
  7. Concept was well-researched [supporting data]   20 points

There would be three rounds of judging in which individuals and teams would rotate from table to table for each new round, allowing students the opportunity to refine their pitch.

In fact, for round three, students presented their pitch to their peers — other students who voted for the best idea per table. Thus, students would be judged and would judge presentations. The top six teams would compete for various cash prizes offered by Delta Epsilon Chi and other private sector groups the next day.

For the finals of the challenge, the following was required:

1. The final teams will prepare and present to the judges a brief, five-minute overview of their concept as well as a typed two-page summary of their concept.

2. Each plan to be typed, two pages, and include at minimum:

   a. Introduction

   b. Statement of Purpose/Mission Statement

   c. Description of Business Concept [who, what, where, when and how]

   d. Feasibility of Concept [market data supporting concept].

From year 2004–2008, over 600 students and fifty faculty members have participated in the Entrepreneurial Challenge. Over $35,000 in prize money was awarded to students. Student feedback has been outstanding as evidenced by a sample of feedback provided last year. Surveys from students indicate that they overwhelmingly think this is a great event, a good learning experience, and that the event provided a valuable life experience while they learned about entrepreneurship and small business. The Entrepreneurial Challenge served as the basis for my selection in 2009 as a Leavey Award recipient. Based on the success of the Entrepreneurial Challenge, CFEE developed an elevator pitch competition for The George Washington community called "Pitch George."

Pitch George

Pitch George is a risk-free opportunity to sharpen your presentation skills and get important feedback on the viability of your business concept. Even better, the Center for Entrepreneurial Excellence (CFEE) will help those individuals with strong proposals expand and refine their ideas into solid business plans. Pitch George is an excellent introduction to the campus-wide networking and support services that CFEE delivers.

Another objective of Pitch George is to provide its participants a total GW community experience capable of creating alliances, partnerships, and mentorship among the diverse community that comprises The George Washington University. An added feature to Pitch George will be the involvement of, and participation by, members of both The George Washington University community and the GW alumni in the greater Washington area who can either judge, mentor, and/or participate in the event.

How Does "Pitch George" Work?

- Teams and individuals who are part of The George Washington University community at-large, including alumni and local high school students, can participate.

- The Pitch George competition has four tiers: alumni, graduate, undergraduate, and high school.

- Presentations will take place on a designated Saturday in the fall on the campus of The George Washington University.

- Each team or individual will have five minutes to pitch a business idea to a panel of judges. The judges will be metropolitan area entrepreneurs, venture capitalists, and GW alumni.

- The judges will evaluate clearly how each presentation communicates the idea, and how viable the business idea actually is. (See Attachment A for the judging criteria.)

- The three best entries in each tier — alumni, graduate, undergraduate, and high school — will proceed to the final round of judging, which will take place at the Washington Monument. Finalists will have 72 seconds to make their pitch. Judges will determine the ranking of finalists in each tier, according to the first, second, and third placings.

- The three winners in each tier will receive seed funding from CFEE to start up their businesses.

Table 3   Presentation Rating Sheet.

Business Ideas and Context:	Points 1 = Poor – 10 = Excellent
1. Mission statement of the business venture.	
2. Description of the product or service.	
3. Overview of the characteristics of the market.	
4. Overview of how the product or service will stand out from its competitors. What's the "hook?"	
Idea Content and Quality:	
1. Did we understand the idea?	
2. Will it work?	
3. Is the idea innovative/creative?	
Presentation Style:	
1. Was the presentation convincing?	
2. Was the presenter articulate?	
3. Did the presenter sell the idea effectively?	
Total Score	

- Individuals register online for the Pitch George competition at www.PitchGeorge.org.

A rating sheet was developed to assist in the judging. Table 3 displays the criteria that are used to judge all the pitch George participants:

CONCLUSION

Whether you are creating a training outreach program in the government or academic sectors, there are some basic "rules of the road" that one must follow to be successful. After thirty-five years, I have learned that there are five basic steps to creating a successful and innovative training outreach activity. They are:

1. Conduct a Needs Analysis

Among the major flaws that exist in both the government and private sector is the misperception that "we" know about the marketplace needs without any data. Thus, we create programs that are offered at the wrong time, with subject matter either too simple or too complex, often lacking the sensitivity to understand what will work best. To remedy this situation, it is important to first gather intelligence on the intended target markets' needs. Also, if need to, partner with certain groups or organizations to add credibility, as SBA did in creating YES by working with national youth organizations.

2. Develop a Networking Strategy

The key to any training outreach program is ensuring that you have developed a strong network of supporters, evaluators, and resource partners. The key is to get "buy in" from everyone by getting them to believe the new program is their idea. My mentor at GWU claims, "people support what they help create," which usually translates into everyone pulling together. Meet with lots of people, get their input and support early on, and then hold a planning meeting where those assembled echo your concept, thus creating the perception that it was always their idea. Don't be afraid of emailing or calling veterans in the small business entrepreneurial education field for guidance and advice. They have been there, done it and can help you plot a course for success.

3. Leverage Existing Resources — Human, Fiscal, and Material

The key to a successful program is the ability to leverage resources: human, fiscal and material. Even if you have all the needed resources, sharing the load strengthens everyone's commitment. If everyone has "skin in the game," then the motivation to succeed is greater, and partnering with or leveraging other resources may bring more effective and efficient use of resources to the program. GWU partnered with IdeaBlob to enhance outreach and financial support for "Pitch George." When the SBA developed the BIC Program, they partnered with Entrepreneur Media, who offered a discount on their extensive library, allowing the SBA to open more centers with a limited budget. One of the keys to leveraging resources is finding a mentor who can provide you tips and guide you through the traps and snares of undertaking entrepreneurial program within bureaucratic organizations.

4. Create a Multifaceted Promotional Campaign

Getting the word out is key, but even more important is creating a 'buzz' before the event happens. In the 21st century, we must exploit the Internet, mass email, Facebook, blogs, and other low-cost, high-impact viral marketing strategies. The key is determining which promotional outlets offer the greatest "bang for the buck."

Keep in mind that the message must parallel the goals of the training program. Remember that using your partner's credibility in the marketplace adds a sense of trust that the participant expects quality and relevant training programs. The George Washington University ensured that the "Entrepreneurial Challenge Program" promotional materials were co-branded with the Distributive Education Clubs of America (DECA).

5. Analyze Outcomes with Follow-Up Evaluations

Often training programs are created, and then someone thinks about evaluating the success or failure. More times than not, they measure outputs, such as how many people attended, rather than outcomes, such as meeting stated training goals. While at the SBA, I initiated a number of evaluations to measure the economic and social impact of training and other outreach activities. It is neither easy nor cheap, but evaluation must be undertaken to ensure continued support from funders and supporters.

In closing, build upon the collective knowledge of the "wise old Turks," and avoid "reinventing the wheel." Blaze your own path, and good luck...

"We are what we repeatedly do. Excellence, then, is not an act, but a habit."

Aristotle

Chapter Seven

Global Entrepreneurship Education: What I Have Learned about Entrepreneurship Education in Asia!

By Leo Paul Dana

Dr. Leo Paul Dana is a worldwide entrepreneurship educator whose main academic appointment is at the University of Canterbury in Christchurch, New Zealand. He is currently at GSCM Montpellier on study leave. He also holds an appointment as an Adjunct Professor at the University of Regina in Canada. Dana earned his BA and MBA degrees from McGill University in Canada, and his Ph.D. from the Ecole des Hautes Etudes Commerciales. He has also held academic positions in such diverse, worldwide institutions as McGill University in Canada, the University of Pittsburgh Institute

for Shipboard Education, Nanyang Technological University in Singapore, INSEAD and ICN Graduate School of Business in France, as well as the Institut d'Administration des Enterprises in Strasbourg. He is a Senior Advisor to the World Association for Small & Medium Enterprises and the Founding Editor of the Journal of International Entrepreneurship. He is the author of the books "Entrepreneurship in Pacific Asia: Past Present & Future" and "Economies of the Eastern Mediterranean Region." Dr. Dana has been a keynote speaker at a number of international entrepreneurship conferences.

ENTREPRENEURSHIP IN SOUTH-EAST ASIA

Success depends on good timing, a proper environment, and people in harmony.

Chinese proverb

Although governments around the world recognise the importance of entrepreneurship and entrepreneurship education, their respective promotion and development efforts differ greatly, reflecting national priorities, demographic factors, and cultural values. Likewise, the entrepreneurship sectors in each country and their individual participants reflect vastly different historical and cultural factors, as well as vast differences in education and public policy. In addition, social norms have a vast influence on entrepreneurship and entrepreneurship education and development.

In the following discussions in this chapter, we shall outline the key differences in entrepreneurship education and development from country to country in the Asian Region. We will also discuss the specific and unique methods of entrepreneurship development and education that work very well in each of those countries, the problems that limit the development of entrepreneurship from country to country, and what is being done to try to solve these problems.

To many of the countries we discuss below, it is now obvious that the ability to produce wealth is more important than simply being endowed with natural resources. The production of wealth however, requires institutions and the efforts of individuals.

Many of these countries are beginning to recognize the importance of entrepreneurship to the development of their economies, and are taking steps to build up a culture of entrepreneurial success. Many countries have much more to do.

Cambodia

In Cambodia, the Khmer Rouge extinguished entrepreneurship during an intense period of anti-capitalism. The sector is re-establishing itself in an environment of uncertainty, yet Cambodia is still amongst the least developed countries in the world. Culture (particularly French culture) has been important in promoting innovation in Cambodia.

China

In China, entrepreneurship is being promoted as a supplement to the socialist economy, yet the state is still a major player in the economy. China's ability to attract foreign direct investment has increased entrepreneurship in the country. SMEs have transformed China and increased international entrepreneurial activity. In a very prosperous region of China, the Pearl River Delta (Hong Kong, Macau, and Guangdong Province), it has become part of local culture for many to want to be their own boss. There is an increasing gap between rich and poor in this big country.

India

In India, entrepreneurs and their SMEs are helping the country become a superpower. The middle class is gaining unprecedented economic power here. Rapid internationalization of the Indian economy has occurred. The global success of the Indian software industry that has occurred through international entrepreneurship is unprecedented; knowledge, intent, and networks are important determinants of the internationalisation process of small and new entrepreneurial firms.

Indonesia

Indonesia is one of the richest countries in Southeast Asia in terms of natural and cultural resources. Islamic religion greatly impacts the entrepreneurial activity in this country. International entrepreneurship in the tourism and investment sectors has huge potential in Indonesia. Given that the Chinese minority has been at the forefront of entrepreneurship, the state has been trying to promote entrepreneurship among the Indigenous *pribumis*. This however, has alienated many entrepreneurs of Chinese ethnicity.

Japan

In Japan, small-scale entrepreneurship complements large corporations, and cultural values propagate inter-firm linkages. Entrepreneurs seldom stand alone in Japan; rather they are linked into networks in which loyalty and harmony prevail.

Korea

Korea has been divided into two countries for over half a century. Credit policy in South Korea resulted in *chaebols* squeezing many entrepreneurs out of business; government measures have since intervened to assist small-scale entrepreneurship. Meanwhile, North Korea remains loyal to communist values.

Laos

In Laos, cultural values discouraged entrepreneurship among Lao men, resulting in opportunities for women and foreigners. Laos is among the least developed nations in Asia.

Malaysia

In response to the domination of entrepreneurship in Malaysia by ethnic-Chinese entrepreneurs, Malaysia adopted a policy of giving preferential treatment to Indigenous *bumiputras*. Some Chinese entrepreneurs are bitter about this discrimination. Nevertheless, Malaysia has prospered by transforming its industry to focus more on exports. Government-supported internationalization activities in the SME sector has encouraged entrepreneurship.

Myanmar (Burma)

Myanmar is rich in natural resources, but its people are not prosperous. Despite its lack of natural resources, poverty prevails. A principal export for this country is rice, and the state holds monopoly over this. The price of rice doubled during 2008, but supply was reduced, as the country's bowl was devastated by Cyclone Nargis in May that year. Myanmar is East Asia's last country to fully realise the potential of globalisation.

Philippines

The Philippines is the only Christian nation in Asia, and this has impacted entrepreneurial activities. Legacies from the United States have also impacted the language and politics of businesses in the Philippines. The Chinese minority dominates the entrepreneurship sector of the Philippines. Many Filipinos work overseas and send money home to relatives.

Singapore

Despite having a small landmass, Singapore is one of Asia's leading economies. Singapore's strong legal system, educational system and security, brought prosperity to its immigrants; later, multinationals saturated the domestic markets, forcing the internationalisation of formerly local entrepreneurship. Many Singaporeans do not become entrepreneurs, citing the opportunity cost caused by high salaries and job security with large companies in the island republic. The strong emphasis on the international economy means that Singapore performs well in business surveys of the best places to do business.

Taiwan

Similar to Singapore, Taiwan provided law and order. In the absence of many multinationals, this in turn facilitated entrepreneurship. Taiwan has more entrepreneurs per capita than any of its neighbours. Taiwan has achieved high export growth rates. The focus on technological innovations in Taiwan has spurned new innovations in this country. Furthermore, government incentives have shifted the focus of the Taiwanese economy to the international market.

Thailand

Thailand is among the few nations in Asia that were never colonized. Politics have influenced entrepreneurship here. The free market economy in Thailand has led to a strong focus on international markets. The Thai government's vision is to make Thailand a knowledge-based society by 2010 through entrepreneurship and innovation.

Vietnam

In Vietnam, entrepreneurship was introduced as a complement to socialism. To circumvent regulations, some entrepreneurs in Vietnam have resorted to smuggling. Nevertheless, Vietnam has encouraged entrepreneurship whilst complementing the political situation in the region. Through remarkable policy improvements, the Vietnamese economy has achieved a strong international growth rate.

COMMON PROBLEMS FOR PUBLIC POLICY

As we have discussed, many different governments have designed a variety of programmes to promote the development of entrepreneurship. Much of their spending, however, is in vain, as entrepreneurship development programmes alone are insufficient.

Programmes may be useful to those who know about them, but often, **those who could use them the most are unaware of their existence**.

Furthermore, policies that are not implemented fairly consequently fail to bring about desired effects on society. In some economies, **bribery, excessive taxation and regulation can inhibit entrepreneurship**. Key factors that could facilitate entrepreneurship in all Asian countries include enhanced entrepreneurship education, reductions in barriers to entry, the reduction of excessive regulation, bureaucracy and corruption, flat taxes, the freedom to compete, and a stable legal framework.

A priority for governments should be to determine the appropriate degree of regulation to enact and to enforce, such that the benefits to society exceed the costs of compliance. John Stuart Mill (1869) argued that the only purpose for which power can be rightfully exercised over a member of society, against his will, is to prevent harm unto others. While some regulation is required to ensure order, excessive intervention is counter-productive.

Where import duties are considerable, smuggling becomes popular — as is the case in Myanmar and in Vietnam. Even a culture supportive of entrepreneurship benefits from an optimal (often more minimal) level of regulation and government intervention.

It appears that the optimal level of regulation and government intervention is culture-specific. Policy-makers should therefore keep in mind that the success of a policy or programme in the West does not guarantee equal success elsewhere. For this reason, it is crucial to avoid trans-locating these from one environment to a different one. To be effective, policies and programmes should be appropriate to the culture of a society.

The religion of a country can play a major role in the development of entrepreneurship and in creating a successful economy. Where a religion lays stress on experimentation, material values, productive investment, thrift and honesty in commercial relations, upon experimentation and risk-bearing... it will be helpful to growth, whereas insofar as it is hostile to these things, it tends to inhibit growth. Where Theravada Buddhism is the backbone of social and cultural values, it may have a restraining effect on the accumulation of wealth and the rise of an entrepreneurial class.

Thus, policy-makers should be aware of the cultural attributes of different ethnic groups and religions, and different policies should take these differences into account.

Economic development programmes have been introduced in different contexts. Experts have become sceptical of targeted economic development programmes, because these often subsidise the wrong people, with no lasting benefits. It appears that micro-finance programmes will have greater success. In any case, no funding should be distributed in transitional economies without **post-loan or post-grant training**. Recipients should be familiarised with finance, tax, and payroll issues. Otherwise, of what use is capital unless there is knowledge to invest it wisely as an entrepreneur?

Many economies face the problem of social inequities, which may limit future economic development. The challenge these countries face is to identify ways to broaden participation in economic development. Priorities should include:

• Reduction of poverty by accelerating agricultural development, and in some cases by controlling population growth

• Improvement of training and vocational education

• Improvement of property rights

• Improvement of legal basis for commerce

• Improvement of infrastructure

• Further liberalisation of trade

• Revision of policies to attract foreign investment

• Improvement of the management of government expenditures

• Reform of tax policies, such as to broaden the state's revenue base in a fair manner.

IMPLICATIONS FOR ENTREPRENEURS

If there is one generalisation that can be made about doing business in Asia, it is that across these vast countries, transactions and profits are a **function of networks and relationships**. Preferential treatment — when reciprocal — reduces overall transaction costs, thus increasing efficiency, competitiveness, and profitability. This is generally true, regardless of the specifics of an environment. Nevertheless, one must be cautious while attempting to generalise across cultures.

In the West where the firm-type sector prevails, societies tend to take a form specific to them. They resemble each other in their value system, class structure, family organisation, governance, and economic models. We have come to refer to this as globalisation. Modern economies in the Occident are democratic, and their mainstream society is secular.

Across the nations of Asia, there is more diversity as compared to other parts of the world. Capitalism in Asia does not necessarily come with democratisation. Political reform is not necessarily part of economic transition. Some governments choose to have greater control than others.

Likewise, some societies are more religious than others, and there are important differences between religions. Attitudes toward business also vary greatly. Zingales argued that "Buddhism and Christianity seem most conducive to capitalism, and Islam the least." He wrote, "Jews, Buddhists, Catholics, and Protestants (in that order) support competition, while Muslims and Hindus are strongly against it."

Nevertheless, capitalism has been very successful in Indonesia and in Malaysia. Badawi explained, "Islam is well suited to economic, social and personal development... as long as we interpret it correctly."

Perhaps the most valuable advice one can give to potential entrepreneurs, and to those developing entrepreneurship education, is that the importance of cultural differences must never be underestimated. There is neither one Asian culture, nor one Asian model. Just because these people live in the same region does not mean that they share the same views about entrepreneurship. There is not one standard approach to transition in Asia either.

This is further complicated in pluralistic societies, which, unlike cultures, each have their own implicit and explicit assumptions. Risk also varies with different types of pluralism. Melting pot pluralism — the situation prevailing when minorities adapt to a secular mainstream society — is stable. In contrast, when ethnic groups do not share a mainstream society, polarisation can result in violence, as has been the case in Indonesia, Myanmar, and elsewhere. Again, there is no obvious consistency across nations.

Nor is there consistency across time, and those seeking to develop entrepreneurship should keep in mind that in some transitional economies — such as Myanmar — the newly emerging private sector lacks professional, financial, and economic structure. Rules change frequently. What is legal today may be banned tomorrow, and vice versa.

Often the ownership of property is not clearly documented, and the liquidity of immoveable assets is often delayed. Where acquisition is not practical, foreign investors may enter markets via networks. Given that communist planners traditionally emphasises vertical integration, managers in a market economy might find it necessary to explain how synergy often comes from horizontal integration.

Western management has mastered the art and science of doing business in the firm-type sector. In Asia, many opportunities are found in the bazaar and in the state-controlled planned sectors.

In the bazaar, the movement of raw materials, processing, distribution, and sales are intertwined activities. The **focus on relationships** supersedes the products and services that are being exchanged. A sliding price system results in prices that are negotiated, reflecting not only the cost or perceived value of a good or service, but also negotiating skills, the relationship between the buyer and the seller, and possibly the time, as well. It is also important to have an understanding of the parallel sector.

IMPLICATIONS FOR ENTREPRENEURIAL EDUCATORS

Much education has been aimed at teaching managerial content. This is inadequate. Emphasis should also be placed on values, as well as technical content. In the absence of the values related to sustainable long-term entrepreneurship — such as asceticism, frugality, thrift, and work ethic, managerial skills are not being put to optimal use.

Where privatisation and downsizing of state-owned enterprises cause mass unemployment, there is often a mismatch between market demand and skills available in the workforce. The workforce needs retraining in skills that are in demand. Consequently, the technical content of courses needs to be adapted to changes in the economy.

Due to the lack of employment opportunities, and in the absence of appropriate retraining, many people have become self-employed, often in informal or covert activities. Legitimate entrepreneurship is confused with illegal transactions. It would be beneficial therefore, for educators to promote acceptance of entrepreneurship in the context of a legitimate, honest path to economic success and independence.

Where a vibrant entrepreneurial class is absent, this may be due to the public policy environment, or to the lack of inherent entrepreneurial characteristics. Where the entrepreneurial spirit exists, new venture programmes may further enhance the environment for entrepreneurship, as is the case in the United States. However, in a transitional society with little experience of legitimate entrepreneurship, education should first focus on encouraging an entrepreneurship-friendly ideology.

As the economy of a nation becomes increasingly complex, marketing functions will mature and become more specialised. Training will be required to help entrepreneurs solve new problems of planning, distribution, and transportation.

CONCLUSION

Entrepreneurship does not guarantee prosperity for a nation. It is important to examine the broader picture. While economic growth has been prescribed as the remedy for poverty, experience shows that growth creates problems of its own. Of what good is rapid transition if its adverse effects are uncontrolled? It is useful to look not only at the creation of wealth, but also at its distribution. Myanmar is an example of a rich country with a population that is mostly poor. Class mobility, in such an environment, is often a function of access to bribes rather than productive creativity or economic innovation.

It would be a fallacy to attempt to understand entrepreneurship or innovation in isolation. There is no global formula for entrepreneurship education and development, or even entrepreneurship itself. What must change, and what need not? The answer depends upon the historical context and the current situation, as well as the result desired. A variety of models are means to achieve different results.

Classic theories cannot simply be taken and injected into transitional economies in neglect of the environment in which they are to be placed. Even among members of ASEAN, there are important differences. Historical, socio-cultural, and economic contexts appear to be important factors affecting the environment for business; societies cannot all adopt legitimate entrepreneurial systems at an equal pace, nor should they be expected to.

In each economy, the nature of entrepreneurship will evolve in time with help and encouragement from entrepreneurial education, but one should not expect entrepreneurship to converge across societies. There is no one formula for a "best" policy to promote entrepreneurship. Entrepreneurship is embedded in society, and the latter is affected by historical experience and cultural values. To understand the global nature of entrepreneurship, we must move beyond a universal model or a Western model. Entrepreneurship must be understood in the context of national development. Most importantly, policy-makers and educators should take note that to be relevant, policies must be culturally sensitive.

"If people only knew how hard I work to gain my mastery,
it wouldn't seem so wonderful at all."

Michelangelo

Chapter Eight

Teaching Global Entrepreneurship through Action-Based Learning

By Len Middleton

Len Middleton is a faculty member at the Stephen M. Ross School of Business at the University of Michigan and an advisory board member of the Samuel Zell and Robert H. Lurie Institute for Entrepreneurial Studies.

He is an experienced entrepreneur who teaches courses in entrepreneurship, family business, strategy, international field studies, and the Executive MBA project course. Len co-teaches the Executive Family Business course and two entrepreneurship courses in Hong Kong. Len is the Co-Director of the Global Projects course. His research interests are entrepreneurial studies, family business, and private equity. He works closely with Enterprise Ireland and two Israeli incubators in the Global Projects course where

MBA teams do projects in business development and planning, market entry strategies, marketing plans, and strategic plans.

He is on the board of several for-profit and non-profit organizations, and is a gentleman farmer.

THE GLOBAL PROJECTS COURSE

The MBA 2 Global Projects course, taught at the Ross School of Business at the University of Michigan, works with startup companies in Ireland, Israel, Jordan, China, India and the United Kingdom. This innovative course provides business development assistance to these companies by deploying teams of MBA students to work directly with start-up companies. This entrepreneurial project-based course fulfills a dual mission:

1) prepare intelligent, motivated MBA students for successful careers as future entrepreneurs, while giving them firsthand knowledge of what it takes to work in a global setting and

2) provide a startup company with exposure to the latest business frameworks, techniques, and models along with unbiased findings and top-notch recommendations that are actionable.

This course is part of the Action-Based Learning approach that is the cornerstone of the Michigan MBA experience.

In an Action-Based Learning course, students gain practical experience by working directly on a business issue for a startup company in a real-world setting. The students work in teams and are responsible for co-creating their knowledge by applying their core course classroom knowledge and business skills to evaluate a real-world business issue. The students learn firsthand what it means to be an entrepreneur by being directly involved in the development of the company.

Action-Based Learning requires students to first ascertain a basic understanding of the situation by gathering data through secondary research using computer databases and industry information. They continue to build their knowledge of the project through primary research by interviewing thought leaders and industry experts, and/or using survey tools.

After accumulating the information, the students apply the frameworks, models, and tools that are taught in the pre-requisite core courses. Toward the end of the project the students develop recommendations that will help the startup company grow over the next few years.

These projects provide a rich management education that emphasizes rigorous data collection, situation analysis, critical thinking, multidisciplinary learning, and developing a set of recommendations that have impact for the startup company.

The lecture and case study method is an important teaching tool at the start of an MBA student's education process because it provides the core business concepts and terminology required for understanding the entrepreneurial world. This pedagogical approach should not be replaced. However, as the MBA student's education progresses, providing all of the information to the student and allowing only partial analysis does not allow them to fully apply their skills in a real business situation while still having the advantage of faculty guidance.

Action-Based Learning

In the Action-Based Learning approach the students experience a fuller learning opportunity by providing the following benefits:

- Working with high-challenge, pressure-filled, time-sensitive challenges

- Enhancing the student's ability to communicate through interviews with industry leaders and influencers

- Taking business issues/problems from abstract to concrete, ambiguous to clear, with impact

- Multi-disciplinary and multi-cultural interweaving of personal experiences, intuition, creative problem solving and analysis, using frameworks and tools from the MBA core courses

- Participating in rigorous data collection, interviewing, detailed analysis, and findings

- Assessing strategic and operational options and presenting specific recommendations with persuasion, support, and clarity

- Team building and leadership development as key components

- Generating professional deliverables, presentations, and a written report.

Each project team works in conjunction with a Business School entrepreneurship faculty member and a business communication faculty member. The role of the faculty in an Action-Based Learning course is very different than in a classroom environment. Here the faculty does not readily give out the answers. This may be a hard role for some faculty members after coming out of the classroom environment where they are the knowledge expert and used to providing answers or giving direction.

A faculty advisor can help shape questions to give clarity or suggest resources that might be available, but it's the students' responsibility to find the answers. **It's important**

for the students' learning process to find the answers on their own.

The companies chosen for this course are at various stages of the startup process. Some of the companies may have a technology idea and need to understand the commercialization process and the market potential for such a discovery. Others may be at the true startup stage, where they have a working model concept, but need a feasibility assessment to determine the market viability or are ready for a full business plan on how to start the company. Some other companies have initial sales and need to expand the product/services offerings or consider a market entry or country strategy growth plan.

"Over the past 12 years, 231 Michigan MBA students have prepared 51 business plans and strategies for penetration of the marketplace for our projects. It has resulted in a win-win situation, providing the students real world, hands-on experience, and providing the incubator companies with documents that have proved to be extremely helpful in their goal of gaining entry into the marketplace."

Oren Sela, Project Director

Yozmot HaEmek Technological Incubator

Yozmot HaEmek, Israel

Getting Started: Setting-up the Projects

The Global Projects course works mainly with business incubators where startup companies have access to office space and business support. Working with incubators streamlines the project acquisition process, as there are many startup companies housed within each incubator. The process begins with the incubator management doing a first screen of their companies to determine who is interested and committed to working with an MBA team. The incubator management will know which companies can benefit from the help.

Next, a faculty member will meet with the companies several months before the course semester begins to ensure the proper level of commitment from the companies and to explain the course process. This face-to-face vetting of the companies is most important because a company that is not fully committed to the course process will continue to be difficult when the students are trying to work with them.

It is important for everyone involved to understand that this is a collaborative relationship between the incubator, company, faculty, and the students. This is not a fee for service like a consulting project. The client word never used, this is a collaboration where everyone benefits from the projects. The students are making a large time and financial commitment through their tuition to be involved in this type of course. The incubator management is investing time to support the student teams and help the company. The company must make a time commitment to support the students. Lastly, the faculty commits a lot more time and resources to these projects than a normal classroom course.

One area of difficulty is the **misconception that the students will not have the ability to do these types of projects.** MBA students at the Ross School of Business normally have five years of work experience and are approximately 28–32 years old. This course is taken during the second half of the final year of MBA education. They have had all of the core courses that have given the students foundation knowledge required to use in the projects. The faculty has approximately ten years of teaching experience in an Action-Based Learning course. The energy and work experience of the students, coupled with the capability of the faculty, sets a high-bar standard for working with these companies.

As the faculty member meets with the company executives in this period, a basic project scope is developed. It is not important that the project scope be completely defined at this time. The focus will come either at the start of the course or after the student team meets the company in-country. What is important is to encourage the companies to want a full project scope. This can be slightly narrowed once the project begins as the team and faculty better understand the company's current situation and future goals.

At this time it is helpful to get the company to send all former business plans, brochures, and company materials as a pre-read for the students. This information is not always available for a company in the early stage of development. These materials help promote the students' interest in a particular project and facilitate the students' learning curve in understand the company and its needs at the start of the project.

Team Formation

Another task to complete in this period is the project team formation. The students are introduced to the projects available through special classroom sessions where the faculty member gives an overview of the company and the project scope. The students are given the basic project scope and some high-level company information, but nothing confidential is divulged at this time. The team selection process ends before the semester starts.

Project Funding

The final piece to complete in this period is to arrange project funding and budgets for each team. The funding to cover travel expenses comes from a variety of sources such as foundations, institutes, and alumni donations. The average project cost is approximately $12,000–$18,000. The budget information is communicated to each of the students along with the university expense guidelines for the course. A support staff person begins buying economy airline tickets and arranging hotels for the teams. The accommodations are two to three-star hotels in safe areas.

The funding for the course is the most difficult part. The incubators do not have extra funds and the startup companies have very tight budgets as well. The funding for the Israel projects is provided by the Frankel Foundation of Detroit, and the Ireland projects are funded by the Samuel Zell and Robert Curie Institute for Entrepreneurial Studies at the Ross Business School. These two sources make it easier to offer these types of projects to MBA students. Faculty travel is covered by the Ross School of Business.

All student teams are required to do an expense report. They are given a set per diem for meals. All traveling participants are told to be mindful of the donors' gift.

Project Task Setup List

Below is a summarized list of tasks that need to be completed to prepare projects before the course semester begins:

- Initial screen of companies (incubator management)

- Face-to-face meeting with companies (faculty and company management)

- Prepare preliminary project scope (faculty and company management)

- Assemble background materials (company management)

- Project team formation (faculty and students)

- Arrange project funding, budgets, and travel (faculty and staff).

Course Semester: The Learning Begins

The Global Projects course is a 14-week course, 5–7 days of which are spent in the host country working directly with the startup company and doing primary research. The semester is divided into three phases during which the teams concentrate on different aspects of the project. Below are the different phases of the process in this course:

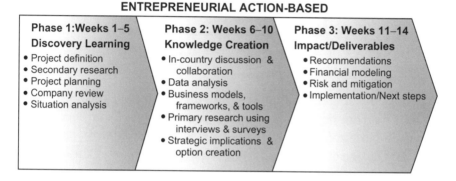

ENTREPRENEURIAL ACTION-BASED

Phase 1: Weeks 1–5 Discovery Learning	Phase 2: Weeks 6–10 Knowledge Creation	Phase 3: Weeks 11–14 Impact/Deliverables
• Project definition • Secondary research • Project planning • Company review • Situation analysis	• In-country discussion & collaboration • Data analysis • Business models, frameworks, & tools • Primary research using interviews & surveys • Strategic implications & option creation	• Recommendations • Financial modeling • Risk and mitigation • Implementation/Next steps

Phase 1: Discovery Learning

The first phase of the project is called the Discovery Learning phase. At the start of the project the students are enthusiastic about working on this type of learning opportunity. There is real excitement in the air. Usually by the end of the first week of the project however, the students begin to understand how much they do not know and that the only way to overcome the inherent project ambiguity is to dig into the project by doing secondary research and asking questions.

At the Ross School of Business, we have about 105 databases available to students. Each student team is assigned a librarian. Even the librarians bid on the projects they want to support. Secondary research involves using business databases to understand the business landscape. Primary research, in contrast, utilizes interviews and surveys to get information from industry

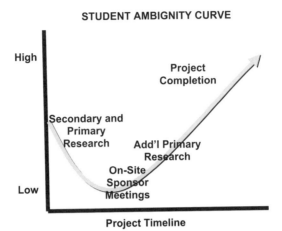

experts, potential customers, or anyone who may provide insight to the project. As the students move from secondary research to having a site visit with the company to doing primary research by talking with industry experts, their confidence in their knowledge and ability grows.

The students need to understand the startup company, its technology, product/service offering(s), and the external environment in which they operate. The process begins with a conference call with the team, faculty, and company to discuss where the company is in its development as well as any background information on the industry along with the company articulating their project needs.

By the end of the first week, the team will prepare a letter of engagement, project scope, team charter, and work plan. Teams are required to provide a pre-formatted weekly status report to the faculty and communicate with the company on a regular basis. These documents and the ensuing discussions will ground the team on the needs of the project.

The teams will have weekly or biweekly calls with the company over the next month to better understand the company and to share what the team has learned through secondary research. The librarians do a classroom session on how to use the database resources that are available. These sessions are highly popular with the students because for many of them it is the first time they learn to use the vast resources available online. A few of the more relevant places to start are covered in Appendix 1.

Project planning is another component at this phase of the project. The students need to develop a work plan that includes a research agenda, and interview guide. The work plan can be a simple, high-level week-by-week plan that determines internal team deadlines. The research agenda will show the tasks needed to ascertain project knowledge. Finally, the team should develop an interview guide that outlines the interview contacts, types of questions to ask, and the information allowed to be discussed by company founders with the outside world so that no confidential information is unwittingly given out.

During the first five weeks, the teams are doing secondary research into the external business environment. The students have access to industry reports that further build their project knowledge. The situation analysis checklist in Appendix 2 enables the students to use a focused secondary research approach in order to have collaborative discussions with the company. This analysis of the business environment in which the company operates will help the students, and later the company, understand the external environment and the issues the business may face. Some call this mapping the business landscape or analysis of the external business environment. No matter what the process is called, the goal is to understand the market, industry, competition, and customer environment into which the company is trying to enter.

Knowledge from secondary research, a few primary interviews, and the initial company discussions allows the team to develop a PowerPoint presentation that outlines the situation analysis and the current state of the company to use during the first day

with the company while in-country. This first in-country presentation will help facilitate the discussion on what the student
team understands about the project and gives the company a
clear understanding of how to fill the students' knowledge.

The next phase will be spent creating tools to assess the company,
the current options available, and any potential solutions. This is
where the team applies the frameworks, models, and tools they
learned in the required MBA courses.

Phase 2: Knowledge Creation

In the Knowledge Creation phase, the team conducts primary
research while in-country, and moves from findings to options to
solutions. They begin the creative process of articulating the
information through the use of business frameworks, models,
and tools to convey the information. The students are required
to do two presentations to the company during this phase.

The first task the team has after arriving in-country is to present the PowerPoint slides they developed during Phase 1. This
presentation should cover the following topics:

- Project Scope Discussion

- Situation Analysis Learning — Using Secondary Research
  Methods

  - Market Analysis

  - Industry Overview

  - Competitive Analysis

  - Customer Groups

- Company and Project Learning

- Project Timeline

- Next Steps.

Part of this first discussion will be spent on the project scope. Some project scopes will have been finalized weeks ago; others may need to have further discussion and refinement while the team is in-country. It's perfectly fine if the project scope is not defined until the students meet with the company in-person. The worst thing to do is to force a project scope because of an arbitrary deadline, causing the students to work on the wrong project scope and lose valuable project time. Once the students understand the issues at hand, the project scope is the easiest thing to write.

Data acquisition and analysis can come in many forms. The two common methods to conduct primary research are through interviews with industry experts and thought leaders and the use of a survey, if it is applicable to the project. The objective is to find credible information and build the student team's knowledge of the company. This occurs during the 5–7 days in which they are in-country.

*Melding Prior Knowledge and Experience
with New Knowledge*

The students now apply the educational learning from their earlier required core courses. The frameworks, models, and tools taught in these early courses are essential at this stage because they can help the student team assess the data by benchmarking the current situation and providing insight into the potential options available for the company.

For example, once the students understand the issues and need to gain more insight into the project challenges, they may decide to use a marketing survey to further measure required customer features on a new product. This type of learning exercise allows the students to create a survey instrument, collect the necessary information, and aggregate the data in the useful form.

The students in this phase learn to hone their interviewing and listening skills across multiple project stakeholders, influencers, constituents, and organizations. These skills will not only help them with recruiters, but will give them an advantage in their future career because they will know how to find, gather, and articulate the requests for information.

Before the team leaves the country, a second presentation is provided to the company organization will reaffirm the knowledge gained during the in-country meetings and they will communicate the work plan for the rest of the course. The second in-county presentation ensures the students, company, incubator management and faculty are all in agreement on the project scope and the necessary next steps to be accomplished by the team. These presentations build credibility with the company and also focus the discussions.

As the team moves toward strategic options, and eventually potential solutions, many of these frameworks enhance the decision-making ability of the team and give the companies a great deal to consider. This is critical because many of the companies know their technology can be used across multiple industries or markets, but they may not have the time, resources or capability to properly assess the right market entry point. This is a good exercise where the team can provide the company a lot of focus and set-up the sequential steps over time to knockoff the other markets. The key at this early stage for many of the companies is to stay focused on the best market to enter.

By the end of this phase it's important for the student team to share what it has learned with the company and the faculty, as well as revisit the project scope to make sure they are staying on-track. Students fully understand the company and the issues it faces. With this knowledge the students can develop potential solutions as a means to illustrate the pathways available to the company. At the end of this phase, however, it is easy for a team to get off-track. Sometimes the research on interviews take the students outside of the project area because they find information that is fascinating, but not needed for the project. Carefully rereading the project scope should keep them grounded to the needs of the project.

Phase 3: Impact/Final Deliverables

A team's final deliverables must have impact and be actionable! This final phase is the most stressful because the clock is ticking to finish the semester and prepare the final deliverables to present to the incubator management and the company executives. Hopefully, the team is beginning to slow down or stop the quest for data to focus on the final deliverables.

The first place to begin is to create an outline that can be used as a baseline document for both the written report and final presentation. The faculty uses this document to help guide the final deliverables. The hierarchy of topics methodology is used to tell the facts in a logical flow. It starts with the background information on the external environment, moves to the current state of the company, and finally takes the audience through the potential solutions to the final recommendations with risk assessment, financial modeling and a timeline for the next steps. Each heading sets the stage for the next heading of the final deliverables.

These outlines can be as short as one page or as long as five pages in length with several levels of subheadings. Below is a typical outline format for a startup company project:

- Executive Summary (fully detachable)

- Introduction or Overview of Project

- Situation Analysis

- Company Overview or Current State of the Company

- Solutions Chapter (this depends on the type of project)

- Financial Model (if applicable)

- Risk & Mitigation

- Recommendations

- Next Steps

- Conclusion.

Introduction will consist of the project scope, research approach, research methodology, and the general background of the project. The Situational Analysis section outlines the external environment facing the company. This will include insight into the market analysis, industry dynamics, competitive analysis, and customer groups. The Company Overview section has the following topics: mission/vision statements, SCOT analysis, product/service summary and evaluation, company structure, and the value proposition.

The next heading(s) will depend on the type of project being done for the company. This section should make clear the potential options and solutions available to the company. If it's a marketing plan, the focus will be on the segmentation, targeting, and positioning of the product/service or the market/country options available followed by the marketing mix. In a pure business plan it can be several sections that outline the internal development of the company such as its operations, technology, and organizational needs.

All of the projects will have some level of financial modeling and possibly funding requirements. The projects working with early-stage companies will have very high-level models and pro-forma statements because so much is unknown regarding the technology costs and market viability. Those working with later-stage companies will produce a full set of pro-forma financial statements, ratios, breakeven analysis, sources and uses statement, and a funding required timeline with the projected amounts needed to sustain the company.

Not all teams will do scenario planning because the project scope may not require it, but those who do may use Monte Carlo simulation software to model different scenarios. It is a nice tool to use with the financial modeling section of the deliverables because the software allows the student team to show the different permutations available and gives the startup company better decision-making ability as they build the company.

Every startup company faces risks because no business model or technology is perfect. The Risk and Mitigation section is a short section that outlines 3–5 risks facing the startup company and the ways to mitigate or overcome those risks.

The most important section is the recommendations. This section will give the full details on how to implement the solutions.

- Time versus sequential

- Degree of difficulty

- Resource capability

- Funding requirements.

The teams working with startup companies are required to do an implementation section in the final deliverables that gives a timeline for implementing the recommendations. No project would be complete without a game plan on how to execute the steps recommended by the student team. These recommendations in a timeline format are very well developed with a full understanding of the startup company's capability and resources.

Every project has a full Executive Summary that is more than just a summary of the recommendations section, but a guidepost of the key pieces that developed throughout the project that led to a summary of the recommendations. No page length is set on this document, but they are typically 2–4 pages in length. This is an important document and is always written last.

The students are told to have no surprises during a final presentation. This means the student team should continuously communicate its findings, options, solutions, and recommendations with the company. This open format creates an environment where healthy discussion ensues at the end of the formal presentation.

One question students always ask is the page limit for the written report and a slide limit for the PowerPoint presentation. No length is predetermined. The proper length is determined by what it takes to convey the appropriate information. One previous team had 350 slides and did four full scenarios for an Israeli biotech company. It made the faculty consider a limit, but the information was very well developed and presented.

Final presentations are usually done by either a conference call or a videoconference with the company and the incubator management present. The team will send the PowerPoint slides via email to the company executives and the incubator management the day before the presentation, which gives them time to review the materials before the presentation and have informed discussion about the content covered in the presentation.

A written report is required of all teams. The final written report is professionally bound and sent to the companies along with a CD of all relevant materials at the end of the semester. The teams will also send the final deliverables via email.

> *"I've had four teams with two different companies. Each team gave us a strategic plan for the future that, on review, made complete sense and helped us move to the next stage of development."*

Enda Keane, CEO

TreeMetrics Ltd

Cork, Ireland

THE CHALLENGE OF TEACHING OUTSIDE THE CLASSROOM

The challenge of an Action-Based Learning course is allowing the outside world into the learning environment. **Not everyone is comfortable with this teaching and learning style** because it's very different than the typical classroom setting where the professor has almost total control of the information being conveyed.

Many faculty have not developed this type of teaching style, and this is a limiting factor when trying to further this type of pedagogy. This is where the bridge between theory and practice is built, but most faculty are focused on academic research within just their particular field.

The outside world can change the dynamics of the learning environment even when everything is predetermined with a solid project scope and commitment from the company. For instance, the company could be bought or acquire a strategic partner at the start of the project which may change the project scope, location, or time commitment from the sponsor company.

During the second Gulf War, the Israel-based projects had to move to a U.S. location because of safety and security issues at the time. This was a major refocus after airline tickets and hotels were booked for international travel. The Israeli entrepreneurs were also rightfully worried about their families and country.

Confidentiality is at the heart of all projects. Since the start of the course, no issues have arisen with the confidentiality of any project. All entrepreneurs are asked if they want the students to sign a non-disclosure agreement.

Sometimes a company will want to block or even strongly influence a recommendation. This is where the incubator management and faculty can be helpful to negotiate a better solution. A team may place the materials in a separate document, but at no time are the companies allowed to use the report or presentation in a way that does not include all of the information presented.

A team coach is hired in case a team has internal communication issues. The coach is available throughout the course, but is rarely needed. Most of the students work out the differences in communication, work style, and commitment using a team charter approach. A team charter is developed the first week of the course and guides the team if internal issues arise.

Achieving Impact around the World

"Partnering with the MBA school in Michigan has enabled WebSpirit Ltd. to advance strategically by 1–2 years in our thinking. It has been hugely challenging and beneficial to our business and enabled us to think big."

Grainne Barry, CEO

WebSpirit Ltd.

Limerick, Ireland

It's amazing to watch the changes in the students as they grow in self-assurance, poise, savvy, critical thinking, and decision-making capability above and beyond the functional expertise needed for the project. **These entrepreneurial Action-Based Learning projects build a different type of confidence that will stay with the students beyond business school**, and more importantly, will enable them to have successful careers because they know how to apply their knowledge and work without a clear set of objectives in the business world.

The biggest benefit is watching the students understand what it takes to be an entrepreneur and the issues they face. By the end of the project, the students are asked to stand in the place of the company entrepreneur and make recommendations as if they were running the company. This focus gives the students real experience about what it takes to start and manage a company.

A former student who currently works for a major pharmaceutical company did an Action-Based Learning project her first year with an Israeli biotech startup company and was in the Global Projects course her second year where she worked with a company in Jordan. Having an Action-Based Learning experience her first year in the MBA program impacted her summer internship with the pharmaceutical company. She says it gave her a real advantage because she not only knew how to get data, but also knew how to apply the information from her experience with the startup company project. Her competition that summer for one full-time position after graduation was against five other MBA students who were from top business schools. She was the only student that received a full-time offer that summer. She credits the project course for making the difference.

The Human Support Input

Support of the student teams comes in many forms. One of the reasons these entrepreneurial projects are so successful is the relationship with the incubator management and the support they provide to the students and the companies. The incubator management knows the companies and can assist the student teams when clarification is needed or when the startup company is composed of mostly technical personnel who do not have the requisite business background. This support, along with the faculty, provides the student teams the best learning environment because the students get access to the appropriate information and knowledge of the startup company.

Additional Benefits

The startup companies and incubator management benefit from the experience by not only having access to young, smart talent, but also from being exposed to the latest business frameworks, models, and tools. The student energy in the incubator creates a buzz of excitement. One of the incubator executives has commented that he can't wait each year until the students arrive. The final deliverables give the company a real roadmap for the future.

Some companies have been able to use the project results to obtain their next round of funding from investors because of the depth of research and the game plan that is projected for the company.

These projects have been instrumental in focusing the companies as well. A few companies each year will have created a product or products that can be used in multiple markets. It is difficult for a startup company to determine which market is the easiest to enter and has the greatest potential for growth and profitable revenue. The company does not have the time or resources to enter multiple markets. The students will work with the company management to determine the best entry strategy.

A few of the projects over the years have been involved directly with the incubator, with incubator management being the sponsor. In Israel, a team has helped review the process of how the incubator supports a company. Another project team in Israel wrote a business plan for a new biotech incubator. Two other project teams have worked with an Irish incubator to look at how they support the startup companies and develop a growth program that would help startup companies with 1 million Euros in sales grow to the next level. These projects are outside of the norm of what is usually accomplished in this course, but they show the true partnership that has been built.

> *"The world comes to Limerick to learn about business incubation and innovation. The University of Michigan came asking how they might help us further develop our processes. Since our partnership commenced in 2002, we have worked together on a number of challenging assignments to look at issues like 'how do we increase the rate of growth of our start-ups' or 'how do we improve our business start-up processes.' In addition, Michigan has helped a number of our client companies with a strategic review of the client business and direct contacts with potential customers."*

> *"Our relationship with Michigan has opened our minds to the world, and in particular, helped us improve our systems and processes."*

John Dillon

High Potential Startup Manager

Enterprise Ireland

Life-long friendships have developed between the students, company executives, and incubator management. Many of the students stay in contact with the companies for years to come. Some former students have been able to use their contacts in their current position to open doors for the company with which they did their project or even other companies in the incubator. Students and company executives alike have said that the experience has had a profound impact on their future.

CONCLUSION

"The Michigan Global Projects programme is a highly effective entrepreneurship development exercise in that students get to work with international entrepreneurs on real life business issues that are critical to their businesses. The entrepreneur, on the other hand, receives high-level advice from a multidisciplinary team and faculty from a world renowned business school."

Patrick Munden, Director of Business Development

Ryan Academy for Entrepreneurship

Dublin, Ireland

This Global Projects course (and other Action-Based Learning courses) is sometimes referred to as the course that never ends (see Appendix 3). To do it right, **this is an eleven-month course**. The relationship management piece with the incubators or the companies in particular never ends because understanding the needs of the incubator and its companies is an ongoing process.

The upside is that it is rewarding to be deeply involved in working with students and companies and being close to practice. It's an amazing learning process for all those involved.

Since this program started in 1992, over 1,800 MBA students have worked with 300+ companies to develop business plans, marketing entry strategies, and growth plans for these companies. This program is the signature piece of the Michigan MBA experience. The Wall Street Journal has ranked Michigan's MBA program number one the last three out of four years because of the Action-Based Learning courses.

The course is for all those involved — our students, the companies, the University, the incubators, and the Faculty involved!

APPENDIX 1: RESEARCH APPROACH — WHERE TO BEGIN

1. Trade Associations and Trade Shows

2. Industry Conferences

3. Industry Studies

   - Books, Magazines, and Periodicals

   - Investment Analysts

   - Market Research Data: Industry Statistics and Reports

4. Business School Cases

5. Company Sources

   - Product or Service Brochures

   - Annual Reports and SEC Filings

   - Public Relations/Promotional Materials

6. Internet Web Sites

7. Government Sources

   - Patents, Legal and Tax Documents

   - U.S. Census Data

- Regulatory Agencies

8. Library Databases

- Frost and Sullivan

- Thomas Register

- Dun & Bradstreet.

Keep a log on where the information was gathered and the date of the source. Stay organized!

APPENDIX 2: SITUATION ANALYSIS, OR MAPPING THE BUSINESS ENVIRONMENT MARKET ANALYSIS

1. Define the PEST+G trends (Political/Economic/Social/ Technological and Global)

2. Economic

3. Social/Demographic

4. Technology

5. Global Issues

6. Actual and potential market size

7. Market growth, sales levels, and profitability

8. How attractive is the market or industry?

9. The cost structure of the market place

10. The distribution system: major channels, trends, and developments

11. What are the current and future key success factors (e.g. cost, branding, packaging, quality, distribution, etc.)?

Industry Analysis

1. How do the five forces affect the industry?

   a. What is the Rivalry among Existing Competitors?

   b. Threat of New Entrants

   c. Threat of Substitute Products/Services

   d. Bargaining Power of Suppliers

   e. Bargaining Power of Buyers

2. What industry trends are significant to strategy?

3. What environmental opportunities and threats exist?

4. What are the major strategic uncertainties?

Competitive Analysis

1. Who are the key Direct and Indirect players?

2. Who are the existing and potential competitors in this industry?

3. What are their sales, share, and profits?

4. What similar products/solutions are being offered today to your "target" market?

   a. From whom and at what price?

   b. Product benefits and features (quality, technology, location, service, availability, and reliability)

   c. Through which distribution and delivery channels?

5. Are there alternate and substitute ways of meeting the market need?

6. Define the strategic groups (players) by characteristics and strategies

7. What are the growth trends?

8. What are the strengths and weaknesses of each competitor?

9. What are their marketing strategies?

10. How do they compete?

11. Are there any significant changes happening?

Customer Analysis

1. Who are the customer groups that will buy your product/service?

2. Who will be the first customer(s), and why?

3. Define the different customer types

4. Relative size of targeted customer groups

5. Segmentation of the market

6. What is being solved?

7. Need served for each targeted group

8. The critical issues and influencers

9. How to reach, motivate, and capture each group

10. How will you measure and track market information?

    a. What are the major product segments?

    b. Define the customer motivations

    c. Information on customers

11. What are the critical trends or unmet needs?

APPENDIX 3: COURSE TIMELINE

- Month 1 — Course Startup Phase

  - Update brochure and course syllabus

  - Sponsor plan

  - Review course planning process

- Months 2–3

  - Setup sponsor meetings

  - Project scope acquisition

- Budget project expenses

- Communicate opportunities to students

- Months 4–5

  - Travel and logistics

  - Student, faculty, and librarian bidding process

- Month 6 — Course Launch

  - Start team meetings

  - Project scope refinement

  - Funding acquisition

  - Review current sponsor materials

- Month 7

  - Student travel to company location

- Months 8–9

  - Project execution

- Month 10

  - Project grading

  - Sponsor and student project debriefs

- Month 11 — Course Completion

- Complete course financial audits.

"Discipline is the bridge between goals and accomplishment."

Jim Rohn

Chapter Nine

Social Entrepreneurs: Born or Bred? Capitalism that Makes a Difference!

By David Bussau

Master Entrepreneur. Philanthropist. Humanitarian. Founder, Opportunity International. David Bussau built his career in the construction business in Australia. By age 33 he began to ask himself of his accumulated wealth, "How much is enough?" He has dedicated the next thirty plus years of his life to helping less fortunate people throughout the world to have a chance at entrepreneurship and realize their dreams! Opportunity International makes about $385,000,000 in micro-loans to poor people in 28 countries of the world. Their payback rate is 98%! Women receive 85% of the micro-loans. He was recently honored as Senior Australian of the year.

Philippa Tyndale authored a biography on David Bussau, titled "Don't Look Back". Some of his comments below are adapted from that book.

THE FUNDAMENTALS OF ENTREPRENEURSHIP

A world without entrepreneurs would be like watching Star Wars Episodes I, II, and III without the light and sound effects. Comprehensible, but terribly unexciting.

Entrepreneurs introduce new and interesting ideas into the marketplace. They are sensitive to the real or imagined needs of the market and are able to find ways to fill gaps. They have mastered the practical application of supply and demand. The need for quick meals gave us fast food, television addicts have TiVo so as not to miss any of their shows, and the need for faster, more reliable, and improved communication has given us the Internet. Entrepreneurs are driven by creativity, innovation, curiosity, risk, failure, and the stubbornness not to fail again.

A simple definition of an entrepreneur is "somebody who identifies and finances commercial enterprises to make a profit." Entrepreneurs are intimately familiar with the concepts of market forces, competitive advantage, interest, increased productivity, and leverage. As innocuous as these terms sound, they are also the very same terms that have sometimes put business in a "dirty" light. **Entrepreneurship is sometimes equated with cut-throat competition or an endeavor where profit is the only goal and conscience is largely absent.**

This perception is unfortunate, and one I reject absolutely. Commerce, business, and enterprise in themselves are neither "dirty" nor "bad" concepts. I believe it is the type of business and the negative outcomes that may taint business.

THE SOCIAL ENTREPRENEUR

In the last few years, a more acceptable type of entrepreneur has emerged. The social entrepreneur, or social capitalist (terms I use interchangeably), shares the same basic characteristics and skills used to turn a profit as the entrepreneur, but the motivating forces and heart are vastly different.

Social Entrepreneurs, or social capitalists, are people who apply marketplace principles to creatively and sustainably solve social problems. These can range from the big global dilemmas such as poverty, slavery, corruption, and the environment, to more localized issues of illiteracy and children's health. In social entrepreneurship, there is a conscious effort on behalf of entrepreneurs to harness their skills and resources and use them in a broader context than the business in which they were learned. **It is far beyond charity. It is a worldview that proclaims that their abilities towards the wider benefit of the social community is just as much a part of their current businesses as turning a profit.**

The Brick Workers of Pakistan

Some of the desperately poor people I have encountered in my work in micro-enterprise development are the brick kiln workers of Pakistan. They were the poorest and most marginalized of all Pakistanis.

The laborers took the jobs in the kilns, and the kiln owners agreed to pay a cash advance to cover the worker's outstanding debts. Little did they know that in joining the kiln, they would be locking themselves and their children and grandchildren into bonded labour, effectively turning them into slaves to the kiln owners.

Whole families spent the entire day in 45°C (110 degrees F) heat digging mud and mixing it with water and straw to make the clay they formed into bricks, as they had done since ancient times. I saw an old man, the grandfather of the family, carried out into the sun on a stretcher so he could spend the day on his side, reaching into the mud to mold his share of the days' bricks. He had made bricks since he was six and would soon die making bricks.

There was no sense of community, although families were out and about together each day. It was a mechanical action all day, every day. There was no spare energy for laughter or companionship.

The Social Entrepreneurial Solution

Having been an entrepreneur all my life, I tried to think of an entrepreneurial solution to the problem of slavery and poverty. If we buy the workers out of their debts it might free some families, but how are they going to support themselves? Many only knew about making bricks and lacked the confidence to dream of doing anything else. Eventually a seed of an idea germinated in my mind — we could build our own brick kiln and let the workers work their own way out of bondage.

This meant having to raise the money for the brick kiln. In 1986, we raised enough money to lease land for the brickworks, buy dozens of the workers out of bondage and buy land in a nearby village to subdivide for the workers' houses. The money allowed the group to build a clinic and provide each family with a milking goat. Bishop Michael and I then assembled a board, a group of business leaders, to oversee the project.

Within the year, the new brick kiln was operational, built on land leased for ten years. Soon, teams of kiln workers and families from other kilns in the district arrived at the new kiln. They had heard this was something new, but their expectations for a life outside drudgery were low. When our group paid out the workers' debts at the old kiln, we became the new owners of the kiln workers. I had played many roles, but never before had I owned bonded workers!

Under the new system, workers were credited with 10% of all the bricks they produced each day, which would then be used to build their own houses on the land near the village. With this system, it would take the workers 18 months to pay back all the debt, and by then each family would have enough bricks to build a small house. We agreed to supply roofing iron, a clean water supply and a nursery at the kiln. This improved working conditions and reduced the health problems. Workers were more motivated, being now able to see the end of the road of indebtedness. The workers worked a little harder because they were healthier and happier and as a consequence, brick production was vastly increased and the brick kiln more profitable.

Strategic impact is imperative in social enterprise. In the Pakistan project, it would have been much easier to pay the indebtedness of these bonded laborers. While this would have still been a valid philanthropic effort, it would not have addressed their problems, which were caused by a faulty system that left the workers without viable skills to get themselves out of their situation.

Are Social Entrepreneurs Born or Bred?

Stated differently, can all entrepreneurs be social entrepreneurs? The ability to look beyond one's profitable interests does not always flow naturally. **I believe social entrepreneurship must be in a person's DNA.** Among the biggest defects of man is shortsightedness, especially when self-interest is involved. A person can be a very successful businessperson and not be an entrepreneur. An entrepreneur can be very creative and innovative and not be a social entrepreneur.

A social capitalist believes that there is an interconnectedness between his business and the society around him other than the simple law of supply and demand. The most effective social capitalist does not bifurcate or segment society. He or she is able to see the place of the business in society as a whole — not simply as a means of meeting a need, but having a larger purpose.

In my experience with a wide variety of social enterprises, there are some basic characteristics and attributes that form part of a social entrepreneurs' make-up. I believe that these characteristics can lie dormant in an entrepreneur for a lifetime unless coaxed out by experience and exposure.

CHARACTERISTICS AND ATTRIBUTES OF A SOCIAL CAPITALIST

Spontaneous and Impetuous

On 26 December 2004, the Asian tsunami — one of the worst natural disasters on record — hit several countries almost simultaneously. One of the hardest hit coastlines was that of Aceh Province in Indonesia, where over 300,000 Indonesians perished. Many relief agencies responded quickly; non-profit agencies and foundations came in with specific programs to help the survivors of the disaster. Donations poured into Banda Aceh in abundance.

Early in 2005, Opportunity International (OI), a global microfinance organization, along with a group of businessmen, invited me to visit the provincial capital, Banda Aceh, to see how we could contribute to its rehabilitation. Housing was the obvious and most pressing need. Many aid agencies, including the International Red Cross, World Vision, Zero to One, and Habitat for Humanity Work already in Banda Aceh mobilizing it's own people to help build homes. To build the needed homes, they would need a variety of fixtures within a very short span of time. We had entered into a partnership where:

- A local non-profit organization (YDS) would retrain the survivors of the tsunami and teach them to make doors, windows, and other fixtures that would be needed to build homes.

- OI would provide micro-credit to YDS and survivors so that they would have the capital to invest in the business of making the fixtures that were needed to complete the Agency's housing project.

- Commercial supply contracts were made with the agencies to purchase the fixtures from the production units of YDS.

- An internet cafe was established with its own satellite link to serve the NGO community and train locals in internet skills.

This business solution addressed several of the societal issues that arose from the effects of the tsunami. The response was comprehensive, quick, and determined. Catastrophes and disasters such as the 2004 tsunami are the typical environment for social entrepreneurship to flourish, ideal for spontaneity and impetuosity to bring about positive results.

Empowering

Entrepreneurship is vital to sustainable economic growth at all socio-economic levels of society, and those who create innovative enterprises are key to enabling and releasing the latent entrepreneurship in others. Some people impede and stifle creativity, while others release and inspire. Each successful entrepreneur has to make that decision as to which one they will be.

Successful entrepreneurs must enable and equip others and then release them into the operation of the business so the burden of making a business profitable is shared. This leveraging of talents develops and releases potential and allows the entrepreneur to manage their time to do what they do best — creating marketplace solutions. A social entrepreneur is no different. He/she will empower, coach, and mentor the people involved in a social enterprise.

In 1991, Mt. Pinatubo in Zambales, Philippines erupted, resulting in massive destruction caused by lahar and volcanic ash. Thousands perished and many thousands more were displaced. Several years after the disaster, a group of businessmen discovered a commercial use for the tons of volcanic ash that covered miles of land. Agriculturists discovered that certain vegetables would grow surprisingly well on the ash and lahar, but even more profitable was that the volcanic ash could be used to make decorative and highly marketable items. Local communities were organized by non-profit organizations so that skills to make something out of nothing could be taught. Filipino businessmen involved themselves in the marketing of the agricultural and other finished products. To this day, volcanic ash items are sold in the Philippines and exported abroad.

As observed through the Mt. Pinatubo experience, **Social Entrepreneurs show an uncanny knack of knowing what they are good at and the ability to engage others with the skills to complement and complete the task**.

Creative

People are either pioneers or farmers, builders or maintainers. **An entrepreneur is a pioneer who thinks out of the box for unusual, unorthodox solutions to problems**. For many entrepreneurs, the challenge is paramount. Ho-hum solutions are boring and unacceptable.

Several years ago, the Indonesian market was deluged by poultry from big producers in the area. These large producers flooded the market with subsidized poultry priced at unrealistic rates in order to capture a larger market share. At the time, we were helping small poultry producers, and we read the writing on the wall and knew that our small poultry producers could not compete with the big producers. If the small producers sold their chickens immediately, they would suffer big losses from which they would not be able to recover. At the same time, we realized the large producers could not sustain those prices, so we decided we would wait it out rather than disadvantage the small producers.

The solution we came up with was to build a snap freezer (a large cold room) and abattoir. We then purchased the poultry produced by the small producers and froze the poultry until the market surplus diminished. We took the risk of selling the poultry once the subsidized products increased their prices. We were able to recover our investment by selling the frozen poultry to hotels and restaurants.

Sensitive

Social entrepreneurs are equally sensitive to the fluctuations in the market and to the needs of society and the community around them. The focus is not only on profit, but also on how much they can give back to society.

Social entrepreneurs know that **eventually every ideal is exploited by commercialism and consumption, and that every good and pure idea will eventually be captured, contorted, and commercialized**. They carefully take steps to guard against this so that the ideal is not lost on the altar of commerce. There are many examples of hospitals and schools set up by communities where the original intention was for social impact, but they have ended up serving an elite sector of society who can afford to pay for their services.

Sensitivity requires that an entrepreneur be able to sense nuances and slight changes in the internal and external environment of the commercial enterprise so that action may immediately be taken to avoid compromising the ideal.

Daring

George Leigh Mallory was a mountain climber who gave a legandary reply to the question, "Why do you want to climb Mount Everest?" He replied: "Because it's there." A similar question may be asked of social capitalists: "Why do you engage and address societal dislocations?" and most certainly their reply would be, "because it can be done." Social capitalists dare to go where others dare not. They are firm believers that we miss 100% of the shots we never take, frown on such a statistic, and take strides to improve it.

When I was 35 years old, **I felt I had built enough personal wealth** and wanted to use my skills and money for the common good. An earthquake in Indonesia gave me the excuse to put my entrepreneurial skills to work. My wife Carol and I started with a few small loans to villagers with our own money. It was risky for a Westerner to provide loans and expect a return on that loan, but I did get returns on my investment. That was 30 years ago. **Today, Opportunity International, which was a result of that little experiment, makes one million small business loans annually and impacts nearly five million people each year**.

Many have asked me why I did the things that I did and I often say that **"We have no control over how we die, but we certainly have control of how we live, and I would I like to live a life that makes a difference."** I simply move ahead towards the goal I set for myself. I believe that we should stop analyzing life. Just live it. Analysis is what makes it complicated. If I had stopped to think before making that first loan, who knows what would have happened?

People come in all different sizes, shapes, and forms. We are driven by a variety of motivations and passions. Some people have 500 hp engines but are only getting 50 hp out of them, or even worse, they have their foot on the accelerator and the brake at the same time. I feel that this is a waste of energy and effort. As a social entrepreneur, I forge on at full throttle to impact society.

Steadfastness

Steadfastness is **perseverance times ten**. It is more than never giving up. It is never, never giving up and finding a new way to do what you want to do each time you reach a dead end.

If an entrepreneur's stubbornness motivates him or her to keep working on a business concept until it is profitable, a social entrepreneur has an even greater motivation, which is making both a profit **and** a difference in society and people's lives. Here, we do not talk about success so much as satisfaction. Success is a measure decided by others. Satisfaction is a measure decided by an individual.

When we first started microfinance on a grand scale, we were told repeatedly that the poor were not bankable, that we were fools to invest so much money on people with no education, no apparent business acumen, and trapped in such abject poverty that they could think of nothing but where they could find their next meal. Now, 30 years later, the microfinance industry is not only within non-profit circles, but involves local and international banks, multilateral agencies, and governments as well. Microfinance is a now core tool in alleviating poverty. We didn't come out of those

30 years unscathed; there were wounds and scrapes enough to discourage us that perhaps the naysayers were correct, but 30 years have proven us right. The poor simply needed us to stand by them, walk alongside them, mentor, and teach them.

Social entrepreneurs are more like marathon runners than sprinters. They stay for the long haul.

Common Sense

Many years ago, the Kingdom of Tonga was hit by a cyclone. The community we were working with was devastated. Trees were torn from their roots, crops ruined, lives destroyed. In trying to come up with ideas on how to help them, the answer was so obvious we almost missed it. Upon looking around the community and seeing trees strewn on the ground, we realized that the economic solution to their problems was right before our eyes. So many trees were felled by the cyclone that it made sense for a group of businessmen to finance the building of a sawmill. The felled trees were gathered by the community and brought to the sawmill. From devastation the people of Tonga found a way to earn their livelihood and rebuild their lives.

While entrepreneurs are daring and pioneering, they should not be without common sense. Sometimes the most exciting and relevant solutions to problems can be the most obvious if we only look with both our minds and hearts. **We must learn to build on our islands of strength and not focus on our weaknesses.** Conservative ideas took flight not because wealthy philanthropists were suddenly willing to finance them, but because they identified actual problems and offered sensible solutions.

Passion for People

They are not just for business and profit. Social entrepreneurs must know that to be successful they must invest in people, not just a cause. They must be willing to look for potential in people and not expect all solutions to come from them alone. They must build and rebuild relationships, as no program will fly if there are broken relationships that are unresolved. In my experience, healthy relationships will self-organize, and if you have healthy relationships, change becomes easier.

Nothing can be accomplished without people who are willing to work on a good idea. Robert Kaplan is known to have said: "Big ideas, particularly bold ones, are hostage to the quality of their execution." This quality is directly relevant to the extent of their creativity, dynamism and innovation.

Vision

I think that quite a few projects fail because of a lack of vision. When a person doesn't know where he or she is going, it doesn't matter whether they have funds or the technical know-how, they will lose their way. Vision is important to keep focus on our purpose for existence.

I also believe we should not wait for a vision to occur to us because I do not believe that life is a process of discovery. It is a process of creation.

When Carol and I gave our first loan in Indonesia, we had a vision of a community of people who were empowered, equipped, and enlightened. We fell in love with the children of the people in the community in which we lived and desired a future for them free from indebtedness, and free to pursue their dreams. The plan to provide credit was merely a stepping-stone to achieving that vision we created in our minds, resulting from the relationships we established with the people in the community. Having created that vision, we had no choice but to act on it; otherwise our vision without execution would only be delusion.

THE CATALYST FOR CREATING A SOCIAL ENTREPRENEUR

I would like to think these characteristics are already embedded deep within most entrepreneurs, and that it only takes a small catalyst to push an entrepreneur over the edge and into social entrepreneurship when faced with the gravity of society's ills. I have had the privilege of witnessing entrepreneurs take giant steps outside their own interests and reinventing themselves to become champions of the poor and the oppressed. There are some things that can be done to encourage this type of a conversion that have proven effective in my work:

- **Exposure trips** — I try never to travel alone to places where I am to observe crisis situations. I bring with me as many friends and colleagues as are willing to go on the adventure with me. I document these visits either in film, photographs, or letters. If for some reason they are moved to do something, then it will be a win-win situation.

- **Attending workshops, seminars, and forums** where like-minded individuals share their experiences. If there is no such event, I organize it myself. I do my best to make myself available to speak at all manner of events where there is a chance of influencing an entrepreneur to involve him or herself in addressing social issues. I have met a number of entrepreneurs in these events, which has resulted in programs being established in Asia, Africa, and Latin America.

- **Mentoring/Coaching program** — I encourage entrepreneurs to take someone under their wing, preferably someone from the community that is being served. Whether it is to pass on business skills or personality development skills, the one-on-one relationship helps to breed a desire to do much more.

GETTING OUT OF THE BOAT

Social Entrepreneurship is not a magic bullet to eliminate the problems of our societies, but it is key to creating the momentum for the start of the outward journey. The values and attitudes of successful entrepreneurs impact the lives of those around them. Their characters reflect the depth of their understanding of their purpose for being.

If we want to walk on water, we have to get out of the boat. It's pretty scary, but it's so exhilarating you will be fulfilled beyond your wildest dreams!

"We make a living by what we get, we make a life by what we give."

Sir Winston Churchill

Chapter Ten

Entrepreneurship Educators Need to be Enterprising!

Innovative Entrepreneurship Education through "Bioneering and Bioneers"

By Chris Collet and Barra Ó Cinnéide

Professor Collet introduced the Bachelor of Biotechnology Innovation degree program at Queensland University of Technology (QUT) in response to industry demands for a different genre of graduate. It is a unique and innovative program that aims to train the next generation of Bioentrepreneurs. He has received two prestigious Australian National Teaching Awards in recognition of this exceptional new program, including the Best Entrepreneurial Educator Award. He has been a research scientist at the Australian National University, Indiana University, and CSIRO. He has

published widely in refereed journals in the areas of molecular and evolutionary biology, and most recently in the discipline of teaching and learning.

Professor Ó Cinnéide is Managing Director of IAIN, Irish Australian Innovation Network, and Emeritus Professor, University of Limerick, Limerick, Ireland, where he was the Dean of the Business School for many years. Prior to entering the educational sector, he was employed in research and development roles with a number of Irish governmental agencies. He joined the University of Limerick in 1975. In 1995 he was appointed to the first Chair of Entrepreneurship in Ireland. He has authored/co-authored or edited nine books and over 150 other publications.

INTRODUCTION: SETTING THE STAGE

It has been considerable time since Thomas Garavan and Barra Ó Cinnéide called for a much higher level of innovative initiatives in the Small & Medium Enterprise (SME) sector. In their 1994 article, these authors wrote:

"There is now a wide acceptance within the European Union that future prosperity hinges on the creation of vibrant indigenous businesses that are deeply rooted in the local economy. For this to occur there is a need to expand the pool of local entrepreneurial talent to develop and manage new business ventures. For the aspiration to become a reality, support structures are required to harness local initiatives and nurture new enterprises that are capable of creating sustainable employment. In the past, emphasis was (and continues to be) primarily placed on the corporate entity, with the area of small business being largely ignored."

Regrettably, the problems that were then observed within the field of Entrepreneurship Education and Training are even more relevant today. With the rise of the Eastern mega-economies such as India and China, there is now, more than ever, a pressing need for revitalized initiatives to enable the Western world to respond to this challenge. This has been recognized at the highest levels of government including the European Union (EU), the USA, Canada, and Australia. The EU Green Paper on Entrepreneurship in Europe, also known as the 2002 Lisbon Accord, recognized the **need for a radical transformation of the economy towards a more entrepreneurially-inclined society.** Subsequent reports from the European Commission have extolled the involvement of education in the process of revitalizing Europe. In particular, the notion of including entrepreneurship and management courses in non-business curricula has been encouraged.

The European Commission has suggested that this fuelling of the entrepreneurial mindset would "contribute to better commercialization of industrial research results through spin-offs and more start-ups in knowledge-based sectors." In addressing the call for the EU to become a more entrepreneurial society, the objective of this chapter is to promote and introduce a range of entrepreneurship education and training programs that will embrace the objectives of the Lisbon Accord, envisioning Europe as a forerunner in business sector initiatives, with particular emphasis on the technological and entrepreneurial competencies of SMEs.

IAIN, the Irish Australian Innovation Network, has been established to specifically promote new approaches to innovation and enterprise within both the educational sector and the business world. Its aim is to encourage fresh initiatives in entrepreneurship education and encourage international research programs in the field. With the Queensland University of Technology (QUT), Brisbane, as a lead partner, a consortium of European universities has been established under the aegis of IAIN to undertake a major initiative involving joint research on the effectiveness of adopting the QUT template in entrepreneurship education. A range of disciplines, including Information Technology, Manufacturing, Creative Media and Bio Sciences, has been chosen for this unique international comparative study.

ENTREPRENEURSHIP EDUCATION: OPTIMAL INPUTS?

The tertiary teaching system takes, as a cultural reference, students' preparation for salaried employment, and focuses on the training of graduates for employment in industry and government. In this context, educational methods are essentially adapted to preparing future workers for all levels of companies/administrations. In this regard, the **educational system is not geared for the training of entrepreneurs** and does not encourage the entrepreneurial mindset in graduates. The educational system can however, play a prime role in promoting two essential components of entrepreneurship: responsibility and risk-taking. Gibb, in his seminal 1992 article titled 'The Enterprise Culture and Education,' revealed two extreme pedagogic models: one 'didactic' and the other 'entrepreneurial.' Contrasts between a university/business school learning focus and that required in an entrepreneurial situation are presented in the accompanying table, which illustrates the differences between the two approaches.

The Didactic model is widely used in most tertiary environments as it is, undoubtedly, the easiest to conduct. Traditionally, management and entrepreneurship have been treated as two very distinct disciplines. However, over the last quarter of a century, business schools have taken on the mantle of teaching entrepreneurship. In many instances, the discipline of entrepreneurship has been from a theoretical perspective with didactic teaching and learning of case studies of success and failure.

Teaching Methods: Gibb's Characteristics of 'Didactic' and 'Entrepreneurial' Models.

Teaching Methods

Didactic Model	Enterprising Model
Learning from teacher alone	Learning from each other
Passive role as listener	Learning by doing
Learning from written texts	Learning from personal exchange and debate
Learning from 'expert' frameworks of teacher	Learning by discovering (under guidance)
Learning from feedback from one key person (the teacher)	Learning from reactions of many people
Learning in well organized, timetabled environment	Learning in flexible, informal environment
Learning without pressure of immediate goals	Learning under pressure to achieve goals
Copying from other discouraged	Learning by borrowing from others
Mistakes feared	Mistakes learned from
Learning by notes	Learning by problem solving

The emphasis in many business schools is on program components such as critical judgment, analysis of large amounts of information, making assumptions about behavior in order to develop models, feedback, and seeking correct answers. This traditionally takes place in a classroom setting with information from authoritative sources and evaluation by written assessments. Over several decades, there have been expressions of disquiet and concern in the literature about the design of such programs from several eminent commentators.

In contrast to the business school management approach, the 'real' entrepreneurs with limited resources are operating with their gut feeling, trying to understand the filters through which information passes, recognizing the hidden agendas in terms of other peoples' goals, and, because of this, making decisions on the basis of judgment of the trust and competence of those involved. Only some of their information is from authoritative sources. The rest is gleaned personally from any and everywhere, with success (evaluation) being achieved through the personal judgment of others and/or by the marketplace. Moreover, the pressure is always there to find appropriate solutions promptly, and often under severe constraints.

In a significant step in the evolution of entrepreneurship education, Gartner and Vesper crystallized the arguments of many commentators in the discipline when they wrote in their frequently quoted 1994 article that the *"the heart of entrepreneurship involves action."* Furthermore, one of the current authors went on to make the call that faculty must be thinking constantly of implementing innovation within curricula, particularly in terms of *"action learning approaches, rather than the more traditional, non-participative teaching role."* It is somewhat ironic however, that much of the entrepreneurship literature is filled with calls about what is needed rather than what has been accomplished through action.

Student business plan competitions have been paraded as one of the great successes of action learning within entrepreneurship education. Business plan competitions are exceedingly popular as students deal with ambiguity and complexity while developing the skills required to manage a business. In reality, the focus is on short-term "success" often based on a non-technological product. Research on the outcomes of the business plan competition approach has not been systematically undertaken, and there is little, if any, evidence of broad-scale entrepreneurial activity by participants.

The question remains as to what constitutes success. Even anecdotal evidence is thin on the ground. By the end of 2005,

10,000 tertiary students had participated in the Business Plan Competition of the US-based National Collegiate Innovators and Inventors Alliance (NCIIA; www.nciaa.org); only 75 of the student groups had gone on to form viable companies. From a pedagogical perspective, business plan competitions can be considered to be a convenient tool to evaluate student performance and output in a structured non-sustainable framework. In this regard, business plan competitions lend weight to the argument that business planning without enterprising behavior is not entrepreneurship.

The roles and perspectives of entrepreneurship educators impact heavily on the entrepreneurship education sector. A common problem is the use of faculty members and trainers who are neither schooled, nor interested, in entrepreneurship per se. It would appear that entrepreneurship teachers need to strive for an effective balance between academic and practitioner perspectives. It has been argued that educators committed to fostering real entrepreneurship are somewhat unique vis-à-vis their peers, tending to be less theoretical in orientation than most faculty members. It is understandable that the content of entrepreneurship education and training programs varies according to the educator's experiences and personal preferences as to definition and scope.

At the practical level a case has been made, for motivational and informational reasons, that entrepreneurship programs require more interaction with entrepreneurs, team teaching, and significantly more input from guest speakers. If entrepreneurship education and training is to be effective, it must be so not only through factual knowledge and the skills acquirable in the classroom, but also through stimulation of new ventures and increasing the capacity of the budding entrepreneur to pursue even greater success.

Entrepreneurship Education in Non-Business Schools

Within the above framework of entrepreneurship education, Gibb called in 2002 for a 'Schumpeterian-style revolution' in entrepreneurship education that embraced new paradigms within a wider University context that focused on enterprising behavior rather than entrepreneurship per se. Business schools, he claimed, were slow to react to the demands of current social, political, and economic needs. Essentially, Gibb argued that entrepreneurship education would be better conducted by tertiary faculties other than schools of business and management as the latter had failed in training entrepreneurs. Gibb's call could also be interpreted as a tacit recognition that the practice of entrepreneurship requires an innovative idea coupled with risk-taking and drive. Entrepreneurship, as traditionally taught by Schools of Business, is disconnected from both the process of innovation and the required understanding of the basis of the underlying technological advances.

Universities have begun to embrace the notion of recognizing and developing the concept of enterprising behavior within non-business disciplines and have introduced subjects on entrepreneurship into all facets of non-business curricula, including the sciences, engineering, law, and the creative industries. Initiatives are, however, normally limited to the introduction of business planning, management, and venture financing topics bound together as a one semester course, often masquerading as entrepreneurship, in the final year of a degree program. While there is an increased awareness of non-business students to the principles and practice of entrepreneurship, there is little, if any, evidence of entrepreneurial activity. After two or three years of conservative, didactic learning, it is difficult to foster the entrepreneurial mindset which requires the combined characteristics of opportunistic risk-taking and taking ideas from conception to market.

There are some interesting findings from embedding entrepreneurship in non-business school curricula as reported in the literature. For instance, it has been is noted that students often opt for the entrepreneurship modules, seen as an easy option to the harder, discipline-based subjects. Exit surveys show that these students consider the notion of a career as an entrepreneur interesting but the predominant career preference is for security/stability. On the other hand, several papers have argued that such modules have an empowering influence on graduates who are already entrepreneurially inclined and considering establishing businesses. These arguments are questionable, as they do not explore actual entrepreneurial outcomes since the surveys are often based on future intentions at course exit. Understandably, these intentions, more often than not, fail to be translated into actions for a variety of personal, financial, and economic reasons.

Postgraduate courses at Masters/Graduate Diploma level in business which include commercialization and entrepreneurship present another avenue for non-business graduates who are entrepreneurially inclined and/or interested in commercialization and technology transfer. When positive outcomes of effectiveness have been shown, these have generally been based on exit surveys of intentions and not on post hoc entrepreneurial activity. Again, to a large degree, the lack of rigorous research has hampered the credibility of such entrepreneurship programs. Therefore, a sine qua non must be long-term studies on the effectiveness of entrepreneurship education.

A Commentary on Entrepreneurship Education and Training Research

A problematic feature of the entrepreneurship field as it is currently constituted is that it has no single overarching theory.

The following observation by Gartner in 2001 summarizes the problem:

> *"Despite the creation of more theory in entrepreneurship, scholars have noticed the difficulty of integrating entrepreneurship theory-development efforts into any coherent scheme."*

The discipline that is entrepreneurship is "adolescent" (to use the term phrased by Low in 2001) and, as noted above, legitimacy remains the biggest recognized issue despite an increasing number of entrepreneurship programs in the education sector and an increasing amount of research into entrepreneurship. A disturbing conclusion realized by Ubhasaran and Westhead in 2001 is that:

> *"There is growing concern that entrepreneurship is fragmented among specialists who make little use of each other's work."*

Several initiatives have made major steps towards creating frameworks for the cataloging of entrepreneurship education efforts, the sharing of experiences and contexts, and, more noteworthy, providing financial support for research into the efficacies of entrepreneurship education and training. In the USA, the Kauffman Foundation (www.kauffman.org), Stanford Technology Ventures Program (stvp.stanford.edu) and the National Collegiate Inventors and Innovators Alliance (www.nciia.org) provide nuclei for the coalescence of like-minded individuals at national conferences. In the UK, the focal point has been the National Council of Graduate Entrepreneurship (www.ncge.org.uk). In tandem with these initiatives, the annual global research conferences of IntEnt (Internationalizing Entrepreneurship Education and Training; www.intent-conference.com) and Frontiers of Entrepreneurship Research (Babson College; www3.babson.edu/eship) make a valuable contribution to dissemination of developments and networking in the domain.

The Global Entrepreneurship Monitor (www.gemconsortium.org) also serves as a major source of information on entrepreneurship, worldwide. The main objective of the GEM reports is to address questions concerning factors that promote and inhibit entrepreneurship in a broad range of countries with different demographic, cultural, and economic backgrounds. A particularly relevant Global Entrepreneurship Monitor commentary promoted the viewpoint that the challenge is to create quality education programs by incorporating findings from developed effectiveness studies on enterprise courses. This includes testing entrepreneurship theories, models, and methodologies that go beyond traditional approaches by being applicable to both practitioners and educators. It is apparent from a series of consistent findings in GEM reports, year on year, that there has been a high level of association between educational attainment, confidence in one's skills to implement a start-up business, and participation in entrepreneurial initiatives.

Cataloging of activities and outcomes and collaboration on a global scale (albeit in a disparate mode, currently) may provide the greatest impetus for evolution of the discipline of entrepreneurship and the gain of academic legitimacy. A particular pressing need is to engage in research related to curriculum development and to undertake longitudinal comparative research across international boundaries and cultures. In particular, the efficacy of entrepreneurship education needs to be more rigorously examined using control groups to compare program participants with individuals who did not experience formal entrepreneurial educational interventions.

THE CHALLENGE TO DEVELOP EFFECTIVE ENTERPRISE/INNOVATION PROGRAMS

Internationally, there is a **heightening awareness of the need to engender a culture of innovation and entrepreneurship through education programs.** In the context of increased global competition, backed by Government policy and funding initiatives, the need for entrepreneurship education is a given. The business world has become increasingly complex as a consequence of both the increased regulatory and compliance issues and the need to look beyond traditional borders and products to maintain a competitive edge. As a result, **it is the cross-boundary perspective/integrated approach that needs to be incorporated in Entrepreneurship/Innovation Education programs.** Increasingly, business corporations are seeking employees who are able to think like entrepreneurs and who can facilitate in-house Innovation, embracing a new approach to Entrepreneurship/Intrapreneurship, in addressing global competition and technological changes.

As a consequence of the rise of high-tech industries such as IT and biotechnology, the value of science and technology-led opportunities in building local and regional economies has been increasingly recognized, with many countries committing billions of dollars to research on emerging technologies. There is universal recognition that, rather than small increments in existing technologies, it will be emergent technological innovations which will create opportunities for new industries, drive jobs growth, and fuel economic expansion. New ventures such as start-up companies or new projects in existing SMEs require champions with a sound knowledge of the technology and a strong entrepreneurial ability.

While the call for a more entrepreneurial culture is being made, new industry and government-backed funding is directed towards increased innovation and the generation of more intellectual property, while the potential synergy with expansion and efficacy of entrepreneurship education is overlooked. The implication is that either the entrepreneurial mindset will spontaneously ignite among the inventors, or that industry will immediately see the relevance of the technology and invest heavily in its R&D. Neither implication is close to reality.

Established companies can view emerging technology from a number of perspectives that reflect the firms' beliefs in the prospective versus established markets, and their subsequent commitment can be radically different depending on past experiences and future outlooks. Similar technologies competing for the same market can further hamper uptake by a jaded industry. Furthermore, technologists and scientists are good at science and do not, by and large, make good business people. Indeed, it is of no coincidence that the introduction of venture capital in the early stages of spinning out a company often sees the inventor relegated to the role of Chief Scientific Officer and a new CEO take the helm.

One of the major barriers to technology transfer and commercialization of research innovation is the lack of understanding by the proponents along the business continuum; that is, the process of product research, development, and commercialization. At one end, the scientist/technologist with a potential product usually lacks knowledge of the commercialization process. At the other end, the venture capital and industry manufacturing groups often lack an understanding of the nature, novelty and worth of the complex science. Are the current pathways and programs of entrepreneurial education and training offered in either the business school environment or in the non-business curricula effective enough to provide the cadre on innovators and entrepreneurs required to commercialize complex, innovative science and technology? We believe that the answer must be in the negative! What is required is a radical, new set of pedagogic initiatives, especially designed to provide the technologically-savvy innovators needed to drive the commercialization of emerging technologies.

An Emergent Technology Meets a Gap in Education

Branded the 'new IT,' biotechnology is seen as a major pillar of economic growth in many countries. While the Western world focuses on medical and agricultural aspects of biotechnology, even some of the world's poorest countries have rich forests of unknown biotic species which may yield the next cure for cancer or an infectious disease. While each of the major pharmaceutical and agricultural biotechnology companies have large R&D departments, with appropriately large budgets, it is widely accepted that the bulk of the innovation originates and undergoes initial development in the SME environment. Thus, **SMEs in the guise of start-up companies are the driving force of regional biotechnology industries**, and the larger, cashed-up companies expand their base through an 'innovation-by-acquisition' philosophy. In many instances, a biotechnology start-up company comprises fewer than ten multi-skilled individuals undertaking multiple roles in the business environment. Like many other nations, the fledgling Australian biotechnology industry has a special requirement for graduates with a strong technological skills base, but also an entrepreneurial flair to facilitate the development and commercialization of emerging technologies.

In seeking feedback on tertiary science curricula at the Brisbane-based Queensland University of Technology (QUT), the major theme advanced by industry representatives was the lack of appreciation of the commercial imperative by biotechnology science graduates. While generally satisfied with the high level of technical skills, industry peers noted a lack of understanding and skills appropriate for the demands of the commercial environment. Besides a lack of real world business acumen, graduates are not entrepreneurially inclined, preferring instead to pursue careers focused on science. In this regard, the average biotechnology science graduate is generally considered as not suitable or capable of operating in the commercialization environment between research and the market that is the focus of biotechnology start-ups and established SMEs.

Besides basic business skills, skills in product development, commercialization, management, and intellectual property law were also considered desirable by industry. There is, however, little scope within a three-year science-based biotechnology undergraduate degree to build-in the industry requirements for business skills. Of the dozens of undergraduate biotechnology degree programs in existence in the 39 Australian universities, only a handful had any business-related subjects, and none had modules encompassing entrepreneurship. Double degrees involving science and business do not appear to answer the criticisms of industry. While the four or five-year courses allow students to obtain skills across broad areas, feedback from students is that they are often unsure on how to marry and make connections between the two disciplines and market themselves to potential employers. Synthesis of the disparate disciplines and the understanding of relevance come after years in the industry.

Feedback from industry was that the new graduate employees were not prepared for working in the chaordic environment (from chaos comes order — www.chaordic.org) of SMEs or new project management where skills related to multi-tasking at different levels, initiative, and decision making in the context of equivocal situations are prized. Without doubt, biotechnology industry feedback showed that the tertiary education sector, in general, failed to answer the needs of the employers. Clearly, a new type of degree was required — one that would instill the entrepreneurial mindset in science-based students.

The 'Bioneering' Model of Entrepreneurship/ Innovation Education

To achieve the *desideratum* of instilling the entrepreneurial mindset in science-based students, **an innovative 'whole-of-course' approach to technology-based entrepreneurship education was implemented** by the Science Faculty at QUT in 2001. The **four-year Bachelor of Biotechnology Innovation**

(BBI) degree aimed to produce science-based graduates who can drive commercialization of research outcomes.

The degree has been deemed unique, not just in Australia, but in world terms, in that it is an immersion-style course that seeks to train biotechnology entrepreneurs who could be business-savvy scientists, or could operate in the gulf that is the commercial world between laboratory bench and global marketplace. Alternatively, it is geared at students who could start their own companies to bring their new products to the marketplace. All these potential roles serve to develop and strengthen the local biotechnology sector. The students and graduates of the BBI degree **call themselves "Bioneers"** as they regard themselves as pioneering a new era in biotechnology, and the term is now synonymous with the students and graduates of the degree.

In curriculum design it was considered essential to maintain the high level of technological knowledge and expertise given the complex and fast-evolving nature of the science, and thus the BBI degree contains the same amount of 'hard' science subjects as the core of a normal three-year science baccalaureate program. Basic business subjects introduce management, accounting, and marketing, and lead onto advanced units in innovation, entrepreneurship, market development, and commercialization. Intellectual property (IP) and contract law are also dealt with in a stand-alone subject. The ultimate semesters allow for industry-relevant project work (see below).

In contrast to double degrees, synthesis of these disparate disciplines is driven through a unique experiential learning framework, the Student BioEnterprise Scheme (SBE), **involving formation of virtual companies that serve to contextualize subject content and provide start-up company experience across the four-year course.** SBE companies are encouraged to think about potential biotechnological products (real or unreal), research ideas, and their potential in the marketplace. The SBE companies are required to operate under normal company rules where hiring, firing, and changing positions within/between companies are all part of the process, and biannual reports on progress towards a product are required. Running the SBE Scheme is handled through whole-of-course weekly meetings throughout the teaching semesters. The SBE company environment serves to develop team-based operations where students apply the theoretical knowledge learned in mainstream subjects to their own product and company development. For instance, in the business subject on product development and innovation, students develop their own product ideas and undertake market and competitor analyses and feasibility studies.

In the subsequent Venture Skills business subject, students draw up comprehensive business plans around their company. The biotechnology business subjects also allow SBE companies to explore models in business finance, development, and commercialization using industry case studies. The biotechnology science units form the basis for idea generation and exploring potential products of real biotechnological worth. The students undertake the various subject-based assignments and projects as the company team. The student and the company team immediately see the relevance of the theory in each subject and gain the experience of putting theory into practice in a team-based environment.

Since the heart of entrepreneurship has been deemed to involve action, then the most important enabling learning tool may be the activities associated with the SBE scheme. The SBE companies act as emerging organizations, and therefore the student learns, enjoys, and becomes accustomed, at no financial burden, to the consequences of turning equivocal situations into nonequivocal events.

Importantly, the SBE environment prepares the teams for undertaking industry-based, consultancy-style projects in the ultimate year of the degree. This team-based approach to industry internships ensures the projects have both the scope and depth that inevitably provide outcomes that value-add to the industry partner. For any one project, tasks can involve review of the patent status and research status of technologies, establishing IP position, SWOT (Strengths, Weaknesses, Opportunities and Threats) analysis, identification of critical success factors and risk assessment, identification of target markets, financial planning, competitor analyses, production costing, identification of potential licensing arrangements, examining venture capital arrangements, and compiling documentation for due diligence.

Examples of SBE projects include:

- SBE *Agnis* developed a test kit for Bovine Spongiform Encephalitis (leading to mad-cow disease) contamination of livestock on behalf of a local industry partner. Agnis's project report remains part of the company Genetic Solutions' potential growth portfolio.

- SBE *Innoteq* explored the feasibility of using patented growth factors in the billion-dollar cosmeceutical industry and provided tissue therapies with a new market focus representing as large a market as the wound-healing sector being targeted.

- SBE *Genero* examined the patent status on blood testing held by the Australian Red Cross Blood Bank and was able to recommend a pathway for product commercialization that involves strategic partnering. Student companies have completed substantial initial phase commercialization projects for Brisbane-based medical research institutes, other universities, and industry as far away as Hobart.

The success of the SBE companies in providing tangible outcomes for real biotechnology companies has seen industry volunteer appropriate projects. Existing industry partners continually affirm their commitment for more SBE companies to work on their projects. From the students' perspective, these consultancy-style projects cement the real-world learning experience. Professionalism is further facilitated by other 'action learning' facets of the course. A BBI-industry networking evening (called *Stellar Start Ups*) is held once a year, where SBE companies present to an audience comprising biotechnology industry representatives, IP lawyers, venture capitalists, research scientists, and recruitment agencies.

SBE companies can present their own company ideas or their industry-based project (confidentiality permitting) or, acting as a group of consultants, make pitches to gain industry support. Attendance at seminars, networking events and local and national conferences is highly encouraged under the old adage *"it is not what you know but who you know."* With the reluctance of the national body representing the industry to cater for student interests, BBI students were also instrumental in establishing a student-oriented organization, the Australian Biotechnology Students Association, which hosts industry and student networking events.

Therefore, in contrast to traditional approaches discussed above, **the concepts of innovation, enterprising behavior, and entrepreneurship are woven into the fabric of the BBI degree**. All the approaches and activities in the BBI instill a **"hands-on/real world"** applicable knowledge and skills base required for a "start-up" philosophy. Furthermore, the whole-of-course virtual companies facilitate student empowerment, reinforced accelerated learning, and support networks. The BBI students also develop and refine the many "soft" skills, such as networking, communication skills, and working in teams, required by the emerging biotechnology industry populated largely by SMEs.

This focused, team-based approach to learning is contrary to traditional science courses that concentrate attention on the individual. Importantly, and very clearly, the BBI graduate is very different from the average science graduate in levels of generic skills and confidence, approaches to problem solving, critical thinking, and their motivation. Comments from QUT academics within the Faculties of Business and Science are that these students "think very differently" and operate at a higher level than the other students, more like those on MBA programs.

Demonstrable Outcomes from the BBI Degree Include

a) **Consultancy-style (value-adding) projects for industry**, as described above, where SBE companies have devised potential products for biotechnology companies, assessed new markets for existing products, analyzed the status and science of new IP, and determined pathways for commercialization or otherwise.

b) **Potential spin-off companies from the BBI course** include

* SBE *Bionyx*, which is undertaking the initial stages of commercialization of the QUT IP enabling ureaplasma detection and blocking of sperm adhesion. As a group, they are looking to spin the company out and develop a diagnostic that detects the common bacterial infection of men and women that leads to infertility during assisted reproductive technologies.

* SBE *Xest* is interested in micro-propagation of plants for the ornamental flower industry to improve on current methods which are slow and labor-intensive. Where

many others have failed, Xest has succeeded in micro-propagation of tissue culture material and regeneration of plantlets, which can greatly facilitate the marketing of existing rare varieties throughout the world and allow, through mutagenesis, the creation of new varieties.

c) **Impact on government** has been evident as prominent promotion by the State Government of the degree in national newspapers, annual reports, and departmental broadsheets. The State Government claims the degree as an innovative program helping skill students for jobs of the future and first among a group of initiatives aimed at broadening business skills and instilling entrepreneurial skills. A news brochure emanating from the Department of Premier and Cabinet featured a photograph of the first cohort of graduates across a double-page spread with the heading *"The future face of biotech."*

d) **Outstanding graduate destinations** including careers as business development associates with biotechnology companies, commercialization officers with technology transfer arms of large research institutes, biotechnology advisors with Australian and multinational investment banking houses and venture capital firms, policy development officers in national and state government departments, and patent reviewers. The first job of one graduate was as Policy Advisor to the Minister responsible for biotechnology in the State of Queensland. Approximately one-third of graduates have elected to undertake postgraduate courses either as PhDs on commercial projects or in areas of technology management or IP law.

e) **A new career pathway** into the exciting world of commercialization and technology transfer of emerging technologies is perhaps the most notable outcome. BBI graduates have moved into technology transfer positions in commercialization offices and start-up companies where previously a PhD and a MBA was a required qualification.

The **"Bioneers"** of the BBI are the first products of an experiment in training entrepreneurs in a science-based environment, and their current success suggests that they may well add a new dimension to the growth of the local biotechnology industry in Australia. The program boasts a 90% uptake into the biotechnology industry compared to the regular science-based undergraduate degree in biotechnology, which has an uptake of 5%. This also demonstrates acceptance of the course by industry. All employers have reported nothing but positive comments concerning the high standard of graduate capability, with some looking for more graduates to join the organization. All graduates consider they have their "dream" job.

Innovation Development — A New Approach

The **Bioneering Model** serves as a successful model of entrepreneurship education in non-business environments. In intent and outcomes, the Bioneering model answers the calls of the EU Lisbon Accord of 2002 in developing a more-entrepreneurially inclined society. While biotechnology is the chosen sector of QUT's approach, the course intent, framework and activities can be applied to any discipline. With a wider applicability in mind, an international collaboration began between Irish universities and Brisbane QUT to promote implementation of the Bioneering model in a broad range of science and technology disciplines and in different contexts.

Why Ireland? The GEM reports note that, as a nation, the Republic of Ireland is one of the most entrepreneurial countries in the EU; second behind Poland. Statistics support this label: the proportion of owner/managers within the adult population of Ireland (10.1%) is higher than in the UK (8.2%), and is very

close to that in the US (10.3%). Evidence for total entrepreneurial activity is also high at 7.75% for Ireland in 2003. This
means that in a population of just four million, approximately
a quarter of a million individuals in the age range 18–64 were
actively involved in either planning a new business or had
recently set up a new enterprise in the previous 3–4 years. The
economic history of Ireland since joining the EU underscores
this view and explains why the Irish economy is also known as
the *Celtic Tiger*.

Strong university-business linkages, a history of philanthropy, innovation, and entrepreneurship work in favor of the
development of new initiatives in entrepreneurship education. This is a stark contrast to the Australian environment,
where national business is more conservative and less interested in investing in research and development. This is an
interesting situation given that Australian scientists are
renowned for innovative approaches and discoveries, but
explains why the majority of Australian inventions are sold
off-shore at early stages of the developmental and commercialization process.

IAIN, the Irish Australian Innovation Network, has been
formed as an international consortium to provide a new framework within which initiatives in the enterprise domain can
be encouraged and implemented. The broad aims of IAIN are
two-fold:

1. To introduce fresh initiatives in entrepreneurship education
    through encouraging 'best practice' approaches in promoting
    innovation, enterprise formation, and business development;

2. To promote and undertake research studies on the efficacy of
    educational and training programs geared to innovation and
    enterprise.

In line with the EU objectives in the Lisbon Accord, the IAIN network plans to provide an international focus for collaboration between European campuses concerned with innovation and entrepreneurship education. Partners from Europe include Poland, Germany, the United Kingdom, and other campuses within Ireland. The IAIN Foundation has prepared a detailed submission for funding to the European Commission through the Framework Program. The submission seeks funds to implement entrepreneurship education initiatives on the campuses of the consortium partners and to fund research, on rigorous pedagogic bases, of the effectiveness of entrepreneurship curricula in bridging the lacuna between, on the one hand, science and technology and, on the other, management and business disciplines. While based on best practices, it is a given that any education initiatives implemented in the different regions would have to be context sensitive and specific for the industry based in that region.

It is believed that the European Commission will be very supportive of the initiative for a number of reasons. The outcomes of the **Bioneering** model have had a major impact on the SME environment of the biotechnology industry in the Brisbane region, and these outcomes can be replicated in different technological sectors in the EU. The IAIN submission to Brussels has been formulated so that partners across the EU will, between them, embrace a range of Science and Technology disciplines. This will enable the consortium to compare pedagogic outcomes across a spectrum of interest areas, allowing multiple centers to each choose similar discipline areas such as biotechnology, agribusiness, engineering, and information technology as their choice for coupling with topics such as innovation, enterprise formation, and business development.

CONCLUSION

Entrepreneurship and innovation must go hand-in-hand for the technological advances to traverse from laboratory bench to the marketplace. Innovation creates IP, but entrepreneurship creates business from IP. Existing entrepreneurship education programs, those based in business schools or those that occur as a single module in the non-business curriculum, do not appear to have a significant far-reaching impact on local SME environment.

The successful outcomes of the QUT "Bioneering" model show that entrepreneurship education programs in a non-business school environment can create a technologically-savvy graduate who comfortably operates in the SME environment focused on developing the potential of innovation. Effective entrepreneurship education programs can impact significantly on the local industry environment and consequently, there is a critical need for rigorous, enhanced research geared to measuring the effectiveness of academic programs in the field. Even failures are an important part of curriculum development. Indeed, failures in themselves are an essential part of a learning process for the entrepreneurship educators! As a wise sage has coined it:

> *"A mistake is only a mistake if you repeat it twice.*
> *The first time is a learning experience."*

Featuring the success story of Australia's **"Bioneering"** program highlights one example of how initiatives in entrepreneurship education are possible with foresight and pedagogic innovation. As a result, the recently formed Irish Australian Innovation Network has been established as a foundation to provide an opportunity for European 'best practice' initiatives with emphases on technology transfer and commercialization.

There is immense scope for new ideas, initiatives, and approaches to teach and learn the behavioral patterns required by the nascent entrepreneur. For this to happen, as indicated in the title, entrepreneurship educators must be enterprising!

"Trust your hunches. They are usually based on facts filed away just below the conscious level."

Dr. Joyce Brothers

Chapter Eleven

The Celtic Tiger Economy of Ireland: A New Perspective

By Ted O Keeffe

Ted O Keeffe is a seconded national expert with the Directorate General for Research and Technological Development (DG Research) at the European commission based in Brussels. Primary duties and responsibilities include the development of future research policies for Small to Medium Enterprises (SMEs) on a European-wide basis. Having completed his primary degree in Chemical Engineering, he went on to study Mechanical and Nuclear Engineering in France and Switzerland. He completed two Masters and a Ph.D. on how individuals and organisations learn.

More recently, he has written a book entitled "Towards Zero Management Learning Organisations: Developing tomorrow's successful leaders today." At the core of this text is a detailed perspective on the extent to which firms can best achieve sustainable competitive advantage. He has held down senior post of responsibility in industries as diverse as textiles to fast breeder nuclear reactors, and even though the individual challenges encountered throughout his extensive career may have varied from easy to resolve to highly complex, each experience proved to be an invaluable learning curve in itself.

The success he has enjoyed in a wide-ranging career spanning four continents that often required more cultural understanding than specific technology interventions on a range of issues, he puts down to his upbringing and sense of fair play instilled in him from his youth. He still remembers the wise council of his father: "a chatterbox learns far lesser than the listener!" He believes it is his willingness to listen and observe rather than espousing a particular point of view that has often being the difference between success and failure, particularly so in multicultural work environments. He may not say so in so many words but it is obvious to those that know him that he is of the firm opinion that the primary reason God gave man two eyes, two ears, and one mouth is because he would like individuals irrespective of their status to listen and observe twice as much as they might like to expound on a particular topic or concern.

INTRODUCTION

Over the previous two decades, from 1987 to the present, the **Republic of Ireland** had, and continues to have, **one of the fastest growing economies in the world**. Many commentators have even expressed the opinion that the performance of the Irish economy in recent years is more akin to an economic "Miracle" than anything they have witnessed to date.

Some have coined the term, **"Celtic Tiger"** to describe the phenomenal economic growth of the country in so short a time — **from one of the poorest countries in the European Union to being at or near the top in most economic criteria.**

These same commentators compliment Ireland's noteworthy economic success in recent years, yet they are somewhat at a loss as to the genesis of this economic miracle. However, if these pundits took but a few moments to really examine the cultural inheritance of the Celtic Irish, they would have discovered a **tradition of learning, innovation and creativity** spanning a thousand years, which had been cruelly stifled by the English invader for almost three centuries.

I would submit that it is this heritage that has played a major role in catapulting Ireland to such incredible economic success. I would also suggest that we can learn from this and look carefully at the cultural and inborn, though often repressed, spirit of people in many other less developed lands of the world. If we look carefully, we may well find that they too, deep down inside, have the entrepreneurial spirit and intellectual capacity to escape the bonds of poverty to economic freedom and success through entrepreneurship in conjunction with sufficient seed capital.

In other words, **there are potential economic tigers hiding in many places in the world**! Entrepreneurship, and the right cultural ambiance, regulatory environment, and political support, can cause change.

This writer has a different perspective on the factors surrounding the Economic Miracle that is "Ireland Inc." today. Unlike the leading economic commentators, many of whom are unfamiliar with Irish history, or have adopted an Anglo Saxon perspective of it and consequently can have no real understanding of the underlying hypothesis of the "Economic Miracle" that is Ireland today, I firmly believe **it was always but a factor of time and the availability of sufficient resources to kick-start it.**

The modern day transformation of the Irish economy **is not a miracle**, as many would lead you to believe, **but the result of a young, independent nation getting its act together** after enduring three hundred years of direct British rule that brought a once proud nation to the edge of an economic, cultural, and spiritual abyss.

Ireland's elevated status on the global stage today is a prime example of a proud nation retaking its rightful place among the nations **in a time frame as little as two generations** from the moment it achieved full independence in 1949. **From a situation of abject poverty to being the wealthiest European country per head of population next to Luxembourg** in half a century is no mean feat, especially for a small, open economy such as Ireland.

The economic achievements of the Irish economy over the previous two decades are frequently held up to the developing world as the way forward. However, the economic miracle that is Ireland today **has its roots not in the late 1980s, but in the late 1950s and early 1960s**, when the then Taoiseach (Prime Minister) Séan Lemass made a **courageous move to open up the economy to free trade, and in doing so, gave Ireland the opportunity to discard its old economic and political shackles that had severely retarded the progress** of a proud nation for more than a quarter of a millennium.

In a little over two decades, the building blocks of effective economic performance had once more been put in place in the form of a young, **highly-educated workforce**, thanks in no small part to the advent of free, extremely high-quality secondary education in 1967, a corporate tax policy that was far reaching to say the least, and sufficient seed capital from Brussels (the EU) to kick-start a stalled economy.

A look at the history leading up to the economic development of Ireland today gives us great insight into the steps that made it happen — and that **can also be followed by others in the world in their own situation**.

Europe's Primary Seat of Learning

What many commentators fail to realise is that Ireland has a longstanding tradition of learning going back to when it was Europe's primary seat of learning that lasted for more than half a millennium from the 5th through to the 10th centuries. While the collapse of Roman authority left Europe in a mess, it had little or no impact in Ireland.

Throughout this period, Ireland remained a relatively cohesive society centered upon monastic settlements and seats of learning rather than cities per se. While the whole of Europe had been plunged into the Dark Ages, the light of civilization shone brightly throughout the Island of Ireland.

This Dark period in European history became the "Golden Age of Learning" in Ireland, in which the future rulers of Europe were sent to Irish centers of learning such as the University of Clonmacnoise, which dates back almost 1,500 years and is situated at the crossroads of Ireland in the County of Offaly. Here Irish and foreigner alike learned Latin, Greek, and Brehon Law.

Through many centuries the Irish thrived and prospered — until the British conquered and repressed the freedom of the Irish spirit. From that moment onwards, the existence or establishment of monasteries in Ireland was all but forbidden for another 300 years. The British tried to win the hearts and minds of the Irish people by destroying their seats of learning, forbidding them to practice their religion or to speak their native language.

It seems that the lessons of history continue to fall on deaf ears since the instigators of every conflict in the intervening years always fail to recognise the simple truth: that **you can only win the hearts and minds of people through education and learning, not by bullet or bomb**.

The English made a concerted effort to colonize Ireland in the 17th century, and they achieved this by giving the confiscated lands of the native Irish to English settlers who were planted in large numbers across the landscape. This led to a split in Irish society between the local landless or nearly landless Irish-speaking population and the newly arrived, English-speaking landed gentry.

By the middle of the 18th century, English Ireland was thriving to such an extent that Dublin had become the second city of the British Empire. At the same time, English legislation developed into an out-and-out attack on the indigenous Irish culture, in which the Harp was outlawed and penal laws both written and unwritten made life for Catholics and speakers of Irish extremely difficult.

Brehon Law

Prior to English rule, Ireland had its own indigenous system of law dating from Celtic times, which survived until the 17th century, when it was finally supplanted by the English common law. This native system of law, known as the Brehon law, developed from customs that had been passed on orally from one generation to the next.

In the 7th century AD, the laws were written down for the first time. Brehon law was administered by Brehons, who were the successors to Celtic Druids, and while similar to judges, their role was closer to that of an arbitrator. Their task was to preserve and interpret the law rather than to expand it.

Brehon Law derives its name from the Gaelic word "Breitheamh," meaning judge, and though we do not have a precise birth date, there are sufficient clues to indicate that it developed during the Bronze Age. These ancient Irish laws were viewed as one of the most comprehensive legal systems of its time in Europe.

Brehon law covered both civil and criminal aspects of Irish society. Although the English despised Brehon Law, it was well received by the Irish, as very few cases of defiance towards the judgments that were handed down have been recorded. The strength of Brehon Law lay in the **equal and indifferent justice it handed down to one and all, irrespective of one's status**.

The reason for its durability was primarily due to the people themselves and the **respect the Irish people had for law and order** and their abhorrence for unjust decisions. As late as the beginning of the 17th century, Sir John Davies, the Attorney General for King James I, was recorded to say "there is no nation of people under the sunne that doth love equal and indifferent justice better than the Irish." The penal system of justice that the English imposed shortly thereafter brought with it the greatest misfortune to ever blight the land.

The Famine

The Great Famine in Ireland began as a natural catastrophe of extraordinary magnitude, but its effects were magnified by the inactions of the Whig government in London then headed by Lord John Russell in the crucial years from 1846 to 1852.

Altogether, about a million people in Ireland are reliably estimated to have died of starvation and epidemic disease between 1846 and 1851, and some two million people emigrated in a period of a little more than a decade (1845–55). Comparisons with present day famines establish beyond any doubt that the

Irish famine of the late 1840s, which killed nearly one-eighth of the entire population, was proportionally more destructive in terms of human life than the vast majority of famines in modern times.

In almost all present-day famines, only a proportion of the population of a given country or region is exposed to the dangers of death from starvation or infectious diseases, and then typically for only one or two seasons. However, in the Irish famine of the late 1840s, potato blight robbed more than one-third of the population of their usual means of subsistence for four or five years in a row.

The potato famine of 1845 to 1849 was a pivotal event in Irish history from which the stature of Ireland never recovered — until the last two decades of the twentieth century. Within a few years of the famine, the population of Ireland had dropped from eight million to less than five million, with three million either starved to death or forced to emigrate to the US and lands further afield. This is why today, some 50 million Americans claim some degree of Irish heritage.

After the terrible famine years, Irish became the language of the peasant, while English was embraced by the upwardly mobile, and as a consequence of the huge emigration to the US, Ireland faced west, and American influence has been increasing ever since but never more so than from the time Ireland re-opened its economy to foreign direct investment (FDI) in the early 1960s.

Home Rule in 1922

By the beginning of the third decade of the twentieth century, the larger part of Ireland had won autonomy from the British Empire. The Southern 26 counties became the Republic of Ireland.

Despite the fact that the most industrialised part of Ireland, namely the six north-eastern counties, had been cut off from the rest of the island under partition, the newly formed Irish government of the day did not recognise the significance of this fact until many decades later.

As the twentieth century unfolded, a realisation began slowing dawning on the powers that be in Ireland that if ever the Island of Ireland was to break free from its economic dependence on Britain, it would have to develop a fresh approach to the staid, prevailing agricultural policy of the day. **It would have to develop a modern industrial policy that would absorb the huge numbers of agricultural workers being forced off the land through mechanisation and automation.**

From the very beginning right up until the late nineteen seventies, more than half the workforce was employed directly in agriculture. With each passing decade of the twentieth century, the decline in agricultural-related employment continued unabated, and still the governments of the day could not be persuaded away from their rigid fiscal policy of balancing the books at all costs.

Throughout this period little or no consideration was given to meeting the long-term needs of the populous in terms of job creation, as Ireland Inc. had a ready-made market for its unskilled and highly educated labour force across the water in Britain. It was not until the late nineteen fifties and sixties that a whole new approach to education and wealth creation was set in motion that would transform the country in a little more than a quarter of a century.

Protectionism and Trade Barriers

The new government formed by Fianna Fail in the 1930s until the late 1950s was contradictory to say the very least, with government policies often being subject to political rather than economic concerns. The De Valera government of 1932 brought in protectionism and an anti-foreign ownership investment strategy that was not reversed until 1958. In the early years protectionism actually boosted employment. However, by the 1950's, despite the fact that employment in manufacturing had doubled, the cost of these policies would be revealed with the advent of free trade.

By the late 1950s Irish industry, long protected from external competitive forces, had become inefficient, expensive, and produced poor quality goods. The biggest indictment of the protectionist policy was the fact that nobody had the vision to encourage companies to develop export markets for their goods and services. Furthermore, nobody in government or business circles had their eyes on the bigger picture.

Throughout this period, Ireland continued to export cattle on the hoof in their millions to its nearest neighbour without a moments thought for the huge loses in added value that such an export strategy was having on the total economy. It took two more decades before the realisation that the development of large scale meat processing plants at home would enhance added value, create thousands of much needed jobs, and help swing the balance of payments in favour of Ireland.

Free Trade

However, as Ireland began opening up its economy to free trade in the 1960s, a new reality emerged that much of the indigenous industry could not compete with the higher quality and cheaper nature of the numerous imports that quickly flooded the market. Nevertheless, all was not lost, as the Irish government of the day did not stand idly by and let the unfolding catastrophic situation develop beyond the abyss.

By the early nineteen seventies Ireland was becoming increasingly successful at attracting foreign direct investment, particularly from the US and Germany. Today multinational companies from these two countries continue to constitute more than 50% of the total number of MNCs with manufacturing facilities in Ireland.

Throughout the seventies the Irish Development Authority (IDA), tasked with replacing the uncompetitive native industry, was happy to attract manufacturing companies per se. By the early 1980s, with a **burgeoning highly educated workforce, thanks to the introduction of free education for all in the late sixties**, a new phase of industrial policy was set in motion, which would become the catalyst for the "Celtic Tiger" economy that continued to roar for a further 15 years right up until 2007.

By the nineteen eighties the Irish government was very clear in its understanding that despite the fact that **favourable tax breaks would continue to attract industry to Ireland, it might not suffice to keep them here**, particularly those medium to low technology firms, now that wage rates throughout Ireland were rapidly catching up with those of mainland Europe.

INDUSTRY/ACADEMIA PARTNERSHIPS

To overcome the outflow of manufacturing companies operating in Ireland to low wage countries on the Asian Pacific Rim and the newly emerging countries of Eastern Europe, the Irish government switched their attention to **attracting high-tech companies** through more generous grants, **especially to those organizations willing to relocate R&D facilities to Ireland**.

By the end of the twentieth century it was becoming very obvious to all concerned that Ireland Inc. could no longer be considered a low-wage economy; consequently, new ways of providing sustainable development had to be put in place. In this regard, a series of **specialist industrial centres of excellence were specifically targeted by region so as not to have all the economic eggs in one basket**.

In each location the **local universities and third level colleges were consulted** regarding the ongoing development of industrial academic pathways and partnerships to meet the changing and often highly specialised needs of the surrounding industrialists.

At the same time a new realisation was dawning upon the planning authority that if something was not initiated immediately regarding the third world infrastructure, the country would choke to death from a logistics point of view. Consequently, a progressive programme of infrastructural development was initiated, the mismanagement of which would ultimately prove to be the chilles heel of the best performing European economy.

The Language of R&D

The language of high-tech research and development initiatives, be they industrial or public research activities, continues to be English for the most part, and in this regard Ireland Inc. has a huge advantage. Not only is English spoken fluently in Ireland, the Irish have a clear linguistic advantage in that all Irish people enjoy bi-lingual education up until the age of sixteen, with tri-lingual education being the norm until students have completed their secondary education.

This **linguistic exposure from early childhood gives the average educated Irish person a far more sensitive ear for linguistics and greater exposure to the art of listening**, a skill that is more often underutilized or missing entirely among many of the English speaking people around the globe.

The Irish secondary education system demands that students study at least six different disciplines in reasonable depth, which allows the individual to better target the third level specialism he or she would like to pursue as a long-term career.

The numbers of people entering third level education in Ireland is very close to 50% of all school leavers, and the diversity of third level programmes being made available is reviewed regularly to ensure sufficient numbers of places are being made available to meet the changing needs of industry and society at large.

A Young, Highly Educated Population

Fifty-percent of the population of Ireland are under the age of 25, and 47% of all second level students transfer onto third level education. The Irish government has a wide-ranging action plan to take full advantage of ICT in the promotion of social and economic objectives.

The overall education policy is aimed at developing strategies that will produce an educated, informed, and skilled citizenry by **improving the enterprise of education**. This policy requires investment, not only by government at all levels of the education system, but **engagement by all stakeholders including the private sector**.

Innovation and creativity through education and skills development rely heavily upon human capital, particularly the talent and creative skills of individuals and teams. Creativity is a vital ingredient in the innovation process and an invaluable source of competitive advantage for service and manufacturing companies alike.

Creativity therefore needs to be cultivated from an early age, from primary and secondary education learning curricula through to vocational education, university programmes, and lifelong learning initiatives. This understanding requires a **partnership approach between the relevant agencies and stakeholders** in the delivery of sufficient numbers of skilled individuals across all sectors of society.

The next question that must be addressed concerns the overall balance between the needs of society and industry at large; in this regard **Ireland Inc. is not capitalising on the strengths and desires of future generations**. Fifty years ago, if anyone achieved two honours in their final secondary school examination known as the Leaving Certificate, they could pursue any course of study on offer from the National University of Ireland and or Trinity College Dublin.

This approach meant that students themselves could decide which course of study they wished to pursue at third level, resulting in a far higher percentage of individuals with qualifications they were happy to engage with throughout their working career.

More recently, due to the increasing numbers wishing to further their studies, a points system was introduced, which meant that only those with 570 points out of a maximum 600 could choose medicine as a career, and so on with all highly sought after profession qualifications.

The points race has become so intense in recent years that those students wishing to secure top marks will often undertake as many courses of study as possible in what are deemed easier subjects to score high marks rather than taking on the more relevant but more difficult subjects in line with their future needs.

This leads to far higher levels of drop out, in some cases as high as fifty-percent. In other cases, such as medicine, we have far too many "qualified" doctors that cannot relate to their patients in any meaningful way, while many of the real humanitarians fail to secure their place in medical and related humanitarian courses based on a points system that doesn't take into account that individual's ability to relate to the individual needs of the patient.

To eliminate the increasing level of mismatch in third level institutions, the points system must be turned on its head, and Ireland must re-establish the very effective system of yesterday in which any student with an average grade at 60% or higher can pursue any course of study at third level. This would lead to an initial imbalance in the first decade or so, but thereafter the whole system would rebalance itself as all students with above average intelligence could once more choose their course of study rather than having the system decide who can study what.

Flexibility in the Workplace

Technology has always played a key role for regional and national economic development, and nowhere is this more evident than in Ireland. It helps in shaping industrial performance, determines productivity growth, creates markets for skilled labour and helps industries to compete on the international stage.

While emerging technologies are driving globalisation, they in turn increase competition by compelling organisations to incorporate and adopt new developments into their manufacturing and services applications. Those organisations willing to invest in creating thinking, new technologies, and in harnessing the capabilities generated by those technologies are establishing the standards that the rest of the world will have to adopt, or fall prey to entropy.

There is an increasing need to enhance our understanding of the range of incentives or barriers to productivity that can be utilised in developed, developing, and emerging regions. Technology transfer is not simply concerned with effective technology utilization, flexibility, innovation, diffusion, and ethical dilemmas surrounding global issues, it also must address the interface between man and machine.

Issues of critical importance in relation to technology transfer are increasingly encountered by boundary spanners and by those who manage the interface between man and machine. This is where the vast majority of all difficulties and concerns arise.

A well-oiled machine will never go on strike: on the other hand, a "well-oiled human" has real potential for disruption and chaos given the correct set of circumstances. **Flexibility in the workplace provides a platform for new ideas and developments to be explored without loss of face by individuals or groups**.

Increasing competition and sluggish productivity growth are greatly influencing the way goods and services are being delivered. **What could be described as science fiction just a few short years ago is increasingly becoming commonplace in a wide range of industries**.

At the same time, very few fully understand the learning imperative that accompanies technological displacement, and while automation will continue to impact the vast majority of jobs in the immediate future, it will not bring as much unemployment in its wake as was predicted just a few short years ago.

The statement that held true twenty-five years ago will continue to hold true for the next twenty-five year period, i.e. that three-quarters of all jobs in which people will be engaged by the year 2030 have not yet been invented; therefore institutions of government, industry and education will have to achieve greater integration if tomorrow's graduates and future employees are to be in a position to avail of the opportunities this constantly evolving environment will bring in its wake.

Access to Market

Ireland as with any other European country, has open access to the biggest market in the world for its products and servicers, and the current rules governing the **four freedoms of movement for goods, services, people, and capital** are not sufficient to achieve the objectives of the Single Market. These objectives can only be fully achieved if national and European policies create a favourable climate for businesses to grow and prosper across national borders.

Firms need to be confident that they can compete on a level playing field and that appropriate legal structures exist to allow all businesses, whatever their size, to operate effectively across the EU. In this regard, the European Commission is committed to improving the regulatory environment within which business operates, and in so doing, help companies to compete successfully in global markets.

Harmonisation of the rules relating to company law and corporate governance is a key element of this policy in **reducing red tape**, and in so doing, assists companies to operate throughout the EU on the basis of a single set of rules and a unified management and reporting system. The single market cannot function effectively without transparency and confidence in corporate governance, enhancing the protection of investors, employees, and the public against corporate cheating, fraud, and mismanagement.

Likewise, EU law on public procurement aims to increase competition and transparency in a key sector of the European economy by modernising and opening up markets across borders, which will mean more opportunities for business, better value, and higher quality services for all.

Other areas in which Europe is committed to improving the regulatory environment for business and removing obstacles to cross-border trade include contract law and taxation.

Low Tax Regime

Ireland has the lowest corporate taxes in the developed world, and this has been one of the five pillars that triggered the Celtic Tiger. As late as the late nineteen eighties, as few as 1.2 million people were engaged in full-time work in the economy, a figure that had changed very little since the foundation of the State (Irish Independence from Great Britain) in 1922. Currently, there are 1.8 million in employment, a fifty-percent increase in less than two decades.

Where did the huge numbers of new labour force members come from? Many were returning emigrants who were forced out through the lack of suitable work in the seventies and eighties.

The Ireland they left behind was one of high tax and high unemployment brought on by low growth and less opportunity. In a period of time spanning less than two decades, the economic landscape of Ireland is unrecognisable, not the least because of its low-tax regime that has released energy and enterprise and **a new self-confidence that has lifted the nation in terms of job creation and higher living standards**.

Not A Miracle, But Certainly An Astounding Growth and Change

The shift in the fortunes of the Irish economy since its low point of the mid-nineteen eighties represents **one of the most remarkable transformations by any developing economy ever**. In the mid-nineteen eighties the living standards in much of Ireland were less than two-thirds of the European Union average, and less than a quarter of a century later, the Irish economy progressed from being one of the poorest to becoming one of the richest member states, second only to Luxembourg in head of population terms.

THE PILLARS OF THE IRISH SUCCESS

The reasons for that economic success are six-fold:

- Low corporate tax regime

- A young, educated, English-speaking workforce

- A previously untapped large female labour force

- A shift away from the traditional learning model in Irish universities

- Government recognition of the importance of having a strong indigenous Small to Medium Enterprise (SME) sector working in harmony with Foreign Direct Investment by the large multinationals

- The huge injection of cash from Europe to prime the economic pump sufficiently.

All of the above provided the stimulus for rapid expansion in employment with the clear understanding that the output in the form of products and services would have unhindered access to the single market, particularly for foreign multinational companies who were keen to take full advantage of Ireland's low corporate tax, low-labour cost base, and open access to the expanding European market.

At the same time, Irish universities and technical colleges are increasingly producing specialised business, science, computing, and engineering graduates to match the changing needs of industry.

THE FUTURE?

It is this same flexibility that will ensure that Ireland Inc. will maintain its competitive advantage in the longer term now that the death knell of the Celtic Tiger is nigh. The lessons learned over the previous twenty years have not been lost, but mislaid for the time being as the Economy struggles to drive forward in the wake of the sub-prime disaster.

Nevertheless, the first steps in the recovery process are currently being put in place in that there is a clear understanding that **what was successful in the past will not suffice in the future**.

Increasingly there is an emerging understanding that **the critical organizational resource** is no longer capital per se, people, or technology. But rather, it **is the untapped innovation streams in the form of knowledge repositories that walk out the front door each evening and who may not return for a variety of reasons**.

Long-term economic success or survival for any organization or country cannot be guaranteed, but those companies wishing to be around for the foreseeable future **must move beyond incremental learning and best practices to developing a strategy for transformational change within self-directed learning environments**.

Coping with the loss of status or power is perhaps the greatest challenge individuals and organizations face today, yet it is something that cannot be avoided in operating environments that continue to evolve at break-neck speed.

The only certainty, apart from death and the need to pay taxes, is that whatever worked in the past will not suffice to ensure continued prosperity into the future. Your competition will not waste time and resources debating where responsibility lies, but will actively be developing more cost effective products and or services.

CONCLUSION: WILL IRELAND INC. SURVIVE THE WORLD ECONOMIC SCANDALS, ETC.?

The answer to this question is a definite yes for many reasons, but primarily because entrepreneurial flair is alive and well in the modern Ireland of the 21st century. The current down turn will cause a lot of pain in the short-term as thousands of individuals lose high paying jobs, which will cause the economy to shrink further, but this correction in any case was long overdue, and in fact, if the truth were to be told, was underway a full year prior to the sub-prime disaster that sideswiped the world at large in 2008.

The very factors that brought Ireland Inc. to the foreground from an economic perspective are still in place and will resurface over the coming years as Ireland Inc. comes to terms with the new reality and repositions the key building blocks for the next phase of the county's development. Ireland will become more competitive once the excessive costs that had been allowed to build up over the last ten years have been peeled back to realistic levels.

If it had not been the sub-prime disaster it would have been something else that would have triggered **the new reality that must be addressed worldwide**, which will not be confined to the banking sector alone. Builders, speculators, professionals including solicitors, and doctors alike will have to take corrective action as increasing numbers of their customers will no longer be willing or able to pay their exorbitant fees in these recessionary times.

However, post the world's economic crisis, a new perspective of the world will hopefully emerge, one that will bring better understanding of what constitutes long-term sustainably for all rather than the privileged few.

The notion of long, uninterrupted production runs of highly-standardised products are well and truly over, and while traditional mass production processes made economic sense in the past as such systems lowered unit costs, they have remained too inflexible and unresponsive to rapidly-changing consumer taste in which batch sizes of one are increasingly becoming the norm.

Thanks to innovation and the flexibility of modern automated equipment, **economies of scale are finally giving way to economies of scope** and are best achieved by flexible manufacturing systems that are capable of producing small batches, as little as single units, of a range of products on the same equipment.

However, flexible manufacturing systems are only as effective as the people that operate and maintain them, and, consequently, Ireland Inc. is well placed to take full advantage in the certain knowledge that advanced technology in capable hands tends to be trouble-free.

"No one can really pull you up very high. You lose your grip on the rope. But on your own two feet you can climb mountains."

Louis Brandeis

Chapter Twelve

The Miracle of Changing The Mindset for Young, Would-Be Entrepreneurs!

By Jose M. Romaguera

Professor Jose M. Romaguera has been a professor at the University of Puerto Rico for 25 years and specializes in teaching creativity and entrepreneurial innovation and new venture development. His education includes a BSBA from the University of Puerto Rico at Mayaguez, an MBA from the University of Connecticut, and a PhD from Durham University in England. He is former Dean of the College of Business Administration of the University of Puerto Rico at Mayaguez where he continues as Professor and is the Director of the University's Business Center. His leadership in the area of entrepreneurship and small business includes his work

as Executive Director of the Puerto Rico Small Business Development Center, Chair of the Board of Governors of the National Association of Small Business International Trade Educators (NASBITE), and President of the International Council for Small Business (ICSB). His work on behalf of developing entrepreneurship, particularly amongst youth, has been presented in six continents. His recent book on opportunity recognition ("Chispa Empresarial"®), published in 2006, is currently in its third printing. Professor Romaguera's business experience includes work at the global headquarters of a Fortune 500 company, Executive Vice President and General Manager of Puerto Rico's sole brewing company, and multiple consulting engagements for small, medium, and large companies.

OBJECTIVE OF THE CHAPTER

The objective of this chapter is to share some initiatives that have worked for us in Puerto Rico to change the mindset of fledgling entrepreneurs, mostly of youth, to start their entrepreneurial journey in a decided and enthusiastic manner. First, some background notes are presented about why we now focus on "changing the mindset." This is followed by an overview of the wide range of initiatives that can be undertaken to foster entrepreneurship amongst youth — ones that have worked for us. These include initiatives to **change the mindset of a complete country** into an enterprising culture and special initiatives to **change the mindset of youth** both inside and outside the classroom.

An incredibly challenging task, you might say, but one we have taken on, learned from the experience, and enjoy sharing our experiences, which some would say have been a great successes.

Why the Focus on "Changing The Mindset"?

The great challenge of creating entrepreneurs, as the title of this book suggests, is the art, science and process of making miracles happen. It is most rewarding to work in initiatives that make miracles happen, and, in our experience, this results when someone discovers he/she can indeed become an entrepreneur and decides to pursue an enterprising endeavor.

One of the miracles behind "creating" entrepreneurs is facilitating very concrete opportunities to help someone in the process of changing the mindset. For example, going from a mindset of: "I want to have a good/secure job working for someone else" to one of: "I want to have my own business." Another example is moving from a: "I cannot become an entrepreneur, it is far too difficult and I do not have what it takes" to one of: "I can be an entrepreneur, **now, starting with what I have at hand**." Initiatives to change the mindset are crucial for creating entrepreneurs, and thus, for making miracles happen.

Let's Begin by not Getting Frustrated

First of all, I must confess that it took quite a bit of frustrated efforts and some time to come to the realization of the importance of changing the mindset as an initial and crucial step in assisting would-be entrepreneurs. For many years, we were very busy developing programs to assist current and would-be entrepreneurs. These programs went for training and counseling, curriculum development at the undergraduate and graduate level, and "road shows," where several players from the banking community, government, and business assistance entities met face to face with entrepreneurs and would-be entrepreneurs to bring multiple levels of help to assist in the development of their businesses.

With so many needs to attend to, and so little time and resources, it was a never-ending quest just to try to keep our heads above water. **In many ways we were spinning our wheels** and not getting as far as we wished in producing results. Needless to say, it was very taxing on those of us that attempted to undertake initiatives to foster entrepreneurship.

Perhaps the reader has experienced this type of anxiety: trying hard to make things happen and never being sure if the return on investment of time, effort and resources is really there. Thus, we hope that sharing some of the background and examples that we have undertaken could be of assistance to the reader. There is no doubt in our mind that one can always benefit from the lessons learned in other settings, and in the process reduce waste of energy and resources, minimize frustration, and focus on results.

What is the Mindset of Your "Client"?

It is very important to understand your client's current mindset. What, if anything, is in his mindset about becoming an entrepreneur?

We checked the obvious, such as demographics, as we proceeded to design entrepreneurship programs. One experience I will briefly share, however, provided the opportunity to **learn directly from a "client"** a great lesson about **the need to focus on the mindset**.

In the midst of a semester at my teaching job at the University, which was particularly difficult as our Island had suffered from the worst hurricanes to hit our shores in a century, I was on a flight with some students for a youth entrepreneurship conference in Chicago. One of the students surprised me by asking: "what do you want to achieve with all of the entrepreneurship programs you work with?" My quick response was an even bigger surprise. I simply said: **"I want to change the world."**

I was puzzled and surprised by my response and, by the look of the student's face, it was obvious he was even more surprised and confused by it. The Chicago activity was very rewarding, and on the return flight the student said: "Professor, remember your response on the previous flight about you wanting to change the world? I honestly thought you were nuts. Now however, I understand what you meant."

Since I also felt that my response had been on the wacko side, I was really interested in learning what the student had finally understood the response to mean. He elaborated:

"I thought you were crazy to think you could change the world because I took your response to literally mean you wanted to change the whole world. This educational trip has changed the way I think about being an entrepreneur ... so *my* **world has indeed been changed!** Now I have an entrepreneurial mindset, and thus, now I understand your response.

"By changing one person's mindset, you can change his world."

What a powerful lesson!!! It is a lesson I will never forget and I trust will be of value to the reader.

The purpose of all we plan, develop, and undertake in terms of entrepreneurship education and development, at the end of it all, is about helping to change the mindset.

It makes so much sense. It is so simple, and yet so powerful. From that moment on, we have a rather simple and straightforward process for developing entrepreneurship education programs and entrepreneurs.

Step one is to understand where their mindset is now for the group we intend to impact.

Step two is to visualize where you need to take the mindset next.

Then in step three, one can begin to work on ideas or initiatives that may be of help in moving the target group's mindset from step one to recognizing that they can be an entrepreneur.

The following section presents an overview of the types of activities that can be undertaken to foster entrepreneurship amongst youth. The chapter then presents various initiatives we undertake, at various levels, to move "clients" from one particular mindset to another one, all in the process of creating entrepreneurs.

OVERVIEW OF THE INITIATIVES TO FOSTER ENTREPRENEURSHIP AMONGST YOUTH

There is a wide range of initiatives that can be undertaken to foster entrepreneurship amongst youth. There are so many in fact, that just listing them can be a challenge. The initiatives, for example, may by presented using as a basis **the types of entity that carries them out**, namely, those undertaken by the government sector, the private sector (including business associations), educational institutions (say, for students K-12, and university level students), and by entities such as banks and other non-governmental entities.

Another way to characterize them is by **the types of initiatives undertaken**, which include programs for orientation, training, mentoring, loans, promotion, competitions, and awards.

Other possible ways to present the youth entrepreneurship initiatives is by **the types of objectives they pursue**. These may be as general as "to promote awareness of entrepreneurship to youth" as a whole, or more specific as "to provide financing options and counseling programs tailored to 18–25 year olds as they simultaneously undertake the development of a business while pursuing their undergraduate degree at a university".

The following figure summarizes the range of options for supporting young entrepreneurs.

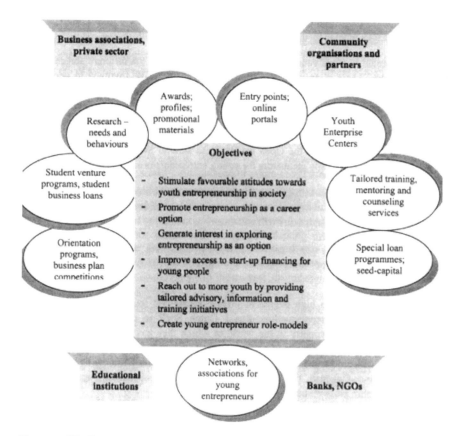

Range of Policy Measures and Options for Supporting Young Entrepreneurs

Source: Louis Stevenson and Anders Lundstrom (2002) "Beyond the Rhetoric: Defining Entrepreneurship Policy and its Best Practice Components"; volume 2 of the Entrepreneurship Policy for the Future Series, Swedish Foundation for Small Business Research, page 187.

The figure above is part of the outcome of a comprehensive study by the Swedish Foundation for Small Business Research whereby an analysis was undertaken of the entrepreneurship policy and practice in a group of ten economies — six members of the European Union (EU) and four members of the Asia-Pacific Economic Cooperation (APEC). The study included an analysis of policies and measures dealing with various target groups, namely youth, women entrepreneurs, ethnic/minorities and immigrants, aboriginals, the unemployed, people with disabilities, and veterans. The findings on pages 176–177 of the publication mentioned above state that:

"Young people are the only demographic group targeted with at least some entrepreneurship promotion or business support measures by government in all ten cases [studied]. Governments are doing this for a number of reasons, one of the most significant of which is the higher than average level of unemployment amongst the youth segment of the population. It is also in response to the changing nature of the labour market and the likelihood that some form of employment option for young people who have finished their educations."

"Authors ... recommend that a more systematic approach to Young Entrepreneur programmes should be taken ... including awareness-raising programmes, promotion of age-relevant role-models, enhanced educational and learning opportunities, and appropriate start-up support services."

What follows is an example of one initiative we have undertaken for a decade. It was designed to provide a "systematic" approach for awareness-raising, and the identification and promotion of age-relevant role models via the **integrated use of various media**, as well as of key entities from both the public and private sector.

CHANGING THE MINDSET OF A WHOLE COUNTRY: THE PUERTO RICO EXPERIENCE FOR PROMOTING AN ENTREPRENEURIAL CULTURE

The Need — The Problem

As the quote above explains, the reasons for undertaking initiatives to promote entrepreneurship in many economies is the high level of unemployment amongst youth and the changing nature of the labor market. In the case of Puerto Rico, an island the size of some 100 by 35 miles in the Caribbean with historical ties to Spain, cultural ties to Latin America, and political and economic ties to the USA, the economic development of the latter half of the 20th century was mostly via attracting manufacturing operations of large multinationals. These provided employment opportunities for the population of approximately four million people. Those with jobs in turn paid taxes to help the economy grow.

The mindset of the country as a whole, thus, was that economic development and jobs were mainly the result of attracting large multinationals. The "formula" for attracting these multinationals was mostly via tax incentives from Puerto Rico as well as from the US Treasury as the profits where repatriated to the USA. This "formula" worked for many years and to some extent precluded the Island from understanding the changing realities of the labor market experienced by many economies.

Thus, as other nations realized that small and medium enterprises were providing the majority of the net new jobs, and responded accordingly, Puerto Rico continued to promote a status quo mindset and to put all or most of its efforts into continuing to focus on providing incentives to attract multinationals to its shores. In the process, the Island neglected to aggressively undertake initiatives to foster entrepreneurship and enterprise formation, including initiatives to promote entrepreneurship as a viable career option, **early** into the mind-set of the population.

The **big jolt** that finally awakened most in Puerto Rico about the need to revisit the economic development strategy was the decision by the US Congress to phase out the US Treasury incentives on profits made in Puerto Rico. After the initial shock, reality set in — there was an urgent need to work towards changing the culture and changing the mentality of the country. The previous culture, whereby people desired to have a secure job, **had to give way to a new mindset** where people seriously consider and take action to become an entrepreneur and decide to initiate and develop a new venture.

Early Efforts

Culture takes time to change. The situation described above, however, required urgent action. We had undertaken some initiatives to assist in the process of starting and developing businesses. Looking back, however, these were isolated and splintered "one-off" initiatives to take care of a specific need and not necessarily to change the culture as a whole. We needed to change the mindset of a country.

One of the initiatives began in the mid 1980's via the Small Business Development Centers program (SBDC's), which appeared to fill mostly the "remedial" needs by providing counseling and training services to help small businesses that were trying to survive or were facing growing pains.

Another initiative was the development in the mid 1990's of various university level courses about entrepreneurship, innovation and creativity, and business plan development, among others. These courses were thought of as a "preventive strategy," whereby students are assisted in planning, initiating, and developing a business in the right manner, thereby avoiding the types of results that warranted the "remedial" services mentioned before.

These courses by themselves, although a step in the right direction, were not enough. Students often questioned the need to undertake entrepreneurship as a career option and felt they were going against too many odds in their quest to become entrepreneurs. Why?

They felt alone, with minimum support from their friends, parents, and society as a whole, which explicitly or implicitly favored the traditional "get a job" culture, which was the collective mindset of going for the time proven, "ideal" strategy of attempting to go for a secure job in a large company — even if those opportunities were rapidly diminishing given the economic scenario described previously.

Working to Change the Culture

The experiences of the initial efforts, including those described above, highlighted that **much more was needed to create a real change**. It was at this point that it became very evident we needed to undertake a **comprehensive effort to try to change the culture**, the mindset, **to one of embracing of entrepreneurship by all sectors**.

The use of **media was the keystone to the effort**, so as to secure massive communication of a "new" awareness of entrepreneurship in an effort to have society as a whole embrace it as a common goal for all to pursue.

The overall results of this initiative will be shared first, in an effort to show the elements that resulted in a positive change of the culture. Then some of the details of how this was accomplished will be shared, along with some of the lessons learned which may be of interest to the reader that wants to consider similar initiatives.

The Strategic Use of Print Media

The "formula" utilized was a competition to identify and recognize on a yearly basis **THE collegiate entrepreneur in Puerto Rico**. Various media, such as the national newspaper with the largest circulation, magazines, and radio stations highly promoted the competition itself and the many prizes the winner would receive.

The element of changing the culture and the mindset comes into play mostly with the results of the competition. The most important and visible result of this initiative is produced by the competition's main sponsor: the largest newspaper in Puerto Rico.

The newspaper publishes a Special Edition of their weekly Business Magazine focused on youth entrepreneurship, with the cover story being the student entrepreneur who wins the competition. All of the articles of the Special Edition feature other student entrepreneurs, a compendium of all the finalists, follow up stories as to the continued success of the winners from previous years, and articles to foster the importance of entrepreneurship and the need to promote young entrepreneurs.

The mix of articles in the Special Edition of the Business Magazine cohesively promotes an entrepreneurial culture. It recognizes young entrepreneurs, and in the process, **makes them role models for all**, and even perhaps heroes for both younger ones and older ones alike. Their stories showcase how they recognized opportunities and turned them into successful ventures.

The fact that they overcame obstacles and triumphed while undertaking their undergraduate university degrees "validates" that the focus is not about either studying for a higher degree vis-à-vis starting a venture, but **about doing both simultaneously**, thus "proving" the desirability of considering entrepreneurship as a career option.

The other articles of the Special Edition of the Business Magazine strategically address issues pertaining to changing the culture. In the first year of this program for example, an article showcased how the parents and family members helped some of the student entrepreneurs featured in the publication. The overall emphasis of the article was to showcase that **all in the family have a role to play** in assisting entrepreneurs and their ventures.

In another year, an article dealt with what the various universities were doing to educate would-be entrepreneurs. This put the spotlight on the universities and called for the need to establish more initiatives to facilitate entrepreneurship.

In yet another article, on another occasion, government entities dealing with permits and regulations were interviewed and quizzed as to how they plan to eliminate barriers that hinder enterprise development. These types of features question what is being done, launch an agenda for fostering enterprise development, and serve as a follow-up mechanism to monitor progress in future editions of the business magazine.

As a whole, thus, the various articles of the special edition publications cohesively and consistently address the need to change the culture to one that fosters entrepreneurship.

The publication of the special editions of the business magazine makes **entrepreneurship newsworthy**. Further, the credibility of mainstream media to all parties, including youth, parents, government agencies, educational entities, and other media, is simply invaluable towards the goal of changing the culture.

The Impact of the Awards Ceremony

The strategy to change the mindset includes a very **high-impact Awards Ceremony** held at the facilities of the newspaper. The attendance is by invitation only, and it has developed into a **must go event** to learn firsthand who the winner of the award is. The audience includes the heads of the sponsors and all key players in the business scene of the Island, who are identified and thanked publicly for their valuable support.

Also present are the Presidents, Chancellors, and Deans of Puerto Rico's Universities, **all of whom now value the impact of having one of their students win** the coveted award. Those academic entities that failed to have a student entrepreneur recognized in a given year work very hard to identify and support their student entrepreneurs so they may have one of theirs recognized in the future. **Peer pressure works!** In sum, all the universities want to be amongst the winners in terms of supporting young entrepreneurs, and many use this distinction to advertise to future students the benefits of their particular entrepreneurship programs.

Cinemas Further Showcase Entrepreneurship

The Awards Ceremony is filmed and a news clip about it is shown on the giant screen of the halls of the **largest chain of cinemas** on the Island as previewing entertainment. This shows to all audiences, particular to youth, the very high-impact awards ceremony where the heads of business and higher education join to toast the student entrepreneur that is honored every year.

The big screen news clip clearly presents the image of the desirability and success that is possible for one to be an entrepreneur, from early on, and the acclaim from society as a whole for such an undertaking. This is a very powerful method for changing the mindset, as it provides a name and a face to the "new ideal" of becoming an entrepreneur. It showcases the fact that it is approved and recognized by society as a whole to be an entrepreneur, and it is culturally valued to support entrepreneurship and to aspire to become one.

Other Media Exposure Ties It All Together

Other media is also used to complement the strategy to change the mindset, including the web page www.exitoempresarialpr.com. When people visit the page, they come into contact with the stories of the winners from previous years and the articles mentioned before, thus providing a lasting effect to the original coverage of the newspaper. The compilation of so many stories in one web page makes the page **a reference point** many faculty ask students in entrepreneurship programs to visit, further impacting new generations of would-be entrepreneurs. It fosters an entrepreneurial mindset, and the competition has been very effective at creating entrepreneurs. Competition breeds excellence in entrepreneurship.

The **celebrity status of being a successful student entrepreneur**, conferred by the mix of media recognition mentioned above, provides a lot of attention and credibility to the student entrepreneurs and makes them great spokespersons for entrepreneurship. They go on to share their entrepreneurial experiences on highly-rated TV talk shows and make presentations to professional and service organizations and others, including students from various educational levels.

Lessons Learned

We could continue sharing about this initiative, but we trust what has been presented provides a good overview of the process and results of initiatives to change the mindset of the country by attempting to change its culture to one of valuing and supporting entrepreneurship. The lessons learned include:

- **Use credible and high-impact media** to send your message.

- **Focus on the person, not on the enterprise.** Why he/she started the business, how they got started, etc. It is a story of a person aimed to impact other people, versus a story of a business trying to impact other businesses.

- Undergraduate entrepreneurs are in the middle of the age spectrum, thus their stories inspire other undergraduates while younger ones, say in high school, look up to them, and older ones, including their parents, are left thinking **"If they could do it, so can I."**

- **Impact all players**, including youth, their parents, teachers, entities related to enterprise formation such as governmental, private, and public, banks, and support agencies. In short, your local society as a whole is your target.

- After the news articles are printed, **keep the story** alive via other media such as cinemas, web pages, personal presentations, etc.

- **Develop strategic alliances** such as with the number one newspaper, number one cinema chain, and number one bank. This helps you to effectively bring out, **as a continuous and cohesive message**, that entrepreneurship is desirable, is achievable, and is recognized and celebrated by all — as highlighted in the mix of media.

- **Undertake a long-term, consistent, and comprehensive effort**, rather than a piecemeal approach, in order to have a long-term effect.

Networking — A Critical Tool

Another lesson is the value of networking. A **network of sponsors** makes the communications prior to the awards possible. We need to promote the awards so student entrepreneurs learn of them and compete. The network of sponsors provides the awards the winner receives, such as free advertising in the number one newspaper, use of a cellular phone for a year, and reimbursement for business trips. The network further provides a united front to validate the key message of the desirability of embracing entrepreneurship as a career option.

Research Proves the Success

It is appropriate to mention that ongoing research underpins the work we have undertaken. The research provides the basis for themes for possible articles for the special edition of the business magazine of the newspaper. The research undertaken also follows the evolution of the student entrepreneurs, winners and finalists alike, to learn more about their challenges and the results of their efforts. The research keeps us posted on results such as the number of student entrepreneurs that completed an academic degree or continue in their studies (90%). We learn how many continue with their business (**87%**) and the fact that some **50%** have started other businesses besides their original enterprise.

These are stunning results — a veritable miracle in our small island economy!

These findings further provide input for the editorial content of the newspaper, data of interest to sponsors, and measurement of the results of the efforts to change the culture. All of this further provides a picture of where the mindset is and where we should attempt to move next, thus serving as the basis for further initiatives to develop entrepreneurs.

What follows are other initiatives developed as a result of this ongoing research geared to changing the mindset and methodology of the student-faculty encounter.

CHANGING THE MINDSET OF THE STUDENT-FACULTY ENCOUNTER

The key theme of this chapter is that the miracle of creating entrepreneurs, from our experience, is changing the mindset. The first example shared was to change the mindset related to the culture of a country by going from a mindset of: "I want to have a good/secure job working for someone else" to one of "I want to have my own business".

Since the objective of this chapter is to share some initiatives that have worked for us in the process of changing the mindset, mostly of youth, to start in a decided and enthusiastic manner their entrepreneurial journey, it is appropriate to focus on the need to change the mindset of the student–teacher encounter.

Education programs are clearly in the arena of services, where you have a service provider and a client. Unlike the situation whereby a person purchases or obtains a product, for the most part a student/faculty encounter takes place between the service provider and the customer. This service encounter has been referred to by many as the **"moment of truth."** Traditionally, to one extent or another, the education encounter of student-faculty has been one where the faculty is the one that knows and thus shares knowledge.

In the case of entrepreneurship education programs **this needs to be revised**.

Entrepreneurial Experiences Count

Many entrepreneurship education activities follow the typical "formula" of most educational programs. That is, "teaching" is mostly done by the faculty to a mostly passive student. After much introspection, and given the results of the efforts undertaken to change the mindset of the country mentioned above, it has become evident that we needed an experience with a different approach. We have changed to a student/teacher approach that we to refer to as the **"entrepreneurship learning encounter."**

For this to happen, we need to change the mindset: from the goal of "teaching" to making it one of "learning." In that process, the focus shifts from the teacher that has the right answer to the student that, probably to his/her own initial surprise, has a lot to share and **thus helps to "teach" his fellow classmates**. The end result is not the traditional "teaching experiences," but rather **learning experiences** that we refer to as entrepreneurial experiences.

The following are some specific examples of entrepreneurial experiences we have developed throughout the years and adapted to regular use. Other experiences, like the elevator pitch, were learned from others and have been adapted from them. These are not meant to be great examples, nor the only examples, but rather some activities we have used and recommend you try as you find the right sort of entrepreneurial experiences to help in the process of changing the mindset within your own situation.

The Business Card Experience

The business card experience is meant to change the focus of the student-faculty encounter. The objective is to **shift all eyes from the professor** "who has all the answers" to ALL of the students as individuals and members of a network who have resources to share.

The way we have developed the exercise is by having students complete an index card with their basic student data for the instructor to collect. This is something they are used to doing, in one way or another, as part of the traditional faculty-student encounter. Then we ask the students. "What is the benefit of this index card? Who benefits from it?" After some discussion it is clear that only the instructor benefits from having this data and that the communication process has been one way (student-faculty).

In contrast, we ask how entrepreneurs share basic information. The response, obviously, is by exchanging business cards with other entrepreneurs. At that moment students are asked to prepare their own business cards and to bring copies to class and exchange them amongst all. The business cards should include their names and contact information (usually cellular phone and e-mail). The card should also have the name and slogan of their enterprise (usually an idea they have dreamed about or, if no idea is in their minds yet, they must make up one ... just to have a complete business card).

Students later present their business idea and share their business cards. The networking really takes off as students realize one's business idea may be a service or product required by a business of one of their classmates. Further developments of their business endeavors emerge as possible strategic alliances or referrals take place amongst them. The **value of a good network comes to light** as students provide feedback to others and share ideas about the plans other fellow students have in mind for developing their businesses.

This networking begins and is encouraged to take place at the classroom. It can also continue and develop amongst them as the business cards have the information required to continue networking. The contrast of completing and sharing one index card with the instructor versus a business card with all in the class is a very effective way of shifting to a different type of student faculty encounter. Most importantly, it provides a whole new way of having students change their mindset ... away from a student mindset (represented by the one index card prepared for the instructor) to a mindset of an entrepreneur (preparing, distributing, and obtaining business cards from all). This opens the door for a shift from a faculty-to-student "teaching" to a student-to-student learning via a networking experience that starts in the classroom and carries on.

The business card experience provides a good mix of many skills: short presentations (or "elevator pitch"), networking, and student-to-student mentoring. These types of entrepreneurial experiences are explained next.

Elevator Pitch — With a Twist

The concept of an elevator pitch has been used as a way to have someone present their business effectively in a short time. It starts with the assumption that you encounter in the elevator the very key person you need to develop your business further. What would you say to him/her during the brief time (say 90 seconds) you have before this person exits the elevator?

We have used the elevator pitch concept as a way to assist in our strategies to change the mindset on campus and outside of the classroom. A competition has been established and advertised on campus for all students. Some students that may have participated in the business card experience mentioned above get enthusiastic about presenting their idea in such a forum.

Preliminary rounds take place, and the final competition is judged by key persons from the business community. The obvious beneficiary of the activity is the one who presents at the competition **who opts for a shot at the title of winner** and receives some awards and feedback from the judges.

By making the final competition open to the public, and by engaging them during the competition, all in the audience participate in a mindset changing experience. The audience witnesses the presentations and benefits from the feedback the judges provide after each presentation. This allows those in the audience to compare their views with those of the judges.

Some audience members get a chance to make their own suggestions to the competitors, and all in the audience get to vote at the end for the "people's choice award." At the end of the activity, both the judges' award and the "people's choice award" are presented. The result is a different kind of educational experience that promotes a change of mindset for all, those that participate as competitors, as well as for those that participate as part of the audience.

One of the awards for both the winner chosen by the judges and the recipient of the "people's choice award" is to receive mentoring. This sort of award highlights to all the importance of receiving advice and mentoring from others. We have been incorporating student-to-student mentoring as a way to change mindsets, as presented next.

Mentoring — Student-to-Student Mentoring

An entrepreneurial experience designed to have students view themselves as part of a network that can be of assistance to each other is **student-to-student mentoring**. This is consistent with the goal of the business card exercise explained before, which aims to change the mindset of the student-faculty encounter to one of a student-to-student encounter.

Various modes have been put in place to achieve this. In some cases the mentoring takes place in the classroom, as the instructor sets aside class time for the students to pair up and provide mentoring to each other regarding their business ideas. In other cases, the mentoring has taken place outside of the classroom. In some circumstances, students have undergone a combination of both mentoring in and out of the classroom. Likewise, this mentorship experience has taken place as a required activity of a course, as a voluntary exercise, and as a combination of both.

The initial reaction of the student is one of shock as they question his/her abilities to be an effective mentor. One way to deal with this anxiety is to provide a workshop on mentoring techniques. Experience has shown that once they conduct the initial mentoring session, they realize they are equipped to ask questions about the business idea of their peers.

The results of this experience indicate that:

- Students favor the experience of being a mentor, as it provides them with the opportunity to **put into practice what they are learning** — to learn by doing.

- Students favor receiving mentorship from another student because their questions and observations **provide feedback** about their business venture from what may be their potential customer.

- Students, in both the role of a mentor and one obtaining mentorship, feel they can be **more open** amongst themselves than with a faculty member.

The student-to-student mentoring experience has been proven to be a key step in our efforts to change the mindset.

Another proven entrepreneurship exercise to assist in changing the mindset is the entrepreneurial mission experience, presented next.

Travel — Or "Entrepreneurial Missions"

The Department of Commerce of most countries and business trade groups like Chambers of Commerce periodically organize trade missions to various countries of the world. These missions are focused on possible matching up of entrepreneurs and businesses from the two regions to explore business opportunities.

One entrepreneurship experience we have developed is something similar to a trade mission which we call "Entrepreneurial Missions." Students travel to another place (in some cases another country or another continent) with other students to better understand the culture and the ways business is conducted elsewhere. **Entrepreneurial opportunities immediately become evident to the students**.

The initial reaction of most students is "I can not afford to make the trip." Our response is to have them focus on whether they want to make the trip or not. IF they want to make the trip, we work along with them in the fundraising activities to make the trip a reality. This in itself represents a mindset change as students engage in enterprising activities to make the trip a reality. In the process leading up to the trip they work as a team with others interested in making the entrepreneurial mission a reality, thus developing the basis for a lasting networking base that further develops during the entrepreneurial experience, and lasts long after the trip concludes.

After the trip, students get to report to other students and to sponsors that help make the trip a reality about the entrepreneurial opportunities they identified. These presentations often include testimonials about how they once thought it was impossible for them to make such a trip, as they initially did not have the money to pay for it.

Students further explain how they focused on making the trip a reality and were able to participate in the Entrepreneurial Mission. This experience, they come to realize, is the preamble for understanding that they can initiate their business if they really want to, even if they initially do not have all the resources. Again, it's about a change of mindset, and the Entrepreneurial Mission experience is one way to help achieve such a change of mindset.

Some of the Entrepreneurial Missions undertaken include a yearly trip to the Collegiate Entrepreneurs' Organization Annual Conference (mostly to Chicago). A participant of this trip is the winner of the collegiate entrepreneur award (the one resultant from the competition explained early in the chapter, which is part of our strategy to assist in the efforts to change the culture of the country). The participation of the winner of the collegiate entrepreneur award allows the students to meet face-to-face and share with someone their age that is already a successful entrepreneur. Again, this is very powerful experience in terms of changing the mindset of the would-be entrepreneur.

What's Next?

Exploring methods to effectively change the mindset of young people, and in the process develop entrepreneurs, is a never-ending process, and one we are certainly committed to. One way to keep enthused in this endeavor is the ability to learn from others. The sharing of experiences has proven to be most beneficial and refreshing in the pursuit of this goal. One way to do so is by using the Internet. In our case, we are using the online environment for the "open source" development and sharing of educational modules found at www.cnx.org. In that space, under the "lens" of "entrepreneurship" (http://cnx.org/lenses/eactoolkit/ entrepreneurship), we have posted various modules sharing some of the activities utilized to assist in the process of changing the mindset into one that fosters innovation and creativity and leads to an entrepreneurial mindset. Feel free to visit, add, translate, adapt, and share your own modules. We look forward to learning about your initiatives and experiences.

CONCLUSION

The objective of this chapter is to share some practical, real life experiences for developing entrepreneurship education programs, and in the process, developing entrepreneurs. It is not meant to be a "how to" do it. It is appropriate for you to consider your own needs, resources, circumstances, and goals for such undertakings, and perhaps use our success stories as the basis for your own efforts.

The chapter does not claim any or all of the experiences shared to be correct, perfect, nor a "best practice." It is simply a sharing of initiatives that have worked for us and, perhaps to some degree, may work for you, or at least serve as a spark from which to ignite your own set of possibilities.

As explained at the beginning, one way of looking at the challenge is to understand that the purpose of all we plan, develop, and undertake in terms of entrepreneurship development is about helping to change the mindset. Thus, in this chapter we shared initiatives that have worked for us in the process of changing the mindset, mostly of youth, to start, in a decided and enthusiastic manner, their entrepreneurial journey.

These initiatives have been used to change the mindset of our target groups in Puerto Rico. We trust they will help in your quest for ideas to change the mindset of your own target groups. With each of us attempting to change the mindset in each of our regions, we can, collectively, change the world to one where entrepreneurship flourishes to allow all to recognize and turn opportunities into realities through youth entrepreneurship.

"Some people see things as they are ask, 'why?' I dream of things that never were; and ask, 'why not?'"

George Bernard Shaw

Chapter Thirteen

Entrepreneurship for Non-Traditional Youth Entrepreneurs

World Entrepreneurship Education from the Yukon to the Middle East: The Curry BizCamp

By Robert Warren

Robert Warren is a Master Entrepreneurship Educator who has led his Stn Clark Entrepreneurship Center to worldwide involvements and recognition since 1995. He has successfully endowed the center, and his students have an international reputation for their successful new business ventures — winning over 40 international competitions and over $1,000,000 in prize money. More importantly, his students have launched

businesses with a market cap in excess of $300 million. He co-authored a marketing text with Dr. Phillip Kotler of Northwestern University, and is a frequently sought after media commentator, including regular columns in magazines. He has an international reputation for his innovative programs fostering entrepreneurial thinking, and the formation of new enterprises.

INTRODUCTION

The Curry BizCamp in Entrepreneurship is the major outreach program offered by the University of Manitoba's Stn Clark Centre for Entrepreneurship. It was launched in 1998 at the request of a London, England-based donor, encompassing aspects of similar programs the donor had seen in the United States. This program has over 1,200 Manitoba youth graduates between the ages of 13–20.

The major difference between the Asper Centre's program and those in the United States is that the Curry BizCamp places more emphasis on helping the youth develop an entrepreneurial lifestyle and less on encouraging them to launch a business. This change was made based on cultural differences between Canada and the United States. Small business startup and ownership is not seen by Canadians in the same positive light as it is in the United States, and the odds of a successful business startup by youth in the target age range are low.

Youth selected for this program are drawn from a variety of groups identified as exhibiting some sort of **at-risk behaviour or coming from disadvantaged circumstances**. Examples of youth invited to take this part in this program include recent immigrants to Canada, youth living in lower socio-economic areas of Winnipeg (primarily the downtown core), youth identified as either being part of or potentially joining a street gang, youth with truancy issues, high school dropouts, Aboriginal youth, and former sex trade workers. The mixture of youth in any given camp tends to vary, but over the course of the past decade the Curry BizCamp has recruited from each of the areas listed.

Recruitment is aided through a **series of partnerships the Asper Centre has developed with social organizations and government departments**. For example, Stn Clark Centre staff have developed contacts with approximately 75 schools in Winnipeg that have been identified as having a student body consisting of one or more of the target groups. In some cases, these schools refer the Stn Clark Centre to outreach programs they offer that are specifically aimed at our target group. As part of this arrangement, the teachers identify the youths they believe could benefit from the program and arrange an information session delivered by Stn Clark Centre staff. These sessions last for approximately one hour and cover the application process along with the program's key components.

Other partners of the Stn Clark Centre include the City of Winnipeg Police Service, Winnipeg Aboriginal Sports Athletic Association, and private organizations that deal with young offenders, teen mothers, recent immigrants, or active or former sex trade workers.

The Stn Clark Centre has also received support in the past from groups like the Boys and Girls Club, Western Economic Diversification, the Business Development Bank of Canada, and Big Brothers/Big Sisters. The Stn Clark Centre uses a similar process as is used in the school system to make youth recommended by these groups aware of the program and its goals.

In 2007, Stn Clark Centre staff met with approximately 80 groups between the beginning of May and mid-June. Over 1,000 youth attended these meetings, including one entire school in a lower socio-economic area. 755 application forms were handed out at these meetings, and over 150 returned. The Stn Clark Centre's three-part application process is the main reason so few youth recruited actually apply. This process was installed for one simple reason — they only want the most dedicated youth to enter the program. This stringent process results in very few participants leaving the program once it starts.

APPLICATION PROCEDURES

The application process consists of a form that asks basic information about the student, for example, name age, address, school, etc. This information is used to both contact the student and to ensure the camps are balanced in terms of gender, background, age, and area of the city represented. This section also includes a brief essay by the student describing why they want to attend the camp.

Even if a student's writing skills are weak, it is easy to spot those who are interested in learning from the program versus those looking for a way to spend one to three weeks, depending on their age, during the summer.

The second part of the application process consists of the youth's parent or guardian agreeing to their application. This section is not necessary for youth over the age of 18.

Part three of the application is an **endorsement of the application** by the youth's teacher, parole officer, a representative from the agency recommending them, or someone recognized by the Stn Clark Centre as a neutral and responsible third part, e.g. a priest or social worker.

Once all the applications are received, they are reviewed by the Manager, Youth Programs and the Stn Clark Centre's I. H. Asper

Executive Director, who together determine which students are offered admission. Typically, 30 applications are extended for each camp, as the goal is to start each camp with 25 youth. Five additional youth are selected because experience has shown this is the number that either rejects the acceptance due to other commitments (e.g. they have obtained a summer position), family circumstances, or failing to show on the first day. There are a variety of reasons for failing to attend, but it primarily results from the youth having obtained a summer job.

Over the ten years the program has been in existence, **95% of those youth who started successfully the program graduated.**

THE METHODOLOGY

The Stn Clark Centre offers **two versions of BizCamp. A three-week version is aimed at youth between 15 and 20, while a one-week version targets 13–14 year olds.** Both camps contain the same major elements. **The change in length is due to the attention span differences between the youth involved.**

Youth that participate in the one-week camp are eligible to return for the three-week camp in later years if they receive a new referral. This is just another way we attempt to keep youth interested in the entrepreneurial lifestyle. Typically 10–15% of the participants in the three-week program are graduates from the one-week program.

Program Elements

The Curry BizCamp in Entrepreneurship involves **five elements**. Four of these take place during the one- or three-week camp while the **fifth is a series of ongoing support programs**.

#1: *Teaching the Fundamentals and Testing*

The main purpose of the BizCamp program is education and, in particular, teaching the participants how basic entrepreneurship and business skills are a part of their everyday life. To accomplish this goal, participants spend about 50% of their time in classroom lectures and related exercises. These cover such topics as basic math skills, such as calculating a rate of return or a markup percentage, reading comprehension, and writing skills.

Participants are taught reading skills by providing them with a daily newspaper, The National Post. One of Canada's two national business papers, the National Post is provided under a partnership deal between the Stn Clark Centre and the publisher. Participants are asked to review the day's key stories and keep tabs on a stock they chose to follow on the camp's first day. Their writing skills are tested by a variety of writing exercises that include everything from preparing a memo listing the contents of the briefcase they are given on the first day to preparing a resume under the supervision of a representative from the Asper School's Career Services Centre.

One day is devoted to teaching the importance of teams to an entrepreneurial venture. This lesson is taught using a series of games and activities. Over the years this exercise has been conducted by representatives from the police service, the Canadian Armed Forces, and BizCamp staff.

It's not enough, however, to simply teach these lessons; participants will also be tested on how well these lessons are being absorbed. To accomplish this goal, the Stn Clark Centre uses a series of tests throughout each camp.

The most important of these is the **pre- and post-test** given to test the math, reading, and business knowledge of the participants.

The same 40-question test is given on the first and last day of each camp and the Stn Clark Centre measures the level of improvement. **In 2007, the level of improvement averaged 68%**, with some students recording almost a 100% improvement. This is in keeping with our results from previous years.

Participants are also tested after key lessons either through oral quizzes or short written tests. Students are encouraged to do well on these through a series of **financial and other incentives, for example movie passes or a restaurant gift card**. The Centre's experience has been very positive with these incentives, as the participants put considerable effort into the tests and become quite competitive to obtain the rewards available.

Interestingly, centre staff haven't found that it results in participants shunning lower performers. On the contrary, they've found the better participants, together with the camp's instructors, will help participants with difficulties in an effort to improve their scores. The Stn Clark Centre encourages this behaviour by awarding a certificate to each participant at graduation listing their most outstanding characteristic. The subject of these certificates includes perseverance, teamwork, and calculating ROI.

#2: The Speaker Program

To make the camp seem less like a school environment, **external speakers** are brought in on a regular basis. These speakers are drawn from the local entrepreneurial community, as well as government and private organizations that support business or career development. In the case of entrepreneurs the Stn Clark Centre is **careful to use speakers representing the various subgroups** present in the camp.

For example, one speaker is a high school dropout. This entrepreneur discusses how he started his career as a fry cook but realized the only way to improve his position and income was by returning to school. This person returned to school and not only finished high school, but went on to obtain a college degree and become an executive with a major quick service restaurant chain.

Another speaker addresses the issues faced by people on social assistance and how he worked within the system to get a good job. A third speaker discusses the challenges she faced as an immigrant to Canada in the 1970s in terms of learning the language and adjusting to Canadian culture. She discusses how, by blending aspects of her culture with Canadian culture, she was able to create a series of businesses across the provinces of Manitoba and Saskatchewan.

Other speakers are brought in from the provincial and municipal government to discuss the legal and regulatory issues involved in launching a new business. Professionals are also brought in from the legal, accounting, and financial services communities to discuss the role they play in starting a business and the participants' everyday lives. All discussions are followed by a question and answer session where the participants are encouraged to ask questions and rewarded for asking tough or probing questions.

#3: *Business Visits*

BizCamp's third major section involves site visits to a variety of locations where participants can **see classroom lessons in action**. In the three-week camp, participants take part in three such visits, while in the one-week camp, due to the limited time available, only one site visit is offered.

One visit is made to a **local market**, where participants learn what it takes to establish a retail operation. Topics covered include occupancy costs and how the management of the market determines which entrepreneurs to invite in.

Participants visit a **manufacturing or service facility** to learn about process and the importance of inventory control. Locations visited in the past have included a local bus manufacturing facility, a furniture maker, and the airport.

The one visit common to both camps, and by far the most popular with the participants, is **Costco, a local wholesaler**. While at Costco, participants learn what it means to be a wholesaler and how to apply the lessons they've learned about markup and profit margins. They also learn about budgeting and consumer tastes during these visits.

The students have a special exercise that involves purchasing inventory for a **small retail operation they run during the camp**. Students in the three-week camp run this operation for three days.

How they perform on this exercise helps determine their **class standing**. This is important because their standing is one of the factors used to determine the **scholarship winner for that class**. This scholarship, worth **$2,000 towards tuition at the University of Manitoba**, is given to the top student in each class and is valid for five years. To date, ten scholarships have been activated. For students in the one-week camp, this retail operation forms the basis of the business plan produced as the capstone exercise.

#4: The Capstone Project

The final component of the camp period is the production of a **business plan for a proposed new venture**. Participants in the three-week camp produce these plans **individually**.

The Stn Clark Centre reserves the right to make an **equity investment** to a maximum of $400 in these ventures if the participant can prove to a panel of judges they are interested and able to launch the venture.

Four such investments have been made recently. These include purchasing a sewing machine for a young woman that wanted to make birthing blankets and repair children's clothes for people living in her area and an inkjet printer for a young man that started a business to print tickets, notices, and other material for his school's student council. Both of these businesses proved to be quite successful.

Unsuccessful investments were also made in a custom car painting business and an asphalting service firm. The custom car painting business was forced out of business when the principal was convicted of auto theft, while the second business failed due to unfavourable weather conditions, in particular, an early snow that cut the construction season short by three weeks. Failure is a learning process too! Participants in the one-week camp build their plans in teams of five based on their retail operation.

Plans are judged by panels consisting of local business people and media. Typically, each panel consists of four members who evaluate the ideas presented based on investment potential. Participants are given 10 minutes to pitch their ideas using PowerPoint for the three-week camp, or overhead template transparencies in the one-week camp, followed by a 10-minute question and answer session.

This often proves to be the toughest exercise in camp, as presenting in front of a group frightens some participants. To overcome this, the staff spends considerable time working with the teams to develop their presentation and rehearse. Despite this effort, **this is the only time during the camp that dropouts tend to occur.** On average, one student per camp tends to drop at this point. To help them graduate, they are invited them to come back at a later time and present to a smaller group of experienced judges that know how to put participants at ease and effectively engage them in a way that explains their idea.

To encourage participants in the preparation of their plan, **cash prizes are awarded for the top four plans**, $300 for first, $200 second, $100 third, and $50 fourth, and for the one-week camp, an additional $50 prize for the fifth-place team.

#5: Continuing Support

BizCamp's fifth component is the support program starting approximately six weeks after the end of each year's camps. These services include arranging mentors from the business community for interested graduates, the previously described venture fund, and regular meetings. Meetings are held every six weeks and involve a luncheon together with a guest speaker to discuss a business issue or their career.

A special Christmas luncheon is held that allows BizCamp graduates to bring their children or siblings to meet Santa Claus and receive a gift. Every attendee receives a gift of an article of clothing, fresh fruit, candy and a surprise donated by a local firm, e.g. compact discs, hockey tickets, or movie passes. It is our experience that these follow up sessions are critical for supporting the lessons learned during the camp and encouraging graduates to continue following an entrepreneurial lifestyle.

Attendance at these events is highest for current year graduates and gradually drops off over the five years the Stn Clark Centre tracks BizCamp graduates. This drop off occurs for many reasons including the fact BizCamp graduates often move without leaving a forwarding address, changing lifestyle decisions, and lack of continued interest in the program. An average event attracts between 25–45 graduates depending on the time of year, location of the event, and speaker, while the Christmas event draws approximately 100 people each year.

Evaluating BizCamp

To accurately assess the impact of the BizCamp on participants, the Stn Clark Centre applies a variety of measures. These include such immediate measures as graduation rates and the pre- and post-test results. A variety of qualitative measures are also used to judge the program's effectiveness, including interviews with key stakeholders, attendance at regulary scheduled events, and comments submitted by past participants.

From the beginning, however, the Stn Clark Centre realized the real proof of the program's effectiveness was in the long-term impact it had on the participants' behaviour. With this goal in mind, the Stn Clark Centre implemented a five-year tracking study of program graduates.

CONCLUSION

The results show, both in the short and long-term, that BizCamp has had a positive impact on its participants. Whether it's the knowledge of basic business terms and concepts that are measured by the pre- and post-tests or encouraging them to further their education, BizCamp has helped Manitoba youth improve their skill sets.

It has also helped them to develop their sense of self-esteem and prove to themselves they can accomplish things they once thought impossible, for example starting a business or attending a post-secondary institution. Although it has not been entirely successful at curbing the incidence of teen pregnancy, it does appear to have decreased the rate of legal issues faced by participating youth.

These results are one reason the **program has been adopted** by Carleton University in Ottawa, Ontario, Bow Valley College in Calgary, Alberta, and Hebrew University in Jerusalem.

In Israel, two versions of the program are offered. The first targets recent immigrants to Israel, while the second is aimed at Palestinian girls living in the areas surrounding East Jerusalem.

In addition, the Stn Clark Centre is currently working with former Canadian Prime Minister, Paul Martin, on his plans to **offer entrepreneurship training to Aboriginal high school students across Canada**. Specifically, the Stn Clark Centre has agreed to host the teacher training sessions using the NFTE curriculum and instructors for this initiative.

The success of the BizCamp program also explains why the Stn Clark Centre was able to launch a **version** of this camp in 2002 **for middle and upper-middle class children**. Offered in conjunction with the Mini-University program and known as the Asper New Venture, the program is aimed at 10–12 year olds living in Winnipeg. Despite the fact that it is the most expensive non-hockey program offered by Mini-University, the New Venture Adventure program is **always over-subscribed**. It has reached over 300 youths since its launch and was expanded in 2008 to include an advanced course for previous program graduates.

In January 2008, the Stn Clark Centre launched a new program using a version of the BizCamp curriculum. This **new program** is being offered in conjunction with the John Howard Society's Restorative Resolutions program. This program will teach twenty-five **convicted felons** how to turn their life around using the principles of entrepreneurship.

"We must dare to think unthinkable thoughts. We must learn to explore all the options and possibilities that confront us in a complex and rapidly changing world."

James William Fulbright

Chapter Fourteen

Five Classic Challenges for Entrepreneurial Leaders: Coaching and Mentoring Entrepreneurial Winners!

By Marshall Goldsmith

Dr. Marshall Goldsmith is a world authority in helping successful leaders get even better: by achieving positive, lasting change in behavior for themselves, their people, and their teams. He is the co-founder of Marshall Goldsmith Partners, a powerful network of top-level executive coaches. The American Management Association named him as one of the 50 greatest thinkers and leaders who have influenced the field of management over the past 80 years. Business Week listed him as one of the most influential practitioners in the history of leadership development. He served on the Board of the Peter Drucker Foundation. Marshall's twenty-three books

include his latest, "What Got You Here Won't Get You There,"
which was named a N.Y. Times Best Seller, the WSJ #1
Business Book, and the winner of the Longman award as the
Best Business Book of 2007. He teaches executive education at
Dartmouth's Tuck School and began his career as a professor
at Loyola Marymount University.

INTRODUCTION

As the business grows, it can be very difficult for successful entrepreneurs — especially founders — to make the changes needed to take their company to the 'next level' of success.

Any human — in fact any animal — will tend to replicate behavior that is followed by positive reinforcement. As entrepreneurs become increasingly successful, they become more and more likely to fall into the 'superstition trap'. Mathematically speaking, superstition is merely the confusion of two terms — *correlation* and *causality*. What does the 'superstition trap' sound like for founders?

"I started this business. I behave the way that I behave. I have been very successful. Therefore I must be successful because of the way that I behave — and will continue to be successful if I continue behaving this way."

Wrong!

To begin with, every successful person is successful because of doing many things that are brilliant and in spite of doing some things that make no sense. Entrepreneurs are no different. Their overall success can easily mask flaws that can come back to haunt them later.

Even more importantly, as the business grows, entrepreneurs need to 'let go' and realize that past success may have been because of *ME*, their own brilliance and contribution. But in the future, because one person can only handle so much, their success will become a function of *THEM*, the brilliance and contribution of the other professionals that are hired to ensure the continued growth of the business, as well as their own contributions.

Peter Drucker once told me, "We spend a lot of time helping leaders **learn what to DO!** We don't spend enough time helping leaders **learn what to STOP.**" Following are five classic challenges for entrepreneurs — that can often appear on their "Things to stop" list.

Winning too Much

Successful entrepreneurs are among the most competitive people in the world. They love to win! While there is absolutely nothing wrong with winning 'big battles', **the need to win 'all battles' can become a classic problem**. As the business grows, leaders need to learn to let others win and take pride in the victories of their staff members.

Bob is one of my favorite entrepreneurial founders. While being generally seen as an excellent leader, he received 360° feedback from direct reports and co-workers that indicated he had an annoying need to 'win' and 'be right' all of the time — which shut off the flow of honest upward communication and honest dialogue in the organization. As I discussed this feedback with Bob he immediately went into the 'they are wrong' mode.

"What do they mean I discourage honest dialogue?" he snorted. "No one loves a debate more than I do! I was even the captain of my debate team in college."

This annoyed response — combined with his feedback — painted a clear picture for me. I went on to illustrate how his 'debating' felt to the other person. "Imagine that I am three levels below you in the company. In front of the Executive Committee, I have the courage to present an idea that you might not love. Then you, the CEO, immediately leap into 'debate mode' — in front of everyone — and begin shooting down my ideas so that you can 'win' the debate and prove that I am wrong."

"What is wrong with that?" Bob countered. "What's wrong with a healthy debate?"

I replied, "There is nothing wrong with a healthy debate if it is a 'fair fight'. Here is the problem. You are the founder and CEO. You are highly respected. You are this person's boss's, boss's boss. You were the Captain of the debate team at one of the world's best colleges. While you may choose to believe that you are engaging in a 'debate', the other person feels like he is being 'stepped on'. His co-workers, who are watching this drama, feel that you are stifling communication and exhibiting your excessive need to 'win' and 'be right' at the expense of the company."

As Bob reflected upon his feedback, 'the light bulb went off'. He realized that while his 'debating' intentions may have been good, the outcome of his behavior was damaging to the company.

As their businesses grow, entrepreneurs need to learn to 'win' the big battles and, as hard as it may be, let others 'win' the rest.

Starting with 'No', 'But', or 'However'

The 'good news' is that successful entrepreneurs tend to be driven. The 'bad news' is that their desire to win and be right can translate into stubbornness. One of my coaching clients had a tendency to 'win too much' and 'be right' all of the time. When I was reviewing his 360 degree feedback his first reaction was, "But, Marshall, I don't do that."

"That one is free," I said, "The next time I am speaking with you and you begin a sentence with 'no', 'but', or 'however', I am going to fine you $20."

"But," he replied, "that's not..."

"That will be $20!"

"No, I don't..." he started to try to argue.

"That's $40!"

"No, no, no," he protested.

"That's $60, 80, 100 dollars," I laughed.

Within an hour, he was down $420. It took another two hours before he finally understood and said, "Thank you."

This gentleman got so much better at being viewed as more open to different ideas — and much less stubborn — after learning this simple rule. Don't start sentences with 'no', 'but', or 'however', if you really want to hear what other people have to say.

If someone is trying to speak to us and the first word out of our mouth is 'no', what message do we send to the other person? You are wrong! Not, I disagree or I have a differing opinion — but you are wrong!

If someone is trying to speak to us and the first word out of our mouth is 'but', we have subtly said, "I would like to disregard everything that you just told me." The word 'however' is just a fancier version of 'but'!

On another note, most of the challenges that entrepreneurial leaders have at work also show up at home. If we are stubborn and opinionated at work, it is highly unlikely that we become excessively open-minded when we go home!

A suggestion for entrepreneurial leaders — who are perceived as stubborn — is to start having everyone that they know 'fine' them for starting sentences with 'no', 'but', or 'however'. Many entrepreneurial leaders have entrepreneurial children! Teenage children will love this system for helping their parents get better — while they are making a few bucks!

Punishing the Messenger

A worse habit than starting with 'no', 'but', or 'however' is punishing the messenger. When leaders punish messengers, we not only show we are stubborn — we prove that we will 'lash out' at anyone who gives us the bad news! In the short-term, punishing the messenger may make us feel better. We get to 'vent' — and don't have to hear what we don't want to hear. In the long-term, punishing the messenger can be a disaster. We stop learning what we need to learn — often until 'bad news' comes too late.

I will give you a personal example of a case when I totally failed in 'practicing what I preach'. I was frantically driving to the airport. My wife, Lyda, was sitting next to me in the front seat — with my two kids in the back. Lyda (who, to make things worse, is a Ph.D. Clinical Psychologist) saw a red light ahead and yelled, "Look out — there is a red light up ahead!"

Rather than just say, "Thank you!" I snapped, "I know there is a red light ahead, don't you think I can see!"

For some reason, as I departed for the plane, Lyda didn't seem interested in talking to me. I didn't get my normal goodbye kiss. Both kids gave me their best "what an idiot" look!

After landing in New York — and feeling ashamed of my stupid behavior — I called Lyda and apologized. I assured her that the next time she corrected my driving, I would just say, "Thank you."

"We will see!" she replied with a healthy dose of skepticism.

Sure enough a few months passed. I forgot about this event. Lyda looked and said, "Watch out for the stop sign!"

My face turned crimson, I grimaced, starting breathing hard, and yelled, "Thank you!"

I am a long way from perfect, but I am getting better!

Entrepreneurial leaders can benefit from a simple strategy that I share with my corporate clients. **When people tell us what we don't want to hear, get in the habit of just saying 'Thank you'.** This will give us a chance to back away — really think about what we are hearing — and recognize that, just sometimes, the message that we least want to hear is the message that we most need to hear.

Adding too Much Value

My friend, Dr. David Ulrich, is a highly-respected thought leader, wonderful person, and perhaps the world's top HR consultant. Dave once taught me that effective performance can be seen as a function of the quality of an idea times the employee's commitment to make it happen ($EP = QI \times C$). One hundred percent commitment to a good idea will often result in higher performance than fifty percent commitment to a great idea!

Leaders, especially entrepreneurial founders, often get so enamored with sharing insights — aimed at improving the quality of an idea — that they forget about the impact that these insights may have on their employee's commitment to execute the idea.

When I asked one new CEO what he had learned about leadership in the past year, he sighed and sadly noted, "My suggestions become orders. If I want my suggestions to become orders, they are orders. If I don't want them to become orders, they are orders anyway!" While this learning is true for all leaders, it is especially true for respected founders of the business.

As his coach, I then asked him to name the lesson that he had learned from me that he felt was the most useful. He smiled and replied, "You helped me understand one lesson that not only caused me to become a better CEO — it helped me to have a happier life! The lesson was simple, **before I speak — I need to stop — take a breath — then ask myself, 'Is it worth it?'**" He went on to note that fifty percent of the time that he asked this question, he decided, "Am I right? Maybe! Is it worth it? No!"

As leaders, our first reaction upon hearing an idea from direct reports may be to say, "That's a great idea, BUT..." and then add our brilliant insights. What we fail to think about is that our attempt to improve the idea may do more harm than good. If we aren't careful, the idea will no longer be their idea — it will become our idea.

Two suggestions for entrepreneurial leaders are:

- The next time you are working with a direct report or team member and you start to "improve" upon their ideas with your insights — take a deep breath and ask yourself, "Is it worth it?"

- When communicating with direct reports, don't just ask for understanding — search for commitment. Listen to the tone of their voices and look at their faces. When describing a project ask the employee to rank their level of enthusiasm for executing the plan. Ask them a simple question, "How can we work together on this project in a way that will lead to your highest level of commitment?" Listen to their ideas. Be willing to trade off some of your insights on content to gain their commitment and enthusiasm.

As Peter Drucker sagely noted, "Most leaders I meet manage knowledge workers. These are people who know more about what they are doing than their boss does."

As Lao Tzu sagely noted, **"When a true leader's work is done — the people will say they did it themselves."**

When managing knowledge workers in an entrepreneurial company, keep this thought in mind — if they don't believe that they did it themselves — it probably didn't get done very well!

Goal Obsession

Entrepreneurs, almost by definition, are obsessed with achieving their goals. **Goal obsession occurs when the achievement of a *goal* may come at the expense of the *mission*.**

One classic danger for technically gifted entrepreneurs is 'falling in love' with products and becoming so focused on their goal, creating a great machine, that they forget about their mission, making money!

Another danger for successful entrepreneurs is to become so focused on their work life that they damage their family life. One successful leader I met was complaining because he had to work so many hours. When I asked him why he was working so hard he snarled, "Why do you think that I work so hard? I want to make lots of money!"

"Why do you need so much money?" I asked.

"I have been married three times. You have no idea how much I have to pay in alimony and child support!" he retorted.

"Why have you been married three times?" I asked.

"Because none of my wives understood how hard I had to work." he sighed.

In California, many entrepreneurs work incredibly hard for years to acquire financial value. They then proceed to ruin their marriages and immediately lose fifty percent of everything they made. **How smart is that?**

Even worse than financial damage, this type of goal obsession can cause personal damage. Entrepreneurs are just as human as everyone else. When I have asked, "What is the most important thing in your life?" to business leaders, "Family" comes out as the number one response. Yet, leaders can get so obsessed with achieving business goals to help their families that they can lose the families that they are trying to help.

A wonderful example of entrepreneurial leadership — and goal obsession — can be found in the Academy Award winning movie *The Bridge on the River Kwai*. The main character, Colonel Nicholson, is a classic entrepreneurial leader. He is a prisoner of war in Burma who leads his men to build a bridge for his Japanese captors. Like many entrepreneurial leaders, Nicholson has high integrity, is dedicated to excellence, and is creative enough to create a wonderful product with limited resources. He skillfully inspires his men to build a near-perfect bridge.

By the film's end, he finds himself in the painful position of defending the bridge from attack by fellow British officers who want to destroy it — to prevent Japanese trains from using it. There's a chilling moment of realization, right before the bridge is detonated, when Nicholson (played by Alec Guinness) utters the famous line, "What have I done?" He was so focused on his goal — building the bridge — that he forgot his larger mission — winning the war!

Our drive to achieve our goals can become a paradoxical trait that is usually a source of our success, but taken too far, can become blatant causes of failure.

Entrepreneurial leaders should continually review their goals — and the amount of effort they are applying to achieving these goals — against their mission. They should also reflect upon their larger mission in life and ensure that their business goals are supporting — not destroying their mission as a human being.

IN SUMMARY

Winning, adding value, being stubborn, and achieving goals can all be wonderful — until they are taken too far. Of all of the leaders that I have met, entrepreneurial leaders would rank near the top in terms of their desire to win, add value, prove they are right, and achieve goals. **Their major challenge is not 'turning on' these desires when they are needed — it is 'turning off' these desires when they do more harm than good.**

By continually asking, "Is this battle worth winning? Is this value worth adding? Should I be listening to this messenger?" and "Is this goal worth achieving?" entrepreneurial leaders can help make the transition from the founder of a small firm, who is driving the business through personal desire and ability, to the leader of a larger firm, who is building the team required to move the business to the next level. They can 'learn to learn' from all of the great people they have hired to move their company to the next level of success!

"When I dare to be powerful, to use my strength in the service of my vision, then it becomes less and less important whether I am afraid."

Audre Lord

Chapter Fifteen

The Entrepreneur's Ethical Survival Kit

By Arthur Gross-Schaefer

Dr. Arthur Gross-Schaefer is truly a "man for all seasons" in many respects. He is a JD, a CPA, a Rabbi (with an active Temple in Santa Barbara), an M.H.L., has been a Professor of Law and Ethics at Loyola Marymount University for 29 years, and is the Chairman of the Marketing and Business Law program at LMU. He is also extremely active in the Ethics activities at LMU. In addition to teaching and writing about law topics, including constitutional, employment, and general business law, he has done substantial instruction and publishing in the area of ethics for lawyers, accountants, and business and religious professionals. Professor Gross-Schaefer lectures for various state bars, accounting societies, law firms, legal administrators, businesses, and religious organizations. His current research centers on such topics as spirituality in the

workplace, issues surrounding clergy sexual misconduct, and the effectiveness of ethics education.

INTRODUCTION

One often does not ordinarily think of the **need for a survival kit** unless one is going for a long trek in the wilderness or is experiencing a major natural disaster where normal support systems are disrupted. One thinks of needing basic items such as food, shelter, warmth, and information so that one can endure and make informed decisions that one hopes will ultimately lead to a **place of safety**.

An entrepreneur is in a similar situation and needs an ethical survival kit.

As one chooses to be an **entrepreneur**, one is **by definition going into uncharted regions where it is easy to get lost and overwhelmed**. Accordingly, one should plan for these eventualities by **thinking ahead and taking essential moral, mental, and ethical tools that will be needed to overcome those challenges**. At the same time, like a natural disaster, many obstacles may be unplanned and catastrophic. One requires that the ethical tools be flexible, easy to use, and effective. Thus, the entrepreneur should have an internal ethics toolbox to meet the known and the unknown tests that will certainly be placed in one's entrepreneurial journey.

Unlike many academic articles that are well-documented with theories and discussion, this chapter is meant to be practical, effective, and very user-friendly. Because entrepreneurs need to move fast and carry only what is needed, so too these tools will not slow one down. On the other hand, these tools will be critical to one's business and personal success. Here is a path to take in building one's Entrepreneurs Ethical Tool Kit.

Articulating a Destination: Personal Mission Statements

The first part of the kit is a personal mission statement. There is an old saying: "If you don't know where you are going, you'll never know when you arrive." Businesses and institutions historically have felt the need to have mission statements so everyone is on the same page and the goals are generally understood.

Similarly, every individual needs to take time to focus on goals in terms of business, as well as in regards to family and individual objectives. One does not live by bread alone, and similarly, one does not live by their business or career aspirations without **appropriate considerations regarding who one is and who one wants to become**, especially in relation to those they care about. In a personal mission statement, one is able to communicate goals, motivations, dreams, as well as challenges that need to be addressed. Here is an ancient mission statement that is powerful in terms of career, but does not include issues of family and self.

Before I begin the holy work of healing the creations of Your hands, I place my entreaty before the throne of Your glory that you grant strength of spirit and fortitude to faithfully execute my work.

Let not desire for wealth or benefit blind me from seeing truth. Deem me worthy of seeing in the sufferer who seeks my advice, a person, neither rich nor poor, friend or foe, good man or bad. Of a man in distress, show me only that man.

If doctors wiser than me seek to help me to understand, grant me the desire to learn from them, for the knowledge of healing is boundless. But when fools deride me, give me fortitude.

Let my love for my profession strengthen my resolve to withstand the derision even of men of high station. Illuminate the way for me, for any lapse in my knowledge can bring illness and death upon your creations.

I beseech You, merciful and gracious God, strengthen me in body and soul, and instill within me a perfect spirit.

On the other hand, here are three sample mission statements from business students that present a more balanced focus:

I feel duty to help my fellow man. I accomplish what needs to be done. I manage my life to achieve proper balance. I challenge myself. I learn because of want, choice, privilege, and obligation. I always look at the bigger picture and take unimportant things in stride. I find humor in life and its many situations. I am not infallible; moreover, when I make mistakes, I fix them if I am able to do so. I cultivate relationships to have a healthy personal life and to learn about myself and others. I love my family. I am successful in my professional life. I act in a manner befitting of an ethical person. I keep an open mind. I always try to learn about other cultures, identity, and history to fully understand my fellow man. (D. Cline)

My mission is to lead a balanced life centered by the principals and morals taught by my family and my religion. I will strive to do the right thing even when it is hard. I will follow my dreams and aspirations, yet remember what is most important to me is my husband, my children, my family, and my friends. I will continue to build a future for my family financially, spiritually, and emotionally. I will live in the present, enjoy life, and thrive from whatever life brings me. I will remember that when times are tough, I am strong and I share my strength with those who need me. I am a mentor to many and compassionate to all. (E. Hook)

I endeavor to be seen as both trustworthy and kind. I hope to be a good son, brother, friend, and companion. In all of these relationships I intend to be loyal and helpful. In my work I hope to be attentive to detail and hardworking, while constantly growing and not remaining stagnant. I also wish to strive to be knowledgeable and understanding of those I work with and around, while providing myself with a financially stable and comfortable life. (N. Smith)

Mapping the Route: Personal Core Values

After the creation of the business mission statement, a **list of core values should be established that reflect the mission statement**. Personal mission statements are important but may be forgotten or ignored when making decisions due to the length of the statement or the lack of clear direction that can be applied to a specific situation.

Core values, on the other hand, are a quick way to remind one of those touchstone concepts meant to direct one's journey. **Core values are generally one or two words** that express essential values such as honesty, integrity, promise keeping, compassion, excellence (a more expansive list is found below). Not only will this list of core values be easier to remember, but it can also be more easily applied when using the values decision model described below.

Generally, a short list of six or seven core values is preferable to a long grocery list that, through its efforts to include all values, loses its impact and usefulness. Some individuals and businesses list their core values on the bottom of their stationary, both as a reminder to themselves and as a public announcement of their commitment to ethical considerations in their business practices. Here is a more expanded list of values. As stated before, these are all important values. Nevertheless, the entrepreneur needs to keep the tool kit light and adaptable by selecting six or seven core values that are of prime importance for inclusion in the tool kit.

- **honesty** — truth telling, candidness, openness

- **integrity** — acting on convictions, courage, advocacy, leadership by example

- **promise keeping** — fulfilling the spirit of commitments

- **fidelity** — loyalty, confidentiality

- **fairness** — justice, equal treatment, diversity, independence

- **caring** — compassion, kindness

- **respect** — human dignity and uniqueness

- **citizenship** — respect for law, social consciousness

- **excellence** — quality of work

- **accountability** — responsibility, independence.

The Bridge Over Troubled Waters: The Personal Values Decision Model

Following the creation of an individual mission statement and core values, a values based decision model can be introduced. The least complicated ethics decision-making models simply **presume that all decisions will be made public on national television and that one's parents and colleagues will be watching.** If one still feels comfortable with his or her decision after the make-believe broadcast and the decision is in line with their personal core values, **then the actions will probably have some ethical validity.**

However, this simplistic type of model does not utilize core ethical values significantly, nor does it really help one think through various options or better appreciate the perspective of those who may have a stake in the decision.

The following ethics decision model is offered simply as an option. This model has been published previously and effectively used for businesses, legal and accounting professionals, medical situations, as well as individual decisions. However, while this model has proved very valuable in a variety of situations, **it should only be used as a guide, since each individual should take time to create a model that is tailored to their own needs, specific, comfortable, and useful**. A user-friendly decision model is much more practical than a complex and cumbersome one that looks good but is rarely utilized.

A Suggested Strategy for Ethical Decision Making

Define the problem carefully, and be certain all of the pertinent information has been gathered. Too often we act without taking time to obtain the necessary information.

- **List all the parties** you believe may be affected by the decision (stakeholders). A decision that does not take into account the way in which it will affect others is not an ethical one regardless of its actual consequences.

- **List all the personal and work-related values** that are involved in the decision. One may want to consult the list of values presented earlier in the article.

- **List all the possible alternatives** of what you can or cannot do. Often, we believe we have only a limited number of options when really there are several others. Alternatives may resolve the situation in a way that produces either the greater good or the lesser harm.

- **Chose and prioritize.**

  - **Of all the parties** you listed above, **select the one** that you believe is most important for purposes of making this decision.

  - **Of all the values** you listed above, **select the one** you believe is most important for purposes of making this decision.

  - **Of all the options** you listed above, **select the one** you believe will cause the greatest good, or least harm.

- **Make a decision** based on the above priorities.

- **Devise a strategy** that will effectively implement your decision.

This model is useful both for making decisions and for conflict resolution. Should other co-workers utilize this model, there will be a commonly accepted step-by-step process allowing for dialogue as well as provide a logical procedure that will help reduce conflicts that are all too often the result of emotional quagmires. This model is **no silver bullet will certainly not work in every situation**, but it sure is an important and proven tool.

BUILDING A BASE CAMP
THE CREATION OF A MORE ETHICAL
WORKING ENVIRONMENT

Even with the best of intent, the pressure to lose one's way, to forget one's mission, can be very powerful, even overwhelming. Accordingly, **one needs to consciously create**

a supportive environment. Here are four elements that have been found to be highly useful:

1. Six Months Income in the Bank

This is very hard when one is an entrepreneur and probably using all their assets just to give their business a chance. When one is faced with a difficult ethical choice, one is already **tempted to take the course of action that will create the most personal benefit**, however that benefit is defined. Add to that pressure a financial dimension, and the strain can become almost unbearable. For example, if one is already at one's financial limits and lives from paycheck to paycheck, a threat of losing one's project may prove beyond one's strength to resist, especially if there is a family involved. Therefore, it is **essential to have some money in reserve**, such as six months income, so that one will know that if they do stand up for their principles, there is a reserve. **This may provide just enough of a cushion to enable one to follow their higher values.**

2. Friends Outside of Business Associates

We are all so busy that we not only spend most of our time at work related activities, but also with work related individuals. Rather than hanging out with friends, we are often spending time with work associates. One of the concerns with this reality is that the values of the workplace, as adapted by the employees, become reflected by those around us.

For example, the workers in Enron and Arthur Anderson reduced the significance of the illegal and unethical actions they were involved in due to the **rational that everyone else around them was doing the same things**. It is therefore important to keep oneself surrounded by people not associated with one's work. People who will be able to **provide a more objective assessment** and hopefully be strong enough to **raise red flags and ask good questions** that may protect one from engaging in inappropriate activities.

3. Activities Outside of Business

The motivations to act unethically can be quite complex and stem from a variety of factors. A key factor includes one's self-perception, as well as how one is perceived by others. While **many might believe unethical actions are prompted by monetary gain, they may ignore the powerful social influences of acceptance**. People generally like being viewed as successful and might act unethically to retain such status.

One person in prison shared how he **liked being seen as successful and would actually do**, some illegal and **unethical actions to uphold this perception**. However, if there are other involvements outside of work, such as with a church or a non-profit-foundation, they can continue to be successful, but in alternative venues. **Being involved in other activities where one can shine may reduce the motivation to engage in inappropriate conduct at work.**

4. Values Audit

No matter how strong and well-developed one's personal values have become, the **environment at work will sorely put our values to the test**. The assault from the values found at work may be either subtle or quite obvious depending on a variety of factors. Either way, one must **be fully aware that there will be a battle, even a war, of values that will be triggered when one enters the work place**.

Rather than be passive, one needs to **take a proactive approach** by not only appreciating the existence of the conflict, but also taking time to monitor and discern the existing workplace values. One can certainly do this through observation and inquiry of others.

Another technique that is more detailed and effective is through the use of a 'values audit.' This tool is generally used by businesses as a training and self-assessment tool. Its details will be discussed more fully later on in this monograph. A modified version can be created in which one's personal values are laid out and a series of questions are constructed to assess the ethical environment of the company they are about to enter or partner with.

While some entrepreneurs may never choose to work for others, these questions are critically important to help guide the creation of their business so as to be both a setting that they can be proud of as well as an attractive environment to future employees. Following are some sample questions:

- To what extent would I be comfortable in this work environment?

- To what extent would I be able to honestly represent this company?

- To what extent would I be proud of the work I am doing?

- To what extent are the company's morals and mission in line with my own values?

- To what extent would I feel comfortable with the position that I would be in?

- To what extent would my family feel proud of the work that I am performing?

- Do the company's activities contribute to society?

- Is the work environment fair?

- Can I succeed at this company without compromising my ethics?

- Will I be treated equally?

- Will I be happy for the next five years working for this company?

- Will I have my boss' support?

GOING PUBLIC — INCORPORATE VALUES INTO YOUR BUSINESS

After an entrepreneur has developed an ethical identity with a personal mission statement, core values, and decision model, one has a **foundation, a strong base**, from which to infuse ethics into the business activity. One can incorporate, with integrity and ingenuity, the importance of values into the business enterprise.

The first major step, as discussed earlier with the individual, is to create a new or revised mission statement for the organization that will recognize the additional focus on values and spirituality. Rather than a top-down process, where the CEO or management simply announce a new mission statement, a stronger approach would be one that allows for employee input from the very beginning.

Perhaps one could create a bottom-up process with a working group to review or create a new mission statement that would embody a vision of the company **including values and spirituality**. This process would send an important message of the priority being given to the areas of values and spirituality, as well as to signal and begin the modeling of a collaborative decision making process.

After the creation of the business mission statement, a list of business core values should be established that reflect the mission statement. Rather than focusing on more personal values such as integrity and honesty, other core values may be introduced such as excellence of product or a culture of appreciation. As previously suggested, mission statements are important but are often forgotten or ignored when making decisions, and this is often due to the length of the statements or the lack of a clear direction.

Core values, on the other hand, are a quick way to both remind workers of, and announce to the public the values that govern the business. As with the mission statement, a bottom-up process that allows input in its formation sends a powerful message of collaboration. A company may even want to reward workers for their involvement in the process including their suggestions. It may want to institutionalize a process of reward for workers' involvement and contribution of ideas in the development of an ethical environment.

Here is an expanded list of appropriate core values that may be appropriate for a business enterprise to consider adopting. As expressed previously, it is better to have six or seven core values/goals to help focus the institution rather than a larger number resulting in is a lack of focus.

• Professionalism

• Quality product/ingredients

• Collegiality

• Promise keeping

- Compassion

- Loyalty

- Respect for life

- Fairness

- Honesty

- Integrity

- Honest and full communication

- Trust

- Being a good citizen/respect for law

- Equal responsibility for management/administration

- Balance between family and work

- Slow growth

- Value diversity of members

- Culture of appreciation

- Joy in work

- Accountability for decisions

- Mentoring/legacy

- Consistency of policies

- Quality representation

- Responsibility.

Following the creation or revision of a company mission statement and core values, a values-based decision model can be introduced. The decision model presented earlier, for example, could be introduced to the workforce as well as the officers and directors. This will give a common language and an effective tool that will help to resolve conflicts and announce that values are an important aspect of the business enterprise.

Once one has a sense of values in the work environment, one can now make an assessment. Perhaps the values are, by and large, consistent with one's own values, and there is little conflict. Or, **if the values gap is large, one can decide if it is a place that may not be an appropriate work environment**. Either way, the person becomes aware and can make a more informed decision about the future.

CREATION OF A MORE ETHICAL WORKING ENVIRONMENT

Similar to the individual tool kit, a business enterprise has the tools to create a more ethical working environment. Nevertheless, **there needs to be an analysis of how seriously ethical considerations will be applied in the daily operations**. Any individual working in an organization will feel constrained and guided by the perceived values of that organization. Whether it is a multi-national corporation or a small-town grocery store, each establishment has its own ethical environment. **People know by simple observation what their organization's ethical priorities are and act accordingly.**

In general, people will act based upon how they perceive the culture of the organization as a whole. If the organization rewards one's behavior, ethical or unethical, such a system will influence how an employee will perform. Yet, in spite of this reality, there is rarely a bona fide, agreed upon, and accepted system that allows an organization to consistently focus and refocus on whether or not it embodies the values it professes. **Clearly, individuals and organizations have great difficulty implementing a holistic self-examination.**

In the article, *The Moral Manager*, the author made the following conclusions about companies in general:

- Few organizations step back often enough to assess the character of their workplace.

- If such an assessment were properly and objectively conducted, it could be very revealing as to the organization's character.

- An assessment of an organization's workplace character is probably the most serious exercise an organization will ever perform.

Therefore, based on these conclusions, it is essential for an institution to observe their respective workplace character in order to better understand their institution's ethical environment. Also, it is important to remember people do not exist and make decisions in isolation. Hence, it is imperative that organizations **utilize internal audits** that combine the context of individually-based ethics with the social systems within which their employees operate.

Moreover, any audit that purports to examine ethics inside an organization **must look outside the organization** as well, since situational and environmental factors have a significant impact upon the ethical behaviors and subsequent policies of an organization. What is clearly needed within an organization is an ethics audit that goes beyond individually-based ethical theory and includes the dimensions of the organization, the social system, and the milieu in which the practice operates.

An ethics audit should be viewed as a firm's wellness tool. The creation of such an audit develops a system of awareness, while simultaneously acting as a self-regulating tool. The ethics audit raises the self-awareness of unethical behavior, thereby heightening ethical actions and preventing corruption within the institution. When an institution uses the audit, it can become a very powerful force for change.

Key categories which must be included in an ethics audit are: areas of social responsibility, open communication, treatment of employees, confidentiality, respect of employees, community values, vendor relationships, leadership by example, human investment, and ecology. The following are sample questions from an ethics audit that attempt to incorporate the aforementioned key categories.

THE ETHICS AUDIT: SAMPLE QUESTIONS

Consider Open Communication

Do we keep organization members informed honestly as to all relevant matters?

- Are decisions made in an open and honest manner with an opportunity for input from all relevant sources?

- Do the employees feel they have free and open access to the organization's leadership?

Audit Confidentiality and Respect for all Members of the Firm

Do we avoid gossip and cliques, and do we maintain confidentiality?

- Is private information about employees (emotional stability, marriage and financial status, etc.) kept confidential and used appropriately?

- Does the organization's leadership actively avoid engaging in gossip?

Look at the Human Investment

What is the provision for the physical, psychological, and economic welfare of present, potential, and former (including retired) employees?

- Does the organization provide fair benefits (pension, social security, medical, etc.) for all of its employees?

- Does the organization have an employee handbook that clearly sets forth its policies for vacation, sick days, family leave, disability, etc.?

- Does the organization handle contract negotiations in a timely and ethical manner?

What is Your Impact on the Ecology of Your Environment?

Efforts to minimize the negative impact of your operations on the natural environment.

- Has the organization taken sufficient steps to conserve natural resources?

- Does the organization attempt to support energy conservation and recycling activities?

And Finally, How Would You Describe The Ethical Status of Your Firm?

- How seriously does the organization take the consideration of ethical issues?

- Does the organization provide an ongoing ethics education program?

- If the activities of the organization were to be made public, would you be proud of your association?

The time taken to **create and implement both an ethical decision model and an ethics audit** is time well spent improving the organization's workplace culture. Creating these ethical tools and using them as aids for measuring and **understanding dissonance between a person's values and a person's actual activities** will help curb employee frustrations and dissatisfaction, while ultimately cultivating a healthy workforce. These internal **ethics tools are not meant to be sources of guilt, but rather as wellness devices** that enhance the achievements of the modern entrepreneur and their firm.

OTHER CONSIDERATIONS

In addition to the mission statement, core values, decision model, and values audit described above, there are many additional arrangements that can be used to create a stronger ethical and values focus; for instance, there are many tools that can also be used to help create an increased focus on ethics and spirituality. There are therefore a variety of tools that can help with the general goal of augmented meaning.

The first step begins in the hiring process. Rather then simply hiring to fulfill a particular job description, **begin to 'hire for mission.'** Hiring for mission suggests one not only hires skilled and highly-motivated employees, one also attempts to hire workers whose core values mirror, for the most part, the core values of the workplace.

Hiring for mission also presupposes that an effective workplace environment is made up of individuals whose perception is not only more closely aligned, but also who seriously understand that what they are doing has meaning and make a positive contribution to society. In this way, the synergy will create more creativity, excitement, and energy. Honestly, this focus on the meaning of one's work is a spiritual focus.

When one understands whatever they do can make the world a better or kinder place and co-workers are other spiritual beings to be treated respectfully and with a sense of wonder, the workplace is transformed. Workers form stronger and better teams and there is a greater sense of partnership and pride.

There is a need to **provide ethics education on a regular basis**. Education programs provide basic skills, such as using the decision model in making difficult decisions. An ethics education program also makes a strong management statement that ethics is important and is to be considered a central part of the business enterprise. Finally, training in ethical principles may reduce employee theft and internal misreporting. Ethics training is perhaps an even more fundamental tool that can be used to enhance the internal audit effort and meet the common objectives of that function and the organization.

Supplementary **techniques include a peer review system, setting achievable goals, and utilizing job rotation**.

Providing feedback from co-workers who have similar experiences provides appropriate and honest advice without the often-faced aspect of inappropriateness when job performance evaluations come from supervisors who may not have sufficient comprehension of current needs or technology.

And, if the **peer review** includes training on using positive feedback and "I" statements, the process of evaluation turns from a focus on judgment to a **forum for improvement**. Setting realistic goals that are generally agreed upon, as opposed to oppressive goals that stretch one to the breaking point, reduce stress and increase creativity and job satisfaction.

In many ways, the manner and the reasonableness of the expectation teaches an employee about how they are viewed by management. A top-down continual demand of "more and more" clearly conveys employees are objects that are expected to wear out and be replaced. A more sensible **partnership-based approach** evidences the fair treatment of employees is central and their perspectives are to be considered.

Job rotation, while not always practical, can be another way for management to demonstrate employees are individuals who can become bored with the work routine. Developing opportunities aimed at keeping employees interested and excited helps to not only renew their energy, but also their resourcefulness, which translates into greater job satisfaction as well as job performance.

If job rotation is not practical, there are additional methods to enliven the work experience such as **supporting participation in philanthropies** and encouraging workers to **guest lecture or teach at local schools**. Furthermore, offering training on topics such as time management, a healthy balance between family and work, and spiritual practices all send very positive messages.

Adding a focus on space, such as providing a **meditation room**, combines to form an environment that will promote workers' mental, physical and spiritual well-being. Simply put, an ethical/ spiritual environment combines attitudes, practices, programs and environmental considerations.

CONCLUSION

Whether an entrepreneur works in a garage or in a large business organization, our actions will often be tied up with ethical considerations. The question will deal with how aware we are of the ethical implications, and how well we have created an ethical survival kit to help us successfully meet the challenges.

Will our interactions reflect our core values, the values we hold to be most significant? Too often we do not take sufficient time to step back and truly look to see if there is a gap between our conduct and our core values. By not taking time to identify and understand the reasons for the gap between our convictions and reality, we risk losing sight altogether of what it was we sought to accomplish.

When one acts outside the boundaries set by one's core values, the individual's own character and self-image become compromised. Ultimately, one's goals and very effectiveness can be undermined. Rather than pursuing a direction charted by our principles, we often allow the gale of pressing problems or political currents control our destiny and how we effectuate our values. This disparity, even if not fully apparent, can produce antagonism, hostility, disenchantment, and simple frustration. Before long, we wonder why we acted the way we did and why we have not been able to actualize our highest convictions.

In psychology, the term 'cognitive dissonance' is used to express the uneasiness one feels when one does not act in accordance with one's values and beliefs. It is that very feeling of being at odds with oneself that we often feel in our daily lives.

For example, if a woman is working full-time and cannot find the balance between her professional life and her role as a mother, she may feel cognitive dissonance. More commonly, when one buys an expensive item, there may be a feeling of cognitive dissonance stemming from the fact that he might have spent too much money or that there was a better product he later became aware of. This is a dangerous situation for both the individual and the organization the person works with because often, when the goals of the individual get lost, the effectiveness of the enterprise diminishes as well.

Organizations, too, have 'core values' which are either enhanced or diminished by the actions of its prominent players. Business professionals are major actors in any organization, and their actions affect the implementation of the institution's values. When such a person acts in his or her capacity within the institution, those actions not only represent, but also in effect control, direct, and alter the expression of the institution's values. If a business professional is unaware and unable to follow his or her own core values, so too may he or she be incapable of following the organizational core values. Over time, the professional's actions may corrupt and impair the institution's ability to follow its own principles.

Thus, **the entrepreneur** and the organization within which they lead **ought to take the necessary time to create** and use the tools offered in this article to help insure the creation and maintenance of **an ethical environment**.

Ethics, when intentionally combined with the actions of entrepreneurs, **will provide significant benefits to the entrepreneur**, managers, executives, employees, customers, and the entire working environment.

"The highest reward for a person's toil is not what they get for it, but what they become by it."

John Ruskin

Chapter Sixteen

Making Entrepreneurial Finance Relevant and Interesting for Aspiring Entrepreneurs

A Users Guide for Helping the Entrepreneur to Find the Pot of Gold for Starting their Business

By David Choi

David Y. Choi, Ph.D. is an Assistant Professor of Management and Entrepreneurship and Associate Director of the Center for Entrepreneurship at Loyola Marymount University. David has worked nearly 15 years as a management consultant and executive at Fortune 500 companies and entrepreneurial ventures. He received his Ph.D. in Management

from UCLA, and an M.S. & B.S. in Industrial Engineering from UC Berkeley.

OOOOH! WHAT A COOL SUBJECT!

It's no secret: Entrepreneurial Finance is a tremendously exciting, thrilling, stimulating, and electrifying subject! It's a topic I talk and think about day and night. I enjoy thinking about it more than sports, vacationing, or partying. I talk about it over dinner, drinks, and dessert. My friends and I even get excited chatting about the deals that our friends, or we, have completed, failed, or are currently pursuing. We talk about the deals we should undertake next, while laughing about the ones that we dropped or did not pan out. (I should mention that I don't have many hobbies.)

And why wouldn't Entrepreneurial Finance be an exciting subject? It's a subject that holds secrets as to how to creatively access valuable resources, unlock growth potential of a business, and achieve personal wealth in the process. The subject deals with such appealing aspects as formulating a vision, selling your idea to others, developing creative strategies for negotiation, and coming to an agreement, among many others. Each one is so exhilarating that I think Hollywood movies should be made of them.

Entrepreneurial Finance is a critical expertise for today's entrepreneurs. In today's competitive business environment, entrepreneurs need to be not only passionate, courageous, visionary, risk-taking, bold, etc. to succeed, but **also finance-savvy**.

By "finance," I am not referring to financial theory like the Capital Asset Pricing model or the Modigliani-Miller Theorem, which business students are taught in Corporate

Finance classes. These are important topics, but in reality are not relevant to most entrepreneurs and venture financiers. The finance skills necessary for entrepreneurship are those that are of direct practical value to financing, operation, and growth of entrepreneurial ventures — Entrepreneurial Finance.

Most entrepreneurship educators I have talked with share similar experiences.

Some of the most common questions from aspiring or practicing entrepreneurs have been about money, e.g., "How do I get the funding I need?" In my experience, **the most common regrets among entrepreneurs also have to do with money**.

I have known far too many entrepreneurs who could not cash in on their own success! Many were unable to grow their business because of their **inadequate understanding of what investors want**, how they think, or how the capital market operates. On the other hand, some of the smartest entrepreneurs I have met were able to build substantial enterprises through very creative methods of financing.

So I pose the questions: Why aren't most entrepreneurs more skilled in Entrepreneurial Finance? And why aren't more Entrepreneurship students thrilled about the class?

One obvious reason as to why more of today's entrepreneurs are NOT familiar with the subject is that, until recently, there were **hardly any courses offered on this subject**. Compared to most subjects in business (and even compared to other Entrepreneurship courses) Entrepreneurial Finance is of a very recent vintage.

Second, a **majority of the teaching and courses** on this subject still **miss the mark**. They are often too theoretical, academic, and

do not offer the practical and useful insights that to day's entrepreneurs need in order to finance and grow their businesses.

Other courses are too narrow in scope, covering only a certain
type of financing or a particular industry, potentially limiting
the career options for some of the students. And unfortunately
the fun, thrill, and seat-of-your-pants excitement associated
with Entrepreneurial Finance is not shared in the teaching
process. Consequently, the only people who tend to find the
course interesting are some Finance students, while the
Entrepreneurship majors — representing many of the aspiring
entrepreneurs — find the course boring, intimidating, overly
technical, and irrelevant.

Personally, I have been fortunate to have had the opportunity to
advise and work with several prominent investment firms in Los
Angeles and Asia over the years. My involvement with these
firms has permitted me to actively participate in numerous meetings with entrepreneurs as well as financiers including venture
capitalists, hedge fund managers, and investment bankers.

I have worked on early stage investments, project financing of
multi-hundred-million-dollar energy projects, mergers and acquisitions, and several IPOs. From this vantage point, I have been
able to observe some of the top finance professionals and entrepreneurs at work and learn first–hand some of the skills needed
to succeed in the world of Entrepreneurial Finance. These experiences have also shaped my opinions and perspectives of how
undergraduate and graduate courses in Entrepreneurial Finance
can be improved.

COMMON PROBLEMS WITH MANY
ENTREPRENEURIAL FINANCE COURSES

In order to diagnose the state of Entrepreneurial Finance education, I **surveyed** about a dozen courses being taught at major

business schools in the U.S. and Asia. As expected, some teachers were doing a fabulous job, while others seemed to be struggling or not adequately meeting the needs of the students. The following are several reasons for which I feel some courses were falling short of success:

Too Much Focus on Theory & Techniques

Entrepreneurial Finance courses, especially those taught by former Finance professors, fill the syllabus with a study of various ratios, formulas, and theories. These "foundations" create the veil of a respectable course among the teachers' peers and the Finance curriculum committees.

From the teacher's shoes, it is actually easier to teach theory and mathematics than anything else. I concede, too, that students do often need to be able to refer to some of the most common ratios. Unfortunately, however, students typically end up with a medley of mini-courses somewhere between accounting, financial analysis, and business law — far from what should be the core focus of Entrepreneurial Finance. As a side note, most of the prominent investment professionals I work with do not know many of the formulas and ratios by heart.

Too Much Focus on Venture Capital Funds

This topic was a concern brought up at an annual meeting of the Global Consortium of Center Directors (GCEC) a couple of years ago: Too many academic researchers and teachers seem fascinated with who venture capitalists are and what they do. This fascination is also reflected in entrepreneurship academic literature, where an overwhelming percentage of research in Entrepreneurial Finance is about venture capitalists.

While venture capital might be sexy and interesting, most students in the U.S. and around the world will likely not ever deal with professional venture capitalists. Even in the U.S., where venture capital is most prevalent, **only about 10–20% of Inc. Magazine's 500 Fastest Growing Companies typically receive venture capital.**

I am not proposing that venture capital is not important. The methods and tools that venture capitalists use are prevalent among investment bankers, angel investors, and high net worth individuals. However, a large percentage of the students will be involved in a wide range of business enterprises, including franchises and low-tech ventures, where standard venture capital is not applicable. Other sources and topics in financing, including various forms of bank loans, angel financing, factoring, project-financing, or bootstrapping deserve more class time.

Not Enough Emphasis on the Most Relevant Skills

Most employers and investors would find it strange that a business major or an entrepreneur is not proficient in certain key practical skills, one such skill being the **ability to create a presentable pro-forma income statement.** Along with some of the investors I work with, I have met several top MBA-school graduates working on funded entrepreneurial ventures who were **disgraceful in putting together sensible financials.** Anyone who takes an Entrepreneurial Finance course should work on being able to develop pro-forma financials that are realistic and presentable to investors.

Putting together pro-forma financials takes more than being able to use Excel. Students have to **search for and obtain sensible, accurate data.** It also provides a great opportunity to discuss what **realistic assumptions** are in terms of how quickly (or slowly) a business will stabilize and grow. Most students will underestimate the time and effort it takes to grow a company. Students also underestimate marketing and operational budgets needed to get traction. They need to learn that the job with pro-forma financials is never finished — that there is always room to re-evaluate and improve one's financials.

Not Enough Excitement for Entrepreneurship Students

There are usually two main groups of students interested in taking my course in Entrepreneurial Finance: Entrepreneurship students and Finance students. I do believe that a course or two in Entrepreneurial Finance is really beneficial to the Finance students interested in careers in investment banking, banking, venture capital, and private equity. Many of them tend to be solid students with strong quantitative skills. I have had students who entered the field of investment banking and later wrote me that they were better prepared for a career in investment banking than students from Ivy League schools because of what they learned in the course.

A colleague of mine once told me that teaching a large number of Finance students defeats the purpose of teaching an entrepreneurship course. I disagree. It is the investment professionals that will advise and fund entrepreneurs in the future. Moreover, in my observation, many finance professionals later become entrepreneurs.

However, **teaching Entrepreneurial Finance** to Entrepreneurship students **takes special effort**. Many Entrepreneurship students are not as proficient in quantitative subjects as are Finance majors. There will always be a few aspiring entrepreneurs who, despite their serious curiosity for the subject, will lose interest as the course becomes more technical. Some become outright intimidated by their Finance peers' quantitative prowess and never develop comfort with the subject. Entrepreneurial Finance therefore becomes predominantly a class for Finance majors with no aspiring entrepreneurs in sight.

Educators need to prevent this situation from occurring by **keeping the courses less dry and more interesting** — after all, **Entrepreneurship is *exciting***. Otherwise we, as educators, run the risk of many aspiring entrepreneurs not acquiring the raw skills and knowledge they will need.

COMMON CHALLENGES ASSOCIATED WITH TEACHING ENTREPRENEURIAL FINANCE

Unfortunately, it is **no easy feat to address all of the aforementioned problems**. Some of the common pitfalls in most universities include the following:

No PhD's in Entrepreneurial Finance

As far as I know, there are no universities that offer a Ph.D. program specifically in the field of Entrepreneurial Finance. It is therefore very difficult to find professors who can teach the subject with the mastery, authority, and comfort that Ph.D.s tend to assert.

From my survey, I conclude that some of the best teachers of the subject have been retired investment bankers or venture capitalists. Adjunct professors like Bill Cockrum of The Anderson School at UCLA (a former investment banker) and Jerome Engel at The Haas School of Business at UC Berkeley (a former venture capitalist) also bring their interesting and eclectic personalities to the profession. Several other schools have shrewdly delegated the teaching of the subject to adjuncts, such as local venture capitalists.

I myself learned most of the basic skills not in the classroom, but while working as a consultant and venturing professional inside a large, deal-happy company. But I do believe that academic types with interest in this subject can teach it after some preparation. An example is the Harvard Business School, which uses tenured or tenure-track professors, with publications in journals like the Journal of Private Equity, to teach the subject.

Organizational and Territorial Issues

Political issues inside business colleges can make it even more difficult to offer courses in Entrepreneurial Finance, or at least to offer the types of practical and useful courses that are necessary. Many Finance faculty members are not capable or interested in offering a course in Entrepreneurial Finance. Moreover, the preparation for a brand-new course takes valuable time and effort. I also know of Finance professors who believe that the subject isn't rigorous enough because there aren't enough established theories on models.

At the same time, though, they are unhappy when a non-Finance faculty member — such as someone in Entrepreneurship or an adjunct with an MBA — wants to teach a course with the word "Finance" in the course title. They may reject having such a course, or demand "rigor" in its curriculum, which means the inclusion of excessive theory and formulas.

The Lack of Suitable Textbooks

One of the biggest problems facing the development of Entrepreneurial Finance courses has been the lack of suitable textbooks on this subject. Several books have been introduced to the marketplace by major publishing houses in recent years, most of them written by Finance professors who probably had **little practical experience**. Many of the books seem theoretically sound, and some contain all the techniques one may need in a lifetime. To me, most of the books seem to be **compilations** of various chapters from books in Finance, Financial Analysis (accounting), and Business Law.

I find there are several problems with the existing textbooks: They

- **are too boring**, failing to make the topics relevant, and are certain to bore most Entrepreneurship majors;

- **do not contain** many of the various **topics that are important;**

- **contain topics that I would never teach** in an Entrepreneurial Finance class, such as detailed SEC issues with respect to becoming a public corporation;

- **are too expensive**, and therefore do not offer a good IRR (internal rate of return), a topic I discuss extensively in my course.

TEACHING RELEVANT AND INTERESTING TOPICS

I have no solution for dealing with the lack of Entrepreneurial Finance Ph.D. programs or the political difficulties inside different colleges. One hopes that these issues will diminish over time. However, I do have suggestions as to how to make Entrepreneurial Finance more relevant and interesting. One of the first steps on this path is to **choose the right set of topics** to be covered in an Entrepreneurial Finance class.

My preference is to **cover** — whether over one course or two — **a wide range of practical subject matters** that will offer a broad introduction to the field and profession. This means that the class should encompass financial issues facing entrepreneurial business ventures at all phases of their life cycle, from initial idea to the ultimate harvest.

I also **cover firms in a diverse set of industries** including high technology, low technology, and service. While students may not become experts in one area of venture finance, they will develop a feel for the range of interesting opportunities and challenges. Some of the key topics I cover include the following:

- **Opportunity Assessment.** I believe that this is an ideal topic for students interested in an entrepreneurial venture, new product development, or getting a job in the investment world. When this topic is taught correctly, it could be one of the **most popular segments** of the course, touching on both hard (e.g., numbers) and soft (e.g., people) aspects. Evaluating a business opportunity involves examining not just the financials, but also the market demand, the competition, the people involved, the deal structure, and the issue of "fit" between various parties, among others. The exercise also forces students to read financial projections and draw deep, practical insights.

- **Small Business Finance**, *e.g., how to buy and finance a small business, including franchises.* I believe that this is a topic that is **relevant for the majority of the class**, whereas venture capital might only be applicable for a minority of the students. Furthermore, even the most unprepared undergraduate students can relate to buying and financing a restaurant, while project financing for an oil refinery may seem foreign and unfamiliar. Thus, beginning the semester with this topic can be a good preparation for more advanced discussions relating to the acquisition or financing of larger businesses.

- **Developing Pro-Forma Financials** *for a new or growing venture.* As a big part of the class grade (25%), I assign my students to develop pro-forma financials (income statement and cash flow statement) for a real business. This exercise provides students with the chance to sit down with business owners and project their companies' growth plans, allowing them to develop a feel for the resources and the time it takes to grow. I explain the importance for business majors to be good at this. I tell them that if they got together with an engineer to start a new technology business, it would be they (the business majors) who would be responsible for developing all the financials. Jokingly, I ask them not to tell anyone that they took my course if they ever find themselves in a situation in which they are unable to develop adequate financials.

- **Boot-Strapping**, *i.e., starting and growing a company with as little financing as possible*. This is a topic that is overlooked by many venture capital courses in the U.S. Students should be taught that they should foremost **be frugal and last as long as possible without other peoples' money (OPM) to build "sweat equity."** Once they have received OPM, they need to be taught to **spend it like their own**.

- **Understanding the Various Sources of Capital.** My course covers a wide range of different sources, e.g., angels, venture capital, banks, hedge funds, etc. and their associated benefits and disadvantages. We also discuss the existence of specialized investment companies, e.g., angel funds and venture firms that only invest in socially responsible companies.

- **Doing the Deal.** This topic consists of two parts in my class: First, I present typical **term sheets** offered by venture capitalists, angels, and banks to discuss the various components and mechanics of term sheet negotiation, e.g., what "liquidation preference" is. After understanding the language, we can discuss innovative structures of deals in the news to emphasize the "creative" aspects of the deal.

- **Ownership and Stock Options.** Students who have taken Entrepreneurial Finance should be familiar with ownership structures of companies. I use a case study where the main character needs to decide between starting a company and joining another company for a certain number of stock options. This is a scenario that many students will undoubtedly face, and therefore, is a useful topic.

- **Growth or Later Stage Financing.** In my class, we not only discuss startup financing for a brand new venture, but also growth financing for a relatively established, profitable company. A course on Entrepreneurial Finance should **cover companies in all phases** of their development to introduce students to the various financial and financing issues of high growth companies. Students are often surprised that companies making profits need outside capital to grow. Exercises include **developing a fund flow statement** to analyze how much equity or bank financing a business will likely need to pursue its business plan.

- **Valuation**, e.g., the venture capital method or the standard DCF model (Discounted Cash Flow). As done in the real world. My class has traditionally **emphasized the Venture Capital Method** (e.g., pre-money valuation, post-money valuations, and comparables) over the standard discounted cash flow (DCF) valuation model taught in most finance classes. However, we do use the DCF model in one of our cases in which we explore a more mature company.

- **Harvesting & Exit.** We spend two or three lectures discussing exit strategies, including the sale and the initial public offering (IPO). When extra time is available, I also screen a video, "E-Dreams," the story of Kozmo.com, which was preparing itself for a scheduled May, 2000 IPO when the stock market crashed in April, 2000.

- **Alternative Methods of Financing.** We discuss alternative methods that include reverse mergers and leveraging foreign markets (i.e., IPO in a foreign market), to offer a taste of the various opportunities that exist. **The intended message here is that one can be creative**, and it is not always necessary to follow conventional paths.

- **My Own Research Papers.** I have written papers on Entrepreneurial Finance topics such as whether investors add value to ventures, how socially responsible entrepreneurs make money, or how Asian-American founded technology ventures are funded and perform, etc.

MAKING THE COURSE RELEVANT AND INTERESTING FOR ASPIRING ENTREPRENEURS

My goal is to make the course interesting for aspiring entrepreneurs, and I believe this should be the focus for most Entrepreneurial Finance courses. Aspiring entrepreneurs want content that is tangible, practical, and relevant. **They derive no satisfaction from solving interesting mathematical problems.** Many professors, as well as some engineering and finance students, might find challenging math problems worthwhile and satisfying, but entrepreneurial types will just be bored. I know that when my Entrepreneurship students are excited, my Finance students are excited as well, while the reverse is not often true. The following are the ways in which I try to achieve my goals:

Minimize Prerequisites

Aspiring entrepreneurs need to understand Entrepreneurial Finance whether or not they are strong in mathematics, and whether they are Finance majors or film majors. I don't see the point of eliminating students who will benefit most from the course. Officially, my course requires the basic Accounting and Finance classes as prerequisites. However, **anyone who wants to learn** the material and is willing to work hard **is welcome** to my class. After all, there isn't much overlap between Corporate Finance and Entrepreneurial Finance.

(Over-)Communicate Each Topic's Relevance

While it may be obvious to a professor as to why a topic is important, it isn't always so to the students. I make a note of **"selling"** **a topic** before I begin discussing it. Students appreciate knowing why a certain subject is important to their overall business education and how it may help with their future careers. Of course, it is much easier to demonstrate a topic's relevance if it is really of practical value.

Maximize the "Experiential" Aspect of Case Studies

I am a moderate fan of Harvard Business School (HBS) case studies in general, but I am a much bigger fan of case studies in Entrepreneurial Finance. Case studies demonstrate the importance and relevance of what may otherwise appear to be boring and irrelevant finance topics.

Before each case discussion, I deliver a lecture or two to introduce students to the terminology and techniques needed for the case assignment. For example, I assign a HBS case assignment for which students evaluate term sheets from two different venture capitalists. I spend a lecture or two before the case discussion to discuss various components and issues associated with a term sheet, e.g. liquidation preference and redemption rights. Students pay close attention because they know they will need the knowledge for their case assignment.

To maximize the experiential aspect of case studies, it is vital that the students really put themselves in the position of the actor(s) in the story, assuming an imaginary version of the same risk. **I require my students to take a position** (i.e., pro or con) on the assigned questions. For example, if the question is "Would you invest in this company under the current terms?", the student's answer cannot be "I would consider it" or "I need more data." Students are given a lower grade when they cannot provide a firm answer with adequate justification.

Language, not Formulas

My goal with respect to most students, especially the aspiring entrepreneurs, is not to turn them into finance experts (although I don't tell them that). It would be difficult to do so in one semester or quarter, and the truth is that they will forget most of the formulas in six months. Instead, I try to help them become familiar with the terminology, key players in the industry, and basic tools so that they can speak the language and have enough familiarity with the subject to **be able to ask the right questions**. I don't want my students to be overwhelmed by unnecessary math, but do want them to remain interested in the topic over many years.

Offer a Well-Rounded Course

As made obvious from my discussion above, my preference is to offer a course that covers a wide range of topics. Obviously my recommendation for having a well-rounded course does not apply to MBA programs that really want to offer a focused course on certain aspects of Entrepreneurial Finance, e.g., venture capital financing of biotechnology firms. I am aware that MIT's venture finance course, for example, focuses exclusively on the technology industry.

Make it Current — Use Real-Time Examples

I bring to class examples of recently funded businesses so that students can see just how relevant the course material is. Any instructor **can easily keep track of major deals on websites** like pwcmoneytree.com or TheDeals.com. I would also encourage faculty members to meet venture capitalists and angel investors and to learn stories of interesting deals, particularly in the industries in which students are interested such as digital media and consumer retail.

Use Multi-Media Often (Even in a Finance Course)

Videos can be a useful tool, not only in "soft subjects" like Human Resources Management, but also in Entrepreneurial Finance. I use videos of entrepreneurs who discuss relevant topics like the value of sweat equity, importance of watching cash flow, etc. I use video clips of well-known venture capitalists like Arthur Rock, Vinod Koshla, and Guy Kawasaki found on Stanford's Educator Corner (http://edcorner.stanford.edu) or Harvard's entrepreneur (http://www.hbs.edu/entrepreneurs/) web sites. I also show documentaries like E-Dreams, a venture that missed out the dot-com IPO boom by one month, to discuss the IPO process. Another source of useful videos is the Charlie Rose Show, including one segment in which Dr. Muhammad Yunus is interviewed about micro-lending.

Emphasize Creativity

This is my favorite topic! I discuss some of the most riveting and creative investment structures that I know of or read about recently. I start the discussion with some of the common structures, such as seller-financed acquisitions or business acquisitions using equity, business loans, and real estate loans. Then, we move into more complex and interesting deals. These can include an innovative method by which someone sold his or his friend's company, an interesting Internet consolidation play in China or Europe that received financing, a large project financing deal with a reverse merger into a public shell to access hedge fund money, or an unusual way a venture leveraged foreign capital market to finance domestic growth. **These kinds of examples illustrate the creative and fun aspects of doing the deal.**

Be Controversial

Maybe it is because I envy professors in social studies who enjoy heated debate with students on controversial subjects, but I like offering certain perspectives that **trigger strong reactions from students**. Basically, I try to create controversies in a class that does not have many controversial issues. For example, in almost every class, I introduce one or two quotes or phrases that catch the students' attention. One example is the following: "A feast is made for laughter, and wine makes life merry, but money is the answer for everything." While students agree or disagree with the statement, it provides a good opportunity to switch the discussion to how important financing is for growing companies. What makes the statement more interesting is that it comes straight from the Bible (Ecclesiastes 10:19).

Another controversial or humorous statement I use is the following: "Golden Rule in Life: Treat people like you want to be treated. Golden Rule in Finance: Whoever has gold makes the rules." Besides the statement being funny, it reveals a reality — that investors often have the upper hand in many situations, as reflected often in term sheet negotiations. It also provides a good opportunity to discuss how to turn the table for the benefit of entrepreneurs. Students will remember not just the humorous/outrageous statements like these, but also the discussions that followed them.

Show that You Live it

I like to share how **I live my life thinking about the concepts that I teach in class**. For example, I often tell the story of how broke I was when I was young and dating women. Then, I go on to tell them what I said when I met my wife after our initial few dates in my own romantic way: "You are no longer an expense, but an investment — I moved you from one side of the ledger to the other." I also mention that my wife wanted to know what depreciation cycle she was on — a 5-year or 30-year — and what my yearly maintenance budget for her would be. Besides some students thinking that I am funny or weird — mostly weird — these kinds of examples show students that they can think of topics learned in class in daily life, and thereby make them their own.

"The highest reward for a person's toil is not what they get for it, but what they become by it."

John Ruskin

Chapter Seventeen

100 Or So Simple Ingredients for Winning in Life as an Entrepreneur, Leader, Manager, and Winner!

A Bathroom Reader!

By Fred Kiesner

INTRODUCTION

I started to develop this list some 30 years ago to stimulate the thinking of my entrepreneurial students about their own mind, heart, and soul! It often includes just plain common sense concepts that somehow we often forget!

It seems to be a very useful tool to help my students to abandon their cell-phones and MP3 players, at least for a few moments a day, and think about how they will lead, think, and act in their futures. It is purposely done in quick "sound bites" so that it is familiar territory with modern young people.

I hope you enjoy it, I believe it is a valuable learning tool for "students" of all ages!

The List

To be read after each major failure, after each major success, or annually if neither of the above are achieved! You will really need to read this if you haven't failed or won in a year! Ouch!

The original hope was that this list was supposed to grow to 100 or so items. It is now many more, I guess I lived much longer than I expected, so I keep adding to it. It is full of occasionally corny, sometimes obvious proverbs for making your life and your career work, and for helping you to reach the pot of gold at the end of your target rainbow!

I strongly suggest you keep this list in your WC (bathrooms for you folks that haven't lived around the UK folks in your lives). The idea is that we should always practice synergy — 2 and 2 equals 5! So, you figure it out, you can learn something while you are sitting.

Please, at least once a week, read a block of five of these ideas, cogitate on them, contemplate how they fit your life, and achieve a productive level of synergy!

This list is absolutely, never, never, never to be used as emergency paper!

This little ditty has been developed by old Prof. Fred Kiesner from his own failures, mistakes, and thoughts, as well as ideas appropriated, adapted, borrowed, misquoted, stolen, downloaded, and developed from the thinking of others much smarter than he!

1. **Have vision.** This is the major difference between a manager and a leader.

2. **Have long vision.** Don't just look for short-term profit.

3. **Add value to all you do.**

4. **Never bitch.**

5. **Stay positive.** An optimist may succeed, a pessimist will never succeed.

6. **Send thank you notes.** Spend at least 15 minutes a day saying thank you.

7. **Back your people.** Most especially in times of stress and crisis.

8. **Return phone calls rapidly.**

9. **Answer your own phone when possible.** Just about every call you get is important, so let the caller think you appreciate that when possible.

10. **Remember that change is with you all the time.**

11. **Know that there are no totally right answers all the time.**

12. **Perfectionism is the enemy of the leader.** Perfectionists get nothing done while trying to do everything perfectly.

13. **You must always make decisions with incomplete information.**

14. **You must do what is right, period.**

15. **You must be ethical.** There are no mostly ethical people. You are either ethical, or you are not. It is sometimes harder to be ethical, but much easier to look in the mirror when you do the right thing.

16. **Be especially considerate to front line staff.** Yours and others.

17. **Remember MBWA.** Management By Walking Around is critical to getting to know your people, and letting them know you. Oh, yes, your people are your most critical resource.

18. **Dress for success.** Look around you, see what fits properly in your game in life.

19. **Empower others.** Be an enabler.

20. **Learn to communicate well — written and orally!** Put a different way, take those dumb ear buds out of your ears, put down your cell phone, and talk to the folks around you. You might find that real people are a delight to meet, talk to, and learn from.

21. **Praise in public, and often.**

22. **Criticize in private, and immediately.**

23. **Time is your friend, and your enemy.** Manage it well.

24. **Be humble in victory, gracious in defeat, always.**

25. **Learn to remember names.** Try to never miss-pronounce or miss-spell names.

26. **Have a "kitchen cabinet."** As you assume leadership, often those around you will not be honest with you. Surround yourself with people you trust to give you their honest advice and opinions. Use them for unbiased in times of trouble or major decisions.

27. **Immediately seek out mentors in any position you take on.**

28. **Always honor your mentors.**

29. **Learn to zip your fly.** Become streetwise. Quickly learn the rules of the game you are playing in.

30. **Find the five or six key ingredients for success in any position, firm, industry, career.** Then just simply do them well.

31. **Act on any job, even the lowest, as though you were the owner/president of the firm.** In other words, even at an entry level job, think and do what you would do when you become president. You just might surprise yourself and actually become the top dog if you think that way.

32. **The most critically important ingredient to your ultimate success is your inherent belief in your self and your ability to win.** Know your talents, and believe in your absolute right to win at what you do, if you play the game by the right rules.

33. **Fail fast, and fail often. Never forget to learn from it.** Succcess is getting up just one more time than you fall down.

34. **Surround yourself with people who are smarter than you, and then listen to them.**

35. **Know when to hold 'em, and when to fold them. In short, shut up and back down when it is appropriate.**

36. **Don't ask your people to do something you wouldn't do yourself.**

37. **Get your own coffee.**

38. **Use today's technology.**

39. **Eliminate useless meetings.**

40. **Make decisions, and take personal risk.** Don't depend on committees as a hiding place for responsibility.

41. **Be visible.** Get noticed, make waves.

42. **Make your own phone calls.** Don't insult those you deal with, both employees and your customers, by having others make the calls you really should be making yourself.

43. **Remember, friends come and go, enemies accumulate.**

44. **Network, network, network.** Do it within your company and field, and outside your field.

45. **Work hard, and be sure you play hard.**

46. **Always be sure you make work fun for your people.**

47. **Guard against letting your own personal beliefs totally color all you do.** Be open minded and do "walk in the other person's shoes."

48. **Invest in lifetime education for you and your employees.**

49. **Take at least an afternoon away from the workplace each week.** Escape to a quiet, contemplative place. Think about what has happened, what you have accomplished, what you should have done, and what you should do. In short, my suggestion is that you "go sit on a rock". Go SOAR.

50. **Be an active listener.** Learn to read body language as well as words.

51. **Remember that trouble also usually offers opportunity.**

52. **Encourage and reward risk-taking in yourself and your associates.**

53. **Fight to let go of the familiar, and embrace the new.** Change comes at lightning speed.

54. **Be a mentor to someone on their way up, just as you sought out a mentor.**

55. **Publicly celebrate the accomplishments of your people.**

56. **Celebrate your own major victories for 12 hours, and mourn your major losses for 24 hours.** Then get to work on achieving new targets.

57. **Use "we" rather than "I" when discussing the achievements of your team.** You win only if your employees want

you to win. Never forget that. If your employees don't want you to win, you just simply won't.

58. **Be approachable.**

59. **Keep all promises.** Do not promise what you cannot deliver.

60. **Quality is the key to success in the future.** TQM are key letters to learn, and it is a philosophy of life that will help you win.

61. **Remember, there is nobody called "they."** You can never again say "They ought to do something about this." You must do something about it if you wish to be a winner, and if there is ever to be change.

62. **Look at problems as opportunities.**

63. **Work can and should be fun.** Bring humor to the workplace.

64. **When you hire somebody, you should not be looking in a mirror.** Hire those who complement and contrast with you.

65. **K.I.S.S. is the key to success.** Keep it simple stupid.

66. **Say "I don't know" when you don't know.** Then find out the answer.

67. **Make sure you have good cause to say "Wow!" regularly.** About your own achievements, and those of your associates.

68. **Never underestimate the competition.**

69. **When in doubt, or when unsure, trust your intuition.** The seat of your pants is often telling you something.

70. **Believe and understand that you never get a second chance to make a good first impression.**

71. **Be confident and comfortable in all you do, but never complacent.** Always look over your shoulder.

72. **Recognize the shadow organization in your firm.** Listen to the company grapevine.

73. **Remember that neither you, nor any of your employees are indispensable.** When you think you are, you will soon be gone.

74. **Remember, technology is a tool for success, not the goal.** Do not become a slave to the computer and hurt what you are supposed to be doing.

75. **Perception is just as important as the reality.** Know what message you are really giving out.

76. **Always be on time for appointments.** This applies in both directions, with those above you and those below you. It is a gross insult to act as though your time is more important than that of others you deal with.

77. **Make meetings short.** As Peter Drucker used to say, make them twenty minutes long, and start them at 20 minutes to twelve, or twenty minutes until quitting time. Then everyone will really want to get something done, and not try to posture and look important.

78. **Never think you are infallible.** You are not, period.

79. **Walk the talk.** Do what you tell others to do.

80. **Never burn bridges.** The world is small, and you just may have to cross those bridges again in the future.

81. **Be a futurist.** Think in the future, act for the future. To only protect what you have now is to ensure that you will fail in the future.

82. **Think global.** It is the reality of now, and the future.

83. **Disagree without being disagreeable.**

84. **Work smart, not hard.** "But I worked hard on this" is absolutely no excuse for mediocre work.

85. **Answer questions.**

86. **Question answers.**

87. **Don't play favorites.** Treat all of your employees with dignity and fairness.

88. **Socialize with your people.** Yes it will make it harder if you have to fire somebody, but being sociable with your employees will make you human. People work hard for human leaders.

89. **Demand excellence.** From yourself and from your people.

90. **Learn that anger is a powerful weapon that should be discharged rarely.**

91. **Serve your employees as much as they serve you.**

92. **Apologize when you are wrong. Accept others' apologies.** Then move on and forgive and forget.

93. **Encourage informality and a relaxed company atmosphere.** Work can and should be fun.

94. **Remember that what is right is not always popular.**

95. **What is popular is not always right.**

96. **Make sure you manage, plan, and operate from both a top-down and a bottom-up approach.** Keep your people involved.

97. **Learn how to say no.** Do not over-commit.

98. **Have the courage to fire people when you must.** Also recognize that getting to that point with an employee usually also partially includes some fault on your part.

99. **Smile and laugh often.** It is contagious.

100. **Be proactive, not reactive.** Control your own destiny. Don't wait for somebody else to make sure you succeed. Your mother is no longer able to help you.

101. **Have breadth and depth in all you do.**

102. **Be willing to toot your own horn.** Do it when it is needed, but not too often nor too loud.

103. **Have the wisdom to know what you can and cannot change.** Act accordingly.

104. **Hate company/office politics, and those who survive by politics only.** However, also recognize that it exists, and figure out how to neutralize it.

105. **Don't dwell on the past.** Learn and grow from it.

106. **Conduct an honest evaluation of yourself and your achievements and failures each year.**

107. **Look out for #1.**

108. **Always watch out for #2.** They may be gaining on you.

109. **Accept that some days you are the pigeon, and some days you are the statue.** That thought will keep you humble.

110. **Embrace change, it is the lifeblood of the future.**

111. **Never totally blame your people for failure.** You are the boss. You are responsible, yet you must delegate. If there is a failure, you own a part of it.

112. **Guard your reputation, it can only be lost once.**

113. **Treat every job you do and position you hold as the most important thing you will ever do.** Then you will hold future jobs that are more important.

114. **Understand that we can always do what we dislike for a time, and you must.** Therefore, do what you are supposed to do, even if you have gotten yourself into something miserable that you hate. If you don't, your path out will be down, not up.

115. **If you are a leader, and the toilets need cleaning, clean them.** In short, do what has to be done, no matter what.

116. **Remember, everything you do in life is a portrait in others minds of who you are.** We are good at primping and posing and looking our best for real life photographs. Do the same with the work image you create.

117. **If you are worried about who and what you will be in the future, then make and define your own future.** You need to have a major role in your path.

118. **Never follow the herd.** Always remember vividly the view you get as a follower.

119. **If you choose to become politically correct in life, please never call me again.** I couldn't stand the boredom.

120. **Take a chance on being different and unique.**

121. **Always come to work being willing to be fired for what you believe, and know is right.**

122. **Always bend/break stupid rules from the past.** But understand there is sometimes a tough penalty on those that pave the way into the future and take risks aimed at progress.

123. **When inventing the future, it is often much easier to ask forgiveness than it is to ask permission.** Particularly if what you did works out well.

124. **If you don't like the game you are playing in, then either gain the power to change and improve the rules, or invent a new game for yourself (business, career) that fits your talents and abilities.**

125. **To win in life you must truly love what you are doing.**

126. **Smile a lot, and give an upbeat greeting to strangers.** The cost is low, it sure makes life fun, and the person you are interacting with might be your next big customer.

127. **Live within your means, and within your seams.**

128. **Return everything you borrow.**

129. **Stop blaming other people.**

130. **Admit it when you boo boo.**

131. **Strive for excellence.** Real winners know no other goal.

132. **Be on time.** Don't make excuses if you are stupid enough to come late. Being on time means showing up ten minutes early. Plan for that.

133. **Take the time to be alone.** Learn to be comfortable and happy with yourself.

134. **Be humble, but inwardly very proud of who you are.**

135. **Understand and accept that life isn't always fair.**

136. **"I tried" is a first rate cop out.** Just trying is nothing. In life there is only doing or not doing. Either you did it, or you did not do it. There are no bonus points in life for trying.

137. **Keep skid chains on your tongue.** Always say less than you think.

138. **Make promises sparingly.** Keep them faithfully at all costs.

139. **Be interested in others.** They will then find you interesting.

140. **Be cheerful, always.** Hide your pains, worries, and disappointments.

141. **Preserve an open mind on all debatable questions.** It is the mark of superior minds to disagree and yet still be friendly.

142. **Be known as someone who builds bridges, not fences or bombs.**

143. **If you give your boss a ride in your car, and if because of the smell and mess, they ask you if you have a dog, always say yes.**

144. **Companies will tell you about their standard operating procedures (SOP's). They don't work.** Learn fast how things really get done. The world moves much too fast for you to depend on standard rule books for action that were written decades or centuries ago.

145. **Don't send anything by email that you wouldn't want in your permanent personnel file.** That holds double and triple true for things like YouTube, Facebook, MySpace, etc.

146. **When sending some memos, the only thing that really matters is who you send cc's to.**

147. **Those who refuse to acknowledge the existence of office politics could be at the mercy of those who do.** At least understand the political game, especially when you are the leader, so you can neutralize the politics.

148. **Never complain that you are bored!!!!! Only boooooooring people get bored.**

149. **Always get up in the morning looking forward to going to work.** If you hate going to work, change what you do immediately.

150. **When sending emails, use proper grammar, punctuation, and language.** To most of the world, the cutsie pie texting symbols and "cool" sayings are not impressive. Communicate well in a form that those you want to impress appreciate.

151. **Do not address business associates (either above or below you) by their last names only.** Show them proper respect and dignity.

152. **Put life in proper perspective.** How much money you made in life will not be the final measure of how good you are. Your impact in doing good with your earned power and wealth is the sum total of your ultimate value to the world, and how you will be remembered. The perks and wealth of success are only a side show.

153. **Say hi to the folks you pass on the streets, or when you get in an elevator, or on a plane.** You will be surprised how it brightens most people's days.

154. **Be happy in all you do.** Reportedly it takes fewer muscles than sadness.

155. **Treat even your lowest level employee with dignity and respect.** They can really hurt you if they want to.

156. **Be fair and equal in paying your people, based upon the results they turn in.**

157. **If your firm does well, share the wonderful harvest with your people, as they helped you to make it happen.**

158. **The trend is your friend.** Seek an insight into where things are going, then tie your future course of life to that trend. Be a part of molding it and creating it.

159. **Draw a picture of your future path, but do it with a pencil with an eraser on it.** Things change, for sure.

160. **If you have to endure the buffoon who dominates a conversation with stupid, ill thought out claptrap, develop a quick and dirty put down.** Saying something like "If horse manure were music, that remark would be a symphony."

161. **Most people who say they want to serve God do it in an advisory capacity.** God doesn't need your help and advice, but the world does.

162. **The economics of enough are important.** At some time in your life you must turn from an acquisition/consumption mode to a life of contribution and significance to others and society.

163. **Raw capitalism is simple greed. Value loaded capitalism is good for society.**

164. **Money is like manure. If you pile it up, it stinks. If you spread it around, it grows things.**

165. **The poor are superb money mangers.** Manage and use your wealth as though you could lose it all. You can.

166. **Ten percent of the workforce are entrepreneurs who will create the jobs for the other ninety percent.**

167. **You will make mistakes. Accept that.** They are part of the price of really learning. Don't let fear of mistakes keep you from your full success.

168. **Life is a tapestry woven from yesterday's threads.**

169. **The best way to become the boss isn't to spend decades stumbling up the corporate ladder.** Start your own business, and lead from day one.

170. **Do not summon people to your office, it frightens them.** Go see them in the comfort of their offices, and on the way there keep your eyes open to what you see throughout your business.

171. **Leaders owe a clear statement of the values of their organization to those they lead.**

172. **A true leader must identify, develop, and nurture those that will replace them.**

173. **A real leader makes a meaningful difference in the lives of those who permit leaders to lead.**

174. **Never forget that those you lead can destroy you if they no longer believe in you.**

175. **Teach those you lead: 1. Shared values 2. Common vision 3. Individual accountability.**

176. **The three biggest failures of our corporate executives: 1. Short-term orientation 2. Shallow thinking 3. Quick-fix expectations.** Fix these faults within yourself.

177. **True leaders and winners cause change and improvement in all they touch, even at the risk of their own status quo at times.**

178. **A key responsibility of the boss is to define reality.**

179. **The leader truly must be the servant to their employees.**

180. **Remember what your Mama told you, say "Thank You" often to those you lead.**

181. **Polish, hone, liberate, and enable the talents and gifts of your people.**

182. **Have a purpose in life.**

183. **Share your brains and knowledge. Don't hoard it.**

184. **Fix problems rather than fixing blame.**

185. **Quality is the key to success!** But you must decide how much quality you can afford at your price point, quality has a dear price.

186. **Leaders orchestrate change and are catalysts for change.** Managers simply handle and carry out the change created by others. You must do both.

187. **You must learn to be a survivor first. Then you can become a winner and leader.**

188. **Outstanding people have one thing in common, an absolute and complete sense of their mission in life.**

189. **The five most important words to memorize when learning to be a leader: You did a good job!** Taking a moment to pat someone on the back is worth much more than all the money and motivators in the book.

190. **Never forget that you get the gift of leadership from those you lead.** Are you starting to get my clear message of how important it is to treat your employees right?

191. **Don't tolerate "yes" people around you.** Hire thinking people who will tell you the truth.

192. **With rare exceptions, how you start out clearly determines how you end up.** If you miss the first button hole, you will not succeed in buttoning your coat properly. Set your course carefully in life.

193. **Don't confuse activity with accomplishment.** Just because you put time in on a project does not ensure that you have maximized your action and results. Work smart, not just long hours.

194. **You might fool your boss, you could fool yourself, but it is virtually impossible to fool those who work for you.**

195. **Be who you are, truly.** This suggests that it might be a good idea to figure out who you are, first.

196. **Finding multiple mentors on the path of life is a critical factor in insuring you are a maximum success story.**

197. **Don't be a fool and think you know it all.** Only idiots are convinced they know it all. Are you an idiot?

198. **Be kind, be sensitive, respect others.**

199. **You may not have been responsible for your heritage! For sure you are responsible for your future.**

200. **When you have hired folks around you that are smarter than you are, leave them alone so they can get on with it and make you look good.**

201. **Aim for remarkable results, not just routine good work.**

202. **Success is never final.** Change is certain. You never "have it made!" "Made" changes.

203. **If you put almost as much passion into your life's work as you do your other interests (sports, sex, vacations, travel, etc.) success will come your way.**

204. **Do not confuse excellence with perfection.** Excellence you can reach for and achieve. Perfection is God's work.

205. **Do not follow where others may want to lead you. Go instead where there is no path, and leave a path for those others to follow you.**

206. **Entrepreneurs have fire in their belly, an unbelievable passion that shows in all they do in life.**

207. **Winners believe passionately in themselves and their ability to achieve.**

208. **Passion comes from doing the things you want to do.** Make sure you do work and lead a life that excites your passions.

209. **The best way to predict the future is to invent it for yourself.**

210. **Creativity and innovation do not have to deal only with earth shaking events and ideas.** One can be terribly creative in designing a better way to flush toilets.

211. **You must be reacting to life extremely fast.** Be thinking, creating and innovating 24 hours a day.

212. **Having the world's best idea will do you no good unless you act upon it.** Take the first step towards implementation, or else shut up and go sit down in the back row where the losers are.

213. **Learn to live with uncertainty and ambiguity.** They are the lifeblood of an exciting and fulfilling life.

214. **In the Mandarin dialect of Chinese, the word for "innovation" is very close to the depiction of an open window.** Bring a breath of fresh thinking into your life and business through an open window mind.

215. **When you think you don't have power, ponder this: if you are at all active in the world around you, the average leader is just five phone calls or less away from contacting the President of the United States.** One of my wonderful students taught me this when he somehow managed to get President Bush (the first one — Papa Bush) to come to our campus and speak with our students. Use your contacts when needed, make those phone calls.

216. **Small minds talk about people. Average minds talk about events. Giant minds talk about ideas.**

217. **An old saying: "Don't hire a dog and keep barking yourself."** Don't hire someone and then continue to run their job. Learn to truly delegate.

218. **Success is not measured by how you do compared to somebody else. Success is measured by how you do with what God gave you.** Max what you have, don't worry about what others have.

219. **Follow the "Babe Ruth" principle, the guy with the most strikeouts is also the one with the most home runs.** Success comes through trying and failing and trying again.

220. **Use people and contacts as conduits and conductors for action.** However, do not abuse them.

221. **Some people are really terrific at running the 95-yard dash. Without the last five yards towards success, the first 95 yards of you life are worthless. Don't stop just short of a touchdown.**

222. **Managers are a dime a dozen. Great leaders are scarce.** Which do you have in you?

223. **You must have a long term future orientation.** You must be thinking at least five years out, not just two inches in front of your nose at the bottom line.

224. **To manage and lead others, one must have a sharp mind in a velvet sheath.** Tact and diplomacy counts.

225. **Be a change agent.** Shake things up regularly.

226. **Before one can bend or break the rules, one must know what the rules are.**

227. **The things we have achieved for ourselves die with us. The impact we have had on the world and its people remains and is immortal.**

228. **Never underestimate the power of stupid people in a large group.**

229. **Don't let your sniping, political critics get to you.** Ignore them and prove them wrong by your magnificent efforts.

230. **To be creative you must lose your fear of being wrong.**

231. **Hunches usually have a subconscious basis in fact, so listen to them.**

232. **Employee problems that are solved only with the head often come back to haunt you ten fold. Employee problems that are solved including the heart stay solved.**

233. **You, not the events around you, have the power to make you happy each day.** You must choose what you must do.

234. **You can become what you consciously imagine.** Dream a lot. But then take the action needed to make the dreams reality.

235. **Never bad mouth your competitors, your boss, or your colleagues.** You win by your actions and achievements, not a big trash mouth.

236. **Look for what is good and positive in all who come within your sphere.**

237. **Failure in life does not come from failing to reach your goal.** The biggest failure is from having no goal to reach.

238. **Don't dwell on your past mistakes and failures.** Learn from them and put maximum effort into what you are doing now, and doing it well. That will clearly limit the chance of any future repetitive failures.

239. **Do not fear setting your aim too high and falling short. Rather, fear achieving your mark after you have set it too low.**

240. **Keep away from those who belittle your ambitions.** Hang with winners who make you feel that you, too, can become great.

241. **Ultimately, the end game should not be to get rich, but to enrich the world.**

242. **Character truly shows in what you do on the third and fourth tries.**

243. **Change and improve yourself first, then embark upon changing the world.**

244. **Take your iPod out of your ears. The same holds true for your cell phone.** Then you just might hear some good sounds like intelligent people saying intelligent things to you. It may sound incredible, but you might even learn to speak to others intelligently, yourself.

245. **Note, the turtle only makes progress when it sticks its neck out.**

246. **Always do the things you fear the most. Courage is an acquired taste that takes practice.**

247. **Besides that, the fear of failure stimulates your mind, your heart, and your soul to do your best work.**

248. **Take all your "stuff", your pain, your problems, and your past and use them effectively to change your future.** Truly, good things come out of absolutely horrible situations if we learn from what happened, and never allow it to happen again.

249. **Failure is the condiment that gives success its flavor.**

250. **Use proper punctuation in your emails.** Using text messaging talk doesn't hack it in the world of business. Yes, this is in here twice, now maybe you will remember it. It is that important.

251. **Believe, always, in what you can accomplish!**

252. **Constantly dream of what can be. Then make it be true.**

253. **Move on quickly from your failures.** However, you must analyze them heavily to see what caused them. If you repeat your past mistakes it is time to become a monk or a nun and repent your stupid sins.

254. **Seek and discover the two or three really powerful strengths you have within you.** Then cultivate them and seek out a career path where these talents are of tremendous value.

255. **Taking the first step is the key to achieving impact.** Most just talk. The winner wins because they act.

256. **Fools think god will provide for them.** God is too busy helping those who help themselves. Do your part in the game of life. Give God something to work with.

257. **Travel lets you see the beauty of the world, but it also lets you see the power and capabilities within yourself.**

258. **An old Irish proverb says "Don't cut your throat with your tongue."**

259. **Hang with the best in your career and your life. Excellence is catching.**

260. **Don't chew gum.** You look dumb, juvenile, and unprofessional.

261. **Never, ever, send really really personal emails from work.** Most large firms do monitor what their employees send out with random checks. Wouldn't it be really embarrassing to ruin your career by sending out some silly, dumb thing that gets you lousy negative exposure?

262. **Find the special advantage for you in every situation.** Assess and extract what works for you.

263. **Those who wish to sing with the "excellence choir" find a song and a pitch that fits their power and style.** Find your niche in life that fits your power.

264. **Proofread everything you do.** Nothing makes a star look more stupid than a 2nd grade level typo or spelling error in their work. Spell check helps, but go way beyond that and use your eyes and mind to really double-check important communications. In short, carefully read your own work before you give it to someone else to read.

265.

266.

267.

268.

269.

270.

PLEASE FEEL FREE TO ADD YOUR OWN PERSONAL RULES
FOR LIFE THAT DEVELOP AS YOU GO ALONG THE PATH TO
BEING A WINNER IN THE FUTURE.

*"Why should I deem myself to be a chisel when
I could be the artist?"*

Johann Christoph Friedrich von Schiller

Chapter Eighteen

Entrepreneurship Within a Large Organization

A Streetwise Approach to Unleashing the Corporate Entrepreneur!

By Wesley B. Truitt

Wesley B. Truitt is the author of "The Corporation" (Greenwood Press, 2006), one of ten books in a series by Greenwood Press entitled "The Greenwood Guides to Business and Economics." He is the Series Editor and Chairman of the Editorial Advisory Board. He is also the author of "What Entrepreneurs Need to Know about Government: A Guide to Rules and Regulations" (Praeger Publishers, 2004) and "Business Planning: A Comprehensive Framework and Process" (Quorum Books, 2002). This book was ranked one of the top-ten business books in 2002 and has been translated

into Chinese. Dr. Truitt is Adjunct Professor of Public Policy at Pepperdine University's graduate School of Public Policy, Malibu, California. He was formerly an Adjunct Professor at the UCLA Graduate School of Management and Executive-In-Residence at Loyola Marymount University's College of Business. He also taught at the Claremont Graduate University. He was a senior executive at Northrop Grumman Corporation for over 25 years, where he directed planning, government relations, and international marketing; his final assignment was Vice President, Europe. His Ph.D. is from Columbia University.

INTRODUCTION

Innovate or disappear is the watchword for 21st century businesses. Small companies have less difficulty appreciating this concept than large ones because their entrepreneur founders usually realize that they have about a one-in-two chance of disappearing within the first year. This Darwinian precept is less well appreciated at many **large companies**, whose leaders hubristically **believe they have an entitlement to exist. They are dead wrong!**

Two Tasks for Big Business

Most major corporations have policies and procedures that encourage entrepreneurship for the development of new products and processes to improve sales, market share, profitability, and the like. At the same time, many large companies, knowingly or not, **erect barriers to entrepreneurship** in their organizational structure, product development policies, and their corporate cultures and reward systems. **The first task for large organizations is to determine if they, in fact, stimulate or stifle internal innovation.**

The second task is a more individual, personal one. The corporate entrepreneur who seeks to effect innovation within a large organization must understand the company's formal procedures to use them effectively and, at the same time, utilize his/her own informal personal networks. Even if a company's stated position favors innovation and experimentation, the reality of its structure and culture may inhibit it. Can the innovator find ways within or around the formal structure using personal networking to achieve acceptance of his/her idea? **Allowing flexibility within the structure and encouragement for individual entrepreneurship is the second major task.**

These are the central issues for large organizations explored in this chapter:

1. resolution of the stated ideal vs. the true reality

2. establishment of flexibility for the use of informal as well as formal channels to enable innovation to occur

For large organizations, nothing less than their long-term sustainability — through organic renewal stimulated by entrepreneurial innovation — is what is at stake!

Large companies need to develop and perpetuate an innovation-friendly internal atmosphere to achieve sustained growth. (Moore, "Darwin and the Demon," *HBR*, July–August, 2004)

For the innovative member of a corporate bureaucracy working in mid- to lower-levels, **internal entrepreneurship is a tricky business holding out the prospect of high payoff or high risk for his/her career.** Finding ways to navigate through or around the corporate "org chart," taking chances with senior management to champion the cause, and finally putting it all on the line for acceptance or rejection of the New Idea is probably the greatest challenge he/she will have faced thus far in his/her career.

The stakes in this game are as high as they can be for both the individual innovator and the corporation. If the innovator is, in fact, stymied, his/her career will likely suffer, and, as importantly, the corporation will be denied a possible opportunity for innovation and growth. No venture is risk-free, and containing the risk to one's own reputation and career while managing the innovation's acceptance throughout the internal process requires some streetwise skills.

INNOVATIVE COMPANIES

Let us begin with a brief discussion of some world-class companies that do internal entrepreneurship right and have strong, innovative cultures encouraging it. Beginning in 2005, *Business Week* teamed with the Boston Consulting Group to publish an annual roster of the **world's 25 most innovative companies** based on surveys of large global firms using three primary criteria: process innovation, product innovation, and business model innovation. Of the 25 listed in 2006, 17 were based in the U.S., 3 in Japan (Toyota, Sony, and Honda), and 1 each in Britain (Virgin), Finland (Nokia), Germany (BMW), South Korea (Samsung), and Sweden (IKEA). The list's top 5 were Apple, Google, 3M, Toyota, and Microsoft.

These 25 powerfully innovative companies, all publicly-traded corporations except for three that are privately held (Virgin, IDEO, and IKEA), topped all others in their industries by **instilling best practices and emphasizing product innovation. A few stand-outs also featured process innovation and business model innovation.** Companies having all three were Procter & Gamble, Nokia, IBM, and IKEA. As a result of superior innovative performance, almost all companies on the list produced impressive margin growth and improved stock performance.

Therefore, large companies can and sometimes do institute formal, open, workable, low-risk innovation processes that

result in pay-offs for the firm as well as for innovating individuals within the firm.

Success Example: General Electric

Number six on the *Business Week* list is General Electric. Throughout more than a century of continuous business, this remarkable company has always been an innovation leader. From its founding by the inventive genius, Thomas A. Edison, and throughout its storied history, GE pioneered not only product innovations, but also process and business model innovations. In 1896, when Charles Dow put together his first 12-company list for his Dow Jones Industrial Average, GE was on the list, and is the only company that never left it. In the last decade GE has been voted the "Most Admired Company" seven times. (Anne Fisher, *Fortune*, March 19, 2007)

A spectacular example of GE's innovative skill is the 20-year period beginning in 1981, when GE's CEO was the **change-agent Jack Welch**. Facing aggressive foreign competition, especially low-cost Asian manufacturing, he restructured the company, reducing the number of operating units, cutting in half the management levels between the factory floor and his office, and instituting processes to tear down communication barriers between operating units. Welch made managers into leaders who relentlessly focused their imaginations to make work more efficient. Using his own metaphor, **Welch transformed GE from a lumbering supertanker into a speedboat able to turn on a dime.** (For a discussion of Welch's GE, see my *The Corporation*, Greenwood Press, 2006.)

Jeffrey Immelt succeeded Welch as CEO in 2001 and continues as a change-agent, institutionalizing internal growth as a process. Immelt's goal is to sustain company-wide organic revenue growth at a rate of about 8 percent — 2 to 3 times faster than global GDP annual growth. To sustain this never-before-achieved growth rate at a multi-business company, **he instituted a change process that is working. At its core it seeks to harness individuals' imagination breakthroughs that stimulate innovation** while continuing to implement process efficiency. A huge investment in R&D is being made with new GE Global Research Centers being established in Shanghai and Munich to augment those already in New York and Bangalore. (Jeffrey R. Immelt, "Growth as a Process," *Harvard Business Review*, June, 2006.)

Immelt's results are impressive. For 2007, GE's revenue grew 14 percent, earnings grew 16 percent, and operating profit margin was 16.6 percent. Sales in 2007 were $173 billion. (GE 2007 Annual Report.) The company as a whole performed well, but how have individuals been rewarded? In addition to traditional metrics, **GE now evaluates its top 5,000 managers on "growth traits," including innovation-oriented themes such as "external focus" and "imagination and courage,"** thus adding personal qualities and flexibility to its once notoriously rigid evaluation criteria. (Jena McGregor, "The World's Most Innovative Companies.")

Success Example: Ocean Spray Cranberries Inc.

This is a cooperative owned by about 800 cranberry and grapefruit farmers who **produce two-thirds of the world's cranberries** and who seek the highest possible price for their crops from the cooperative, plus a dividend from Ocean Spray's profits. The pressure for paying a high price for raw material coupled with price competition facing the end product resulted in four CEO turnovers during the early 2000s. Overproduction sank the commodity's price and threatened the viability of the entire cooperative.

In 2000, Randy Papadellis took over as chief operating officer and **instituted a creative process** to find new product uses for cranberries. A new $100 million product line called "Craisins" was made from cranberry husks that used to be thrown away. Company scientists found a way to infuse them with flavor to make a raisin-like fruit snack. Next, Ocean Spray infused husks with blueberry and strawberry flavors for use in muffins, cereals and other baked goods. Today they are used in over 1,000 products worldwide. Light juices and diet juices were next, capitalizing on the fact that cranberries contain almost no sugar. Packaging innovations such as juice boxes and rectangular bottles were introduced, immediately copied by other brands.

Total sales grew 12 percent to $1.1 billion in 2006. **Thanks to innovation, Ocean Spray remains No. 1 in juices.** (Aaron Pressman, "Ocean Spray's Creative Juices," *Business Week*, May 15, 2006)

Managing Innovation for Growth

Both General Electric, the 5th largest company in the U.S., and Ocean Spray, one that is too small to even be on the *Fortune* 500 list, demonstrate the fundamental principles of innovation in a large organization. **Top management of each company clearly stated their desire for innovation as a core necessity of the firm, and top management encouraged flexibility to enable individuals to utilize formal and informal channels** to seek top management approval to effect innovative solutions.

How did they do this? GE's and Ocean Spray's **leaders took command of their growth** by knowing where their revenues really come from, **recognized the need for innovation** to develop new products and **position those products to new growth markets**, and while doing all that **managed their costs.** Critical to their success was **creating a company atmosphere open to innovation and making a commitment to reward those who attempt** it and succeed. Likewise, there was a commitment **not to punish those who fail.** (Michael Treacy and Jim Sims, "Take Command of Your Growth," *Harvard Business Review*, April, 2004)

Failure Example: The Old AT&T, 1984–2000

An example of a large firm that **failed to innovate and died** is the former AT&T, the one that kept that name following the court-ordered breakup of the company in a 1984 antitrust case. This venerable icon of American industry, founded by Alexander Graham Bell in 1876, was a regulated monopoly, providing telephone service throughout most of the United States through the Bell System. In 1984, a federal court ordered its break-up, giving local phone service to seven "baby bells," one for each major region of the United States. AT&T continued, providing only long-distance service nationwide. It is this AT&T that is our focus here.

Suddenly, with the 1984 break-up, AT&T faced an <u>**entirely new external environment**</u> in which it had no experience and for which it was wholly unprepared — intense competition with the loss of government protection. MCI competed for long-distance service, and the new baby bells quickly sought to encroach on AT&T's long-distance near-monopoly. This new situation forced AT&T, in as short a time as possible, to undertake a strategic refocus and achieve precision in execution. By the mid-1990s, its strategy and its execution were both failing. The board of directors hired C. Michael Armstrong as its new CEO, the first outside CEO in the company's history.

AT&T's problems were further exacerbated by the enactment of the Telecommunications Act of 1996, which deregulated the telephone industry, permitting the baby bells to offer long-distance service and to merge with each other. They quickly did both, undermining AT&T's primary position in the long-distance sector. Further, by the late 1990s, wireless communications and cable had emerged as major threats to AT&T's land lines. This **heightened competition necessitated a whole new business model** for AT&T, whose revenues were sinking almost daily along with its stock price.

The enormity of the task of transforming this once staid, highly-regulated type of company into a fast-paced, innovative, multi-service, management-driven company with global reach was too much for AT&T. **Its own 100-year-old culture of conformity inhibited its ability to make changes quickly enough to avert disaster** in this new highly-innovative, competitive business environment. In October, 2000, AT&T announced its own break-up into four companies — one each for wireless, cable, long-distance, and business services, AT&T keeping that name for long-distance service.

A few years later, **SBC Communications, one of the previous baby bells, acquired AT&T for $16 billion** and BellSouth for $68 billion. SBC then took the AT&T name, calling itself the New AT&T. (See my *Business Planning*, Quorum Books, 2002)

AT&T's demise resulted from its leaders failing to innovate in products, processes, and business models fundamentally enough and quickly enough in the face of profoundly altered external business conditions. Failure to execute a flawed strategy is a double-barreled prescription for defeat.

Success/Failure Example: Northrop Grumman Transit Bus Program

We have now addressed innovation in three companies, two in which it is a success, and one in which it failed. Let us now look at an example of entrepreneurship within a large company on **a particular program that was itself a success, but "fit" neither**

that firm's product line nor culture, ultimately resulting in its failure.

When the Cold War ended in 1990–91, Northrop Corporation, a major defense contractor headquartered in Los Angeles, faced an uncertain future. Northrop feared that its principal customer, the U.S. Department of Defense, would place fewer orders for its B-2 stealth bombers, F/A-18 jet fighters, and other weapons. Having approximately 90 percent of its sales in military equipment, the company forecast a gloomy outlook with its major market potentially drying up.

A new CEO, Kent Kresa, established that Northrop would remain principally a defense contractor and adhere to its core competencies related to this field. He also determined that, in the face of an anticipated decline in Defense Department orders, **the company would explore applications of its core competencies in fields other than defense and to non-defense government agencies.** Thus, Northrop began to search for new opportunities beyond its traditional Defense Department customer base.

During this same period, the Los Angeles County **Metropolitan Transportation Authority (MTA) needed a new generation of transit buses** to modernize its aging fleet, the second largest in the U.S. MTA wanted a radically different approach to the design of a new bus based on a clean sheet of paper, not a modification to the existing diesel buses that were mostly 1950s and 1960s designs. Their criteria specified lightweight, low emissions, and low floor. Existing buses were all approximately 30,000 pounds, and MTA desired to cut the weight by one-third to save fuel and street repair costs. Low emissions and low floors were required by the Clean Air Act and the Americans with Disabilities Act, respectively.

MTA approached the large aircraft companies in the Los Angeles area with this concept, believing they, rather than existing bus manufacturers, would welcome the opportunity to apply their skills to their design criteria. **Northrop responded** to this overture, seeing an opportunity to apply its core competencies to a new product area.

At that time **I was Northrop Aircraft Division's Vice President of Business Development and gave the go-ahead for exploratory discussions** with the MTA for what became known **as the Advanced Technology Transit Bus Program (ATTB).** I viewed the ATTB as an excellent opportunity to apply the CEO's vision of alternative technology applications to a real test case. **The bus program <u>fit all the company's core capabilities</u>:** advanced design, systems integration, lightweight materials, computerized control systems, and advanced electronics. Moreover, **MTA was a government agency**, albeit not a U.S. federal government agency; it was a county agency.

My next task was to convince the Aircraft Division's General Manager of the desirability of bidding on the program. To that end **I lined up support from the key departments at the Aircraft Division** (finance, engineering, and planning) whose agreement was needed. Moreover, **I had previously served the former CEO as his Executive Assistant** and therefore **understood the Corporate Office** very well, looking ahead to the time when its review would be undertaken. The General Manager believed that I could gain corporate office approval at low risk to him.

Thus, **my personal network of relationships at both the division level and at Corporate Headquarters was a critical factor in deciding to take the primary risk to promote a radical new venture and the secondary risk to personally seek approval of higher authorities.** The Corporate Office held the power of life or death for new projects.

I utilized my former corporate office experience and **made back-channel pitches individually to the key players** emphasizing the CEO's openness to new applications of core capabilities. These sessions gave me insights as to each person's likely position at the upcoming formal review meeting. I found that I had support from all the key players but one, the VP of Public Affairs. He saw nothing but risk in the project and would not be convinced otherwise. At the meeting he was simply outvoted. **The Corporate Office authorized me to bid on the MTA's development program, but I was forbidden to discuss future production of the bus.**

The design and development of the bus program, expected to take five years, was the **largest government-funded R&D transit program in U.S. history.** Suffice it to say, **Northrop developed an outstanding proposal and won the R&D contract.**

The concept definition/preliminary design contract was signed with a value of $3.8 million, making Northrop Grumman (Northrop had just acquired Grumman) the prime contractor on the MTA's Advanced Technology Transit Bus Program. The projected unit price was $300,000 in 1992 dollars.

It was decided early in the program that **funding for the R&D program would come from both the federal government and Los Angeles County.** The split was 80/20, with the Federal Transit Administration (FTA) providing the larger amount, or approximately $41 million. Northrop was not required to make any investment. **The amounts involved were unprecedented: never before had a county government funded a large R&D program, nor had FTA ever made a commitment for multi-year R&D funding.**

How was this achieved? **Northrop Grumman's core competency in government marketing was brought fully into play.** Working with MTA's lobbying firm in Washington, D.C., Northrop Grumman Washington Office personnel were assigned to support the program. I traveled to Washington frequently to acquaint the lobbying team with the particulars of the program and personally called on Congressmen, Senators, and Congressional staff members to gain funding support. In both **strategy-making and execution**, this was a true joint effort of the customer and contractor working to achieve a common goal — funding the program.

After intense lobbying, Congress added $6.2 million for the first year's work to the Transportation bill, appropriating the funds without their having been previously requested by the Administration or authorized by Congress. This was a most unusual step.

Later that year, 1993, the **Secretary of Transportation was personally briefed on the program, and from that time forward actively supported it**. He frequently referred to the program in speeches as a fine example of defense conversion and **government-industry partnership**. Funds for the next year's R&D work were therefore requested by the Administration and subsequently authorized and appropriated by Congress in the usual manner. **With this support, the ATTB became a national program and gained widespread public attention.**

I began to focus on the prospects of actually putting the ATTB into mass production. For this activity, I had no Corporate Office approval, but I began preliminary analysis anyway.

The U.S. domestic transit bus market varied in demand between 2,000 and 3,000 units of the "standard" bus size represented by the ATTB. At a unit price of $300,000, annual sales would exceed $1 billion per year. I estimated that the ATTB could capture 30 percent of the U.S. market within five years of production start-up. We also considered the European and Asian bus markets but found no partner company willing to produce our revolutionary design.

On October 8, 1996, after nearly four years of development, the first prototype ATTB was rolled out at Northrop Grumman's California factory. A total of six prototypes were delivered by the end of 1997, and road testing was conducted throughout most of 1998 in various cities. The road test program was a major technical success; no systemic failures were encountered.

In 1998 road testing was completed and results were presented to MTA and the Federal Transit Administration, both of which were highly pleased. This ended the ATTB R&D program. The question then was, who will put the ATTB into production?

Northrop Grumman stated from the beginning that it would make no commitment to put the bus into production. Strategic fit was the major consideration. Management also realized the company lacked key skills needed to succeed in this business: experience with high rates of manufacturing production and knowledge of the transit industry.

In the end, the ATTB R&D program was completed and the program office was disbanded. All drawings and prototypes were turned over to the MTA. **The bus was never put into production. The program was both a success and a failure — a radical new bus was successfully developed but never produced, with a waste of over $50 million in taxpayer funds.**

(This discussion is based on the author's personal knowledge and the following: Jose de la Torre and Wesley B. Truitt, "Northrop Grumman and the Advanced Technology Transit Bus Program," in Jose de la Torre, Yves Doz, and Timothy Devinney, eds., *Managing the Global Corporation: Case Studies in Strategy and Management*, New York: Irwin McGraw-Hill, 2001)

Entrepreneurship Lessons Learned

These four cases — GE, Ocean Spray, AT&T, and Northrop Grumman's bus — contain lessons for entrepreneurs working within a large organization and lessons for top management to promote and encourage innovation. **Entrepreneurial innovation was enabled by the six key factors discussed below. In AT&T's case, the absence of these factors was a contributing cause of the company's demise.**

- **Rapidly Changing External Environment.** All four companies faced <u>a dramatic and threatening change</u> in their external business environments that required a response.

  - GE's new threat derived from the growing success of low-cost Asian manufacturing intensifying its competition globally and from a company structure inappropriate to emerging market conditions.

  - Ocean Spray's challenge came from overproduction and falling prices, plus altered market conditions necessitating restructure of the cooperative into a new business model.

  - AT&T's threat in 1984 was the federal court's ruling to break it up, and its threat a dozen years later was the enactment of the Telecommunications Act of 1996, deregulating the industry and fundamentally changing the playing field by increasing competition.

  - Northrop Grumman's threat was the erosion of its major customer base with the sudden end of the Cold War.

- **Encouragement of Innovation by a New Change-Agent Leader.** An atmosphere of welcoming change was fostered

by <u>new top management, opening the door to lower-level</u>
<u>change-agents to innovate</u>.

- GE's new CEO, Jack Welch, the prime mover for change,
  deliberately altered the mindset within the company to
  encourage innovation wherever possible. Jeffrey Immelt
  has sustained this innovation culture.

- Ocean Spray's COO, Randy Papadillas, was the lead
  change-agent, building a consensus to change the business model and encouraging scientists and farmers to
  innovate in product development and product marketing.

- AT&T's CEOs were on record favoring changes to face
  the new competitive realities but were institutionally
  incapable of achieving it. Only under new CEO Michael
  Armstrong in 2000 did AT&T restructure into four operating companies. Yet, the surviving long-distance
  company, AT&T, was incapable of standing alone in the
  face of brutal competition and was internally paralyzed
  by a culture resistant to innovation.

- Northrop's new CEO, Kent Kresa, initiated change by
  asking for innovative use of the company's core competencies. Marketing organizations were particularly
  encouraged to develop new markets and new products
  within guidelines laid down by the CEO. The bus program, though the largest, was only one of more than
  50 such innovations.

- **Formal Approval Procedure for Entrepreneurial Activities.**
  Each company had <u>in place or developed a process</u> to review
  and approve innovations.

  - GE had a long-standing review process for evaluating
    new product and process ideas both at the operating unit

level and at the corporate level. These were not discussed above.

- Ocean Spray's COO established a process for initiating innovations and a procedure for their evaluation and approval, leading to implementation.

- AT&T lacked a formal process for innovation outside of purely technical matters. This was best illustrated by technology advancements at Bell Labs that were divested in the 1984 break-up. AT&T's culture was one of machine-like conformity, illustrated by employees referring to themselves as "Bell heads."

- Northrop Grumman's approval procedure began in the operating unit where the initiative originated. Each initiative was vetted by appropriate division staff, leading to general manager approval. Only then would the initiative be taken to the Corporate Headquarters, which was charged with evaluating and granting approval/disapproval company-wide for major new product initiatives.

- **Informal Processes for Innovation Acceptance and Implementation.** Companies having formal review procedures may also permit the <u>use of informal means</u> to promote innovations and facilitate their acceptance. Entrepreneurs utilizing these informal networks, which often <u>run parallel to formal channels</u>, are two-fold entrepreneurs: they are at once both innovators of new products and innovators of ways and means to achieve their acceptance. This is essentially a <u>political process developed by creative politicians to lobby policymakers</u> for acceptance and implementation of their ideas.

  - GE's formal procedure may appear to inhibit individual entrepreneurs from lobbying for their innovations unless they have the support of senior executives and corporate staff members, yet enterprising individuals will always find back-channels to the top and use them.

- Ocean Spray's small size and openness to innovation foster upward movement of ideas and innovations on a personal as well as a formal basis.

- AT&T's rigid command and control structure and imbedded conformity culture militated against entrepreneurs developing back-channel lines of upward communication.

- Northrop Grumman was small enough ($5 billion in 1991 sales) and open enough to enable those with initiative and personal connections to lobby for new initiatives at senior division and corporate levels. Individuals could pursue an idea using personal networking up to the point where the innovation required formal management approval.

- **Open Culture Permitting Risk-Taking Initiatives.** Firms having a culture of openness to ideas and new initiatives provide fertile ground for internal entrepreneurship. Apple, Google, 3M, and eBay are examples. These companies believe ideas have merit, and, even if they fail to produce measurable success, their authors are neither punished, nor do they lose face.

- GE's Jack Welch fostered innovation and "thinking outside the box" to enliven GE's people to achieve stretch goals, and Jeffrey Immelt's approach is the same.

- Ocean Spray has a culture of try it: if it works — great; if it fails — go on to the next idea. This is as good a non-risk-averse culture as it gets.

- AT&T's management could not begin to grasp this concept. The "Bell head" mentality of conformity and rote execution of top-down command is as far away from an open culture as can be imagined.

- Northrop Grumman encouraged innovation and stimulated it with exploratory funding, awards and prizes, and other forms of recognition for achievement. Failure was not punished; it was accepted as part of the innovation process. One of the two companies (Lockheed being the other) that invented stealth technology could not be otherwise.

- **Favorable Internal Systems Fostering Innovation Execution.** The point here is that a company having a systemic approach to the development, review, and approval of innovations <u>must also have a process for their timely **execution**</u>. Clearly such a systemic implementation process exists at Apple, Microsoft, Target, Toyota, and 3M. Once approved, innovations at these firms are executed, and <u>the entire corporation systematically supports the launch</u>.

- GE's review process does not permit approval of a new product launch unless it is also given full corporate-wide backing, leading to execution of the initiative with maximum probability of success. With GE's enormous global resources ($173 billion in sales in 2007), this is as near a guarantee of success as any product launch could hope for.

- Ocean Spray's limited resources require that any initiative receiving approval must be a winner. Their track record of success over the past half-dozen years attests to solid company-wide backing to execute every new product launch.

- AT&T was a systemic failure in many respects, starting with an inability to stimulate initiatives, and even failure to execute its existing business model. In the end, this was a company in meltdown.

- Northrop Grumman has an internal approval system that ensures that once an initiative is approved it will be backed with the full resources of the entire corporation. The bus R&D program was a success. The fact that it did not go into production was not the fault of the program but the consequence of a strategic fit decision made at the highest level.

CONCLUSION

The six factors cited above are the necessary, but not sufficient, ingredients for successful entrepreneurship within a large business. **Companies possessing these qualities have an <u>improved probability</u> of successful entrepreneurship and execution of innovations**, assuming the initiatives themselves make business sense. **Companies lacking one or more of these qualities have a <u>low probability</u> of success and long-term survival.**

The common denominators for success are:

- A **change-agent leader** who recognizes the altered external environment

- The leader understands **change is needed within the organization**

- The leader then **infuses an entrepreneurial spirit** throughout the company

- The leader establishes **procedures for innovation approval** and organization-wide **follow-through support** during execution

- The leader permits personal initiative networking to promote innovations

In the final analysis, success boils down to **leadership!**

"Believe that you can do it, under any circumstances. Because if you believe you can, then you really will. That belief just keeps you searching for the answers. Then pretty soon you get it."

Wally "Famous" Amos

Chapter Nineteen

Can a Young Person REALLY be an Entrepreneur?

By Brad Keywell

Special Note from the Editor:

Brad Keywell was my student at the University of Michigan He is clearly among my top two best students ever, and I have taught some 15,000 students in my 40 years as an educator (the other one is a multi-billionaire, but in his fifties — Brad is targeting the billionaire status, and is well on his way, but is still in his thirties). Brad is what I would call a "wunderkind"! He came to me as an 18 year old Freshman and advised me he wanted to take my Graduate Entrepreneurship class! I said no! He kept selling himself, and I became extremely impressed with his passion. Rather than failing, as I feared he would do, he was actually the best student in the graduate class, as a Freshman in College! During his stay at *the University of Michigan he started numerous businesses to finance his education, and was actually written up in Business Week Magazine for selling one of his businesses as a Senior for millions. He bought a troubled business after graduating, then started a new business, built it up, and sold it for $241 Million in his late twenties. He is just plain a genius at the entrepreneurial game. I asked him to do this chapter so the reader can gain some insight into what a natural born entrepreneur thinks like. We can all learn from peeking into his thought process!*

Brad Keywell was a Bachelor of Business Administration (BBA) graduate of the University of Michigan School of Business in 1991. He earned his Juris Doctor degree from the University of Michigan Law School in 1993! While at the University of Michigan he obtained an internship with the entrepreneurial genius Sam Zell, and has since worked closely with Zell on several projects, including a short stint with Sam at Equity Group Investments, Zell's investment vehicle. Brad currently sits on the Board of Directors of the Zell-Lurie Institute of Entrepreneurship at the University of Michigan. Brad has founded fourteen business of various sizes in his young years, and is currently in the process of building three businesses: MediaBank, a technology provider to the global media buying community, which currently has $35 billion of media spend on its platform; Echo Global Logistics, a transportation/logistics business founded in mid-2005, which three years after being started has over 750 employees, and is going public in the next year; and ThePoint, a brand new social-networking-meets-collective-action venture which Brad describes as a very fun adventure!

INTRODUCTION

One of my most influential books when I was young is "Letters to a Young Poet" by Ranier Marie Rilke, and it influenced me because I felt like it spoke to me, about the issues I was thinking about at the time, in a way in which no one else seemed to be able to. It spoke about creativity and poetry, not about the technique of poetry, but rather about the need for expression and **the singular challenge** a poet has **to express and create.** I mention this in the context of a book about entrepreneurship because I relate it to the role of the entrepreneur.

The entrepreneur is unique in our society — we rely on entrepreneurs to innovate, to create, and to push our capitalistic society into progress and innovation. But, at the same time, the odds in business are stacked against the entrepreneur, and **very few voices speak clearly and profoundly to those who aspire to create and innovate.**

To me, an entrepreneur is someone who does not merely want to create, it is someone **who NEEDS to create.** Someone who can not fathom living in an environment other than one created by him, someone who has no tolerance for taking things the way they are, but rather has an innate need to question the status quo and strive to create his own status quo.

Wanting versus needing is the key concept here — if you merely want to start a business, but don't need to, and don't have the fire in your belly that totally and completely precludes visualizing yourself on a path more conservative and secure than that of entrepreneurship, then the odds are that you will either

- find a way to not be an entrepreneur,

- sort-of-kind-of become an entrepreneur, and then retreat to the hills once challenge looks you in the eyes, or

- dive head first into entrepreneurship, but fail and go to Plan B.

The odds of success for people starting businesses in the U.S. is staggeringly stacked against the entrepreneur — some accounts are that fewer than 10% of new businesses are still around after five years, and even fewer after 10 years, and fewer still those that are able to sell or exit within this time.

Why do I lay out this grim picture? Because it should serve as motivation, not fear, for the true entrepreneur. The entrepreneur cannot envision herself doing anything other than risking and creating and innovating; **thus the long odds against success serve purely as challenge, not as barrier.** If you find yourself literally unable to contemplate any other livelihood than being a creator, then dig in! If you find yourself weighing creation versus the standard take-a-job and make-a-salary situation, I recommend taking that job and making that salary.

But, if you are like me, and entrepreneurship is literally a definition of the only thing you want to do, then the question is: What can you do to make sure you are as successful as possible? I have a simple answer, one that can be applied to anyone and anything, and one that can serve you well not only in business, but in life. My answer:

- Calibrate Risk

- Calibrate Reward

- And don't let your ego, your emotions, or anything else get in the way!

Once you do this, **use third grade math** to determine what is worth doing, what is not worth doing, and what you should avoid at all costs. **The third grade math is simple, the rewards should be at least 10 times the risk; otherwise, find another idea.**

Let me explain. Most entrepreneurs do a very poor job of understanding what their true risk is, and what their true reward is, when going into a venture. The best illustration is the personal guarantee, where, in order to get a loan, an entrepreneur signs a personal guarantee which guarantees that his entire net worth, all of his assets, and all of his livelihood will go to pay back the bank if the business venture fails. This may sound brutal and extreme, but people across the country sign on this dotted line every day.

Why would you do such a thing? Why mortgage your entire life on the hope that your venture succeeds? The answer, **if done properly, is that the odds of success are so high, and the rewards of success are so great, that it's a good bet.** The problem is that this equation is rarely calibrated properly.

I so often read business plans, and see people starting businesses, where the reward if everything goes 100% perfect is a tiny business. **Why go to bat if you don't want to hit a home run?** If you go to bat, and in your wildest dreams you may hit a single, then you've got a problem. And many businesses, at their most successful states, are singles, which should be the first sign to **not** sign a personal guarantee (and probably a sign to find a venture with more potential reward).

I say to "calibrate" risk and reward because it is a hugely imperfect science to figure out the quantitative side of both concepts, and **the best one can do is approximate.** But, calibrate we must do, and our challenge is to be good calibrators.

A strong entrepreneur should be the first one to entertain an idea, go to the ends of the earth exploring its viability, talk to everyone there is to be talked to in order to understand every aspect of the prospects for success and failure, but at the end of the game should be like a wine collector when making his decision of whether to proceed. A wine collector, very much unlike a wine drinker, does not buy wine because he is thirsty, because he wants to get drunk tonight, or because his wife likes the look of the bottle. A wine collector buys with a ton of knowledge, and buys for value, **weighing the odds** of appreciation against the risk of spoilage.

An entrepreneur should not start a business because it feeds his ego at the time, because it is "cool", or because it can provide him a little bit of money in the short-term. An entrepreneur needs to understand **exactly what can go wrong**, and, of equal importance, exactly what can go right. My advice to all is that if something is worth your time, your sweat, and your good name, **the upside opportunity should be significant and meaningful.** If it's not an upside that you would describe as a grand slam, then go on to the next idea.

So, in a longwinded way, I hope I've offered a brief perspective on what not to do:

- **Don't fall in love with ideas**, as they are plentiful and most of them are worthless. Fall in love with execution, knowing that you have a unique ability to execute in ways that few others can

- **Get everything out of the way** when assessing the risk and reward of a prospective new venture — your ego, the mania of the day (and there is always some business mania going on), your personal fear and doubt — all of this should be muted when you are assessing the risks and rewards of a concept

- Be careful to not go to the plate if the most you can hit is a single. **Give yourself the opportunity to hit home runs**, and grand slams, especially if your risk is significant.

A Little About Me

I am not sure when or how I determined that I was an entrepreneur, but probably sometime when I was in my early years of elementary school!

I started to understand what business was when I would to go to my dad's office. I saw that my dad was the "leader" of his law firm, having founded it, and I really liked the feeling of him in charge.

Later, I refined my ideas about what it means to be in charge and determined that I wanted to be the one making the decisions, not the counselor giving advice to the person making the decision.

I started my first business when I was 6, making greeting cards (my parents supplied the raw materials) and selling them to family friends. I even tried to trademark my logo. When I was 9, I created a board game and sent a letter to Milton Bradley (for those who don't know, this used to be one of the largest makers of board games) to try to get them to make it and sell it. Then I did hourly odd jobs and services, but ending up stopping that business when a customer took the $1/hour rate seriously, and gave me literally one dollar for one hard hours' work (previously I was banking on tips).

My business adventures continued throughout high school and college, including home watch services, a bagel delivery service, campus handbooks and discount cards, graphic arts posters, t-shirts, promotional calendars and many more.

I found true success in college when I had the idea to create a "modern art" version of the block M (Michigan's logo). With little budget, my idea was to have a contest at the Michigan School of Art, and the winner would get the award of having his or her art featured in the poster (in other words, cheap labor — although I did offer the winner a cut of the profits, which resulted in thousands of dollars to her).

Now, nearly twenty years later, I can say that "Painting the Perfect Picture," the name of the poster, is the best selling poster in University of Michigan history, and the sales continue to this day. With this success, **my entrepreneurial blood was really starting to flow**, as I tasted true entrepreneurship, tasted monetary success, and my brain started to figure out how business operated, what formula led to profits, and how it really worked to start a business.

By the time I graduated from the University of Michigan, I had several businesses started and operating at the same time, including a publishing business that had the best business formula of all. I collected the money from advertisers for advertisements in our cultural handbook, and only when I had the money (and profits) in hand did I have to make the investment of printing the book. With an office, employees, and meaningful profits, I did what any fledgling entrepreneur would do (heavy exaggeration here) — I applied to law school!

Why would I apply to law school when what I wanted to do most was start and build businesses? Well, first of all, my father, who is my role model and one of my primary inspirations, was a graduate of Harvard Law School, and successfully persuaded me that a legal education was an invaluable asset for business. And, second of all, Sam Zell, one of the nation's most successful businessmen and a mentor to me, told me of his experience going to law school and how valuable it later was to business. With the strong persuation of both my dad and Sam, law school became my next logical step.

As it turned out, going to law school was truly one of the single most important and valuable experiences in my life, and pays dividends every single day (to this day) in some way. In fact, when I speak to entrepreneurship classes at colleges, I sound like a broken record extolling the virtues of a legal education (and doing my best to persuade the business school students that if they really want to learn about business, they should go to law school).

When I went to law school, it was something I wanted to do for myself, not for a job or a career! It has certainly benefited me today in surviving and winning in the entrepreneurial world

My first entrepreneurial experience, post-law school, began with seeking a business to buy during my second year of law school, then going through three separate investigations/due diligence experiences during the next year. I learned that you can't jump at the first business you see — you need to look at each one with total objectivity, and (as I said above) **remove all emotion and ego from your assessment.**

Finally, my business partner, Eric Lefkofsky, and I negotiated a purchase agreement for the business we ultimately acquired while studying for our law school exams. We moved to Wisconsin to finish the acquisition and take over the running of the business before actually taking the Bar exam. The ironic fact is that I took the Bar exam for the State of Illinois AFTER I had acquired my first business, knowing full well that I would never practice law.

Since then, I have started and grown many businesses, in many industries. My list of experiences, lessons, and insights could fill a book in itself. But the most blatant reflection (and lesson) I have from my experience is that **passion and resourcefulness are the keys to success**, and that **the limits of your capabilities are only defined by the limits of your willingness to take smart, calculated risks.**

I often repeat the maxim, **"Everything comes to he who hustles while he waits."** By this, I mean that if you are constantly thinking, exploring, testing, asking, and learning, even when you are seemingly just passing time, then opportunity will find you.

Down to Business: Can a Young Person Really be an Entrepreneur?

You bet!!!!!

Here are some key thoughts that I feel are critically important to helping a young person believe in himself/herself, and the fact that they not only **can, but will win at the game of Entrepreneurship!**

- **There is no time like the present to act on your gut instincts.** The surest way to not find out what you can do is to not try to do what you think you can do. I often find that the people who "want to be entrepreneurs" are separated from those who **are** entrepreneurs simply because entrepreneurs are able to **do, and not just think about doing.** If you believe in your ideas, do something about it. I'm not suggesting to start every business you think about, but I am certainly suggesting to research, talk about, explore, and conceptualize every single idea you have — the bad ideas will quickly fail this scrutiny, and the good ones will rise to the top.

- **Any belief that a young person can NOT be an entrepreneur is wrong.** In fact, if you study the Forbes 400, you will find dozens of our nation's most successful entrepreneurs started when they were in their late teens or young twenties, and that this start led to a **PATTERN** that, while modest in its beginnings, led to huge success over time. **Age has ZERO correlation to success**, other than the fact that age leads to experience, which leads to higher degrees of success and a more sophisticated utilization of resources. But, **the best time to pursue your unique passion is NOW.** The old proverb says that the best time to plant a tree is ten years ago, and the second best time is right now. In other words, NOW is the time!

- **Entrepreneurs are "tinkerers of ideas,"** constantly playing around with concepts, ideas, and plans for how to make things better, do things better, and solve problems. I am constantly thinking about new business ideas, researching them, writing about them, and visualizing how they might work.

What does it look like to tinker with an idea? Well, here's how I do it:

- If I like an idea, I write it down. The practice of writing it down, thinking about it, organizing it, looking at it, and refining it is a great way to clarify what is the essence of the idea, what are the challenges inherent with it, and whether it passes the "simple test" (is it simple enough to be understandable and achievable).

- If I really like it, I write an entire business plan around it. I think, and spell out, what it will really take to make it work, and in the process explore the dynamics around execution of the idea, and the true risk/reward inherent in the idea.

- If I still like it, I talk to everyone I know (and find and meet those I want to know but don't yet know) who might have an opinion about it, and hear what they have to say.

- And, if the idea survives all of those levels of filter, then it might be time to start a new business!

You should be doing the same thing — tinker with ideas, and make sure you are watching carefully so you don't miss those that have true possibility.

- Great inventors do not get their best inventions when they begin tinkering, but **if you do not tinker, you will never invent**. Play with ideas, talk about ideas, let your ideas play with each other, and watch the ideas of others to see how they overlay against yours. **How will you find out what you REALLY want to do until you begin figuring out what you DON'T want to do?** I often tell friends who have business concepts that I like the idea, but it's not a business, but that they should pursue the idea in order to find out where it will LEAD them. My belief is that one idea leads to another, and that the first level of ideas (like the skin of the onion) is not where the fun (or money) is. The real action is in the middle of the onion once you've peeled back all of the layers. The same is true, too, with entrepreneurial passion. **You need to start with one idea and see where it leads you in order to find the real action.**

- The world's influential thinkers, doers, and entrepreneurs **have many more failures, attempts, and misses than they do successes**, thus you must start now if you want to give yourself the advantage of experience. My best business lessons are from my failures, not my successes. In fact, **failure is much more valuable** (although, unfortunately, not more lucrative) **than success.** Failure lets you see who you are, understand what you can do, and experience the resolve and dedication that makes each of us special and unique. **If you are not prepared to fail, you should NOT pretend to be an entrepreneur!** Failure and success go hand in hand, and both are the natural fruits of an entrepreneurs' labor.

- I've always said **either you are or you aren't an entrepreneur** — and, either way, there's not much you can do about it. Entrepreneurs **must** create, and cannot even conceive of themselves doing anything else other than creating business opportunities for themselves. If you find the prospect of a safe paycheck and a comfortable day-to-day job attractive, you should take it and not waste your time pretending to be an entrepreneur. If you **must** create, and the prospect of not being a creator and innovator is one you cannot fathom, then you are an entrepreneur, and you should **get to work!**

- If you can imagine yourself taking the easy road, getting a job and just making yourself invisible to serve out your tenure, then you should not attempt to do anything on your own. **At the first sign of failure, your brain will find that imagined "easy route" and will paralyze you with fear.** The world depends on entrepreneurs for innovation, progress, and the creation and definition of our future! If the "easy road" is not on your map, then you are an entrepreneur, and one of the people who will help define our collective future with your innovation, passion, and resourcefulness.

What is an Entrepreneur?

This is a very tough issue to clarify! They come in all sizes, shapes, colors, and personalities than you could ever imagine. A multitude of books have been written trying to define the entrepreneur! All have good insight and thoughts. I believe there are **several really critical traits** that the entrepreneur needs! I also believe firmly that **these traits can be developed and honed to perfection.** You don't need to be born with them; you can develop them, particularly with practice. Entrepreneurs:

- Are resourceful people who have the traits of passion, persistence, focus, and drive to make it work, no matter what

- Have the ability to see the simple in the sea of complexity

- Find sources of value in the things they commit to and attach their dreams to

- Devote 110% of their energy to the execution of the idea their mind created

- Have vision and can see the simple solutions to the complex problems they are attacking

- Are risk quantifiers! Notice I did not say "risk takers." They have the ability to quantify both risk and reward better than the average person

- Can choose routes with optimal risk/reward equations in an unbiased manner

- Are the type person who loves the art and science of creation

- Remember that **resourcefulness is the entrepreneurs' strongest and most precious trait.** You must use your resourcefulness to overcome any adversity, including that of being a young person in an old person's world

Is This You?

If yes, then age is no determinant or critical factor!

Key Thoughts of Those I Admire As Winning Entrepreneurs

Profiles in Entrepreneurship! President Kennedy's book was called Profiles in Courage, and celebrated those who took risks based on their internal conviction and devotion to what they think is right; a book about entrepreneurship could easily be called Profiles in Courage as well, as **successful entrepreneurs are champions of courage**, who take risks based on their internal conviction, and who are devoted to what they think is right.

Other key lessons from other great entrepreneurs include:

- **Richard Branson:** Are you willing to devote your creative energies to your ideas, put yourself 100% into your vision, and then expand your vision to the limits of your abilities?

- **Michael Dell:** Are you willing to see the simple in the complex, and take a privileged life and make it complicated because you are so convinced that your idea will truly make a difference in the world?

- **Sergey Brin and Larry Page:** Are you willing to take the world that you see and use all of your intelligence and experience to conceive a better way for that world to work, and then follow your vision?

- **Kirk Perron (Jamba Juice founder):** Are you willing to observe trends and have a great idea, and rather than just talk about it, are you willing to do something about it?

- **Ralph Lauren:** Are you willing to define a space that does not yet exist, and allow your passion to be so strong as to create an image and lifestyle that reflects your idealistic aspirations?

- **Sam Walton:** Are you willing to sacrifice the present in order to deliver your vision of the future, and believe in yourself and your vision despite the doubters and naysayers?

- **Jeff Bezos:** Are you able to dream big, and see not just a small opportunity, but rather a game changing, industry changing revolution?

- **Steve Jobs:** Can you create a picture of the way things should look and feel, passionately translate that look and feel into everything you do, and then convince others that you see what others don't?

Is this you?

Do you see yourself in these profiles?

Then create a new portrait, of yourself as an Entrepreneur!

How Do You Start?

Many people spend their time asking others "what do I do", "how do I do it", or "what should I do first?"

I prefer to turn the question around — if you believe you are an entrepreneur, then, no matter how old or young you are, my advice to you is to **find all of the answers.** No book will tell you what to do, no class will explain to you how to do it, and no single person can tell you whether or not you CAN do it. Only YOU can figure this out.

The primary quality that I see in entrepreneurs that makes them different than everyone else is **resourcefulness!** That's right. Not intelligence, not wisdom, and not math skills. None of these are even remotely as valuable as sheer resourcefulness. In fact, if I had to hope for one skill to rise among others in my own kids, it would be resourcefulness — my hope is that they can figure out **not just what to do, but, more importantly, how to do it.**

You, as an entrepreneur, are challenged with a task that has no instruction manual. Your task, once you decide what business you want to create, is to figure it out. And don't even for a moment think someone is going to tell you how to do it — if they could tell you how to do it, they would do it, and you would not be in a position to reap the rewards of millions of dollars if you figure out how to do it.

You will certainly get it wrong, a lot! I have. But each time you get it wrong, you will learn a little bit about how to get it right the next time.

Failure is a magnificent teacher!

As an example, in a class called **"Failure 101"** at the University of Michigan, with no advice, guidance, or "how to," we were asked to make something out of popsicle sticks and then go sell it on the street — a great learning experience. Creativity abounded, and people learned how to find the answers to what they thought was an impossible assignment. The year was 1988, and it was a concept well ahead of its time. Twenty years later, Donald Trump on "The Apprentice" is doing the same thing — giving people difficult tasks not to see if they will succeed, but rather to observe how they will perform in the face of failure.

I often say that **the best education is** not in any classroom, but **at the door.** Door to door sales of anything, whether the doors are peoples' homes, boardrooms, or local businesses, are the best way to learn about yourself and your strengths and weaknesses. People telling you NO all day long is a sure way to figure out ways to get them to say YES — you see, as human beings, we like hearing "yes" more than we like hearing "no," so your natural instincts and resourcefulness will lead you to the answer of how to create more "yes" and less "no."

Do you have what it takes to hear "no" and keep going?

Can you figure out how to turn a "no" into a "yes?"

You are not an expert at this from birth — no one is — but the only way to get good at it is to try, and, while you're trying, to remember that God gave you a gift (your brain) that will allow you to become great at this if only you will let it reach its incredible potential.

You can easily **not** let your brain help you, by focusing on fear, doubt, self-defeat, and more!

Don't!

What I Know for Sure!

This is a great question that I often ask people I meet, that Oprah has asked many of her guests — **what do you know for sure?** It is a refreshing way to consider where you are on your life path

I am still young myself (38), and thus what I know for sure today will likely be much different or, in other words, much more limited in breadth and depth than what I'll know for sure when I'm 48 and 58. But I know a few things for sure when it comes to business and entrepreneurship, and what

I have learned has allowed me to have some success as an entrepreneur!

Think about these ideas as you plan your future Entrepreneurial conquests:

- **Failure will happen**, but what determines your fate is how you deal with it.

- **Inventory is bad**, if you can avoid it. While some entrepreneurs are gifted at managing inventory, I much prefer managing technology, service levels, and, ultimately, profits.

- **EBITDA and Free Cash Flow are what it is all about.** While there are many financial metrics to put on your spreadsheets, the only two worth losing sleep over are EBITDA and Free Cash Flow.

- **Friends make great friends, and generally lousy business partners.** While I have the rare pleasure of having a lifelong friend who is also my business partner, it is our very unique and complimentary characteristics that make us so effective. In most instances, I strongly advise against going into business with someone because they are your friend. I talk to many young people who are exploring starting a business, and who invariably tell me they have a friend who wants to do it with them. When I probe, it turns out that the friend's involvement makes them feel more comfortable, and they think will let them have more fun. These are no reasons to choose a partner. A 50/50 partnership most often equals confusion and complication. It is the rare 50/50 partnership that works — and if you are the one who is "making it happen," then you should make the call, and you should make more of the money.

- **Find partners based on their talents**, not on how comfortable they make you feel with the risk you're taking.

- **The best ideas are generally not revolutionary, but evolutionary.**

- **Simplicity rules.**

- If you find yourself **thinking that your idea is so good that if anyone else hears it, then they will steal it** and make the millions that you should have made, you should **stop kidding yourself.** Ideas are cheap, execution is priceless.

- The **best businesses** I've seen **are ones dependent on execution**, not on the idea. Great execution makes for great businesses. Rarely is an idea so good that it, in itself, makes for the great business.

- **The most important thing that I know for sure: You can do it!**

If you are taking the time to read this book, it shows that you care enough to take your valuable time to read these words and think about them. This shows that you can do it.

The Main Question Is Whether You Will Let Yourself Do It

- Will you be **paralyzed** by the fear of failure?

- Will you **quit** your journey at the first sign of failure?

- Will you let your **fantasies** of risk and failure get in the way of your vision of success?

- Will you allow yourself the time and patience needed to grasp the full meaning of the concept of **"resourcefulness,"** and let your creative energies find their resourceful side?

- Will you **harness failure** and learn how to use it as the best learning tool around?

- Will you **overcome your first failure**, move on to the next, and walk the stepping-stones to success?

Final thoughts on Winning as a Young Entrepreneur

Make it happen. Now.

Don't force yourself on a business — let a business idea force itself on you, and then pour all of your energy, passion, and RESOURCEFULNESS into it to make it succeed.

Keep your ego and emotion out of the risk assessment.

Make sure that the reward is huge enough that you will be happy you took the risk.

If you simply MUST pursue your ideas, and cannot fathom a 9-to-5 job, then you are ready to change the world. In fact, the world is waiting for you to change it — now.

It's your move. Make it happen!

You Can Do It!

Now Go Out And Do It!

"Were the diver to think on the jaws of the shark,
he would never lay hands on the precious pearl."

Saadi

Chapter Twenty

Being a Winner or a Loser: It is Your Choice!

By Fred Kiesner

INTRODUCTION

Being a successful Entrepreneur is not an easy task! It requires you to commit your entire persona to making it happen. You don't just do it with a partial commitment. **It takes a 110% commitment!!!!!**

Part of accomplishing this is that you seriously look at all you do in life — what choices are you making that would tend to drive you towards being a Winner, versus being a loser?

These choices confront you many times during the day — you must learn to go in the right direction, almost automatically! It is similar to the military, the football team, or the soccer team — practice, practice, practice! Eventually you will begin to just automatically make the right choice between "evil and good," being a Winner or being a loser!!!!!

I hope you will **let me into your head** a little bit during this discussion! I hope you will set up a tiny little spot in the left rear quarter of your powerful, wonderful brain where the thoughts I am going to present below can take root, gestate, grow, and eventually bear wonderful fruit in your actions, achievements and success as a Winner!!!!!

Perhaps some of what you will consider here will strike you as a bit obvious and basic. If so, good! That will indicate to me that you are already well on your way towards being a Winner! You might even think that some of it is corny, or old-fashioned! Maybe, but good old-fashioned values and actions are what lead many of the biggest winners in the Entrepreneurial game towards unbelievable success. Sometimes we need to think about the "corny" things in life!

It is all about learning to control your actions and making sure that your total thrust is towards winning, not diverting your actions towards diffusing the effectiveness of what you do.

I have taunted my students with the following thoughts for about 40 years, and an awful lot of them are exceptionally successful, so **maybe there is some truth to what is said here!**

Take that chance, and listen to what I am suggesting!

Think on these thoughts — they cannot hurt you, and they certainly can really propel you towards success!!!!!!!

I warn you, I try to always be a positive thinker — the Entrepreneur and Winner cannot be anything else. **Negativity is the**

absolute antithesis and enemy of the concept of winning! Never, but never, forget that!!!!!!!!!

I do hope you will let your guard down and let some of these ideas sink in!

- I deeply believe **we are born to win! We condition ourselves to lose through our own actions or inactions!** Thus, we can impact where we are heading and how we get there! If this is true, why on earth would you ever give any thought to not heading for the winning side? Yet millions and millions make that negative choice in their lives every minute! Why? Don't join the crowd, take the high road. Yeah, the road is tougher and steeper, but oh boy, is the view ever grand when you get to the winners' flag at the top of the mountain!!!!!!!!!!!

- You have a **right to be a winner, not a guarantee!** You must earn it, not just expect it!

- You **learn to be a winner**, being a loser comes automatically through inaction and laziness!

- You **learn in all you do**, therefore do an awful lot of stuff!!!!!!!

- **You can change. It is not written in fate!**

- You are truly **charting the course today for where and how far you are going** in the future! If you accept that, invest everything you have in brainpower and talent to lay a most magnificent and powerful foundation for the future! Yet, we tend to think only of what is happening in the now — exams, projects, super date tonight, what is for dinner! Nice things, but the mundane and unimportant aspects of your future.

- You must **set aside time to think on the more profound things in life** that can super-charge your direction and achievements! Try to take an afternoon a week where you go someplace peaceful and quiet with nobody around to bother you, and just think on what you are doing right or wrong, what needs to change, your short-term targets, intermediate, and most important, your long-range goals, targets, and hopes! I tell my students and clients to go "sit on a rock" at the beach — that translates to **"Go Soar!"**

- You must **think about and accept the gifts you have** — not the things you don't have. Then maximize the impact and effect of those gifts! I am talking about the gifts we often treasure (beauty, brains, being from a good home, etc.); these are all given to us, and you did little to earn them. They were in your genes, and while they are neat, great, and wonderful, many of us do little to maximize them, develop them, and improve upon them. Enjoy and maximize what you have been given! You just must do this!

- However, I would submit to you that **sometimes the negative "gifts" we have been given in life can be the most wonderful** and grand stimulators towards excellence and success! If you were born on the wrong side of the tracks, from a poor home, from a split home, with a medical problem, etc. — I would argue that these can actually be the most wonderful gifs you could ever receive!

For instance, I had a massive heart attack at age 32 that ended my career as an Entrepreneur! But, it also drove me into a full-time career as an educator that has been the grandest and most fulfilling life I could ever imagine. Sounds funny, but I thank God everyday for sending me that heart attack!

Also consider this — receiving a "bad gift" in life, such as being born into poverty, is still a gift — if you look on the good side — you learn to survive by your own wits when you live with poverty, which is a critically important talent for the Entrepreneur to own.

On the opposite end of that spectrum, we are often jealous of those who are born "with a silver spoon!" Well, we have an old adage in the Entrepreneurship field, **"Poverty to Poverty in three generations!"** The first generation comes out of poverty by building a wonderful entrepreneurial venture. They turn it over to the children. The second generation doesn't appreciate what they get because they did not have to sweat for it. If the business survives (often they don't thrive), they turn it over to the Grandchildren. To the third generation it is often just a means to live the high life without having to work very hard (they think)! Thus, they end up destroying the business by inattention, and milking it rather than nurturing it. I can assure you that I have seen this happen countless times in my 40-year career of teaching Entrepreneurship!

Both good and bad breaks hone and shape the character and ability of the Entrepreneur!

The only thing that really counts in life is what you achieve with the gifts you get, good or bad. Nobody cares about what bad luck you have had — they do care about how you overcame difficulties, and built up something wonderful with your own abilities.

- **Entrepreneurs never hide behind excuses** for not achieving what they can, which is a grand lesson for us all to remember. They embrace the hand they are dealt, and make the most of it through their own determination and willpower! I know of very few Entrepreneurs who would ever consider going on welfare if they had some bad breaks! They just stand back up, dust themselves off, and start to build their life again from their own talents and resources! Stop complaining and get back to doing it!!!!!!!!

- **Failure is a learning experience to the Entrepreneur!** They want to win all the time, but they also know life doesn't work that way, so they accept the fact that sometimes they will have a setback or a bump in the road along their path to the glory of being a great Winner!

- **Winners pay the price today for success tomorrow!** They fight the temptation we all face these days to have instant gratification — it seems the big mantra today for young folks is **"we want it all, and we want it NOW!!!!!"** In some ways it is easier to take this short-term view, and probably more fun. However, the Entrepreneur with a wonderful future as a Winner knows that if sacrifices are made today to invest in the future, he/she **can win really big in the future**. It is kind of like the difference between having a hot Mustang today versus having a super hot Ferrari someday! Which would you be satisfied with???

- **Losers live for today!** They have excess commitment to short-term gratification — sex, money, cars, etc. They often think only of themselves!

- **Winners are future-oriented!**

- **Winners add substance and value** to all they touch in life. They don't **just take from life, they contribute to life and the world!**

- Winning Entrepreneurs recognize that they are the **major driving force in their future success!** Mommy and Daddy aren't going to ensure it (see above, even if you are born rich)! If it needs to get done, you gotta do it! No one owes you a thing in life but you! Accept that, and watch how far you can go!

- Remember that **everything you do in life is a brush stroke on the portrait of you!** Make sure you are Rembrandt creating a masterpiece!!!!!

- **Entrepreneurs know that image really counts!** Watch your body language, your facial attitude, your eye contact (really telegraphs sincerity), your voice, your tone, your handshake. People form an impression of you in 30 seconds. Use the little things like this to make sure the impression they form is the one you want.

- **Winners are memorable — be memorable in all you do!**

- **Winners associate with Winners!** Find heroes, role models, associate with stars (but certainly not the Hollywood types), but don't be a clone — do it your way! **Then turn around and be a role model yourself when you have won.** I once heard a man talk about how when he was young people helped him, and now he felt a compelling urge to **"toss the rope back over the wall to help the next generation of young Entrepreneurs to make it like he did!"** Boy, is it ever fun and fulfilling to be a mentor and help others! Incredibly fulfilling!

- Following up on the above, **find mentors, and then be a mentor!**

- **You are and will be what you truly believe you can be!** Walt Disney always used to say **"If you can dream it, you can do it!"** Dream big, it will become a **self-fulfilling prophecy!**

- **Winners get in the Habit of Winning!** Crawl before you walk. Start learning your power by winning the little victories, then build on them to obtain the greater victories of life.

- **Be realistic!** Losers want all or nothing! They don't understand that you earn what you get; it is not given to you for doing nothing.

- Winning Entrepreneurs **do not have the lottery mentality!** They don't waste their money on an 80 Million to One long shot. They invest their money in their **best odds chance in life — themselves!!!!!!**

- Those that win clearly understand that **perfectionism is the enemy of success!** The perfectionist often uses that trait as something to hide behind as an excuse for not achieving anything. Yes, you should strive for excellence, but you must do things and achieve a lot. You do not have the time for perfection, you will die before you get around to achieving what you are capable of! Do good stuff, forget about perfect stuff!

- **Winners plan and control the game they play.** Life is a game, find a game (business) you can win at, or move on and find a new game. Early on identify and follow the rules of the game you are in! Have a clear game plan, purpose, focus!

- Entrepreneurial **winners make themselves so very good that life cannot get to them!** Once you start winning, many will go after you, big time.

- Politics, unfairness, nastiness are part of the scene of building a business. **Don't hide behind it, or from it, neutralize it!**

- **Entrepreneurs, as Winners, are excited and exciting people!** Be that in spades, and you will find out how much fun it is.

- **Winners are resilient — they bounce back from defeats!** Get used to it; as you begin winning, many will delight in kicking you in the teeth and knocking you down. Learn to shake it off and get back to work.

- Winners are **doers, not watchers!** If you prefer sitting on the sidelines watching the action in the game, be sure you get a job at the Post Office where you can watch the world pass you by. You cannot be a quitter and cut and run when it gets tough in the path towards being a Winner!

- **Winners don't waste their energy complaining!** If your boat strikes a rock and gets a hole in its side, don't use a second of your precious time lamenting your misfortune — get to work fixing the leak so you can get on with winning!

- Winners remember **to take care of the fine print, as well as the big stuff!**

- Successful people who are Winners think like an owner in all that they do. If you start your career in the mail room, do what you do as though you are the President and Owner in training!!!!!!!! You are, if you figure out what winning is all about.

- Winners quickly **identify what Winners do in their field, and then do it much better!**

- Winning is not as difficult as you think, for **there are usually only a few critical elements in life and your field that you must master!**

- **Winners accept that they can and will have an impact on life and cause big things to happen. It is their destiny!**

- Those who win understand that their **brain and intellect are tools!** They use them just like any other tool, to leverage their ability and achieve something. They don't use their brain/tool just to prove how smart they are and impress others. Impress yourself, not others. Others will jump on your bandwagon as supporters when they see what you have done.

- **Guarding your reputation is critical to winning!** You can only lose it once. It is priceless, your greatest resource!

- Those who win **guard against a stupid, fatal slip!** Winning and success are fragile — always double-check yourself quickly to make sure you are not careless.

- Winners **identify the uniqueness in themselves, their winning ingredients!** Find them fast, then nurture them carefully!

- You must find a void — **do things others have not, or will not do!**

- Winners **never go where the bulk of their competition goes! Create your own special niche!**

- To win big, and stay there a long time, **you must be honest and ethical**. You can't be somewhat honest, or a little crooked! Be a straight shooter. The guy in the white hat!

- In my book, the big Winners in life **win with social responsibility!** I tell my students to tell me when they win big (and I have a lot of kids who are very successful). Then I will ask you what you are doing for society with your success and treasure! That is how I measure success in life — **what you do for the world with your wealth and the power it brings after you have won!** For the first part of your life, you took from society. Then you started to contribute to society. After you win, it is payback time to society!

- Successful people are **not afraid to be different!**

- Winners in life understand that if they **want to change the world, they must get the power to do it first**. Don't waste your time on futile efforts like protesting and picketing injustice and unfairness. Win, and win big — then you will have the influence and ability to fix what is wrong!

- Winners **don't fear criticism** — they recognize it as another tool they can use to grow and improve.

- Successful people are **prepared for attacks and jealousy**. The losers of the world **will** try to destroy you!

- Those who get to the top **manage their ego**. Yes, you need a really healthy belief in yourself, and the self-image to have the confidence to win, but don't let it grow to excess.

- If you want to win, **treat even the lowest person you encounter with respect and dignity!** Often those at low levels have the power to hurt you, and they know it. **One wins only if those who work for them want them to win!**

- To live to enjoy winning, **work very, very hard, but also play very, very hard!** You need the play time to clear your mind and rest your brain!

- Most people waste time. **For Winners, every minute is precious!**

- The **Winner must be able to say, when they die, the world is better for my having been here**. I have seen research that shows that those who are comfortable that they have done good in life (the winners) have a much more peaceful passing! Losers often find dying a terrible and frustrating ordeal because they recognize that their passing will not be noticed. Which way do you want to go to the great beyond?

CONCLUSION

Mahatma Ghandi had a wonderful saying; it went about like this: "In a gentle way you can change the world!" Winners know that, you must accept this.

Another quote of his, roughly remembered, is "Be the change you wish to see in the world!"

Go be a winner, my friends!

Change your world and the world around you!

Wow! What a wonderful ride you can and will have!

"We either make ourselves miserable, or we make ourselves strong. The amount of work is the same."

Carlos Castaneda

Chapter Twenty-One

Creating the University-Based Entrepreneurship Resource Center

By Cal Caswell

Dr. Cal Caswell is the Director of the Small Business Development Center and has been a Lecturer in Entrepreneurship, Management, Marketing, and Logistics at Loyola Marymount University for over twenty years at the graduate and undergraduate levels. His academic career started in 1977 at local community colleges, universities, and military bases. He has taught over twelve thousand college and university students since his first instructional experience in 1977. Dr. Caswell's professional business career was in the aerospace industry, where he spent 20 years. He earned his Educational Doctorate (Ed.D.) from Nova Southeastern University, and his MBA and BBA in Management from Loyola Marymount University in Los Angeles. His dissertation

was based on teaching prison inmates to restart their lives through a program called "My Own Business." In the past fifteen years, Dr. Caswell has taught and counseled over one thousand inmates, enabling them to become self-sufficient through entrepreneurship.

WHAT IS A SMALL BUSINESS ENTREPRENEURSHIP RESOURCE CENTER, AND HOW CAN IT HELP DEVELOP SUCCESSFUL ENTREPRENEURS?

Originally, the Loyola Marymount University Small Business Development Center (SBDC) was created under the College of Business Administration (CBA). Initial program funding was provided through a U.S. Small Business Administration (SBA) grant and university matching funds. LMU was motivated to involve itself in this endeavor from its earlier participation in the U.S. Small Business Administration's (SBA) Small Business Institute (SBI) Program.

The primary mission of the new center was to serve the local area community, from nascent entrepreneurs, to small businesses, to the campus community and the underserved and under-represented populations of the Los Angeles area. After several years of working with the SBA, we have taken our program "private" and eliminated all of our ties with the SBA and its funding. We are expanding our abilities to help the entrepreneurs into a broad new offering of creative new areas and needs, without restrictions — we serve the customer, the fledgling entrepreneur, and provide them with what they want and need in our new regional Small Business Entrepreneurship Resource Center.

Building a Program

We originally focused our efforts on structuring client accessibility and first-rate business consulting on topics ranging from how to create a business plan to marketing plans, financial issues, business law, contract terms and conditions, and accounting practices for nascent start-up businesses. The center immediately began offering short-term seminars and workshops on "How to Start a Business," "Marketing Your Enterprise," "Access to Capital," and "Choosing the Best Legal Structure." The seminars were conducted at **local area Los Angeles County Libraries as well as on campus**.

At the core of the center was the belief that the general economy flourishes when individuals are trained and educated about specific mechanisms for starting or growing a small business. We focused on serving a diverse audience from various income levels, specifically within the South Los Angeles region. 57% of the clientele self-identified as female, and over 50% of the total clientele are of Latino, African American, or Asian ethnic origin.

The second phase of development for the center was to expand the reach of its professional staff and services through a series of geographically accessible training seminars — taking the program off-campus and into the community. Community partnerships were formed that served the intended populations and enabled the Center to:

- Plan and execute generalized small business conferences in south Los Angeles, reaching over 1,000 small business owners and entrepreneurs (cumulatively) from different industrial sectors;

- Create a regular series of fee and no-fee specialized training seminars focusing on advanced aspects of small business development, held at geographically accessible locations throughout South L.A. on a regular, rotating basis;

- Create curriculum modules and obtain supplies for small business entrepreneurs who attend training sessions to use as future reference materials;

- Expand faculty presence to accommodate proposed schedule of training seminars, and to broaden the curriculum to include topics such as small business accounting, international business, and budget planning;

- Develop and print effective communication materials that will promote the training sessions throughout the target communities.

Entrepreneurship Resource Center Expansion

We have created and implemented a series of fee and no-fee high level business development training seminars for small business entrepreneurs by successfully collaborating with organizations such as the South Bay Workforce Investment Boards (SBWIB) and the South Bay Economic Development Partnership (SBEDP) to identify areas within the South Los Angeles area that were in need of economic development, or that demonstrated a propensity toward small business ownership. We identified specific geographic regions where training seminars would be most relevant, and worked to identify specific candidates to invite to both the kick-off conference and subsequent seminars.

To generate a broader interest in the full training series, we initiated plans for small business conferences, which offered a variety of generalized education — training sessions, networking activities, and expert speakers from the business community. These business information conferences were viewed as an interest-building tool for the future training seminars, and as an accessible source of generalized small business education for new and interested entrepreneurs from low to moderate-income communities.

The expansion of the Center and its training sessions were also tailored to the needs of a diverse, often Spanish-speaking population. We customized our small business conference series, training seminars, and workshops to particular business opportunities suited to this region. Specifically service industries, logistics, and international importing and exporting opportunities were targeted by our training programs. Of particular interest was training entrepreneurs to serve the needs of the gigantic Los Angeles International Airport and local area Ports of Call.

Establishing the Center

The first real challenge for the new center was to recruit and hire the right people! That process required several months, and ultimately a professional and experienced team was formed with a complement of five business professionals. Marketing our services was a constant challenge that required internal and external meetings, presentations, advertising, and an endless amount of "schemes" designed to inform potential clients of our services.

During the first two years of operation, the LMU SBDC staff must have answered the **"you mean there is NO-COST for these services?"** question about a thousand times, because our initial operations were totally free to the client!

In spite of a series of start-up difficulties, **much like our entrepreneurial clients**, we ultimately formed a powerful Entrepreneurial Resource Center dedicated to providing full-services to the client. We served over nine hundred and fifty clients in our first nineteen months of operation and provided well over two thousand hours of training through seminars and workshops.

Vision Statement

The LMU Center will be recognized as the area's resource of choice for entrepreneurs. It will be the most professional and competent source of business information, business resources, and analytical services to assist individuals in realizing their business dreams.

Mission Statement

The Center's mission is to provide business planning and evaluation services, professional consulting, as well as educational activities to entrepreneurial business clients in the South West Los Angeles area in order to assist them in achieving sustainable business success.

To accomplish our mission we:

- Provide consistent client focused, results-oriented, and cost-effective core services (counseling, training, informational and referral services), as well as specialized services to meet local needs;

- Maintain a highly dedicated, flexible, diverse, enthusiastic, professional, experienced counseling network;

- Act as a catalyst for sustainable economic development by responding to local business needs;

- Build strategic collaborative partnerships that leverage resources to enhance and expand services to our clientele;

- Work to build awareness of the LMU resource program — local, state, national.

Standard services provided by the center include:

- Business Plan Assistance

- Marketing Planning Assistance

- Strategic Planning

- Marketing Research

- Technical Assistance

- Site Location Assistance

- Loan Packaging

- Business Related Training Opportunities

- Financial Analysis

- Business Resource Library, including Internet Access

- Business/Community Advocacy

- Assistance in Identifying and Accessing Federal, State, Regional, and Local Funding Sources.

Our core values

The core values governing the LMU center include:

- Professionalism

- Competence

- Accuracy of Knowledge

- Business Development

- Professional Ethics and Social Responsibility

- Real Value to Clients.

Business Consultation

We provide one-on-one business consulting, which includes a wide-range of services, including legal advice. Every client receives confidential consultation from the LMU staff. Most clients meet with the staff multiple times, and some clients receive ten hours or more of consulting. We typically provide this service to existing small businesses, small business seeking to expand their business, small business owners, start-ups, and entrepreneurs.

Consulting is usually accomplished via our consultants' specializations. This center purposely recruited and hired professional consultants with unique educational and background experiences in business finance, loan development, marketing, production operations, logistics, management, and business law. All of our business professionals have advanced degrees and five years or more of small business ownership and management experience. Often, our clients need consulting assistance from several members of the team. Whenever possible, the entire consulting team meets with new clients to ascertain their eligibility and to identify their specific business needs.

Business counseling is designed to provide in-depth business assistance in areas such as marketing, finance, management, production, human resources, operational planning, organizational development, business planning, and the never ending search for likely target markets for the client's services or products. We try to allocate sufficient resources to positively impact small business start-ups and current business operation. The standard consulting client goal is 10.0 hours.

This center's experience has shown that many clients truly require five to ten hours of counseling. Many clients enter this center with the expectation that we will be doing all of their business planning, business plans, marketing plans, provide them with loans, and solve their legal issues as well. **It is critically important to fully inform the client at the first meeting that the center provides guidance and assistance in developing business plans and other services, but it is their responsibility to develop a quality business plan.**

It is clear that we lose clients once the client realizes that they need to take responsibility for these activities.

There is no free lunch — our goal is to help to give our clients the recipes for success, but they must create and build their own businesses. For some, this is difficult to understand — they want us to do it all.

In short, the Center makes available one-on-one consultation with our program specialists to all participants of the program. Consultations address participant's needs and provide confidential business advice on topics including: business start-up, company registration, legal structure and contracts (terms and conditions), business planning, marketing, budgeting and financial statements and financial planning, credit, banking and collections, international trade, and more.

Client Qualification, Client Assessments, and Selection

Providing professional small business counseling service is the overall goal of the LMU Center. Client assessment, qualification, and selection are a very critical piece of the service delivery mechanism. Client assessment and program qualification sets the counseling program in motion. Over the last two years we served over nine hundred clients. Approximately one-third of those that visited the center chose to not pursue business counseling services because they were not in a position to begin a business. We give them initial guidance, but we cannot do the work for them unless they have taken on the bulk of the work themselves.

Another third took advantage of the Center's services and primarily attended our no-cost small business courses. The final third of the initial client's actively worked with the Center's counselors, which in some cases amounted to many face-to-face counseling sessions.

The typical daily operating questions include which clients to serve, what projects to undertake, and when to stop. Regardless of the client, these are the questions to which the counselors are required to find answers. This approach is required primarily because the Center operates on limited resources. Therefore, assessing clients to ascertain their skill level, readiness, and intention to act are critical before we can commit our resources to any individual project.

WHAT IS A TYPICAL CLIENT?

Of the nine hundred plus clients that we served over the past two years, no entrepreneur or small business was exactly like another. Entrepreneurs are unique in their own right and have significantly different levels of ambition, skills, education, motivation, sophistication, and business acumen. Similarly, small businesses differ greatly in size, specific types, industries, and stages of development. Entrepreneurs present the most challenging situational issues to our counselors since every new client is so vastly different and there is no boilerplate solution that fits all clients.

Lessons Learned — That Helped us to Deliver Better Service

1. **Clients inaccurately defined their specific problem —** they focus their attention on the wrong issues. They feel that cash flow is the real problem, while it is clear that increasing sales is the solution they are really looking for.

2. Clients often visited the Center with a **misconception that we loan funds**, and that they will leave after the first visit with a check.

3. Clients occasionally **hide or forget critical financial information** such as filing for bankruptcy several years ago — often because of embarrassment.

4. Clients may be totally **unaware of the importance of things like strong FICO credit scores** and other measurements of reliability.

5. Clients may strongly desire to start and build their business but **may be unwilling to do the necessary work**. Writing a business plan appears to be a deal stopper with many of our potential clients. They want to just do it, starting this minute.

6. Clients have to be informed and educated on the **importance of writing a professional business plan** and that most lenders will not talk to them without it.

7. **Clients need reassurance** as they continue the small business counseling process.

8. **Clients need detailed instruction in specific areas** such as completing loan applications, permit requirements, contract terms and conditions, name search, website development, etc.

9. Clients often **need someone to just sit and listen** to their concerns, problems, and frustration in attempting to start their own business.

10. Clients benefit greatly from a thorough **review of many fundamental small business subjects** such as taxation, hiring

policies, where to find capital, learning how to apply for government-funded projects, and what organizational form to choose prior to business start-up.

The Time, Pride, and Speed Dilemma

Many potential small business clients will have limited resources, assets, experience, and time available to implement solutions:

- Many attempt to **avoid formal planning** (business plans, marketing, etc.), become exceedingly frustrated with the lack of progress, and then are plagued by problems and issues that result.

- **Procrastination** is unfortunately very common.

- Clients typically want to jump in right away and want to **learn by doing immediately**, rather than by reading, researching, and/or listening.

- Clients are **often suspicious of authority figures** and government.

- Unfortunately some clients are **late to the market** with their entrepreneurial ideas.

- Client **egos and highly sensitive personal feelings are often a problem**, requiring counselors to utilize their people skills more frequently than one would think.

Target Client Definition

The LMU Center focuses its resources on:

Pre-venture (A): Entrepreneurs who are interested in starting a business seek LMU Center services to acquire the information and management skills needed to establish a viable and sustainable business.

Start-up (B): Entrepreneurs in the process of starting a business or who have recently started a business seek our services to acquire the information and management skills needed to meet the daily specific, pressing, and immediate challenges of operating a viable and sustainable business. This is a critical stage for businesses, and one in which we can have a great impact.

Established (C): Mature business and entrepreneurs whose businesses are past the initial start-up challenges and who have been in business for a few years. These established businesses come to us when they need assistance in growing their businesses or in dealing with a specific challenge.

High-growth (D): Entrepreneurs whose businesses are growing or have the potential to grow at rates of 25% to 50% per year. We aim to help these entrepreneurs plan for and to successfully manage rapid growth. Entrepreneurs in high-growth companies, because they face sophisticated management challenges, usually require in-depth counseling and associated services.

Upon entering the LMU Consulting Program, each client is provided an entry consultation session which enables the consultants to map out a plan to assist the client. This initial activity includes basic information that identifies client and consultant assignments for follow-on meetings. This initial agreement confirms the commitment of both the client and the consultant. Both parties sign the form and set up schedules and assignments for future meetings. At the conclusion of this consulting relationship the client is provided a final consultation which will evaluate their progress and suggested future actions.

Roles of Counselors in the LMU Consulting Center

Skilled, qualified, and experienced counselors play a vital role in the Center's service delivery mechanism. Dedicated counselors contribute greatly to the Center's mission and goals, and certainly to the individual successes of the clients served. We put maximum emphasis on experience, dedication, and a caring attitude towards helping entrepreneurs when we hire our staff.

How do the LMU Consultants help the clients?

- By **focusing on working with clients that have high potential** for business improvement, growth, and economic impact.

- By **assisting the client in developing "scope of work"** for their business. Always mindful of result-oriented and achievable goals with a specific timeframe.

- By **developing a professional rapport with the client**.

- By providing **consistent record-keeping** of all client meetings, project status, and major developments to improve client's business.

- By **providing feedback to the Center Director** on the effectiveness of direct services and suggested solutions to client issues.

- By encouraging **clients to communicate frequently** with their Counselor.

- By **adhering to the LMU Code of Conduct**.

- By **presenting a professional attitude**.

- Hold the affairs of their clients in strict confidence,

- Strive continuously to improve their professional skills,

- Advance the professional standards of LMU's Center,

- Uphold the honor and dignity of the LMU College of Business Administration.

LMU COUNSELOR COACHING SKILLS — WHAT IS EFFECTIVE COACHING?

The Center Counselors fully realize and appreciate the fact that they must create a win-win interaction that fosters an atmosphere of teamwork with their client. This win-win atmosphere allows a counselor with specific professional knowledge and experience to help a client acquire knowledge, skills, and understanding related to his specific business issues and concerns.

Professional Coaching:

- Assists client in **setting attainable goals** and guides them in reaching those goals.

- Enables client to **do more work** on their business development than they would have normally done on their own.

- Helps clients to **focus** more realistically and accurately on their specific problems or opportunities.

- **Provides the tools**, counseling, support, and structure to obtain better and more immediate results.

Work-Assignments:

This technique of coaching clients teaches them how to **break-down the start-up issues** of beginning a business utilizing a step-by-step approach. Coaches must:

- Choose a quiet and reasonably private place to work with the clients while assuring them that their business ideas will be protected.

- Give work assignments that are meaningful and fit the client's specific business needs.

- Adapt work assignments to match the resources of the client.

- Whenever possible, prepare client "Homework" assignments in advance of client meetings.

Critical Elements Counselors Need to Consider in Preparing Client Work-Assignments:

- Determine the Objective of the Client Work-Assignment.

- Assure Understanding of the assignment. It is clear, logical, and doable?

- Set a Time Schedule for each assignment.

- Assure acceptance of the assignment.

- Keeping the door open if/when the client has difficulty in completing assignments.

- Encourage the client to work directly with the Counselor to review progress on work-assignments.

- Problem Solving is not exclusively the client's responsibility. Creating a win-win scenario for the client is essential!

- Identify possible solutions.

- Identify potential barriers that prohibit clients from completing assignments.

- Monitor and support the client's progress.

- Deal with Procrastination. Being encouraging and supportive to keep the client involved in the business development process.

As the work-assessments progress, each active **client should start realizing significant milestone accomplishments**. The typical milestones may vary in magnitude and relative importance to signify the continued development of a business. Significant milestones include: started business, bought a going business concern, copyright obtained, trademark obtained, location change, change in sales, changed legal form, jobs created, business plan completed, etc.

WORKSHOPS AND TRAINING SEMINARS

The LMU Center has also **provided low-cost, or no-cost, non-credit training** to improve our client's business skills and general business knowledge. Classes and workshops are offered from level one to level four depending on the current business skill levels of the class members. The vast majority of our training class and workshops are typically three to four hours in length and attended by 15–20 participants. Some topics require sixteen to twenty hours of instruction, scheduled over four weeks, and many classes have had as many as forty attendees. The majority of the workshops are conducted by the LMU in-house Consultants.

In every case the attendees are provided with useful instructional materials designed to assist them in the application of the workshop topics. Training covers topics such as marketing, business plan development, accounting, management, finance, and legal issues.

A specific training topic list of LMU Center courses is as follows:

Planning

- Business Survival

- Succession Planning

- The Family Business

- The Successful Business Plan

- How to Start a Successful Business

- Stop the Hemorrhaging — Getting Control of Time and Priority Management Issues in Your Business

- Preparing for Next Year and the Year After

- Other — we grow and develop what the customer needs.

Marketing

- Marketing Your Small Business — How to Make Business Presentations

- Four Walls Marketing

- The Business Review

- Target Markets and Marketing Objectives

- Positioning, Promotion, and Advertising

- Marketing Budget, Payback Analysis, and Marketing Calendar

- What is the Target Market?

- Other — we grow and develop what the customer needs.

Financial Management

- How Much is that Business Worth?

- Invoicing and Contracts

- The Art of Money Management — Business Mathematics with Direct Application to Small Business Operations

- Financial Health of Your Business

- Budgeting

- Money Troubles Impacting Small Business

- Accounting for Small Business Owners That Hate Accounting

- QuickBooks for Beginners

- Other — we grow and develop what the customer needs.

Risk Management

- Basic Tax Considerations

- Forming a Corporation or LLC

- Forming a California Professional Corporation

- Family Law and Your Business

- Contract Basics (Terms and Conditions)

- Being Your Own Business Lawyer

- Landlord ABC's

- Legal Issues for Small Business

- Basic Insurance Considerations

- Permits, Licensing, and Red Tape

- Other — we grow and develop what the customer needs.

Personnel

- Basic Employment Issues

- Making Sure a Consultant is Really a Consultant — The IRS View

- Understanding the State of California Employment Determination Guide

- Human Resources in Today's Workplace

- Other — we grow and develop what the customer needs.

International Trade

- Small Business & NAFTA

- Business in Asia

- Business in Eastern Europe and Russia

- Business in Europe

- Business in South America

- Customs and Borders

- Export Basics

- Finding Opportunities in International Trade

- Funding International Deals

- Import Basics

- Other — we grow and develop what the customer needs.

Management

- Emerging Supervisor

- Emerging Manager

- Management Basics

- Motivating the Team

- Moral Issues

- Project Management

- Inventory Management

- Improve Your Product Quality by Using Professional Inspection Methods

- Other — we grow and develop what the customer needs.

Technology

- Small Business and Technology

- Internet Business

- E-Commerce — Can I Make a Living in the Internet Business.

Invention — Innovation

- The Big Idea and How to Protect It

- The Basics: Copyright, Patenting, and Trademarks

- Other — we grow and develop what the customer needs.

CONCLUSION

We are proud of what we have developed in consulting and counseling help at LMU's Entrepreneurship Counseling Center for the fledgling business owner and entrepreneur.

We have tried to present here a comprehensive checklist and idea-provoking series of actions that will help you to develop your own counseling and development center, regardless of whether you are a governmental entity, an academic institution, a non-profit assistance group, or even a for-profit organization.

We hope that we have helped you to help the Entrepreneurs in your realm of influence. They need your help — you can really help them.

"You miss 100% of the shots you never take."

Wayne Gretsky

Chapter Twenty-Two

Listening to the Pioneers
of Entrepreneurship Education

*Life Lessons from the Oral Histories
of Entrepreneurial Education Heroes*

By Brian McKenzie

*Brian McKenzie was born in Kelowna, Canada and grew up in
a family business. He attended the University of British
Columbia graduating with a degree in English Literature.
Brian married his high school sweetheart, Molly in 1970. The
couple opened a retail specialty store, Molly's Spice Shop in
1971 and ran this business until 1981. In the late 1970s, Brian
turned his love of sailing into an avocation as a classic boat
owner, and then into a second career as a professional boat
builder. Brian and Molly moved to Sidney on Vancouver Island
in 1982, where Brian started a new venture, Brian McKenzie*

Boatbuilding, specializing in the restoration and repair of classic wooden yachts. In 1994, Brian returned to school to do his MBA with the intention of using these skills to develop his boatbuilding business. However, in 1996 he felt a calling to teach entrepreneurship and so gave up boatbuilding to pursue his PhD. During his doctoral studies, Brian was a part of a teaching team that won both the Academy of Management Entrepreneurship Divisions Innovations in Pedagogy award and the United States Association for Small Business and Entrepreneurship Model Undergraduate Program award. Brian also assisted in establishing the Entrepreneurship program at Worcester Polytechnic Institute in Worcester, MA during a visit in 1999–2000. His doctoral research was based on the collection and analysis of oral histories of working entrepreneurs. Brian graduated from the University of Victoria with an interdisciplinary PhD in 2003. Brian moved to Hayward, California in 2003 where he teaches entrepreneurship at California State University, East Bay. Brian and Molly enjoy sailing San Francisco Bay in their 40 foot motorsailer, Dorothy.

Editor's Note: *Brian McKenzie has had the extraordinarily wonderful chance in life to interview and chronicle the views of the pioneers of the field of entrepreneurship. Through his insights into these leaders' minds, he provides below some excellent information on just two of them to stimulate the reader's thinking and action in creating their own outstanding contributions to the field of Entrepreneurship and Entrepreneurship Education. McKenzie has dozens upon dozens of taped interviews of other key leaders. For more insight on the leaders in the field we would suggest you contact Dr. McKenzie.*

INTRODUCTION

In 1947, the first academic course in entrepreneurship was offered by Myles Mace at Harvard Business School. Today, there are entrepreneurship courses offered at more than 1,500 colleges and universities. This growth did not happen in a vacuum. The development of entrepreneurship as a rigorous academic discipline involved a host of academics and support personnel working together with purpose and discipline. Academic research programs were initiated, findings were disseminated at conferences and published in journals, and textbooks were created to pass the core lessons of the field to students.

In 2003, I was a newly minted PhD, having returned to school after a career as a successful entrepreneur. I was sitting in a meeting of entrepreneurship academics when I was struck with the insight that I was in the presence of many of the pioneers of entrepreneurship education. I could see that many of these pioneers were getting on in years. I realized that someone should be collecting the valuable histories of these pioneers. In the absence of other volunteers, I decided that the person to do this research was me.

Over the next four years, I was delighted to meet many of the people who developed entrepreneurship education. I was amazed by their generosity in sharing their time with me and their devotion towards the community of academics. As I spent countless hours enjoying the stories of their lives, I was inspired to be a better teacher and researcher.

In this chapter, I hope to share with you the stories of two of the pioneers of entrepreneurship education: Justin Longenecker and Max Wortman. Each of these pioneers played a key role in the development of entrepreneurship as an academic discipline. In 2003, Jerome Katz wrote:

> "The history of entrepreneurship education in America is blessedly brief, but frustratingly disjointed. The disjointedness comes from the isolation of different academics pursuing entrepreneurship in its various forms."

Longenecker and Wortman formed key points of connection in the disjointed history of entrepreneurship education. Justin Longenecker developed the first textbook in small business management. This textbook both solidified the academic discipline of management of small firms and built a link between the disciplines of small business management entrepreneurship. Max Wortman played a key role in the development of the academic infrastructure of entrepreneurship.

Justin Longenecker's Life Story

The oldest entrepreneurship educator that I interviewed was Justin Longenecker. Our interview took place on Jan 16, 2004 in Dallas, TX, where we were both attending the United States Association for Small Business and Entrepreneurship (USASBE) meeting. Longenecker began his life story this way:

"I was born in 1917, if you can imagine that you are going back that far in history... I grew up in a small business of sorts. My father operated what, at that time, was called a General Store, in a very, very small village, unincorporated. My father operated this store that included all kinds of products from food products to clothing, particularly farm-type, blue jeans,

and work shoes and that sort of thing. Also hardware items anywhere from wire to bolts and nuts and products of that kind; feed, some kinds of feed for livestock and we also sold International Harvester implements of various kinds for farmers. We had a gasoline pump and we sold gasoline. We also purchased eggs at one time."

Longenecker learned about small business management in his family's business, I.B. Longenecker & Co. He described how he was tempted to stay in the family business, but realized that there were forces of change in America moving towards urban growth and away from rural life. He described his struggle with the decision to leave the family business in these words:

"The fact is, that was in a sense a dying business because of its rural location. With the emergence of the transportation change, automobiles, it moved to larger cities... At one time I thought I might be able to come into this business, but it was not viable from that standpoint... I could see it clearly enough that it was tempting to go back and think that by having youthfulness in there again and vigor, but then the trends were too much against you. It would no longer have the volume."

Longenecker studied political science in college during the years of the depression and took a job in government service at the beginning of World War II. He was transferred into a civilian position in the US Air Force. At the end of the war, he could see that large numbers of veterans returning from the war with Veterans Preference (legislation from the Civil War era which provides veterans with an advantage in procuring civil service jobs and promotions) would delay his career in government service. He decided to do something considered quite risky at the time. He quit his job and went back to school to study for a Masters in Business Administration at Ohio State.

When he completed his MBA, several professors suggested that he look into doing a doctorate in business administration. Longenecker wondered about the wisdom of doing this, thinking that he might be overqualified for the world of business. He described his thoughts this way: "I said to myself: I don't know. If you have a PhD, you might be in a sense be too qualified for business."

In spite of his reservations, Longenecker moved, with his young wife, Frances, to Seattle and enrolled in the University of Washington. At the end of his first year of doctoral studies, he took a teaching position at Western Washington University in Bellingham to see if he enjoyed teaching. He described the experience this way:

> "It was a wonderful experience. I probably wasn't the greatest teacher, but I could read faster than the students. I was teaching classes that I'd never taken. It was wonderful. Fortunately I'd had about five classes in accounting by that time, so I taught Principles of Accounting I and Principles of Accounting II; Intermediate accounting, if you can believe this, with this very limited background."

When Longenecker took a faculty position at Baylor University in 1955, he was asked to teach a course called "Small Business Management." These were the early days of entrepreneurship education and so Longenecker had to create most of the material in this new course. He reminisced about the experience:

> "I had never in my life taken a small business management class. But this is how I got into it. I really don't know how long they had given this kind of course, but I don't suppose it had been very long... My Department Chairman had evidently taught this class and had identified a textbook published by Prentice-Hall authored by two professors by the name of Kelly

and Lawyer... You have to realize Baylor had a lot of students who had not come out of corporate backgrounds in terms of their parents: a lot of family businesses, a lot of small businesses. They were kind of a more middle-class group of students. So there was a natural interest on the part of those students for picking up something that is more practical than some of this corporate finance and high level accounting that they had been taking."

The focus of Longenecker's course was: "How do you make a small business effective?" He would go over a lot of the material that the students had already learned in their other business courses and showed them how to put it into practice in a small business. His Department Chairman suggested that they prepare a book for teaching Small Business Management. Longenecker reacted in this way:

"Well, at this point I was pretty humble. I hardly realized that ordinary people could write textbooks. I considered myself to be just an ordinary guy. I'm not a genius. Could we do a textbook? Well, he talked to Southwestern Publishing Company, now a part of Thompson Learning, to talk to us. He divided up the chapters and we decided to get going on that."

The textbook "Small Business Management" by Broom and Longenecker came out in 1961. It went on to become the most widely used textbook in small business management.

"Small Business Management" had both immediate importance and a long-term importance in the development of entrepreneurship education. The immediate importance was the creation of a textbook described by a contemporary, Wendell Metcalf, as: "a clear, comprehensive treatment of a neglected subject of school textbooks ... small business management." The long-term importance was the development of small business management as a legitimate field of study in business schools. The publication of David Birch's research, "The Job Generation Process," in 1979 led to a new interest in the development of small businesses. Birch effectively argued that small, independent, and volatile business led the growth of job creation in the US. This finding led to the popularization of the Small Business Administration and a linkage between small business and entrepreneurship. Reflecting this linkage, Longenecker changed the title of his textbook to "Small Business Management, an Entrepreneurial Emphasis." Justin Longenecker was working on the 13th edition when he died in 2005.

Gerald Hills, professor at the University of Illinois, said of Longenecker: "... he was an incredible pioneer. Through his writing and research, especially writing textbooks, he touched the lives of thousands and thousands of students." Longenecker summarized his life spirit in another way. He said: "I try to think young and stay young as much as I can... I haven't lost my zest for life."

Max Wortman's Life Story

Max Wortman began the telling of his life story with a description of the humble circumstances of his birth:

> *"I was born in Iowa City, Iowa. Of all things, in the University Hospital in the charity wards in 1932. My grandparents had money, and they lived in Grinnell, Iowa. And he owned four or five businesses, so he was an entrepreneur, or a small businessman in contrast to an entrepreneur. My grandfather was worth probably a half a million dollars as they went into the Depression, and he lost all of his money during the Depression."*

Wortman showed entrepreneurial initiative as a young man. His energy and salesmanship is shown in this story he told about his work as a young man:

> *"When I was eleven, I would bother my sisters and wake them up in the morning. So my grandmother, because we were living with my grandmother, it was World War II, said "Get him a job." So they got me a job; they got me this paper route. At age eleven, I started this paper route and I had about 60 or 70 papers. And as time went by over the next four years, I had 480 new subscriptions ... By the time I was 15, I lent my folks enough money to put a down payment on a house."*

Wortman's paper route led to a scholarship to Saint Ambrose College in Davenport, Iowa. College exposed Wortman to the excitement of politics. He became active in campus politics and his church. He continued his education at Iowa State, where he studied engineering. However, Wortman discovered that he was not a good student. He explained:

> *"At the end of my fourth year, my college pastor called me in and he said, "Max, you are not cut out to be an engineer."*

And I said, "Why is that?" And he said, "You talk too much."
And so he said, "You know what, I think you need to go and get
some counseling." I'm all done with my engineering degree
except for one course... He goes ahead, picks up the phone,
calls the Director of the Counseling Service and says, "I've got
this guy, I want you to test him out." I had taken this Strong
Vocational Interest Test several times before. So I went over
there and took the test again... Sure enough, he found that
I scored very low in engineering. He said to me: "Why don't you
go into personnel and industrial relations?" So I took another
year and did a Master's degree."

In 1957, Wortman became an instructor in mechanical engineering at the University of Minnesota. He enrolled in a MBA program there with the intention of becoming a personnel manager. At the end of his first year of studies, his Major Advisor cut him a deal. Wortman recounted his advisor's words:

"He said, next fall (the fall of 1958) you start taking PhD
exams, and if you pass them you are going to get your PhD.
If you don't, I'll give you your Masters Degree. What a deal.
From then on, I had straight "A"s in the PhD program."

Wortman completed his dissertation in the summer of 1961 and started working at the University of Iowa in the fall of that year. He did not receive his PhD until 1962, but he was awarded tenure in 1963 ... the same year he was on sabbatical funded by the Ford Foundation.

In 1963, Wortman became a member of the Academy of Management. He attended a record 42 meetings in a row before his death. At the 1967 meeting in Chicago, he was asked to take over the placement service for the academy. This gave him a position as a member of the Board of Directors. In 1970, the Academy of Management moved to the divisional structure that it has today. In 1973, he was elected editor of the Academy of Management Review. In 1974, Karl Vesper led the Academy of Management in the formation of an Entrepreneurship Interest Group. This interest group later became the Entrepreneurship Division of the Academy of Management in 1987. He served as the President of the Academy of Management in 1982 and Chair of the Entrepreneurship Division in 1995–1996.

A submission to the Journal of Small Business Management got Wortman involved in the National Council for Small Business Management Development, the organization formed in 1956 which sponsored this publication. In 1977, the organization was renamed International Council for Small Business. In 1981, the US affiliate, United States Association for Small Business and Entrepreneurship (USASBE) was formed. Wortman described his role in the formation of USASBE this way:

> *"I joined the National Council for Small Business Development in 1965. Before Justin Longenecker, even though Justin is a lot older than I am... Then, in 1980, there we are 15 years later, a guy by the name of Cliff Baumback, who was at the University of Iowa, called me up and said: "You know a lot about national meetings." And I said "Well yes, I know a lot about meetings, yes." So he said, "Why don't you come out here and talk to us?" So I went out and talked to him and Jerry Hills. Jerry Hills was about to become the president of ICSB, and Baumback was about to become the president of the US affiliate... By the end of the morning, I had become Competitive Papers Chair; by Tuesday night, I had become Program Chair."*

Wortman served in a number of roles in USASBE, becoming its President in 1986–1987.

The notion that humble beginnings can lead to an extraordinary career in entrepreneurship education is evidenced in my interview of Max Wortman. Wortman's career also included the honor of being the Chair of the Institute for Certified Professional Managers (1972–1973, 1982–1987) and President of the North American Case Research Association (1985–1986). He published more than 150 articles and proceedings and nine books during his academic career.

CONCLUSION

The word "miracle" is derived from the Latin "miraculum," which means "something wonderful." Justin Longenecker's creation of the first widely-used textbook in small business management shows the way that something wonderful was created by a self-proclaimed ordinary individual. Max Wortman's dedication to developing the academic infrastructure of entrepreneurship shows the impact that an individual can have in the creation of organizations dedicated to doing something wonderful.

Max Wortman died in March of 2005, Justin Longenecker in September of the same year. At the 2006 USASBE meeting held in Tucson, AZ, Robert D'Intino, Charles Matthews, and I convened a special symposium "Remembering Professors Max S. Wortman and Justin G. Longenecker and Their Contributions to Entrepreneurship Scholarship, Teaching, Organizations, and Careers." For this symposium, Matthews put images he had collected to an edited version of the recordings I had made. The meeting room was packed, and there was not a sound from the audience throughout the half hour audio/visual presentation.

When the lights came on at the end of the tribute, there was not a dry eye in the house. Academic meetings are known for their lack of emotions, so this was a very unusual situation. The silence became deafening. Then, quietly, one after another of the members of the audience began to tell stories of how these two pioneers in the field of entrepreneurship had influenced their lives and their careers. These stories showed the impact that Justin Longenecker and Max Wortman had had in "creating entrepreneurs and making miracles happen."

"The best way to have a good idea is to have lots of ideas."

Linus Pauling

Chapter Twenty-Three

The Academy of Business Leadership

*Preparing Our High-Potential,
Low-Opportunity Youth to Become
Our Future Leaders Through
Entrepreneurship Training*

By Anna Ouroumian

*Anna Ouroumian is the Re-Founder, President, and CEO of
the Academy of Business Leadership (ABL), a non-profit social
entrepreneurial venture for underserved youth in Southern
California, and now Zambia, China, and South Korea.*

*Anna grew up in orphanages in Lebanon during the
sixteen-year civil war. She lived under extreme hardships and
danger often without water and electricity with bombs going*

off everywhere, witnessing death for the first time as a toddler. She fled Lebanon alone and came to the United States as a young teenager with only $160 in her pocket, English as her fourth language, and two books: one about Ronald Reagan, and the other about the Harvard Business School. She went on to study at UCLA. She was honored at graduation for her inspirational story and received the Outstanding Senior Award for outstanding academic achievements and service to UCLA and the community. Out of UCLA, she heeded President Clinton's call to join the first class of AmeriCorps, the domestic Peace Corps. Later she joined Building Up Los Angeles. She was a California Governor's Executive Fellow, where she did speechwriting for the Attorney General of California. Anna serves on several boards and advisory panels of key Southern California business and cultural and service organizations. She co-founded the Women's Foundation of California, was elected to the Women's Leadership Board of the Harvard Kennedy School, and was elected to the trustee-ship of the International Women's Forum. She is also the Inaugural Chair for the Harvard Future Women Leaders Fellows Task Force.

Anna has spoken to thousands of students and executives from corporations, organizations, and schools internationally. She has been featured by Forbes Magazine, the Los Angeles Times, The Los Angeles Business Journal, Reader's Digest, and KCET Life & Times Tonight. She was honored on the Tyra Banks national TV show. She received the "Inspiration Award" from the National Association of Women Business Owners (NAWBO), and the "George Washington Honor Medal" from the Freedoms Foundation at Valley Forge. She received the Montel Williams Voices Campaign Award for the five "amazing women using their voices to make a difference." She also received the Conrad Hilton Distinguished Entrepreneur Award as part of Loyola Marymount University's Entrepreneurship Program.

INTRODUCTION

I was put in my first orphanage at the age of one and grew up without water, electricity, and oftentimes without food during the civil war of Lebanon. By the time I finished high school, having skipped several grades, I had been through nine different schools and orphanages, and was even homeless on the streets for one summer. Given the war, I did not know if I would even grow up one day, let alone aspire to live up to my God-given potential.

As a poor young girl, I was told the best I could do was to finish the fifth grade, go work somewhere as a maid, and get married someday. I know it sounds surreal. As I am writing these words, I cannot believe that this was truly my reality then, for I have come a long, long way.

How is my story relevant to entrepreneurship and the work that I do? I guess you could say **my first difficult entrepreneurial venture was developing a business plan for my life!** I had to move myself to a fulfilling life. I had to first get myself out of Lebanon, and then figure out how to learn to navigate the American system.

The odds were stacked against me. I was in this land of opportunity all by myself, barely speaking English, without the emotional and financial support of a family. My lifeline was a nun, Sister Aida, who had been transferred from one of my first orphanages in Lebanon to Los Angeles. So I took a chance and designed a plan to get me out of my circumstances by myself, while seeking the support of numerous individuals such as Sister Aida, to whom I will be forever indebted.

When I stumbled upon the Academy of Business Leadership in 1998 (it was founded in 1991 by Rick Yamamotto, an employee of Southern California Edison, which is still a major sponsor of the program), I was barely three years out of UCLA. The focus of the organization was to get inner-city youth to perhaps one day aspire to go to college, and have an opportunity to run their small businesses, such as a flower shop. ABL's mission was noble; however I felt our undeserved youth should be able to achieve their impossible dreams.

Why not inspire these kids to dream bigger dreams, and even have seemingly impossible ones? Instead of a few kids making it, why not get most of them, if not all of them, to fulfill their God-given potential?

Why can't they one day aspire to grow up and be our future CEOs, MEGA entrepreneurs, and civic leaders of America and the World?

These were some of the questions I grappled with. I am not a social scientist, nor a psychologist. I studied economics at UCLA and had taken a few courses in psychology and philosophy in high school and college. But I know if I as a "girl" could get myself out of an orphanage in a war-torn country in the Middle East to the USA and through college, so too can they get themselves out of their circumstances, with a little help from me.

The question became "how?" I set on decoding what had led me to "make it." Mind you, I too was still "at risk," even as I began running the organization. The kids were just a few years behind me, and I had to be on a fast learning curve to deliver a vision that would inspire thousands of youth and ignite their passion for learning, self empowerment, and giving back through entrepreneurship, business education, and leadership development!

CREATING THE FOUNDATION
OF A STRONG PROGRAM

We give our young participants in our programs extensive discussion about, exposure to, and experience with **core values that anchor them to what is important in life**, and we remind them that they have what it takes to succeed. We also **provide them with entrepreneurial and financial literacy training, leadership development, and social entrepreneurship training**.

Throughout our programs, we provide our kids with **access and exposure to the highest levels of entrepreneurial and corporate leadership**. They meet with CEO's and senior executives from Fortune 500 corporations, as well as movers and shakers of our times in the Entrepreneurial world.

Since 1998, over **80,000** kids from hundreds of middle and high schools across Southern California have gone through ABL's Empowerment and Prosperity Building workshops and presentations. In addition, over **2,800** students have graduated from our Summer Business Institute.

We have year-round workshops, programs, and a summer program, which we will discuss in detail below. Our two year-round programs are **Building Outstanding Leaders Today (BOLT), and The Ambassadors** for the top twenty percent of our students each summer. These programs are designed to further prepare our future CEO's, Entrepreneurs, and civic leaders through extensive business and leadership training, as well as mentoring. In addition, each year we reach around 15,000 students through our Empowerment and Prosperity Building workshops at hundreds of middle and high schools, and about 350 students through our Summer Business Institute.

Our ABL programs have engaged more than **5,000 volunteers** and initiated and created strategic partnerships with groups such as DLA Piper, Edison International, Merrill Lynch, Bank of America, State Street, the Capital Group Companies, PIMCO, and First Pacific Advisors. We have forged collaborations with over 300 corporations, entrepreneurs, and organizations to benefit thousands of youth.

Our Philosophy and Methodology

Our basic philosophy of teaching our young kids is to instill in them the concept of **capitalism with a soul**™ while inculcating in them our seven powerful, anchoring core values.

We live in very exciting times. Our country has just elected its first African American President, and on the other hand, we are on a slippery slope with respect to our current financial meltdown and major problems we see in the economic situation across America and the world! More than anything, what our country and our world need at this time is leadership! We must redouble our efforts to develop our young future leaders, which is what we at ABL are doing.

Young people have unlimited talent, energy, and potential! Thousands of disadvantaged and underserved youth are yearning to make a contribution NOW, with not many positive and fulfilling outlets within their reach. Yet, fundamentally, they have the talent and ability to be leaders in the future. When we harness the talent of our youth, magic happens. Young people can unlock solutions to our current problems worldwide, from the environment to education. We just need to give them a chance to sit at the table.

There needs to be a paradigm shift in our society to see the power and ability of our **youth as assets now, and not as**

liabilities, and there needs to be a paradigm shift in our youth **to see themselves as Leaders Now,** and as agents of change NOW! Our youth, particularly our inner-city youth, need to know that it is their responsibility to **open the doors for themselves, and to not wait for others to do so!** I am convinced that our inner-cities are America's last frontier.

At ABL, using business and entrepreneurial training as a vehicle, we teach our kids to stand up for themselves, to speak up, to see that their voices need to be heard, and are heard. We also teach our kids that it is their responsibility to **give back now**, and not wait until they become millionaires to do so.

We teach them **capitalism with a soul**™, the basics of how to lift themselves and their families up financially while not forgetting where they come from by developing in them a social consciousness, imbedded in action now, no matter what career paths they choose to pursue in the future.

The Core Values of Our Programs

We added seven core values as the foundation of our program because we felt that business and entrepreneurial education, while exciting, are not, on their own, enough to help these kids transcend their circumstances. The **seven core values act as lifelines and anchors beyond our programs**.

1. **Vision**: We teach our young future leaders to **create a vision** to forge a path before them and **fulfill their destiny**. We do so by teaching them visioning and goal setting.

2. **Integrity**: We teach our kids how to have integrity **with their word and their commitments to themselves and others**, how to **see how their words can impact others**, and **how to act and live ethically**.

3. **Responsibility**: We teach them how to **take full responsibility for their lives and not see themselves as victims**. When they assume responsibility, there are **no more excuses**, even for things they have no control over. I know it sounds harsh, but that's the only way to overcome obstacles and thrive!

4. **Passion**: Only by **following one's heart can one have passion!** We teach them how to unleash their passion and apply it to fulfill their God-given potential.

5. **Courage**: We teach them to have courage, to **face fear, and to use it as fuel**. We teach them to have the courage to say "no" and the courage to say "yes" as appropriate.

6. **Perseverance**: We teach them to not give up and to not give in, no matter how difficult circumstances may be! We teach them **that it is OK to fall, but imperative to have the courage to stand up again and keep going**.

7. **Giving Back**: We teach them that they have the responsibility to give back today! We teach them to **be proud of where they come from and to remember their blessings, no matter their circumstances**.

These are my lessons learned along the way that I share with our students to help them create their own journey and lead fulfilling lives!

Our main goal has been for us to capture our students' imagination in order to unlock their gifts and brilliant spirits. These core values have moved our kids to see themselves, each other, and their role in our society with new lenses. **There are no excuses in life.** This philosophy is based upon my background, and where I came from, on my own. **If I can make it**, they have no excuses! **So can they!**

Implementing the Vision

Over the past ten years, we have completely shifted the focus of ABL by centering its vision on harnessing the talent of under-served, high-potential, low-opportunity youth to **see themselves as leaders now!** We teach them to develop the vision and start making a difference in the world today, **now, while uplifting themselves!**

We spend a great deal of time enlightening them to the idea that they **can, and must**, rise to become the future Entrepreneurial, corporate, and civic leaders in America and throughout the globe by persevering and using their passion as a fuel to guide them.

We use a multitude of methodologies to accomplish this, most particularly by giving the young future leaders access and expo-sure to the highest levels of Entrepreneurial and business and community leadership. They get an opportunity to see, feel, and touch winners who have gone before them, and in the process they find out they are good enough, and they develop the courage to stand toe-to-toe with these leaders and hold their own. This is a phenomenal confidence-raising experience for these young minds!

Through various powerful examples, we touch the lives of thou-sands of young people by instilling in them a spirit of courage, inspiration, and hope to "dream big, have no limitations, and reach for the stars."

Our bold vision is to create a movement of overlooked, under-resourced, high-potential, low-opportunity youth as agents of change by shifting the paradigm of our society and our youth to see themselves as leaders now versus twenty years from now. Our thrust is to harness the talent of young people across the globe to thrive economically and make a difference in their respective communities, countries, and the world now. We prepare them to one day rise to the highest levels of leadership in the corporate, civic, and Entrepreneurial spheres.

Our Year-Round Workshops and Programs

While our high schools in Southern California struggle just to get our inner-city youth to graduate, ABL has found ways to not only get them to graduate, but to see themselves as the future Entrepreneurs, corporate executives, and civic leaders of America and the world! In a statement released in 2007, Jack O'Connell, the California Superintendent of Public Instruction, said the Los Angeles Unified School District drop out rate was 33.6% for grades 9–12. The drop out rate for African American youth throughout Los Angeles was 40%, and for Latino students, it was 30%.

How can our country maintain its economic competitiveness in the world when at least a third of our kids are unaccounted for, lost? After participating in ABL, high school graduation and college attendance are no longer an unreachable goal for our students, but a given fact, a done deal!

The new major questions and issues in their lives become "what is their purpose in life, what will their contribution be," and not whether they will be graduating from high school and attending college. This represents a major shift with respect to the expectations set by society in general for our inner-city youth.

At ABL, we help our youth see themselves as Leaders Now! They gain a clear path for their future. ABL graduates are civic minded and engaged, and they make a difference through various Social Impact Contracts™ (service projects) in the community and around the world today!

Each year, we conduct "Empowerment and Prosperity Building" workshops for 15,000 mostly high-potential, low-opportunity students at hundreds of middle and high schools. While we cannot **yet** accommodate thousands of students in our Summer Business Institute, these workshops give us an opportunity to share with them our seven core values as anchors for their life. In these short workshops we try to inspire these young people to take complete charge of their destiny and graduate from high school and pursue higher education. We try to give them a strong understanding of the value of entrepreneurship, and investing as means to financial independence. Our goal is to have these young and exciting future leaders emerge as agents of change now, committed to making a difference in the world Today!

THE SUMMER BUSINESS INSTITUTE PROGRAM (SBI)

Over **2,500 students** from **435** elementary, middle and high schools and **151** school districts **have graduated** from ABL's award winning Summer Business Institute on seven college campuses in the Southern California area. Our university and college partners have been generous hosts for our students. Without them, most of our students would have never had the opportunity to set foot on a college campus, let alone take a course on these campuses. Because of this phenomenal opportunity, our participants can easily see themselves attend colleges and universities.

Participating colleges and universities include:

- California State University, Los Angeles (CSULA)

- California State University, Fullerton (CSUF)

- California State University, Dominguez Hills (CSUDH)

- Loyola Marymount University (LMU)

- Santa Monica College (SMC)

- University of California, Los Angeles (UCLA)

- University of Southern California (USC).

This program takes 11–18 year-old middle and high school students into a loving and nurturing environment **where expectations are set very high**. 70 percent of our kids are from low- to moderate-income backgrounds, and 30 percent from middle- to upper-income groups. 90 percent are from minority backgrounds.

The results? Major transformations from the inside out! Our program utilizes an innovative, low-cost, high output business model.

Talented executives in transition, MBA graduates from top business schools (such as USC, UCLA, and Harvard), as well as bright college juniors and seniors and alumni, along with over 500 active volunteers, ignite our students' passion for learning, prosperity building, and giving back through a new paradigm of self-perception and empowerment.

Students write full-length business plans using *Business Plan Pro* from Palo Alto Software, which they present to executives and venture capitalists.

They also manage fictitious stock portfolios and visit Fortune 500 CEOs and senior executives. They are taught all the intangibles for success such as Power Networking and Connecting, and skills such as how to dress for success and how to develop an Individual College Action Plan.

As an example of our students' entrepreneurial spirit, in 2006, a team of five young students from the CSULA site, who ranged in age from 12 to 17, won the ABL Regional Oral Business Competition. Their business plan idea centered around the creation of a company that produces bio-diesel fuel by recycling used restaurant oil! Subsequently, the team was invited to present their plan at UCLA alongside MBAs and seasoned professionals seeking funding from a prominent group of venture capitalists from the Tech Coast Angels!

Over the years, the kids have come up with very innovative ideas. Some have gone on to implement them as young budding entrepreneurs, while pursuing their college education.

In our Summer Business Institute, through the business plan, stock market, and other various competitions, **around 60% of our students win over $30,000 in cash prizes. They have been sponsored each summer since 2002 by Merrill Lynch.**

An Expanding World Wide Impact — Beginning with Zambia

Up until 2005, the focus of our work had been throughout Southern California, with the occasional out-of-state students. However, in November of 2005, a chance meeting propelled us to create a new initiative that has allowed us to open our hearts and minds and share our best practices with youth from Africa, and to collectively teach us invaluable lessons in collaboration, leadership capacity building, and cultural enrichment.

After a visit by then First Lady of Zambia, the Honorable Maureen Mwanawasa, to the Harvard Kennedy School with the Harvard Women's Leadership Board, where I have been serving as a board member, and after hearing her pleas for her country, we volunteered to bring five young women to America to partake in our Summer Business Institute. Subsequently, in collaboration with the Harvard Women's Leadership Board, the Maureen Mwanawasa Community Initiative (MMCI), and the Oxford School Foundation, we initiated and launched the "Project Africa" initiative.

The goal of this program is to annually bring "vulnerable but viable" talented, underserved young women from Zambia to California to have the opportunity to partake in ABL's seven-week Summer Business Institute (SBI) on college campuses. We strive to help these young women develop their leadership and business education skills and return to their home country empowered with a new vision, which will enable them to uplift themselves, their families, and their communities.

This will ultimately help these scholars build leadership capacity for Zambia while providing an opportunity of a lifetime for American students. Our inner-city youth, who for the most part have never been outside a three-mile radius from their communities, now have a chance to reach out and touch Africa by sharing, collaborating, and exchanging ideas about how to improve the human condition on a global level. Moreover, American students are able to learn from the dialogues and experiences of the Zambian scholars and gain insight, cultural understanding, inspiration, and motivation.

Similarly, in the summer of 2007, through our work with the Zambian Scholars, we formulated the ABL Zambia Ambassadors Program (AZAP) as part of the ABL Zambia program. Through AZAP, the ABL Zambian Scholars will be training 200 high school graduates and college students to reach 4,000 youth. Their goal is to conduct HIV-AIDS prevention education; nutrition, hygiene, and health awareness; and values and leadership training.

And on to China — The Project Asia Initiative

In 2007, in collaboration with the Oxford School Foundation, we initiated and launched the "Project Asia" initiative, where **young women from China participated** in ABL's 2007 SBI. The idea is to expand the horizon of our Chinese Scholars, who will one day become leaders of their country, to give back now, and provide more opportunities for other Chinese youth.

And on to Even More Countries

In 2008, we expanded the international initiative to include **youth from South Korea and Canada in addition to Zambia and China**. The international component constitutes a small part of our work. However, given how our world is increasingly smaller, while we cannot (at this time) literally take our kids to the world, here at ABL, we strive to bring the world to the kids. In 2010, we hope to launch the "Project Latin America" initiative.

And Now We are Impacting Middle Eastern Young Women

For the summer of 2007, as part of a collaboration with the Academy of Business Leadership, I was asked by the Harvard Women's Leadership Board to design and implement a **leadership training program for young Egyptian girls**. This was part of the Harvard University Future Women Leaders Fellows Program (FWLF) that they sponsored to take co-curricular classes at Harvard College.

For the Harvard leadership program, I designed and launched the **Social Impact Contract™** concept and developed a training methodology where youth have an opportunity to **design large-scale, high-impact projects** that entail training other youth **to**

pay it forward, thus affecting the lives of thousands in a relatively short period of time. We have implemented this concept with our students throughout our Summer Business Institute program within ABL for the past two summers, with tremendous results.

In 2007, as part of the Harvard training, young Egyptian girls designed the concept and model for a social entrepreneurial venture they called "Lena," meaning "for us" in the Egyptian Arabic dialect. The mission of Lena is to help youth develop a sense of belonging towards Egypt, tolerance towards all religions, and leadership skills. The Egyptian girls will develop curricula and build partnerships to train 300 college students in Cairo who will in turn work with 3,000 kids throughout Egypt by the Summer of 2009. Furthermore, in 2008, through the Harvard Future Women Leaders Training Program, we reached young women in Egypt, Jordan and Kuwait.

Thus, so far, we have implemented the **Social Impact Contract**™ training program for American, Zambian, Chinese, Korean, and Canadian scholars in Southern California, as well as Egyptian, Kuwaiti, and Jordanian scholars at Harvard.

CONCLUSION

Our programs inspire our youth to take charge of their lives. We are extremely proud of our results.

- 100 percent of our students graduate from high school.

- 99 percent of them attend colleges and universities nationwide, such as UCLA, Harvard, University of Pennsylvania, Yale, Stanford, Duke, Cornell, Princeton, USC, LMU, and others.

We are very proud of our students who have implemented their first entrepreneurial ventures by taking care of themselves first and uplifting themselves to break the generational cycles of poverty by transforming themselves from the inside out. They are being admitted into major universities worldwide, including America's most prestigious Ivy League schools. Many of our alumni are now at major corporations such as Price Waterhouse Coopers, Deutsche Bank, Merrill Lynch, Bank of America, Pimco, State Street, the Capital Group Companies, and others, and some are now implementing their own entrepreneurial ventures.

It has been said that to know the future of a country, one should look towards its youth. Similarly, we would add, **to know the future of our world, we must look towards ALL youth**. At ABL, we are proud and privileged to prepare our urban high-potential, low-opportunity youth to become our future CEOs, Entrepreneurs, and civic leaders in America and the world!

"Start by doing what's necessary; then do what's possible; and suddenly you are doing the impossible."

St. Francis of Assisi

Chapter Twenty-Four

Developing Entrepreneurs Through Mentorship

By Shaun Tan & L. Nicole Landrum

Shaun Tan is a graduate of UCLA with a BS in Business/ Economics. He graduated summa cum laude, finishing the four-year degree in two years. Shaun has been involved in the startup or buyout of seven different companies. Shaun has turnaround experience in leading the successful revitalization of three companies. His role as the managing partner of a buyout firm has allowed him to engage in all different aspects of a deal, including sourcing, deal negotiation, deal structuring, operational improvement, and growth and establishment of a management system and team. Shaun has had the pleasure of working with over 200 members of the Entrepreneur Mentor Society as its leader. EMS mentors young professionals who aspire to be entrepreneurs. Through this organization, Shaun has been able to affiliate with many different organizations, including Entrepreneur Organization (EO), Young President's Organization (YPO),

World President Organization (WPO), Tech Coast Angels, and Tech Coast Venture Network (TCVN). Shaun is presently on the board of the University of Southern California Trojan CEO forum and was previously on the board of Project by Project.

Nicole Landrum is an entrepreneur with an appetite for helping new businesses get off the ground. As the executive director of the Entrepreneur Mentor Society, Nicole has coached and mentored Southern California's most accomplished and exciting young fledgling entrepreneurs. She has also worked with other prominent entrepreneurial organizations, including the Tech Coast Angels, the Entrepreneur's Organization (EO), The Riordan Programs, and the Pasadena Angels. She is a graduate of Loyola Marymount University and received her bachelor's degree in Business Administration.

INTRODUCTION

"Those Who Can, Do. Those Who Can't, Teach."

Life is full of wonderful aphorisms, maxims, and adages. By their very definition, there is always some truth behind each of them. I remember teasing a friend who is an entrepreneurship professor at a local university about the old saying, "Those who can, do. Those who can't, teach." **The reality is that those who can't "do" yet need to ask those that can and have already.** What better way to learn about entrepreneurship than to directly learn from those individuals who have already directly experienced the success of being a winning entrepreneur?

The key to the success of the Entrepreneur Mentor Society is that we bring to the fledgling young Entrepreneur the chance to meet, interact with face to face, be mentored by, and learn from real, live, experienced Entrepreneurial success stories!

I once teased my professor friend that he had it all wrong. I said that he was working too hard preparing all his lectures. To teach

my mentees, I simply had to bring all these experienced entrepreneurs to guest lecture, and my job was done. It was so much
easier to capture the attention of the students when they were
being lectured by multi-millionaires and billionaires than by a
Ph.D. carrying professor.

However, I was absolutely wrong!

The reality is that there is a place for both educators and
successful entrepreneurs in developing and mentoring young
fledgling entrepreneurs.

The advice given by successful entrepreneurs is worthless without the fundamental basics learned in a classroom.

THE ENTREPRENEUR MENTOR SOCIETY (EMS)

To be fair to my professor friend, he doesn't get to screen his
class composition like I get to with the Entrepreneur Mentor
Society, the organization that I founded and lead. EMS is
a 501(c)(3) non-profit organization that was designed to
encourage, promote, nurture, and develop aspiring entrepreneurs. Most of the participants are college students and young
professionals. Applications flood in from all over Southern
California.

There is no credit, no tangible benefit, and no purpose for the
participants to attend other than their desire to learn and
improve their own foundation for successfully starting their own
ventures, impacting society, and winning in life.

Developing Entrepreneurs — Through Mentorship

When asked what element is most effective in developing
a young entrepreneur's intellectual, creative, and social skills,
I immediately respond, "mentorship."

Carl Jung said it plainly: "the meeting of two personalities is like the contact of two chemical substances; if there is any reaction, both are transformed."

Often underestimated, the blending and mixing of youth, passion, and unjaded optimism with years of experience, expertise, sophistication, and contacts can function as the **tipping point** for ambitious young talent, and fulfillment for an accomplished leader.

It's quite amazing, really.

The Entrepreneur Mentor Society, an organization designed to **place young talent with seasoned success**, is a wonderful case in point for exploring this topic. We create a large social network of entrepreneurial companies for new members and alumni alike to tap into and get hands-on mentorship for their business endeavors. The rest of this chapter will discuss the various factors and program details that lead to the success of our Entrepreneur Mentor Society program.

Pique the Curiosity, and the Rest is Cake

The beginning of entrepreneurial development lies in the individual, who should be entrepreneurial in their pursuit of knowledge. The student **must** show a thirst for knowledge, just as a true entrepreneur tries to seek out and create their own opportunities. Socrates once said: **"Wisdom begins in wonder." By taking the wonder already latent in the individual and lighting it on fire, you fuel their desire to learn and to be mentored.** This desire is crucial. Thus, by possessing the spark of curiosity, the individual will engage with the process of learning and continue to seek mentorship. This marks the student's commitment to a mentoring relationship.

About the Students

The most important aspect of EMS is the inquisitive nature of its members. Once the curiosity of its participants is piqued, the rest is easy. It sounds simple enough! It is hard to fail when you are instructing a group that is yearning to learn. The strength of the group is a direct function of the quality of the students.

EMS accepts applications from college students and young professionals. Through heavy-duty interviews we seriously inquire about their goals, intent, and background and determine if there is a fit for them in the program. We accept only **powerful young people** who are willing to grow and contribute. It's amazing to get the best of the best together and let the abundance of natural talent control the environment.

Engaging the Students

The Staying Power of Value: EMS hosts top speakers at six different universities in Southern California and gives hopeful future entrepreneurs a place to incubate their ideas. The speakers are given a series of questions to address before they come speak. Their talks often directly hit the questions, experiences, and concerns the young students have. Furthermore, through an interchange beyond the formal presentation, EMS provides the platform for the students and young professionals to dialogue with entrepreneurs. They talk to accomplished people who have already trod down the path on which they are just starting out. The visiting entrepreneurs give tangible and tested advice and guidelines. This not only engages the students, but it also keeps them coming back.

By teaching them things that cannot be gained just from textbooks and mentoring our students in such a way that they understand their future success in entrepreneurship is not just based upon economic theories or laws of the market, we truly impact our young participants. We also guide them to understand that success also depends on their interactions with other people and cultivating lasting relationships. This also helps us develop an engaged alumni base who, once they have succeeded, come back to mentor the next generation of new, young, hopeful entrepreneurs.

Another valuable asset that keeps EMS members engaged is our showing them that some of the most successful entrepreneurs are ones who have also given something of value to their community or to others around them. **EMS strives to foster a culture of giving back to others and to the community** by instilling in young people the value of doing business in a way that multiplies the good of the community and others. We believe this added benefit truly makes our program successful!

The word "entrepreneur," while borrowed from the French, was first defined by the Irish economist Richard Cantillon. He said that an entrepreneur is a person who undertakes and operates a new enterprise or venture and assumes some accountability for the inherent risks. **EMS encourages young entrepreneurs to explore and grapple with the accountability aspect they must answer to, no matter what venture they pursue.** These young people see the importance of accountability, how those who have blazed trails before them have been held accountable for their actions, and how that has driven part of their success.

Contagious Curiosity: Every person who enjoys mentoring others has undoubtedly been mentored himself or herself. It is the sharing of ideas and the ability to network and exchange thoughts with other entrepreneurs and aspiring entrepreneurs that make a mentorship program particularly rewarding. When a speaker comes to share his or her experiences, the synergy of all the different viewpoints from each person and their different thoughts and opinions creates an incredible interaction that encourages active student participation. The curious and the inquisitive nature of these young people to learn and pursue their goals unhindered is absolutely contagious.

Entrepreneurs are known for being innovative and pioneering. If they are able to be successful in a particular business venture, this will affect many others. This includes the employees, the investors, the market, and the general public who will consume the good or service. Because entrepreneurs are natural leaders who take on the challenges of organizing different resources into a successful working whole, it is natural for them to have a certain **charisma or fire in them that is contagious. In order to think big and dream big for big ventures, they must be optimistic and motivational.** The spirit of an entrepreneur, with all its embodiment of the dreams of the future, must affect and inspire those around it.

By allowing our student and professional members to have **one-on-one and group access to these entrepreneurs on a regular and continuing basis**, we speed the learning and growth processes in our members.

Curiosity and Academia: While bringing in speakers with real-life experience is of great value to the students, there is **something extremely unique and vibrant about the academic environment**. Young college students and young professionals are at a place in life where they are given the opportunity to study whatever they feel passionate about and whatever interests them in seeking their life's dream. They are ready to begin setting down the first steps in their lifelong journey as a contributing member of society. They are aware that the career path they choose will help define who they will become, where they will go, and what they will accomplish.

EMS focuses on university-aged students and young, newly working professionals because **there is an enthusiasm and**

independence in this age group that is a great driving force for these young people. They are young enough to still be curious about the world around them. They pursue gaining knowledge and experience with great fervor, but they have not yet become so set in any particular way or path that the thrill of the next great adventure has lost its luster.

The members of our EMS organization are young and vibrant, but also **old enough to make huge life decisions for themselves**. For most of these students, they are also living away from the homes in which they were raised and are establishing their identities apart from the families and high schools in which they grew up. For the young people who have graduated college and are venturing out into uncharted territory for the first time, they are still excited about the potential of life.

Our goal is to we work closely with the academic community and those who have just recently graduated, to provide the "extra plus" of real life experience and contact that the colleges and universities that teach the economic and business principals that are the platform for the real life experience.

Cross-Pollination

EMS allows students to push the boundaries of not only their classroom, but also their campus. The Entrepreneur Mentor Society incorporates many different students from different schools so that students can learn from each other and their diverse strengths.

Blending Together New Ideas: Mixing together a different variety of students allows the young men and women to be challenged in the way they normally see or view things. They can gain new ideas or concepts by networking with students from other places in life who are learning different things in their classrooms. Some of the older students or newly working young professionals are also able to share ideas, contacts, insights, and knowledge gained from internships and their fledgling work experience.

Crossing and Combining Strengths: When you pull so many different people together, they can learn from one another and the group as a whole will get the best from the best. Students from different schools bring unique talents and skills. For example, a University of Southern California (USC) student might have a flare for and talent in the arena of marketing but can benefit from the strength in technical skills and know-how of someone from California Institute of Technology (Caltech). The cross-pollination of students' different college experiences can be invaluable as they learn from each other and adapt one another's strengths.

The Importance of Dynamism

Dynamic Energy: The young people who make up EMS have a lot of energy and enthusiasm. **We make sure of this in the recruiting process.** These **go-getters** are the ones who will remain committed to the group and will make a long-term entrepreneurial mentorship program really happen. Successful entrepreneurs are the ones who go out and make things happen. They are the type of young people we recruit, train and mentor for a long-term involvement in our organization. They begin by being mentees. When they win in life, we want them to be passionate mentors. An entrepreneurial mentorship program is a great space for fledgling entrepreneurs to practice and learn how to help others someday.

The participants of an entrepreneurial mentorship program should **truly want to learn and should be passionate about learning** how to identify opportunities, how to know when to seize them, about their own limitations and the areas in which they are completely unbound. A mentorship program can only be successful if the culture that embodies the program encourages the group to be a **dynamic and excitable one**. The culture must be one that fosters a myriad of **positive activities**. There is no room for negativism in the entrepreneurship game of life.

Dynamic Culture: A culture where students give back and are supportive of each other's endeavors means success for everyone. We create the right culture to encourage members to be successful, yet fraternal with each other and supportive of the overall mentorship community. Developing an entrepreneur development program outside the classroom using practitioners reinforces a dynamic culture of winning. Yes, **they compete with each other, but they also learn from and help one another other**.

Dynamic Setting: The dynamic quality of colleges and universities allows students to interact with their professors and fellow classmates with concepts and ideas that are unfamiliar to them. They are expected to come in to college and be filled with knowledge and learning. This makes them **unashamedly eager to ask questions** and be in the position of "I don't know, but I'd like to find out and learn." The academic aspect of their learning provides them with knowledge, but no real place to apply that knowledge and see how they will execute the things they've learned according to their own talents and abilities. **It is our job in EMS to provide an atmosphere that is deeply rooted in learning and growing, and practical appreciation.**

Dynamic Opportunity: On the other hand, an entrepreneurial mentor program allows students to take part in their growth and learning and build something with their own effort and willpower. Their ability to create a society or group of like-minded individuals who can effect change and growth and difference in the world will energize and ignite their passion to pursue business opportunities with great confidence.

Through the process of learning how to be a successful and responsible entrepreneur, these students and young people also build relationships with those around them. A professor mentors his or her students through the medium of the classroom. Students in turn can mentor one another and continue dialogue about new concepts and ideas in their study sessions or leisure time. Entrepreneurial mentoring must also enrich the knowledge and exchange of information that takes place in the academic setting. The keys to being a successful entrepreneur are not limited to just the classroom or campus, but through young men and women pushing past the boundaries of their classroom. **A good entrepreneurial mentoring program brings the real world onto campus and into a partnership of learning with academia.**

Speakers and their Insight

Real World Experience & Success: One of the strengths of a good entrepreneurial mentoring program is combining the best aspects of classroom learning with the best aspects of learning from real life experience. In the end, we know that **there are a million things that the real world will make you learn the hard way**. The classroom cannot prepare you for all the real, tough, unexpected problems you will face as an entrepreneur. While attending a university, you may go to classes with other people who all have the same purpose to learn, grow, and graduate. In the real world, you will encounter people with whom you will disagree on things that you thought would never be an issue worth debating. In university life, you can focus on your schoolwork and extra-curricular activities.

In the real world, you will have to **learn to juggle new things**, such as possibly settling down, starting a family, paying off loans, paying bills, and more. In a university setting, you can learn about timeless principles established by economists, sociologists, and mathematicians.

In the real world, you must **learn to constantly change** how you do business, as the world is rapidly changing and the competition is always chasing after you. You must learn to always keep a sharp eye over your shoulder, and the other eye on your goals!

Are they gaining on you???

Textbooks cannot tell you how to interact with difficult clients, find more efficient ways to do things in your specific and unique situation, or the timing of when to make certain decisions. A successful entrepreneurial mentoring program brings in entrepreneurs who have learned from their own life experiences and are able to **share what did and didn't work for them**. **Learning from failure can be most powerful lesson!** While the things that worked for these speakers may not necessarily work for each student, it is our hope that the students see how that entrepreneur arrived at that conclusion, and how the decision led to success or failure.

Seeing the actual products or hearing stories of real services provided by successful entrepreneurs who have made it does a lot for aspiring young entrepreneurs. The actions they took to achieve their success are interesting and important. What is much more important is to **learn what motivated them**, and the insight behind what drives them. Oh, yes, the stories behind their success provide much more depth and insight than just what was done, and they are gripping and compelling!

Insight on People: Some of the timeless aspects of what makes entrepreneurs successful can include things like how to treat your employees and maintain good relationships with investors. **People are a major key to winning**. This includes your people, your customers, your money sources, your suppliers, and so on. Working with classmates in a group project can be a great foundation for learning to work with people but you learn how to manage various kind of relationships from a real life entrepreneur, not a textbook.

Insight that Inspires: If there is one thing that makes all entrepreneurs similar, it is the drive in each person to push forward and make something happen. This drive is comprised of the desire for a successful venture, to achieve greatness, to work hard, the leadership strength, and the pioneer spirit to forge ahead into the unknown and take on risk — all of these are things that make up an entrepreneur. While you can copy a person's steps and procedures, the result may not be the same without a similar drive and motivation. The speakers that come to share their experiences also give some key insight into not just how they did something successful or great, but **also why they wanted to do it**.

Speakers that Truly Want to Give Back

Speakers who are willing to mentor: Another important aspect of ensuring a successful mentorship program is to make sure the **students have the opportunity to follow up with one-on-one mentorship**. Office hours with professors are important because students cannot necessarily ask the questions they want in a large lecture hall, and meeting with mentors and speakers in a one-on-one setting is just as essential.

Find speakers who do not simply fill the minimum of only coming to speak, but find the kind of speaker who is open to following up if needed. Make sure students feel free to contact the speakers directly and are encouraged to do so. If the students note that a **speaker is approachable, sincere, and inspiring**, they might not feel shy about sending an email follow-up.

Speakers that lead by example: If a speaker is approachable and willing to mentor students, this shows that **they are more concerned with the greater success and betterment of many people rather than just a bottom line dollar amount**. Find speakers who are just as dynamic, energetic, and excited about being a part of an entrepreneurial mentor program as the students are.

Multiple Industry Perspectives

Diverse in Many Ways: Just as we have diverse students from different schools, it is important to get speakers from different industries and backgrounds. It is as important to bring in entrepreneurs in their 40s as it is to bring in entrepreneurs in their 60s. Experience comes in all ages. **Gray hair does count, especially in helping young entrepreneurs to avoid the dumb mistakes the gray hairs made along their path to success.** Some things you should look for in terms of how to choose a variety of speakers and mentors include a diversity of:

- Industries

- Technologies

- Backgrounds

- Ethnic backgrounds

- Gender

- Industries

- Different regions

- Different countries.

This is important because as times change, the way we do business must also change. It is important to invite a large spectrum of speakers who have different experiences in different times, places, and environments.

Hopefully, if a student or young person continues in EMS for several years, he or she will be exposed to so many varied entrepreneurs that he or she can determine how the nature of business has evolved over time, as well as glean the timeless aspects of how to be successful. How we do business today is different than yesterday, and will surely be different tomorrow!

For example, having to deal with new things like Sarbanes-Oxley or a newly industrialized and fast-growing country such as China quickly and profoundly changes how people do business. It is critical to deal with these changes immediately, and with solid thinking that is empathetic to the specifics of the changed situation. Hearing, speaking to, and being mentored by a winner who has played this game and won is priceless help for the new entrepreneur.

Technology is constantly evolving and changing how we do business as well. The students of today are always learning a new technology that will help them do business in a more efficient and complex manner. Even as moving from an industrial age into an information age revolutionized how businesses were run, the students we mentor will take some of the principles they learn and adapt them to new cutting-edge technologies on the horizon. Technology and today's economy necessitates globalization. The digital age **introduces tough challenges** such as outsourcing, international laws, and the need to be able to maintain clients or employees in different time zones.

They learn these lessons firsthand in the program, both from the speakers and from mentoring.

ADDED BENEFITS OF THE PROGRAM

Variety: Similar to the strength of cross-pollinating students from different universities and different speakers from different industries, it is important for an entrepreneurial mentorship program to look for speakers and other participants from a wide variety of business organizations and industry sectors. Pooling people and resources from diverse sources is always a good idea in helping young people.

Networking: Every successful entrepreneur has many contacts. No one can be a master of all trades, and it is far better to be a jack of all trades than a master of just one. Networking among other business contacts will allow you to find people who are knowledgeable about legal matters, real estate, the tools for raising capital, the hands-on mechanical everyday management aspects of being an entrepreneur, and much more.

This networking is a two-way street — the speakers help the students, but they also gain a network of bright young people to call upon for help, especially in complex areas of knowledge where the young are so adept. This is a **worthwhile perk for the speakers**.

We help the young mentees chase their dream and prepare to fulfill their wildest ambitions, but we also provide solid benefits to the mentors who help them.

KEYS TO HOW WE OPERATE

You now have a better idea of the EMS mission and purpose. Just as consequential is how EMS runs and operates. There are a few fundamentals that must be incorporated to ensure the organization functions well.

You have to be VERY selective with applicants. When recruiting potential members, be sure to reach out to the places (universities, etc.) where the best and brightest reside, but also reach out to other places as well. Seek out powerful research schools with great entrepreneurship programs, as well as schools with underdeveloped entrepreneurship programs that can really benefit from your interaction with them. Schools with under-developed entrepreneurship programs often have a tremendous need for your help and will welcome and fully support what you are trying to do.

When perusing the applications and meeting applicants, **look for enthusiasm and passion** in their writing and interviews. You want to make sure the students are excited by life and their future, and truly interested in learning and entrepreneurship.

The structure of the sessions — there are eight sessions in one program each semester and there are two semesters per year. These sessions take place every other Saturday and run from 8 a.m.–12 noon. We have two entrepreneurs speak (one from 9 a.m.–10 a.m. and the other from 11 a.m.–12 noon). The hour between the two guest speakers is the opportunity for members to share their start-up ideas with their colleagues to receive feedback, resources, and guidance from the speakers and others.

These meetings are organized by the student leaders. This is a take charge, learn-by-doing organization. From the planning of the sessions, to the follow-up with speakers, to handing out name tags and arranging breakfast and lunch for the members, the student leaders delegate tasks among each other, and the president follows-up with them to make sure it all works smoothly.

The meetings are held at top universities in Southern California. University of Southern California (USC), University of California, Los Angeles (UCLA), Loyola Marymount University (LMU), and California Institute of Technology (Cal-Tech) are our key venues for sessions.

EMS is a registered club at all four universities, so EMS hosts events at these schools and receives treatment as a local college club. We arrange it this way so that the organization can operate as a local college club would, but also, on a larger scale. This allows us to bring together students from all over Southern California, as all members are invited to all programs at all universities.

Entrepreneurs who come to speak know that the organization seeks to put them in touch with young starters who are looking for guidance. With this in mind, we give the members of the organization the opportunity to reach out to the speakers for mentorship. The mentor relationship usually lasts anywhere from two months to one year. Some continue on in the program for several years as students. Because our students are so passionate about seeking mentorship, the mentor relationships that they build often last a lifetime. Often the students come back as mentors after they succeed.

CONCLUSION

As the saying goes, Rome was not built in a day. Cultivating a community for young entrepreneurs, giving them the tools and resources to make them successful, and putting them in touch with very successful entrepreneurs takes time, and a lot of small efforts. In an endeavor like this, every little bit counts. **Treat the development of a mentorship program the way you would treat a start-up.** Remember that the organization is ever-evolving and ever-growing. Most importantly, your measure of success in an entrepreneur-developing and mentoring organization is the results that your students achieve. Are they chasing their dreams, and are they more certain of how to get there because of your organization? That's the test question.

As a result of a program like this, students should both believe in their dreams and better understand the practical steps they need to take in order to make those dreams a reality. And they will gain resources and contacts that will help propel them to success!

"People usually fail when they are on the verge of success. So give as much care to the end as to the beginning."

Lao-Tzu

Chapter Twenty-Five

So What is this Beast Called an Entrepreneur?

A Description — But Certainly not All-Inclusive

By Fred Kiesner

INTRODUCTION

Over the past forty some years that I have been involved in teaching, counseling, and consulting with Entrepreneurs, I have developed a list of **entrepreneurial traits** that I discuss in detail with my students. I use them to stimulate the future entrepreneurs to think about the type of **traits they might want to hone, develop, and stimulate if they do not already have them**.

I make it very clear to the students that they **do not need to possess all of these traits** (in fact some of them are negative traits they may not want). **They are traits that tend to describe what makes up the psyche of successful entrepreneurs.**

I present the list here to give the Entrepreneur, or potential Entrepreneur, **something to think about as they forge forward in finding their place in life as an Entrepreneur**, or, at minimum, an Entrepreneurial person in the larger corporate business, working for someone else. Indeed, it is critically important to the survival of many of our large corporations that they, too, accept and encourage their employees to be entrepreneurial (are you listening, General Motors)?

1. **Fire in the Belly!** Passion is the critical ingredient here! Being an Entrepreneur is not easy — in fact it can be unbelievably tough; thus, you had better be wonderfully excited about what you are doing.

2. **Perseverance, Persistence!** You better be full of determination and a "don't-give-up" attitude if you are to succeed as an Entrepreneur!

3. **Energy!** Oh yes! It certainly does take the maximum amount of energy to be an Entrepreneur! No loafing allowed, even when you have started to "have it made", because they are gaining on you!

4. **Unwavering Positive Attitude!** Want to ruin a business? Fastest way I know is to turn negative — especially when times are tough. You must stay upbeat at all times. A negative attitude is telegraphed immediately to folks like employees, customers, bankers, venture capitalists — the folks you depend on for success!

5. **High Tolerance for Ambiguity!** There are no guarantees for you when you are an entrepreneur — think about it, if times are tough and money is short, the Entrepreneur is the

last one to get paid. If you want guarantees, get yourself put in prison — that is the only place I know of that promises you three meals a day and a roof over your head.

6. **Streetwise!** That most wonderful man, Warren Buffett, has a saying that goes something like this — if you have a four hundred horsepower brain and you only get 100 horsepower applied to the road, you are useless. If you have a two hundred horsepower brain and you apply all 200 horsepower to the road, you are successful. In short, maximize the impact everything you do has on "the street," namely, your business. It is better to be decently (or average) smart and make everything work than to be brilliant and waste what you have. Connect your brainpower fully to the reality of the street.

7. **Action-Oriented!** You must not succumb to the sickness of "paralysis by analysis!" I sometimes worry that we teach our students to depend much too much on analyzing the situation to death. At some point, if you are to succeed as an entrepreneur, **you must act, and act decisively!** Entrepreneurs do things, they don't just study things. They are doers, not stewers! **Take the first step sooner rather than later!**

8. **They are not Perfectionists!** See above. If you are too much of a perfectionist, you may be hiding behind the excuse that "it is not perfect yet!" **The Entrepreneur cannot afford perfection in their business.**

9. **They are Flexible!** They change and adapt quickly to the action around them!

10. **They have Excellent Health!** Who does the work of the leader if the Entrepreneur allows themselves the luxury of being sick?

11. **They are Generalists!** They must wear many hats, and must know a lot about a lot of things. I sometimes worry a lot that we tend to try to force young people into the tunnel of exceptional specialization. This can be the enemy of the Entrepreneur.

12. **They exude Self-Confidence!** The successful Entrepreneur has little self-doubt. They believe anything is possible if they are in control.

13. **They are unwilling to let others control their destiny!** They delight in the belief that they control their own destiny!

14. **Urgency!** In the Entrepreneur's mind, all that they do is urgent, critical, and they are always operating on a rush timeframe!

15. **They often have Superior Conceptual Ability.** We used to call this "women's intuition!" They can see through the "noise" and recognize the critical issues in a situation. They simplify complex problems. Perhaps this is part of the reason why women are doing so well in starting businesses in America.

16. **They have Vision!** They can see the big picture, and their role in it. They are always looking ahead to the future, and always seek ways to impact that future!

17. **They understand and maximize the value of Networking!** You never know when you will need a plumber to fix the office toilet.

18. **They have just plain, old-fashioned Common Sense!**

19. **They are not Self-Defeating!** They do not program themselves to fail! For the successful Entrepreneur, nothing less than being a winner is acceptable. **Nothing!**

20. **They are Poor at Delegating!** How often have you heard someone say "if I want it done right, I have to do it myself." You won't hear this from the successful Entrepreneur! They know they must depend on others.

21. **They have an extremely strong Need to Control and Direct the action around them!** They just plain want to be making things happen. Often this trait is frowned upon in a large corporate setting where they are perceived as out of control cowboys!

22. **They set extremely High Targets for themselves!** And they have no doubt that they will achieve them.

23. **They Win Fast, and They Lose Fast!** They don't waste time excessively mourning their losses and setbacks, and they move on quickly to the next objective after they score a win!

24. **They have only a Fair Degree of Creativity and Innovation!** Many successful entrepreneurs are not excessively creative, but when they have an idea, they know how to quickly surround themselves with talent smarter than they are to help them carry out their dream!

25. **They have a Fertile Imagination!** They dream a lot — and in the dreams they are always solving problems and doing exciting things!

26. **They thrive on having a High Degree of Autonomy!** They are survivors, on their own! They can handle being the Lone Ranger!

27. **They are Moderate Risk Takers!** They are not lottery players — where they have no impact on the risk. They want to control and mitigate the risk. They are very willing to take a risk, if they can see the ability to cut it down with

their talent and ability, and have a dramatic impact on the outcome. They know they can lose, they just don't take the chance of losing with stupidity!

28. **They are Persuasive!** Ahhhhhhhh! Yes, they can sell ice cubes to Eskimos!

29. **They Take the Initiative!** No way they are going to wait for the other fellow to do it. "Get it done" is the Entrepreneur's motto!

30. **They often have Poor Interpersonal Skills!** They quite often treat their employees poorly! (Just plain dumb.) And, if you meet one at a cocktail party and they leave you after just a few words of conversation, it is probably because they will only spend time with people who are of value to them and their success! Diplomacy is often lacking in the Entrepreneur! How sad!

31. **They are often Unconventional!** They are not afraid to be different, weird! Does the name Donald Trump come to mind? In short, they have just sufficient stability to keep from being hauled off to the Looney bin. They have been described as spirited, unconventional, weird, kooky, odd, willing to make waves! Ain't it fun?

32. **They are very Realistic!** The successful entrepreneur must know the facts, good or bad.

33. **They have a Low Need for Status! In the beginning** they will run their business out of their garage or barn, sitting on orange crates to be sure to have the funds to maximize the business. Boy, does this change fast once the business makes it over the tipping point and it becomes successful!

34. **They Have Fun!!!!!!!!!!!!!!!!!** Being an Entrepreneur can and must be fun! If it isn't, get a job with the Post Office!

35. **They Make Their Own Luck!** They absolutely do not have the lottery mentality. They know that if they make it big, it is because they cause it to happen!

36. **They Accept Responsibility for what happens!** They don't try to shift the blame. They are comfortable with the weight of responsibility!

37. **They have a Long Attention Span!** For things they are interested in. They have a one-track mind when involved in their business passion. They are not easily distracted.

38. **They are often Unmarried!** Or, they have a spouse that understands! Sadly, the stresses of creating a business and making it fly can cause great damage to a marriage if you are not careful.

39. **They are Team Builders!** But not in the foolish way the larger corporations do it. They understand that their biggest resource is the Entrepreneurial Team!

40. **Usually They are Lousy Administrators!** You better have a really powerful personal assistant!

41. **They Do Things They Hate To Do!** For the success of the business, the successful Entrepreneur knows there are many things they must do — even clean the toilets if nobody else is available to do it.

42. **They do Presidential things!** They are the boss, they think like the boss at all times, they do not waste their time on inconsequential activities. They do what counts big!

43. **They tend to get in Trouble, or even fired in the large firm for some of the characteristics listed here!** Despite all their talk about wanting to be entrepreneurial, the General Motors firms of the world, deep down, really truly just want "yes men!"

44. **Add your own ideas — no list can ever be fully complete!**

Be aware, dear friends, **this is not by any means an all-inclusive or perfect list**. It is, I hope, a list that will make you think about yourself, your own power, ability, and winning characteristics.

Perhaps, after reading this list, and cogitating and chewing your cud a bit about what these things mean, you will understand yourself a wee bit better!

Remember, if you aren't growing, you are falling behind in the race of life!

Enjoy Growing!

"Have the courage to follow your heart and intuition. They somehow already know what you truly want to become. Everything else is secondary."

Steve Jobs

Chapter Twenty-Six

Fulfilling the Impossible Dream: Breaking into a Targeted Niche Market

A Glimpse into the Mindset of a Groundbreaking, Glass-Ceiling-Shattering, Community-Oriented Entrepreneurial Heroine

By Martha de la Torre

Martha de la Torre is the CEO and Publisher of El Clasificado, an award winning interactive media company that has connected buyers and sellers in the Hispanic marketplace since 1998 through point, digital and experiential media properties. She launched El Clasificado in 1988 with her husband, Joe Badame, not only to build a successful business, but also to provide the

481

Latino community with a valuable tool. That is why, in addition to providing free, low-cost advertising solutions for Latino microenterprises, El Clasificado also contains editorial sections to help readers learn to help themselves. El Clasificado.com also offers free online classified ads to help individuals and small businesses build online marketplaces. Martha is a graduate of Loyola Marymount University, where she earned a Bachelor of Science in Accounting. She became a Certified Public Accountant and audit manager while at Arthur Young (now Ernst & Young) and was the Chief Financial Officer of La Opinion before starting El Clasificado. Banking industry trends, in 2008 El Clasificado grow by 15% to reach revenues of $13 million and through retaining and reingineering has been able to sustain its work-force of 110 with short-term plans to expand its digital workforce. The company under Martha's leadership has been named one of the fastest growing companies in Los Angeles by Hispanic Business, Inc Magazine, and the Los Angeles Business Journal. Martha is currently helping to enrich her community as an active participant on three nonprofit boards: the Los Angeles County Education Foundation, which focuses on K-12 education; Los Angeles Child Guidance Clinic, which provides mental health services for emotionally disturbed children; and Loyola Marymount University's Mexican American Alumni Association, which helps provide scholarships for qualified and deserving LMU Undergraduate Latino/a students. In 2006 Martha was appointed to serve on the Board of Regents of LMU.

Editor's Note: *Martha de la Torre is an outstanding example of how a potential entrepreneur with a dream can win as an entre-preneur, despite having to overcome several additional obstacles that are often thought of as very difficult for entrepreneurs — being a woman, and being a minority. She disproves all stereotypes about woman and minority entrepreneurs. Current research in America shows that women are becoming entrepre-neurs in astounding numbers, far exceeding the level of startup entrepreneurship ventures by men. Minorities are also achieving* *incredible success in the USA in starting their businesses. I asked her to do this chapter so that we can gain insight and understanding of the thought process of this wonderful entrepreneur, and how she overcame exceptional odds and difficulties to make her business succeed. She helps us to clearly understand the entrepreneur's psyche and traits. She also proves so very well that nothing, but nothing, can stand in the way of winning as an entrepreneur — age, gender, heritage, etc. have absolutely no negative impact on success as an entrepreneur!*

INTRODUCTION

The Dream of Having an Impact — The Accidental Entrepreneur

I am not one who has dreamt all their lives about becoming an entrepreneur. I dreamt of becoming a dance choreographer for musical plays. But I couldn't take the risk of graduating from college with few job prospects and a burden to my family. I owed it to my family to be successful and financially independent. My parents and family had sacrificed so much to leave their beloved Ecuador for the United States. They came to Los Angeles to ensure that my generation would have opportunities and a better life. My parents wanted us to live the American dream, and that meant a college education with a bankable degree.

I first met someone who wanted to be an entrepreneur in college. I thought this student was crazy and that to be an entrepreneur was an impossible dream. I thought that only people with a lot of money and an established family with a business could be entrepreneurs. However, I eventually had the wonderful experience as a CPA and manager at Arthur Young to work with CEO's and founders of companies. I learned that many business leaders were just ordinary people: usually very educated, dedicated, and experienced with a great idea and an ability to execute and follow through with a plan. I was fascinated with how some people could turn a vision into a multimillion-dollar company. The vision was always based on observing a need and finding an effective way to fill that need. I admired such people and wanted to be in an environment where I could be of help to the entrepreneurs with an interesting vision and be part of making the vision fabulously successful.

In 1984, I noticed the growth of the Los Angeles Latino population, the routine coverage by local media of Latino art and culture, and the increase in mergers and acquisitions of Hispanic media properties. I was very much an assimilated American and spoke very little Spanish, but I loved Latin art, dance, food, and culture; it occurred to me that maybe I could become an expert in the emerging Hispanic market. So I decided to become an *Intrapreneur*: a person who can help a company fulfill its growth potential through innovation, strategy, and passion for success, but as an employee with a nice and secure weekly paycheck. I left Arthur Young after seven years and became the CFO of one of my clients, *La Opinion*, the largest Spanish language daily in the nation. La Opinion had been my audit client for many years and I felt that as CFO I could help La Opinion expand from its core and break-out into a dominant media company in the Hispanic market.

I stayed with La Opinion for two years. The newspaper grew significantly during that period but my vision for La Opinion was beyond my boundaries as a CFO, so I decided to leave the Company. I was considering getting an MBA so I could become an investment banker and continue with my desire to help other companies reach their full potential. At the same time I contemplated switching careers, I was also thinking of the emerging Latino market and of the many useful products available in English and not yet available in Spanish.

For instance, I wondered why there wasn't a Spanish language classified shopper. At La Opinion the classifieds were the strongest source of revenues. In the general market, Harte-Hanks quite successfully served the local classified needs of Los Angeles with several zoned versions of the nationally recognized, home-delivered Pennysaver. **I wondered why there wasn't a Spanish version of the Pennysaver and thought someone should create one.** I often mentioned this to friends and colleagues who thought it was a great idea and that I should be the one to launch such a venture. **This was a crazy idea because I never wanted to be an entrepreneur. I just wanted to help other entrepreneurs and have the opportunity to join their thrill ride to success.**

A couple of attorneys I knew encouraged me to write the business plan for a Spanish classified shopper and committed to raise the needed capital for the venture. I had the opportunity to be the sweat equity investor. My future husband, Joe Badame, also thought I had a great idea and encouraged me to proceed. Following Joe's advice, I drafted the business plan for El Clasificado and published the first issue on May 4, 1988.

Against My Better Judgment!!!

We launched El Clasificado without having raised the estimated needed capital of close to $700,000, against my better judgment. I kept expecting my original partners who had encouraged me to launch this venture to raise the necessary capital. But my partner's law firm went bankrupt after the launch, **his investment check bounced**, the recession began early in the Hispanic market, and I found myself with a classically undercapitalized company — and now I was an entrepreneur.

The Vision

When I first envisioned El Clasificado, I wanted it to be a publication that wouldn't simply take up more room on newsstands or shelf space in the homes of potential readers. **I wanted it to be a useful resource for the immigrant community**, which, with its enormous concentration in Los Angeles, was essentially the heart of the city. I thought about my parents' experience as immigrants from Ecuador, the hardships they faced trying to integrate into a new way of living in a foreign land where they did not know the language or the culture. What options would be most useful to people with the same challenges my parents had faced? In addition to classified ads in Spanish, I wanted at least 5%–8% of El Clasificado's content dedicated to editorials about health, education, parenting tips, and even English lessons. Anything that would empower Latinos to make life better for themselves was open for inclusion.

Additionally, to succeed, I wanted to go into new marketplaces in Los Angeles. I studied the demographics of Los Angeles and targeted Latino communities where existing competition from other Hispanic print media was minimal or nonexistent. So in summary, we launched El Clasificado as a **classified shopper with valuable and concise self-help editorial content distributed by community zones** in order to differentiate ourselves from existing offerings in the **Hispanic marketplace**.

That was the vision in 1988, and to this day El Clasificado is the nation's only Spanish-language weekly classified shopper with audited circulation in over 24 zones in Southern California.

Twenty one years after those initial startup days from plan to execution, I am proud to say that El Clasificado has become one of the nation's largest classified weekly publications in Spanish, with a multi-cultural workforce of more than 100, annually increasing sales, and a circulation that continues to grow in spite of declining circulations for print publications nationwide.

Moreover, with online products on track to aggregating close to two million monthly page-views and dozens of grassroots community events that we present year-round throughout Southern California, El Clasificado is fast positioning itself as the leading platform for multi-media advertising solutions in the Hispanic market.

PREPARE FOR THE BIGGEST CHALLENGE OF YOUR LIFE

If you are thinking about starting a business, accept the fact that it will not be easy. I don't mean for this to serve as a deterrent to you. Rather, you should prepare and even look forward to meeting these challenges head on. **Nothing you have ever done in your life will be as hard as starting your business.** Despite the difficulty, **it can also be the most fulfilling and fun effort you have ever undertaken.**

The Struggles

After realizing that no one was going to raise any capital for El Clasificado, Joe and I raised capital from friends and family while our few employees ran the operations. I **made cash flow projections daily**. I became the salesperson and marketer, while Joe took care of operations after his day job. **We struggled — we didn't take a paycheck for over ten years**, we made mistakes with our business model, and everyone said I should just give up and go bankrupt. My ethics wouldn't allow me to do this, and if it wasn't for my accounting background I could have never survived to see our present success. The accounting education I received in College, together with the training and experience I received from Arthur Young ensured that, **good or bad, I always knew the Company's financial position. Even when we didn't have money, I at least knew exactly how much we didn't have.**

The recession of the early nineties hit the Hispanic market, my target market, early and hard soon after my business launch, which translated to more than ten years of struggle to keep my investment from going bankrupt, and hopefully making it become profitable. I regularly borrowed money from friends and family to keep from losing El Clasificado. Just about everyone who surrounded me at the time insisted that I give up. They saw the feat ahead of me as hopeless, and for my own good they tried to persuade me to quit before I lost even more money.

If I went bankrupt, how could I face my friends and family that had supported me emotionally and financially? How could we throw our few employees out on the street, many of whom were high school students helping support their families? My ethics, deeply rooted in my LMU education, made giving up and going bankrupt not an option.

It was around that time that I was impressed by the film "Stand and Deliver." The movie demonstrated how **all it took for scores of students to achieve success was for one person to believe in them and challenge them to work hard and believe in themselves**. The point that hit especially close to home for me was the fact that there are so many bright and talented students, not only in East Los Angeles, but in inner cities nationwide, who just need to be given an opportunity to flourish. Headquartered in East LA, **I chose to recruit local high school students as my essential employees because I knew they were intelligent, energetic, and talented**.

Recruiting Garfield High School students turned out to be a win-win situation: the students provided energy and computer skills, and I provided them with opportunities to earn a weekly paycheck, to develop professional skills, and earn advancement opportunities within the company. I am proud to say that **a handful of these students are still with** *El Clasificado* **today and hold management level positions in the company. They are making enormous contributions** to help El Clasificado solidify its position as a leader in Hispanic market advertising.

Achieving the Dream

El Clasificado eventually underwent one of the most rapid periods of growth in its history, increasing in revenues from $237,000 to $2.4 million between 1993 and 1999.

I am fortunate to be able to say **today that I own and operate the nation's largest circulation, free, Spanish classifieds weekly**. Currently, El Clasificado continues to buck the current circulation trend plaguing print periodicals nationwide, having **recently peaked at the all-time high of 360,000 magazines per week**. In 2001, we purchased Al Borde, an eddy and "raw" entertainment publication focused on rock en espanol music, and reaching a niche audience consisting of young, trend-setting bilingual Latinos. We are investing heavily in the websites for both El Clasificado and Al Borde, adding an enormous amount of content and designing them to be more interactive and user-friendly, because we understand that our readers will begin to migrate and rely more heavily on the Internet and less in print.

We have also **recently become an increasingly interactive medium by producing our own community events to continue with our mission of helping our customers and the community**. Our most successful events, El Clasificado's *Su Socio de Negocios* and Al Borde's *Cool Careers for Me* are perfect examples.

Launched in 2006, Su Socio de Negocios (which literally translates to "Your Business Partner") is a series of free small business expos and networking breakfasts for Latino micro-business owners who find themselves in need of entrepreneurial resources and information, much like I did twenty one years ago. Every event offers basic training for new entrepreneurs who are looking for ways to grow their businesses. Because each event has a unique theme, such as technology, marketing, and finance, we invite a panel of experts who can educate our audience on the given topic, as well as answer questions and provide supplemental information and resources. The expos are also a networking area where exhibitors display the products and services they offer our audience of new small business owners. We have found this to be one of our most successful formulas because not only is the material important, but **this service is provided to Hispanic business owners for free** and in **their own language**.

In 2008, we introduced our latest event series presented by Al Borde, which we refer to as **"Cool Careers For Me."** Like our small business training workshops, these events also depend on a great panel lineup of professionals working in a given industry, who volunteer a few hours of their day to visit our headquarters' warehouse space-turned-hang-out-spot, the Al Borde Lounge, and talk to about 100 local high school students about their experience working in the field, obstacles they had to overcome, and also offer advice to the students about how **they** can achieve their career goals. Our first event was about Journalism, and included Syndicated Cartoonist Lalo Alcaraz, ("La Cucaracha"), Syndicated Columnist Gustavo Arellano ("Ask A Mexican"), as well as PR greats Mariluz Gonzalez (Fonovisa) and Josh Norek (Nacional Records, LAMC Cofounder). In true Al Borde style, the students are also treated to two live performances by local rock en espanol groups and pizza to keep up their energy for this interactive event.

We first learned that investing in the local community by providing employment opportunities was mutually beneficial when we began to hire local high school kids and learned how productive and efficient they could be. Events like the ones mentioned above are a major contributor to El Clasificado's success because they are free, and they are a valuable resource to our local community.

WHAT I HAVE LEARNED

Below are the most important tips that have had an impact on the growth and success of my company, either directly or indirectly. These are tips that I have learned along the way through trial and error, and which I think would benefit any up-and-coming potential entrepreneur.

Believe in Yourself and in Your Idea

As I've mentioned, it took El Clasificado about ten years before the company became profitable. In fact, there were several months at a time when I was in danger of losing the company because it was not bringing in sufficient capital to cover all the expenses it incurred. I had to continuously borrow money from friends and family in order to break even.

To those around me, the **logical solution at the time appeared to be to simply give up**. But to me, the idea of giving up on something I had invested countless nerve-racking days and sleepless nights **developing** was **unthinkable**.

In retrospect, what got me through all those difficult years, when I was making cash flow projections daily to ensure that we didn't get ourselves too deeply into debt, was the **belief I had in my company**. I knew that El Clasificado offered services and content that the Hispanic community of Los Angeles was in need of at the time, so I persevered.

Everyone says that it takes a good idea to start a business, **but what keeps a business operating and eventually makes it successful is the amount you as a business owner actually believe in what you have**. If you are thinking about starting a business, keep in mind that you will certainly come across many, many challenges that will test every ounce of strength that you possess, and often it will appear that giving up on your venture is the best solution. During moments like this it is helpful to take time to **focus and reassess** your original goal. **If you believe in it, you will undoubtedly find a way to make the idea work.**

Trust and Good Work Ethics

In addition to understanding and staying on top of cash flow, **a solid set of ethics and social responsibility** is also extremely important. When you are a struggling entrepreneur, oftentimes **your word is the only thing you have to offer**, so you should always make it a point to follow through on every commitment you make.

Following through on even those little, seemingly trivial obligations not only enables you to build up your own solid reputation, but, more importantly, it allows you to **build trust** with everyone you deal with in business, from your lenders and business partners, to your employees, and even the people you hire to do the cleaning.

Toot Your Own Horn!

Once your organization is officially up and running, you should begin to focus on getting the word out about all of the wonderful things your business is doing. Paid PR can be quite expensive and was a luxury that was certainly not in the budget during the first years of El Clasificado. Yet one thing that I found really worked was **researching unique recognition that is available for the type of work you do**. There are hundreds of different promotional vehicles that are available in your community by groups such as your local chambers of commerce and other business networks. These organizations are often seeking to recognize and put the spotlight on new local businesses **and it is free publicity!** What you are doing is news to many — get the word out, and you will be surprised how many people want to hear about your dream.

Once you start receiving this kind of recognition, and you start letting others know all about it, you start to obtain **credibility**.

Early in my entrepreneurial career I secured as much of this free publicity as I possibly could, and I also made sure to call local and national newspapers and to **email** local businesses to let them know what El Clasificado was up to and how our dream was progressing.

These **grassroots, and free, PR efforts** soon proved to be a great way to **gain credibility** without having to spend too much money. You can hire an intern to research the contact information of a few local and national trade publications and/or websites that are relevant to your business, as well as local media and competitors, and be sure to send them a press release every time your organization achieves a new milestone. It's also a good idea to call and follow up with each of the media outlets; if you angle your success the right way, you may even be able to convince them to mention your success story in their news medium!

Network

Attend as many **networking events** as you can. I'm not talking about those big expos with an attendance of 300+ and for which tickets often cost an arm and a leg. Sure, these bigger events usually feature a tremendously impressive list of invitees and keynote speakers, but in my experience I have found them to be rather intimidating to new entrepreneurs. Their mere size can make it difficult for inexperienced business owners to intimately interact with others.

The networking events I am talking about are the smaller ones with attendance of 50–150. Because of their size, these **grassroots networking events** actually provide more successful opportunities for you to interact and connect with other small business owners such as yourself. Look for networking mixers that feature a topic or theme that is of interest to you.

It is important to take advantage of such opportunities in order to gain fresh business perspectives from others in your field, new ideas for you to apply to your own business model, and they also allow you to share your own ideas and insights into what has worked and what hasn't for your business. What I'm leading up to here is the importance of **developing trustworthy, mutually beneficial relationships** with others in the business community. They provide a source of ideas and actions you can emulate and a sounding board for evaluating your own ideas and efforts.

Give Back What You Received

Now that we have achieved and surpassed many of our company objectives, it is satisfying to be able to provide avenues for others to realize their dreams of starting their own businesses. Many of our own clients have found success at our own small business training seminars *Su Socio de Negocios* **(Your Business Partner)**, an event series held quarterly in different grassroots Latino communities.

These events were created by El Clasificado in 2006 to serve as a platform connecting Spanish-speaking Latino micro-entrepreneurs with widely known corporate sponsors that offer resources for small businesses. According to past attendees, our *Su Socio de Negocios* small business seminars have become a valuable tool in saving money and enhancing business operations for two reasons: their size — anywhere between 150–300 attendees — and because they are in Spanish.

In addition to setting *Su Socio de Negocios* apart from other similar events, these characteristics allow many of the thousands of Spanish-speaking small business owners, who attend to network and learn new tools that will help their businesses, thrive **in a non-intimidating environment, and at no cost to them**.

Show Them Who You Are

Oftentimes at business expos you will be treated to some wonderful, exciting presentations by top experts in your field. Don't be afraid to **introduce yourself** to these panelists and collect the business cards of those who you believe you can add to your valuable network of resources. This is a great time to deliver the famous "30-second elevator pitch" that captures the essence of who you are, what you do and, if you're a master of rhetoric, why the person should care and want to invest in you.

The idea of approaching someone who is far more experienced, successful, and seasoned in the business world can seem rather daunting at first, but you will be surprised at how approachable many of these business experts/celebrities actually are.

Think about it! What do you have to lose?! Some of my greatest mentors and the most substantial contributors to El Clasificado's success have been individuals whom I've met at conferences like the Association of Free Community Papers, the National Association of Hispanic Publications and the International Classified India Association.

Follow-up, Stay in Touch

Most importantly, always follow up with the person after you have introduced yourself and picked up a business card. You could have hundreds of business cards from many different influential figures, but these cards are worth little if all they are doing is sitting on your desk. A quick phone call or e-mail thanking the contact for his/her time and anticipating future opportunities for you to discuss ideas shows that you are genuinely interested in what they have to offer, and is a great way to increase the likelihood of developing a productive relationship.

A great way to stay in touch with potential business partners is through online social networking sites such as Facebook,

MySpace, Hi5, or my personal favorite, LinkedIn. All of these are free, and they are also a great way to learn more about a potential business associate because the sites usually contain complete profiles that contain previous work experience, skills, the organizations that person is involved in, and dozens to hundreds of references in the form of 'friends' or 'connections' on the site. Generally these profiles paint a more complete picture of a business contact than a simple resume could.

When You Stop Learning, You Stop Growing

Once you have a business that has taken off, you should **beware of getting too comfortable with the success you have achieved**. Always be on the lookout for new trends and developments in and outside your field of expertise, no matter how unlikely or irrelevant the field may appear to your business. When El Clasificado eventually became a hit among Latino consumers as a print publication, I was relieved and thrilled at the idea that I might actually have a shot at becoming a successful entrepreneur because I had a product that people responded to positively.

In the midst of the dot-com boom, everyone around me was buzzing about the importance of purchasing domain names and creating websites. I have to admit that initially I was very reluctant to even consider trying my hand at something I knew almost nothing about.

I **attended instructional workshops and seminars** and learned enough about this new technology to see its value. Fortunately for me, I had a tech-savvy brother who also saw the value of this new medium and helped us purchase over 100 domain names for me at a bargain rate, and at a time when I did not yet understand what a domain name even was. This early move has enabled the company to launch successful vertical internet platforms to capture advertisers migrating from print to online. Quinceariern.com, a website that helps Latino families prepare for their daughters' fifteenth birthday celebrations, is the most successful to date. Other domains acuired in 1988 like plomeros.com (plumbers) and funeravias.com (funeral) will soon be launch to expand marketplaces for our customers.

Gain Employees' Trust

I think we owe much of the growth of our organization to the **loyalty that most employees feel toward El Clasificado**. It is important to gain the trust and loyalty of your employees because they ultimately hold the key to your company's success. If your employees value your organization, it is much more likely that they will be more productive than employees who think poorly of their place of employment. We have gained our employees' respect and loyalty by adhering to a series of simple, yet often overlooked policies that anyone can emulate:

- **Make employees feel like they are "part of the team."** This policy can be difficult to employ, especially if your company is large and consists of several different departments. Nonetheless, I highly recommend that you try to include EVERYONE in your organization in some of the decisions that affect the entire company. For example, if you are going to change your company's slogan, run it by everyone, from Senior Managers and Directors to Assistants, for feedback. It goes without saying that you will ultimately be the one who makes the final decision, but this will greatly motivate your staff by **letting them know that you value their opinions**.

- **Be available.** As a business owner, I often find myself away from the office trying to make it from one business meeting to another. When I do work at the office, however, I make sure to let my staff know that they are **welcome to step into my office** whenever they need to get a hold of me. In my professional experience, I was always **wary of CEO's who secluded themselves** in enormous offices, barricaded behind large, imposing doors that were always shut. I often felt that this culture of isolation is detrimental to any organization because it can significantly reduce communication within the company. Moreover, there are always employees who rely on feedback and support from C-level executives; this type of employee cannot grow and give his best to your organization if he/she does not feel a sense of direction or support from his/her supervisor.

- **Remove the doors.** In the ten years I have operated El Clasificado, we have relocated three times to three different buildings, and I always make it a point to **remove the doors from my office and to have it located centrally** within the building. In our current facility, **my office almost serves as a hallway** from one side of the building to the other, so I rarely miss my employees on their way into or out of work. I have found this to be an excellent way to stay on top of my business operations by giving staff the opportunity to come to me with questions about a work-related project, and also by giving me the opportunity to chat with those employees with whom I rarely interact.

- **Keep your eyes open — always.** I believe that a good CEO needs to always monitor their business operations closely. I no longer have to reconcile the bank account and prepare daily cash flow projections, but I maintain many benchmarks and dashboards to monitor sales, cash, receivables, and expenses. Over the years I have developed metrics that help me stay on top of our productivity and progress against goals. We always watch trends against our own performance and now are getting better at benchmarking our trends against competitors. Technology and captured online data reveals so much about your business and customers. It is important to review this information for inspiration and strategic decision-making.

ESSENTIALS FOR SUCCESS

I'd like to conclude with a few basic ideas that I have instilled in my sales managers throughout the years, but which I think are applicable to any manager in just about any field. Whether you have 2 or 200 employees, it is important to **always remember the value that they bring to your organization**. It takes a lot of time and money to find and hire top talent... but you must also keep in mind that as a business owner, it takes a lot of investment on your part to keep that person happy and working for you, **and not your competition**.

The primary function of a manger is to **Recruit, Teach, and Inspire**. Focus on these basics, and you will have the keys to success.

- **Recruit.** When Recruiting, you want only the best, only those who show **talent** and who demonstrate a **true passion** for what they do. In order to attract the best, you should always offer compensation that includes the following:

  - **Offer a good mix of Base Pay + Commission** (you should focus on offering a competitive salary if commission does not apply to you).

  - Provide a **Regular Bonus** as well as a **Retroactive Bonus**. Reward your employee even if they didn't meet the actual goal. This will motivate them to increase their performance level.

  - Create learning and growth opportunities. It is especially important to **empower** your employees to make decisions. This will really come in handy if these decisions directly affect your clients because your client will be happy with the level of efficiency, and your employee will be motivated by the **autonomy**.

- **Teach.** Employees should be taught to produce results. When they achieve goals, be sure to reward them promptly and consistently in order to keep them motivated. You should also train employees to deal in a customer-focused approach. By the end of the training period, employees should know how to increase customer satisfaction and understand and anticipate clients' needs.

- **Inspire and retain talent.** I have found that my employees are most satisfied and most productive when they receive **feedback and appraisals on a regular basis**. Employees always like to know where they stand in their place of employment, therefore you should ALWAYS be able to sit down and map out a career plan within the organization with your employee. **Support** is also important, and it should come from Senior management and Supervisors, who themselves lead by example. I always like to remind my management team that **employees don't leave their jobs, they leave their supervisors**.

- **Offer regular training sessions** to improve employees' skills and performance. This gives good employees the opportunity to fully develop their strengths by letting them know what they are doing right when they are doing it, and it also helps underperformers to identify what work habits are not exactly cutting it for the organization as a whole. It is important to remember — especially when giving negative evaluations — that your job is not only to identify weaknesses, but also to offer tips and suggestions for improvements. At El Clasificado, in addition to offering regular appraisals, we also provide constant **training and coaching** in order to ensure that all our **employees have an equal chance at achieving success**.

Don't Put All Your Eggs in One Basket

One other important lesson I learned the hard way is to **be careful against relying too heavily on the strengths of one person that you lose sight of the vast pool of talent that exists among other employees within the organization**. It is great when you find that one person is extremely skilled in many areas, is reliable, and delivers nothing less than his or her very best. When you come across such a remarkable employee, especially if you own a small business, it becomes very easy to look to that person and depend on him or her for all of your needs. This is something that you should try to avoid, however, because it not only comes with the **risk of burn-out for your employee**, but this may also be **detrimental to the many other employees who also have other hidden strengths**.

I like to compare this situation to a box of knives. Have you ever noticed when you buy a new set of knives that there is always one that is sharper than the rest? Usually, this becomes our favorite, and we rely on it for just about everything. Unfortunately, we soon find that not only does our favorite knife become dull from overuse, but we are left with an entire box of perfectly functional knives that remain idle. The same can be said about employees who are oftentimes overlooked. I have found that with the right amount of coaching and training, every person is capable of sharpening his or her innate skills, developing new ones, and achieving their full potential.

A FINAL THOUGHT

What I love best about being an entrepreneur is the opportunity to create new jobs, new careers and new wealth for a family and a community. I am so proud to be an American, so grateful to

God and my parents that I was born in the U.S., and I want everyone in the world to live the American dream!!!

That is not about being rich with money, but about enriching your life and those around you with a sense of independence and self worth.

"It is not what you are, but what you don't become that hurts."

Oscar Levant

Chapter Twenty-Seven

What is it You Want Out of Life?

By Fred Kiesner

A critically important part of the job of Entrepreneurial coaches, educators, advisors, and mentors is to **stimulate the Entrepreneur or the prospective new Entrepreneur to think seriously about what is absolutely important to the Entrepreneur in life**. We have many choices of what we want, and what we can be.

The only problem is, we are often so caught up in life's activities that we just never sit down and think about where we are going, and what we are seeking in life.

For probably thirty years I have required **ALL** of the Entrepreneurs and Entrepreneurial students I have worked with to do the following thought stimulator. I adapted and developed it from a wonderful piece first developed by Dewey Johnson, a wonderful Accounting Professor at Fresno State University in California.

I hope you will do this exercise, putting maximum effort into thinking deeply about what is really important to you in life. You should keep it in a place where you will encounter it every few years — and enjoy seeing how you have progressed, and how your thinking may have progressed on what is important to you.

INTRODUCTION

The purpose of this exercise is to force you to think about the important things in life, as they apply to your future career. We are often so busy worrying about building our careers and grasping for all that life has to offer, that we do not **make the time** to sit back, think about what is important to us, and then put those things into some sort of **priority order that will give us a very basic decision matrix**.

This exercise forces you to do that.

In the following list there are 35 value areas (including blank ones that you can use to add special values that are unique to you).

Organize and assign those thirty-five value areas under the five impact headings on the next page.

There are no right or wrong answers.

This exercise will not be graded.

This is for you only!!!!!

THE EXERCISE

It is recognized that there will be some temptation to say **"they are all of great importance to me,"** and want to put them all into the top one or two categories. **This is not allowed!** You must choose which of these values are of the most importance to you, and then next most important, etc.

If you put some serious thought into this, as you should, it will be a difficult assignment, but fun. It should have some serious impact on your future thinking, and what you should be doing with your life.

Your "grade," or reward for completing this assignment will come in the future! Do not worry about what other people will think about the priorities and rankings you have given these values. This exercise is of importance only to you! Nobody else's ideas or views matter!

You may, however, want to show the results of this exercise to a close and trusted friend and mentor, and see if they see you making your choices, and living your life today, according to these values, as you have listed them.

Your values and priorities will change over time, and particularly as you embark upon your career building years. Keep this little exercise someplace safe, where you will discover it in five or ten years. It will be very revealing to you in the future to see where you were (now) as compared to where you will be in the future in your value system.

Now go ahead and have fun thinking about you, and where you should be putting your priorities and efforts, as you build your most wonderful life and career!

The Values and Priorities List

NOTE: You are not allowed to put more than seven value areas under any one heading. You must distribute them among all the categories of relative impact.

1. **Family** — build a close-knit family group.

2. **Balanced Lifestyle** — have a variety of interests that you spend time on.

3. **Power and Authority** — control the work activities and destiny of others.

4. **Friendships** — develop close personal relationships with others.

5. **Excitement** — experience a high degree of stimulation, novelty, and drama in life.

6. **Help Others** — help people either directly or in small groups.

7. **Moral Fulfillment** — feel that my work, career, and life are contributing to ideals I feel are very important.

8. **Influence People** — be in a position to change the attitudes/opinions of others.

9. **Exercise Competence** — show above average proficiency and effectiveness.

10. **Change and Variety** — have work responsibilities frequently changed in content and setting.

11. **Independence** — be able to determine the nature of the work you do without significant involvement from others.

12. **Challenging Problems** — engage continually with complex questions and demanding tasks, with troubleshooting and problem-solving as a core part of my career.

13. **Profit, Gain, Advancement** — be able to move ahead rapidly, and have a strong likelihood of accumulating large amounts of money or other material gain.

14. **Affiliation** — be recognized as part of particular groups or organizations.

15. **Aesthetics** — be involved in appreciating the beauty of things, ideas, life, etc.

16. **Security** — be assured of keeping my job and a reasonable financial reward.

17. **Knowledge** — engage in the pursuit of knowledge, truth, understanding.

18. **Recognition** — get positive feedback and public credit for my work and achievements.

19. **Competition** — engage in activities that pit my abilities against others.

20. **Stability** — have a life that is largely predictable over long periods of time.

21. **Help Society** — contribute to the betterment of the world as a whole; have a keen sense of social responsibility.

22. **Status** — impress and gain the respect of others by the nature of what I do, my career.

23. **Work Under Pressure, Deadlines** — have time restraints that demand that you produce at your best with no margin for error.

24. **Creativity** — be able to create new ideas and programs using your own initiative.

25. **Location** — live in a place I absolutely love, in the manner that I love.

26. **Protect My Family** — live in a place that is safe for my family.

27. **Love What I Do** — go to work everyday absolutely excited about my career and life's work.

28. **Achieve Success in an Ethical Manner** — maintaining honesty and ethics in all I do.

29. (Add any other items you think have not been covered here that are important to you).

30.

31.

32.

33.

34.

35.

Have fun thinking about your life and ranking your values!!!!!

The Values In Life Worksheet

ALWAYS VALUED	OFTEN VALUED	SOMETIMES VALUED	SELDOM VALUED	LEAST VALUED
1.	1.	1.	1.	1.
2.	2.	2.	2.	2.
3.	3.	3.	3.	3.
4.	4.	4.	4.	4.
5.	5.	5.	5.	5.
6.	6.	6.	6.	6.
7.	7.	7.	7.	7.

Remember, no more than 7 items can be put under any one heading.

Please save this analysis someplace where you will pull it out again in a number of years and review how your thoughts and ideas have changed and been modified by time and experience.

Now go out and use this knowledge about you in determining what you want to do in your life and your career!

"Man can only become what he is able to consciously imagine."

Dane Rudhyar

Chapter Twenty-Eight

Sound Bites and Other Food for Entrepreneurial Thought

By Elissa B. Grossman

Dr. Elissa Grossman is an Assistant Professor of Management and Entrepreneurship at Loyola Marymount University, having previously taught at Baruch College (CUNY) and the University of Southern California. She has taught introductory courses in entrepreneurship, as well as courses in feasibility analysis, business plan development, and new venture growth. When not teaching, she conducts research in the field — exploring, particularly, how entrepreneurs build and extract value from the social networks essential to very early stage resource acquisition. Elissa earned her PhD and MBA from UCLA, an MSc from the London School of Economics, and an AB from Harvard University. She has also worked in brand and marketing management for companies including LiveCapital (a start-up later acquired by Dun and Bradstreet), Sun Microsystems, and Procter & Gamble. Her dissertation

was recognized with the Academy of Management's NFIB Award for Research Excellence. In 2008, she received the Acton Foundation's Entrepreneurship Master Teacher Award and Baruch College's Teaching Excellence Award.

INTRODUCTION

When I first started teaching, I suffered from **"Reinvent the Wheel Syndrome"** — a non-medical ailment that involves trying to prep new classes by building them from scratch. (If you were to look this syndrome up in a book, if that book existed, you would find it listed as sharing many symptoms with **"Too Big for One's Britches Disorder,"** a condition that involves knowing, despite no supporting evidence, that you can, without any experience whatsoever, fix all of the egregious mistakes of your own teachers.)

In my mind's eye, Reinventing the Wheel would be very simple. I'd just track down every teaching material ever developed and jigsaw it together into the best and most creative class in the business world. The students would be bowled over by my genius, and I would receive the highest teaching ratings that any first-time professor had ever received in the history of academia (or, at minimum, the history of my employing university). After three intensive months of preparation and three months of teaching, I had what I viewed at the time as a great epiphany:

Reinventing the wheel is not always the best way to go.

My teaching ratings weren't terrible, but they also weren't going to put me in the Guinness Book of World Records. The bottom line: My students thought my class was creative; they also wished however, that at some point along the way, any point, they'd actually learned something! I shared this depressing (but somehow revelatory) feedback with my father as he had, early in his career, taught advanced physics at the university level.

It turned out that when he'd first taught, only one student had taken the time to complete a ratings form. The student didn't actually fill out the numerical component of the assessment. The student instead chose to provide feedback in the blank space allocated to "Additional Comments." As my father tells the story, "Instead of sentences, the student chose to draw a picture. Of a hand. Giving me the finger." My second great realization thus accompanied what had been my father's first:

Me: Some students can take what happens in class very seriously.
He: Some people major in physics when they should really major in art.

The truth is ... **most educators aren't super-fantastic right out of the starting gate**. And **neither are most entrepreneurs**. There's a lot to learn. The challenge lies in figuring out not just what constitute worthy lessons, but also how to maximize the likelihood that those lessons will be remembered. Several years ago, a student asked me if his wife could attend one session of a week-long class that I was teaching. He later thanked me for what he described as a "very educational" experience. I asked him, out of curiosity, what his biggest learning was. His very earnest answer: "I learned that my wife can go three whole hours without speaking!" After I stopped laughing, it occurred to me:

What you're teaching and what a student learns are not necessarily the same thing.

I use guest speakers in my classes. I used to worry about inviting guests as I'd heard a great deal of collegial concern about visitors whose sole purpose was to "share war stories" while giving the professor a chance to rest his or her weary big brain. I worried that students were being entertained without being educated. I worried that they might not be learning anything.

Finally, I decided to adopt the approach I'd taken with the harried husband. I asked them, "What is your biggest learning from our guest speakers?" And the students told me: "We learned that it's important for entrepreneurs to have PASSION." In a variety of ways, using a variety of words, the students provided the same lesson again and again and again. So I went home, and I wrote up a lecture that ended with a slide that said what I felt (and continue to feel) is a very important additional lesson:

You can't launch a business on passion alone.

Don't get me wrong. Passion is a great thing to have. Loving what you do is a wonderful recipe for happiness in work and in life. I'm a huge fan of the concept! But over-reliance on passion can cloud the following objective facts: As helpful as passion might be (particularly in tough times), passion isn't necessary for success. Perhaps more importantly, **passion isn't enough**. It's very important for aspiring entrepreneurs to understand that the wonders of their job will be matched with real challenges. I feel very passionately about this issue. In fact, I now have a final exam question in which I ask students to list strategic or operational lessons derived from guest speakers ("deductions for students who cite as a key lesson the 'importance of having passion' or equivalent"). The question helped me realize that students really do learn from speakers. For what it's worth, their favorite learning over the years is below (the exact speaker quote, censored for a G rating):

It's not the money! It's the F#&%ing money.

If you tell the average student or aspiring entrepreneur that money is important, you're likely to get a knowing half-smile or rolled eyes. People know money is important. They're as sure of that as they are of the sun in the sky and the high fat content in french fries. Have an experienced entrepreneur tell them the same (ideally, with some profanity thrown into the mix), and it's an observation of pure genius. It's raw and honest and direct and shocking. It's about something other than passion (though, granted, some people do have a passion for money). Perhaps most importantly, **it's about the most powerful kind of learning — the kind that emerges from mistakes**.

My own early experiences in teaching motivated me to seek counsel from successful colleagues. In the process, I realized that my time was better spent trying to build on the foundation of great teachers than trying to avoid the mistakes of terrible teachers. I believe there is an analogue in entrepreneurship:

> **When you learn from others' successes, you also learn from their mistakes.**

I've had the luxury of hearing a lot of entrepreneurs' stories at this point, and I look forward to hearing many more. Their stories, coupled with my own experience, were used to assemble the following — a summary of some of the truths that entrepreneurs and students of entrepreneurship seem to find surprising, informative, or valuable (even if not every truth is a happy one).

HARD WORK

As a part of my research, I interview entrepreneurs. In order to ensure that I interview only active founders, I first ask them to confirm some facts about their work. On one memorable afternoon, shortly after I'd started one of my very first interviews, I asked an entrepreneur: "How many hours per week do you spend on your business?" He answered, "Eighty hours." I then said, in what I thought was a joking tone of voice, "ONLY eighty?" This question prompted a diatribe that doesn't merit repetition in polite company. At the core of this diatribe was the entrepreneur's difficult truth: He'd been working for 100 hours a week, but his wife had threatened to divorce him if he didn't cut back. My comment and his wife's request clearly demonstrated to him a flagrant insensitivity to the true demands of entrepreneurship. (There might also have been something in there about me being a useless, unappreciative human being, but that's neither here nor there…) As he hung up on me, I made a note in my teaching files:

For some entrepreneurs, an 80-hour week is a slow week.

That not everyone understands just what entrepreneurship is all about was recently echoed in the comment of a friend who founded and runs a successful online information service. As he put it, "Not having a 'job' working for a big company is a social anomaly. I try to describe what I do, and people still ask, 'So who do you work for?' Heck, even my mom asks me, 'Are you keeping up your skills so someone can hire you?'" In fact, I've met many entrepreneurs who tell a version of this tale.

To some in the world of cubicles and 9-to-5 schedules, entrepreneurship resides in an uncomfortable "somewhere" between unemployed and gainfully employed. In this view, entrepreneurship is not a real job; instead, it's a vacation in a place full of coffee, biscotti, Internet connectivity, and a lot of busy nothing until something real comes along. Entrepreneurs learn quickly, thus, that their hard work is not always met with understanding or moral support. With that in mind, another lesson in hard work is often shared with my students:

Launching a business takes emotional and intestinal fortitude.

One entrepreneur with a young, successful, and uniquely creative scavenger hunt company recently sent me an email in which he asked: "Did I warn your students that if you get successful, you stop doing the things that you enjoyed and made you want to start a business? You start working with things like 401(k) plans and insurance." Another entrepreneur offered a similar perspective: "A lot of the things you think you'll be worrying about as an entrepreneur get second shift to things that you assumed were mundane — how the heck to deal with the books and the accounting, with taxes, business licenses, and other regulatory stuff, with things like getting your email and making sure your computers are running."

Here's where it's really, really great to have passion. If you love your business, it will help you through those times when you need to focus on the very important, but not particularly interesting minutiae. No matter what, however, **you need to spend time on the minutiae.** That means:

Entrepreneurship requires patience.

It's not just patience with details. It's also patience with what can be slower than expected progress. An investor once told me, "When entrepreneurs predict their time to profitability, I assume they're off by a factor of at least two." Another said, "I always triple entrepreneurs' time-to-profit estimates." **Most first-time entrepreneurs underestimate how long it takes to build a business.** It can thus be a shock to the system when they realize that their dream of a better tomorrow is really a dream of a better several years from tomorrow.

As one entrepreneur reflected, "Back in school, we were repeatedly told it would take seven years for a start-up to achieve success (if, of course, we managed to survive all the threats to our existence through those seven years). And I remember thinking, first of all, 'Where did they come up with such a specific number?' But even more, I remember thinking, 'Seven years? What is that?' When I was in school, that felt like an eternity. I couldn't even comprehend a timeframe that long when it came to work. To my amazement, seven years is exactly how long it took to prove my business." Whether it's seven years or a different number, the fact remains, as Danish physicist and Nobel Laureate Niels Bohr is believed to have observed:

Prediction is very difficult, especially about the future.

In some of my classes, student groups complete consulting projects for new and rapidly growing businesses. One group created an expansion plan for a successful shop whose inventory was comprised almost exclusively of good luck charms. It's interesting, in a world of passion and hard work, to find a business built entirely on a foundation of luck. **But luck — good or bad — has a funny habit of amplifying or undermining the hard work of even the most capable entrepreneur.** As one such capable entrepreneur once commented to me, "Most who succeed attribute their success to skill and hard work. Most who fail attribute their failure to luck." Whether underestimated or overestimated, the reality is ... bad luck can happen to good people (and vice versa, but that's a different conversation).

At times, entrepreneurs need reminders that some things will simply be out of their control. They should also be reminded, however, that some of what people retrospectively call "luck" was really something else — highly unlikely, but still possible (and thus predictable) events for which planning might have been useful. New venture planning is essential.

PLANNING

One of my guest speakers founded a business importing Sicilian blood oranges to the United States. While in graduate school, she invested a tremendous amount of time researching and planning her business launch, addressing what she viewed as every key issue that might be credibly expected to affect the business. There was one problem, however. She never considered a question at the very core of her business: What happens when orange groves are located near an active volcano — and the volcano erupts? The answer in the short-term is not good. In the short-term, ashes get embedded in the orange rind and cause U.S. Customs to turn away cargo-loads of product. In the long-term, however, it turns out there is a good answer. In the long-term, you turn a blood orange business into a blood orange juice business. That's right. Through creativity and flexibility, she turned a bad business situation into what, as it happened, was a better business. She turned lemons into lemonade. Or something like that. The point remains:

Anticipate the unexpected.

Every time I share the volcano story, there's an eruption of discontent among students. As they rightly point out, volcanoes are not typically a make-or-break feature of most businesses. But I hear a lot of these stories. If it's not a volcano, it's a blizzard. If it's not a blizzard, it's a drought. If it's not a drought, it's a fire. If it's not a fire, it's Oprah. Really. If Oprah decides to showcase your business, you better be ready for a tidal wave of demand.

That's what happened to one entrepreneur (a baker and retailer of gourmet cupcakes) who visited my class. As she pointed out, most people worry about what might happen if things go less well than planned, this despite the fact that **challenges also accrue when things go better than planned**. Do you have enough product to service the demand? Do you have enough space in which to store the needed product? Do you have enough staff to handle the product in the space that you have? Overwhelming success can be, well, overwhelming. Entrepreneurs need to be able to cope with it (as the cupcake entrepreneur did, with aplomb).

Don't only plan for the bad times, plan for the good times as well.

I've noticed a tendency for successful entrepreneurs (particularly if they were successful on their first try) to assume that their way will work every time. The challenge with this tendency is that they will tell future generations of entrepreneurs an "ironclad rule" that might not be clad in iron at all. A few years ago, I invited the founder of several successful Hollywood nightclubs to my class. He told my students, in no uncertain terms: "Always buy the real estate on which you build a club or restaurant. That way, if the business fails, you still have a saleable asset." The following semester, I happened (because I've found that students really love nightclubs) to bring in a different founder of several different successful Hollywood hot spots. He told my students, in no uncertain terms, "Whatever you do, don't buy the real estate. You don't want to get bogged down. It's better to rent." There's a valuable lesson attached to both entrepreneurs' advice, but it has nothing to do with buying or renting:

One size does not fit all.

When students or entrepreneurs begin writing business plans, they tend to first look for sample business plans. The request makes sense. They realize (as I didn't when I first began teaching) that Reinventing the Wheel is not always the best way to go. But **entrepreneurs sometimes rely too much on what already exists** — force-fitting their business ideas into a slightly modified version of whatever they've already read. However easy it might seem to make the planning effort, dependence on sample plans can lead entrepreneurs to confuse the quality of the writing with the quality of the planning itself. In fact, too laser-like a focus on completing a plan (for the sake of a plan) can lead entrepreneurs to lose sight of meaningful issues of short- and long-term business implementation. A successful business is the end; a business plan is simply one means to that end. One entrepreneur reinforced this lesson to my students by observing, "A great business plan is like a great wedding. Neither guarantees lasting success or happiness."

A good business is only as strong as its foundation.

It goes without saying that the best plan in the world is pretty useless if the underlying business idea isn't good. **There, I said it.** It's also the case, however, that the best plan in the world is pretty useless if it's never put into action (even when the underlying business idea is great). **"Analysis paralysis" is more than just a cutesy phrase. It's a malignancy** to which the most highly intelligent are vulnerable. It's a malignancy that can cause great ideas to go nowhere.

A few years ago, I met two talented entrepreneurs with a truly unique fitness concept. The entrepreneurs asked themselves (and a host of others): "How can we communicate the value of our services to maximize sales?" They were so aware that the product might be a difficult sell that they spent only limited time selling — this despite the fact that proactive sales efforts might have helped answer their question. Today, their concept remains a great and unrealized business opportunity (though both have gone on to success elsewhere). The point is ... the risk of getting mired in analysis can be greater than the risk that entrepreneurs seek to avoid through analysis. Businesses require action-oriented entrepreneurs. And money. Businesses also need money.

MONEY

If I had a nickel for every entrepreneur who failed because he or she wasn't paying attention to the money, I'd have... Well, the truth of the matter is, I don't know how much I'd have. But I think it would be a lot. That's why it's good to pay attention to money! **It never fails to amaze me how often I see business plans that are incomplete when it comes to the numbers.**

When I remind entrepreneurs that financial planning matters, they assure me it's the very next item on their list of critical to-dos. This reassurance is usually coupled, however, to some variation of the following sentence: "But I don't know where to start." "Can you do it for me?" "Can you help me find someone who will do it for me?" After repeatedly hearing these questions, I caved in and asked one of my larger groups: "How many people here are intimidated by the whole financial thing?" More than half of the students raised their hands; of those who didn't raise their hands, a significant number began to fidget uncomfortably, look sheepish, or stare with tremendous fascination at the ceiling. Their discomfort was rewarded by my none-too-friendly reaction to the lack of financial enthusiasm:

Fear of numbers is no excuse.

Perhaps the most common reason for arithmophobia (yep, there's actually a word for "fear of numbers") is a belief that start-up math is harder than it actually is. Another reason is that numbers can reveal an entrepreneur's self-proclaimed "world's greatest idea" to be, well, a dud. Some entrepreneurs just can't handle the truth. And the truth is... Entrepreneurs who hide from the numbers are like ostriches with their heads in the sand — exposed to the world in a very uncomfortable way, with limited ability to move.

I've found that springing a financial analysis assignment on students is a very good way to activate a **mass freak-out**. As fun as that might be, the response is far more constructive with a little foreshadowing and reverse psychology. For some odd reason, students become much more willing to face the financial challenge when hit with a statement like, "You might not enjoy the upcoming assignment, but running from it will prove you're not an entrepreneur." When reluctant individuals are pushed (or pulled) through a financial exercise, a common reaction is something on the order of: "Hey! That was actually useful!" If you know your numbers, then you know your business.

Mind your own business.

Aspiring entrepreneurs often assure me that, given enough money, they'll be able to launch their great new idea into orbit. When I ask what constitutes "enough money," it's not unusual to get back a puzzled stare, a long pause, and a nice round number clearly pulled from thin air — something like $50,000. If I then ask how the money will be used, I get a similar stare and pause, followed by an answer of simultaneous ambiguity and certainty: "The money will be used to start my business!"

Entrepreneurs have a tendency to underestimate their cash needs, in part because they don't get immersed in the specifics of those needs. But specifics are necessary. Nice round numbers and exuberance are rarely enough to net investor or banker coin. In fact, it can take quite a lot to get investors or bankers interested in a meaningful way — and by meaningful, I mean a way that involves the giving or loaning of money.

Seasoned entrepreneurs will tell my students very clearly, "It's difficult to raise money. Incredibly difficult." An expression of investor interest is not an expressed agreement to give money. An expressed agreement is not a signed agreement. A signed agreement is not a signed check. And so on. Even items in the mail can miss their final destination. Take this lesson to the bank:

Don't bank on expressions of interest. The only real money is banked money.

I once met an entrepreneur who had, through genetic good fortune, been able to escape the trials and tribulations of the entrepreneurial investment hunt. He came up with an idea, requested and received $1,000,000 in seed capital from his parents, spent the money over the next six months, and then went out of business. When I asked him what he'd learned, he said, "Cash is king." He thought he failed because he couldn't get more money. I thought he couldn't get more money because he'd failed.

Whatever the reason for his venture's speedy end, it got me focused on why cash might wear a crown. Herein lies a fundamental misunderstanding of many an arithmophobe entrepreneur — and a frequent cause of untimely death amongst start-up firms. Unsuccessful entrepreneurs make lots of sales whose proceeds are collected after the entrepreneurs' own bills are due. Successful entrepreneurs make sure there is enough cash on hand to pay the bills. Successful entrepreneurs pay attention to the real revenue of payments rather than just the promised revenue of orders. The rules of the game are simple. Pay attention to the cash, because:

Cash rules.

In the best-case scenario, an entrepreneur manages his or her cash, earns a lot of profit, and becomes an acquisition target or IPO possibility. One entrepreneur likes (or dislikes, as the case may be) telling the story of a dot-com venture that he founded in the years when dot-com was booming. Over a period of several years, he secured millions in venture capital investment, built his staff to more than 120 people, acquired a portfolio of well-known clients, and attracted substantial and positive Wall Street buzz. When his company was valued by investors as worth $30 million, a top technology company offered to acquire him for $40 million. Because the acquirer was worth $2 billion, the entrepreneur suggested that $200 million might be a better price. The acquirer saw the gap as too big and walked away. A short time later, the dot-com market imploded. Though the entrepreneur's business did survive that implosion, and he was eventually acquired by a different company, it was several years later and for less than the original offer. His message to the students:

Don't be greedy.

I've heard the entrepreneur tell his $40 million story on several occasions. I've also heard an equivalent $100 million story. While students might at first consider these to be cautionary tales of greed run amok, there's an important lesson that the very big numbers can obscure: What seems greedy in retrospect doesn't always seem greedy at the time. These are not entrepreneurs who wanted more for the sake of more. These are not entrepreneurs who started businesses solely or even primarily for money. When large sums of money are involved, however, decisions can get complicated. Consider, for example, that a market full of highly valued companies is a market in which it's natural to seek a high valuation. A company with 120 hard-working employees is a company whose people arguably deserve a piece of the financial pie. And an idea that grows into an attractive acquisition target is an idea with a lot of stakeholders — including partners, employees, customers, investors, bankers, family, and members of the community. Entrepreneurship involves a lot of people, particularly when big money enters the picture.

PEOPLE

Though first-time entrepreneurs might acknowledge the reality of multiple stakeholders, their original leap into launch often has a hint of the romantic independent. As the founder of a children's clothing line once told me, "I began my own label because I'd gotten to the point where I didn't want to answer to anyone. I wanted the freedom to be on my own, to try something new that didn't involve a boss or politics or endless meetings. I wanted to be really creative." In making this comment, however, she also shared that **freedom from others can be a double-edged sword**.

An independent entrepreneur is one who, in her own words, needs to "wear every hat in the business." But most entrepreneurs aren't good at all of the skills (and don't have all of the resources) required in business. They thus need help from others. And help from others can involve sacrificing some of the very independence that motivated them to start up from the start. Entrepreneurs have business needs that can trump the independent desires of even the most talented founder.

No successful entrepreneur is an island.

Entrepreneurs are not likely to be wowed by the observation that people matter. People are like noses. They're obvious. For the entrepreneur who wants to stay independent, however, it can be difficult to let other people in. I once met an entrepreneur who had launched an innovative, high-end handbag line. In her first season, without almost any help, she designed and produced a series of bags — and sold them into the very best department stores (securing window displays and substantial shelf space). At the end of that season, she discovered that many of her bags had gone unsold to consumers and that the stores were uninterested in purchasing her second season designs. She thus found herself in a quandary: She lacked the requisite knowledge, time, money, and connections to simultaneously get rid of the old bags, fund the second season's production run, sell into a broader set of stores, and start planning for season three. Though she knew she needed help and tried to work with a number of consultants and partners, she ultimately proved unwilling to make the creative or business compromises necessary for effective teamwork and commercial survival. Her wonderful designs ended up in discount bins, passé before their time.

Compromise isn't a four-letter word (except where integrity is involved).

Though the fear of losing new venture control is real and problematic for many entrepreneurs, some are even more frightened that their great business idea might be stolen. For newbies, the potential downside of seeking help is often perceived to be greater than the potential upside. Playing one's cards too close to the vest however, can slow down progress — and that downside is certain. I've lost count of how many experienced entrepreneurs tell my students that they wasted time trying to over-protect their idea when first starting out. As one entrepreneur (the founder of an online financial services company) observed, "Most people lack the time or interest for your idea. Even if they don't, who cares? If you launch a successful idea, competitors will emerge anyway. It's better to get the help you need."

A venture capitalist offered a similar perspective: "If an entrepreneur asks me to sign a non-disclosure agreement, I refuse to sign. It's a naïve request. I see too many similar ideas for it to make sense. Besides, a business is about more than the idea. People need to share to be successful." These comments aren't meant to suggest that entrepreneurs ditch the patent, trademark, or copyright efforts that could protect aspects of their business. But entrepreneurs should recognize that protection extends only so far.

Fear of others can prevent success through others.

For those who are willing to work through others, networking is often seen as key: "It is essential." "It's probably the most important element." "It's everything." When just beginning, however, it's not easy to find people with the desired magical mix of likeability, helpfulness, skill, and experience. This difficulty is compounded by the fact that networking events — a tactic of obvious accessibility for first-timers — tend to be less useful than expected.

As one displeased founder observed, "It's lots of 'give me your card,' telling people what you do, the jealous eye flutter, the 'you don't look like much to me' shrug, and hoping against hope that someone will give enough of a [bleep] to answer your call." **Successful entrepreneurs prioritize the cultivation of real relationships over the schmooze.** They do this through conversations with already valued contacts, a very clear sense of their start-up needs, and a plan for meaningful exchange. As one entrepreneur noted, "Selfish reasons are very good reasons to network, but if you're selfish about it, you can't do it well ... To me, it's 'Can I establish relationships with people that are mutually beneficial, and can I find a way to be of value to people?'"

Find something to exchange, even when you have nothing.

Conventional wisdom has it that new ventures will do better if led by a management team in collective possession of deep experience and extensive functional skills. While I don't disagree with this view, it doesn't fully address just how hard it can be to build such a team — particularly if you're a cash-strapped entrepreneur.

As the founder of a home decoration company recently commented, "It's hard to get good people without a proven business. It's hard to prove the business without good people. Just find solid workers who do what needs to be done and who can learn on the job." Many entrepreneurs echo this sentiment. In fact, some find that more experienced hires can struggle in the flexible and rapid environment of a start-up. As one entrepreneur noted, "The difference between an A and a B performer isn't always obvious. I've hired A people who didn't fit. I've hired people who I thought were B's, but they grew over time into some of my best colleagues." Individuals with the right energy, enthusiasm, natural smarts, and risk profile can grow as a venture grows — even if they don't start out "perfect."

You don't need the dream team to start a dream business.

The co-founder of a technology company recently observed to me that, in his experience, work activities fall into three categories: **"There's what you are doing, what you want to be doing, and what you should be doing."** For overwhelmed entrepreneurs, the urgent almost always displaces the important. In part, that's why having others around can be valuable. Of course, involving others does have a price.

As the founder of a food cooperative said to my students, "It's great to be your own boss, but you still have to answer to someone. A lot of someones." But other people can also ease the burden. In sacrificing some decision-making freedom, for example, entrepreneurs might in fact free up some time — time to focus on what they should be doing and, more importantly, time to focus back on what they want to be doing. Passion might not be enough, but without it, entrepreneurship just wouldn't be all that worthwhile. Ultimately, successful entrepreneurship is rewarding.

REWARDS

I began work on this chapter by emailing a variety of entrepreneurs and asking for their candid views of entrepreneurship — their views of "Entrepreneurship: The Good, the Bad, and the

Ugly," if you will. One very good entrepreneur, who was having a very bad day, immediately answered with some ugly. He suggested that I title my chapter, "The Importance of Strategic Drinking." As amusing as the suggestion was, it worried me (particularly as it came on the heels of a conversation in which another entrepreneur described start-up as "always being on the brink of imminent disaster"). Yikes!

So I asked them, "If entrepreneurship leads you to unhappy happy hours or the precipice of nowhere, then why on Earth would you do it?" The answer: **"It's worth it."** I took a class once in which a professor said, "Happiness is positive cash flow." The students laughed (and I immediately started using the line in all of my classes). But happiness is also supposed to be a warm blanket. And a warm puppy. And lots of other things.

I got a big response from my good, bad, and ugly email. One entrepreneur's response seemed to capture the sentiment of everyone. She sent me a list of bad, along with a list of ugly. She ended with the following: "Fortunately, the Bad and the Ugly are outweighed by the overall happiness gleaned from the Good."

Live Long And Prosper!

Chapter Twenty-Nine

What I Learned in Forty-Five Years as an Entrepreneur, Entrepreneurial Mentor, Teacher, and Coach

A Chronicle of the Conversion of a Corporate Guru to an Entrepreneurial Affecienado, Practioner, and Leader

By John Bailey

John Bailey was born in Preston, Victoria, Australia, the son of a father who conducted a small house construction company. He initially studied electrical engineering at college level, and his first full-time appointment was in Australia's largest packaging company as a customer services engineer. Three years of engineering did not provide sufficient interest, and

John began a very varied career which included high school teaching of mathematics and science, university teaching in business statistics, management, and entrepreneurship, co-founder of six different entrepreneurial companies, founding director of a Centre for the Development of Entrepreneurs, Training and Development Manager for the largest telecommunications company in Australia, CEO of a management consulting company specializing in Intrapreneurship and corporate venturing, mentoring of start-up entrepreneurs, and chairman of a start-up company in the education industry in China. Along the way he attained professional qualifications in engineering, education, and commerce and MBA and PhD degrees. In 2005 he was diagnosed with leukemia and found it necessary to resign from most business activities because of long periods in hospital. Whilst in hospital he recorded his memories of 45 years working in a wide variety of fascinating situations.

INTRODUCTION — EDITOR'S COMMENTS

John Bailey from Australia is one of the pioneers of the Entrepreneurship field! He has spent 45 years of his life involved with entrepreneurs in a multitude of ways, and has an incredible treasure of knowledge about entrepreneurship in his wondrous mind! He has written a grand summary of his life that is a most wonderful read. As he has so much knowledge of the development of Entrepreneurship and Entrepreneurship Education in the world, **we have excerpted here a number of key thought gems and snippets of insight** that should give you great food for thought about how an Entrepreneurship "grandfather" grew and learned what Entrepreneurship is all about.

We present here a summary of what he learned — the lessons learned in life. **Read it in little bunches, taking time to**

think on what you have read, and relate it to who you are, where you are, and where you are going in your life of Entrepreneurship!!!

It will be fun for you to watch how his thinking develops as his life and career unfolds and grows!

THOUGHTS FROM THE SIXTIES — THE CORPORATE YEARS

- When seeking a career, **be adventurous** and don't let traditional thinking prevent you from choosing a path less traveled!

- When you discover that you are not suited for a particular position in life, **move on rapidly** to ensure that you don't frustrate your managers and that you remain motivated yourself!

- The people element of a larger firm is much more interesting to me than the mere accumulation of $ or the manufacture of superior products!

- Working on Can Production Lines from 7 am to 4 pm is **soul destroying** for me! I learned to have an affinity with workers who have no other options available!

- The importance of people skills in the business world became obvious — I learned when it was appropriate to listen, and when it was more appropriate to direct and control!

- The people on a production line have pride and should not be ignored when decisions are being made about the quality of their work. If I involved them in solving customer problems rather than berating them, we made good progress!

- **Being able to rely on people to get a job done is a key quality in building the firm!**

- **Teaching was in my blood!** Every day at work was a new challenge, and seeing young people achieve creatively was the outcome of addressing these challenges!

- **My mentor's encouragement made a profound impact on me** — he imbued in me a level of confidence which was probably unfounded!

- Every situation encountered, every news article read, was **examined for the opportunity that it might offer** to me in life!

- Physical conditions do not have impact on the culture of an organization if an inspiring vision is available to all and the leadership is open and supportive to ideas and personal motivation!

- Young people can be built into productive groups and teams when they are involved with their teachers in the planning of activities!

- **I am not a good, loyal player in large, impersonal organizations!**

- **I need leadership that encourages my creative efforts**, and I will work 24/7 to provide wonderful results!

GROWING INTO THE SEVENTIES — THE TRANSITION, FALLING FOR ENTREPRENEURSHIP

- **An MBA** does not purport to provide detailed knowledge about particular areas of business. Rather, it **assists in**

integrating all elements of business into a coherent whole!

- Mixing and learning with businesspeople and entrepreneurial types drawn from a wide variety of backgrounds provides a very rich overview of the ways in which people with differing cognitive styles solve business problems.

- Now I was meeting people who created their own companies from scratch, the Entrepreneurs! I was fascinated!

- **Take up all invitations and opportunities to be involved with professional associations.** You never know where the network might lead you!

- There is a significant group of players in business who are not understood, not recognized for their importance to the economy, and have not been researched by the academic community. These are the people who create new organizations from scratch — the Entrepreneurs!

- Leading a team of 28 academics, all with expert opinions in their own (and other) fields, requires extreme patience and influence skills!

- Keeping in touch with external consulting professionals and with owner/managers was a great way to stay grounded when designing new academic programs for accreditation!

- Establishing two new businesses in one year taught me a great deal. But in retrospect, it was too time-consuming in a year when the gaining of the accreditation status of the academic program I headed up was paramount!

- **International networks need to be developed** by professionals in all fields. The best way to build the networks is to take the time to visit people in other countries to share knowledge and dialogue together. **They give you more attention if they can see the whites of your eyes!**

- If you are going to conduct research in an area that is on the "fringe" and may offend the sensibilities of the expert academics who need to hold on to their power, spend time discovering how they think and how you need to frame issues so they can say yes.

- I finally discovered that I was much more motivated when starting new initiatives than in managing activities of an ongoing nature!

- 1977 was an incredible year of rapid learning about large bureaucratic organizations, training and development, executive development, and about **how people do or do not remain motivated in a large organization!**

- **I learned that it really was far easier to ask for forgiveness than permission!**

- **I learned the value of skilled facilitation in working with teams!**

- **The large, impersonal, bureaucratic organization is not where I am comfortable.** I should have become aware of this much earlier, but ego and ambition took over in slowing my moment of enlightenment about entrepreneurship!

- **When building an Entrepreneurial consulting practice, tender (bid) for everything! You never know where it will lead you!**

THE EIGHTIES — EUREKA! ENTREPRENEURSHIP IS INGRAINED WITHIN ME!

- **Working with Entrepreneurs and budding Entrepreneurs is the most exciting area of teaching I have ever undertaken!** In teaching we were now seeking a real business outcome rather than just providing learning opportunities for the sake of learning!

- **I received a tremendous sense of satisfaction when a business was actually launched from the courses we taught!** I began to think that if we encouraged and trained more people to do what they didn't think they could do, we would have a multiplier effect on Entrepreneurs in our society! Wow!

- **Never sign a director's bank guarantee if you can get out of it!** If you do, conduct an annual due diligence audit of your guarantees!

- **Consulting assignments emerge because of relationships, not because of heavy promotion or advertising!**

- **Entrepreneurship workshops and classes are hotbeds of opportunity when people get together and link their respective backgrounds and experiences.** It is extremely satisfying to me to see people identify opportunities together that they would never have considered individually!

- **Toward the end, a PhD becomes an endurance test, but if you have chosen a topic that is of real interest (entrepreneurship), it makes the hard grind a little easier!**

- **If you create an innovative idea, know your audience and their preferences before you seek a "yes"!**

- Making contact with thought leaders around the world is not as difficult as it may seem, if you are prepared to take the time to visit them in their home territory. Wonderful, lasting relationships can occur!

- The business plan for a new adventure bears little resemblance to the actual events that occur in the first 12 months of building the new entity. This helped me understand how the Entrepreneur feels as they face the ambiguities and uncertainties of the early years of a new venture!

- When bringing in expert consultants, **bring in real experts, not charlatans!**

- My 23-year, part-time quest for a PhD ended successfully! I learned how important knowing how to juggle many tasks is to the entrepreneur!

- Generation of a positive cash flow is an essential component of any start-up company. It is no good waiting until the seed capital runs out to begin thinking about alternative sources of cash.

- Inventors and idea people need to be assisted to engage in their own evaluation of ideas. We found that helping the inventor to discover the data both trains the inventor and assists the observer with their judgments of merit!

- Social Entrepreneurs can be very useful to communities who need to be rejuvenated! However, not all potential Social Entrepreneurs know how to stimulate opportunity identification and evaluation. They may need assistance with the processes and tools!

- When a larger company takes Intrapreneur development seriously, and puts time, effort, and money into the program, **very valuable outcomes can be generated** for the large organization!

- **Business cycles need to be watched very closely when you operate companies that have an emphasis on something new and non-traditional!**

HERE COMES THE WILD NINETIES!

- **When I was able to listen to noted gurus at overseas conferences, I was able to bring their theories and stories home to Australia and share these with clients!** The Entrepreneur must broaden their horizons and avoid becoming insular!

- **Spread the values message with stories!** This is a powerful and evocative method of teaching and learning!

- I was profoundly affected by the **"reciprocal feedback methodology,"** which convinced me that if I involved group participants in the design of a learning process, **very effective and useful outcomes are attained for all concerned!**

- **The brightest and most intelligent people in the world do not necessarily recognize the difference between expertness and facilitative processes!** The elite business schools would do their students a great service if they conducted some facilitation skill training with their graduates. **It helps a lot to learn how to make things happen, not just know stuff!**

- **Music as a leadership development tool is worthy of further experimentation!** Many people do not believe they can play instruments or sing effectively. However, when placed in the uncertain, risky situations that musical performances require, many people see how they can grow from collaboration with others! How useful this is to drawing "belief in self" out in the fledgling Entrepreneur!

- I have concluded that **"relationship skills" rather than human skills, people skills, or soft skills are what works best!** We need to spend much more time assisting Entrepreneurs to comprehend the importance of relationship management in their leadership and development of their firms!

THE NEW ENTREPRENEURIAL MILLENNIUM BEGINS! WILL IT CONTINUE TO BE THE AGE OF THE ENTREPRENEUR?

- **I discovered how valuable it can be to assist individuals and teams to understand the difference between debate and dialogue!** Debate implies that I am right and you are wrong. Dialogue assumes that neither of the positions being argued is correct and that an exploration of the different positions is worthwhile!

- **I began to realize that I was always anxious to try new initiatives — this is the heart of the Entrepreneur!**

- **Grand Plans and extravagant proposals are exciting, but always fraught with higher risk!**

- **To try something is worth the effort, even though it might be ultimately unsuccessful. Failure teaches one!**

- The Entrepreneurship education and research community suffers from the same disability suffered by many bright, intelligent researchers in other fields of activity! **They are so obsessed with their desire to impress their peers that they are unable to consider how and when the results of**

their research might be used to benefit practitioners in the field. This certainly explains why the academic and entrepreneurial communities remain so far apart and often don't have a positive word to say about each other!

- **Entrepreneurs and leaders like to listen to "new voices" of change!**

- **The conduct of innovation laboratories and workshops is not the only way to help entrepreneurs to become more innovative. Personal, one-on-one mentoring is the most useful way to help entrepreneurs!**

- **The mentoring of younger entrepreneurs became a most satisfying way to pass on my knowledge and experience as I found my energy levels were insufficient to operate at the rate of work I was used to.** With gray hair comes new pleasures of helping others!

- **Retirement has been forced upon me because of health issues but I have learned so well that both mentoring and writing are as satisfying as building companies and developing entrepreneurs when energy levels are limited and time is in short supply!**

CONCLUSION

As I look back across the journey of the past 45 years, three key concepts of life stand out for me:

1. **One's working life, if possible, should be about doing something worthwhile!** When I found myself engaged in activities that didn't seem to make a difference to a situation or to other people, I was fortunate enough to be able to turn away and do something else!

2. **I found my most satisfying work experiences in helping others to be what they wanted to be!** I have always found myself involved in some form of teaching throughout my working life. I find much more satisfaction from assisting a range of Entrepreneurs than from pursuing my own single objective. I guess my selfishness is reflected in my desire to become satisfied by observing the success of others! There is a deep beauty in this.

3. **Mentors and mentorship are critical issues in a person's development!** My mentors supported and encouraged me so that I have lived a wonderful life. I like to think that I have done the same for the thousands of entrepreneurial lives I have touched in my career as an entrepreneurial teacher and mentor!

My work journey of 45 years was totally unplanned and Entrepreneurial! It was a wonderfully satisfying series of careers, actually, I look upon it as 45 careers in one. Being a part of the entrepreneurial field has never been dull! What a grand tour through life it has been!

I am in the twilight of my life! Through my travels in the field of entrepreneurship I have been able to live a privileged life because of the tens of thousand of wonderful people I have met along the way!

I am very content!

"The odds of hitting a target go up dramatically when you aim at it."

Mal Pancoast

Chapter Thirty

WHEW! Pulling it all Together!

By Fred Kiesner

I have had the honor of being an Entrepreneur and an Entrepreneurship Educator during my nearly 50-year career! I love the field of Entrepreneurship and have a passionate belief that it is the **panacea for the economic troubles of the world today in many, many ways!** And we are certainly painfully aware of the world's troubles, today!

As the world struggles with the solutions to its many and complex economic troubles in this first decade of the third millennium, I am not too worried about the long term economic future of the world. I have lived through a number of troubled economic times during the past fifty years of my career. I find that somehow there is usually a "rainbow" at the end of the cloudy times, and the Entrepreneur and Entrepreneurship are often the ones that carry the day once again.

In the not too distant past we have had several major crisis situations in the United States and the world — and the press had a field day predicting the demise of the entrepreneurial sector of the economy.

I remember the days of the eighties when interest rates were up to 22%–25% for small businesses. Stagflation was the buzzword back then.

Or how about the dot-com crash of 2000?

Many predicted that each of these crises heralded the end of the business world.

They missed big! They were so very wrong!

As we now struggle with the predicted "death of business" as touted in some of the world's media, I will tell you that I am not excessively worried. It always looks bad on the downward slide.

In tough times, the Entrepreneurs arise and cause great things to happen!

They jump into the pool!

They read "bad economic times" as **opportunities coming to life!**

They keep their antennae up! They see what others don't!

Chaos spurs the development of a myriad of opportunities!

Entrepreneurship will thrive in the years to come, following the tough times we are having in the end of the first decade of the millennium!

Entrepreneurship will be the solution to the problems of the world, without doubt!

Right at the beginning of this book I strongly stated that we are in the **"Age of the Entrepreneur!"**

Believe it! Act on it! Don't just sit there bemoaning how much money you have lost in the market, or your retirement account (true winners never retire, anyway, they just change what they do), or whatever!

Take action! Take your life into your own hands! **Start controlling your own destiny, as an Entrepreneur!**

This book has been an attempt to provide fledgling Entrepreneurs and those who guide and help to develop Entrepreneurs with a **"cookbook" of recipes** that will help in the successful development of the Entrepreneurial World of the Future!

I invited a number of the most wonderful Entrepreneurial Superstars, who are the movers and shakers in the Entrepreneurial field, to contribute to this book!

I could have had a hundred more — and they have provided the reader with an exciting collage of real life, streetwise advice that will help anyone in the world to become a winning Entrepreneur, and help the teachers and coaches of Entrepreneurs to develop winning Entrepreneurs!

We hope you have enjoyed learning about the wondrous world of Entrepreneurship from this myriad of outstanding Entrepreneurial leaders and educators that joined in the creation of this book. It truly was fun!

My suggestion for you, as you have read this book, is to grasp the incredible knowledge you have received and dive into the wondrous and powerful world of Entrepreneurship.

As I said right at the beginning of this book, we ask the reader to:

Read it in Small Snippets! Never more than a chapter at a time!

Learn! There is so much in this book that will help you!

"Borrow" and make better anything you want from this book! That is what we want, for you to use what we have provided for you!

Adopt the ideas we have given you, as they fit your unique ambiance!

Adapt its content to your life, culture and situation! We have provided some wonderful, neat action oriented material in this book!

But of most importance, after reading this book, **go out and do something wonderful, fun, majestic, and powerful for yourself and your corner of the world!**

So, don't just sit there thinking!

GO OUT AND MAKE A WHOLE BUNCH OF

IN YOUR LIFE AND THE LIVES OF OTHERS
YOU TOUCH!!!!!

"Let your hook be always cast; in the pool, where you least expect it, there will be a fish."

Ovid

List of Contributors

We wanted this book to be of full value to you in causing change in your Entrepreneurial world. Therefore we are providing you with the contact information for each of our authors. If you wish to contact them, please do. I suspect you will find the authors absolutely excited and passionate about Entrepreneurship, life, and the future!

BY CHAPTER

Chapters One, Two, Five, Seventeen, Twenty, Twenty Five, Twenty Seven, and Thirty

Fred Kiesner
Conrad Hilton Chair of Entrepreneurship
Loyola Marymount University
One LMU Drive
Los Angeles, CA 90045
Email: fkiesner@lmu.edu
Tel: 310-338-4569
URL: www.fredkiesner.com
http://entrepreneurship.lmu.edu

Chapter Three

Donald F. Kuratko
The Jack M. Gill Chair of Entrepreneurship
Professor of Entrepreneurship & Executive Director
Johnson Center for Entrepreneurship & Innovation

The Kelley School of Business
Indiana University
Bloomington, IN, 47405
Email: dkuratko@indiana.edu
URL: www.kelley.iu.edu/jcei/

Chapter Four

Charles W. Hofer
Regents Professor of Entrepreneurship
Coles College of Business
Kennesaw State University
1000 Chastain Road
Kennesaw, GA 30144
Email: chofer@kennesaw.edu
Tel: 678-797-2502

Chapter Six

George Solomon
Director, Center for Entrepreneurial Excellence
Associate Professor of Management
The George Washington University
School of Business
2201 G Street NW
Funger Hall, Suite 315
Washington, DC 20052
Email: gsolomon@gwu.edu
Tel: 222-994-3760
URL: www.gw-cfee.org

Chapter Seven

Leo Paul Dana
Professor
GSCM Montpellier (France) & University of Canterbury

Private Bag 4800
Christchurch, New Zealand
Email: leo.dana@canterbury.ac.nz
Tel: 64-3-3642987
URL: http://professordana.homestead.com/1.html
www.mang.canterbury.ac.nz/people/dana.shtml

Chapter Eight

Len Middleton
Adjunct Professor of Strategy & Entrepreneurship
Ross School of Business
University of Michigan
Ann Arbor, MI 48109
Email: lenm@umich.edu
Tel: 734-763-9226

Chapter Nine

David Bussau
Ernst & Young Social Entrepreneur of the Year, 2004
Senior Australian of the Year, 2008
Founder, Opportunity International
Australia
Email: dbussau@maranathatrust.org

Chapter Ten

Chris Collet
Associate Professor
School of Life Sciences
Queensland University of Technology
GPO Box 2434
Brisbane QLD 4001, Australia
Email: c.collet@qut.edu.au
Tel: 61-7-3138-5173

Barra Ó Cinnéide
Managing Director
Irish Australian Innovation Network (IAIN)
Ireland
Email: barrapat@eircom.net
Tel: 011-353-61-377-207

Chapter Eleven

Ted O Keeffe
European Commission
DG Research
Sq. de Meeus 8
1050 Brussels, Belgium
Email: tokeeffe@skynet.be; ted@thelearningmodel.com

Chapter Twelve

Jose M. Romaguera
Professor of Marketing & Entrepreneurship
Founding Director of the Business Center
College of Business Administration
University of Puerto Rico at Mayaguez
Email: chispaempresarial@yahoo.com

Chapter Thirteen

Robert Warren
I.H. Asper Executive Director For Entrepreneurship
Stu Clark Center For Entrepreneurship
Asper School of Business
526-181 Freedman Crescent
University of Manitoba
Winnipeg, Manitoba, Canada R3T 5V4
Email: Robert_Warren@Umanitoba.ca
Tel: 204-474-8422; 204-292-8092

Chapter Fourteen

Marshall Goldsmith
P.O. Box 9710
16770 Via del los Rosales
Rancho Santa Fe, CA 92067-9710
Email: Marshall@MarshallGoldsmith.com
Tel: 858-759-0950
URL: MarshallGoldsmithLibrary.com

Chapter Fifteen

Arthur Gross-Schaefer
Doctor of Divinity, Honoris Causa, JD, Rabbi
Chair, Department of Marketing and Business Law
Professor of Business Law and Ethics
Loyola Marymount University
One LMU Drive
Los Angeles, CA 90045
Email: agross@lmu.edu
Tel: 310-338-2859

Chapter Sixteen

David Y. Choi
Associate Professor of Entrepreneurship
Associate Director, The Entrepreneurship Program
Loyola Marymount University
One LMU Drive
Los Angeles, CA 90045
Email: dchoi@lmu.edu
Tel: 310-338-2344
URL: http://entrepreneurship.lmu.edu

Chapter Eighteen

Wesley B. Truitt
Adjunct Professor
School of Public Policy
Pepperdine University
Malibu, California
Email: Wesley.Truitt@Pepperdine.edu

Chapter Nineteen

Brad Keywell
Co-Founder & Principal, MediaBank LLC
Co-Founder & Director, Echo Global Logistics, Inc.
Co-Founder & Principal, ThePoint LLC
600 West Chicago Avenue, Suite 725
Chicago, IL 60610
Email: brad@echo.com
URL: www.mxbg.com, www.echo.com, www.thepoint.com

Chapter Twenty-One

Cal Caswell
Director, Small Business Development Center
Lecturer, Management, Marketing, and Logistics
Loyola Marymount University
One LMU Drive
Los Angeles, CA 90045-2659
Email: ccaswell@lmu.edu

Chapter Twenty-Two

Brian McKenzie
California State University, East Bay
Department of Marketing & Entrepreneurship
25800 Carlos Bee Blvd.

Hayward, CA 94542
Email: brian@brian-mckenzie.com
Tel: 510-885-2858
URL: www.brian-mckenzie.com

Chapter Twenty-Three

Anna Ouroumian
Re-Founder, President & CEO
The Academy of Business Leadership (ABL)
2244 Walnut Grove Ave.
Quad 2 A
Rosemead, CA 91770
Email: anna.ouroumian@sce.com
Tel: 626-302-1441

Chapter Twenty-Four

Shaun Tan and L. Nicole Landrum
Entrepreneurship Mentor Society (EMS)
11131 Dora Street
Sun Valley, CA 91352
Email: shaun.tan@emsociety.org
Tel: 626-780-8876
URL: www.emsociety.org

Chapter Twenty-Six

Martha de la Torre
Founder, CEO
El Clasificado
1125 Goodrich Blvd.
Los Angeles, CA 90022
Email: mdelatorre@elclasificado.com
Tel: 323-278-5310
URL: www.elclasificado.com

Chapter Twenty-Eight

Elissa B. Grossman
Assistant Professor of Management & Entrepreneurship
Loyola Marymount University
One LMU Drive
Los Angeles, CA 90045
Email: elissa.grossman@lmu.edu
URL: http://entrepreneurship.lmu.edu

Chapter Twenty-Nine

John Bailey
Emeritus Principal Fellow
Melbourne Business School
University of Melbourne, Australia
Email: jbaileycarlton@aol.com
Tel: 61-(0)-3-9844-4466 / 61-(0)-4-1950-8646

Index